PL   Treat, John
830   Whittier.
.B8
Z9   Pools of water,
1988   pillars of fire

$30.00

DATE			
MAY 1990			

© THE BAKER & TAYLOR CO.

The Literature
of Ibuse Masuji

Pools
of
Water,
Pillars
of
Fire

Pools
of
Water,
Pillars
of
Fire

The Literature
of Ibuse Masuji

John Whittier Treat

UNIVERSITY OF WASHINGTON PRESS

Seattle and London

Copyright © 1988 by the University of Washington Press
Printed in the United States of America

All rights reserved. No portion of this publication may
be reproduced or transmitted in any form or by any means,
electronic or mechanical, including photocopying, recording,
or any information storage or retrieval system, without
permission in writing from the publisher.

Library of Congress Cataloging in Publication Data

Treat, John Whittier.
    Pools of water, pillars of fire: the literature of Ibuse Masuji /
John Whittier Treat.
       p.   cm.
    Bibliography: p.
    ISBN 0-295-96625-4
    1. Ibuse, Masuji, 1898–   . 2. Authors, Japanese—20th century—
Biography.   I. Title.
PL830.B8Z9 1988
895. 6'34—dc 19
    [B]   87-33011

This book is published with the assistance of a grant from
the Japan Foundation.

For William and Mabel Hughes

Contents

Preface

This study of the writings of Ibuse Masuji begins with a question: Why and how did this particular author come to write Japan's most acclaimed novel of the Hiroshima atomic bombing? While Ibuse, born in a small village in western Japan at the turn of the century, is certainly one of his country's most prominent modern writers—his name is now regularly mentioned as a leading Japanese contender for the Nobel Prize—his fame at home derives largely from his command of style, his subtle humor, and his great affection for the everyday people who populate his stories. Yet this same author, who in 1929 wrote about a forlorn salamander trapped in an underwater cave in "The Salamander" (*Sanshōuo*), a story widely enjoyed in Japan today, would turn more than thirty years later, with *Black Rain* (*Kuroi ame*, 1965–1966), to a theme that disallows parody, invention, and lyricism: the incineration of a city.

In Ibuse's world, fully formed by the time he published his little tale of an amphibian, what prepared him to become a literary witness to Hiroshima's destruction? My own answer is told in five chapters organized chronologically and thematically, incorporating elements of both biography and interpretative literary criticism. This volume, the first comprehensive critical study of Ibuse outside of Japan, is an inquiry into the life and writings of a man brave enough to attempt a story that, in the view of more than one survivor, "was beyond words."[1]

Ibuse's standard edition consists of fourteen volumes; without judicious pruning it could have numbered twice as many. It is beyond the scope of this initial English study to discuss each of his stories, novels, poems, and essays. I have included, however, not only his best known works—certainly all of those widely available in translation—but also those lesser known works that demonstrate the pervasiveness of his principal themes. Readers without a command of Japanese will find in the Bibliography a list of Ibuse's writings now in English. Ibuse has been served by a number of able translators, most notably by John Bester, whose *Black Rain* (Tokyo, New York and San Francisco: Kodansha International, 1969) and *Lieutenant Lookeast and Other Stories* (Tokyo and Palo Alto: Kodansha International, 1971) have established Ibuse's reputation abroad. While I am grateful for Bester's work, I have used my own translations in quoting from Ibuse to ensure continuity in diction and style and to emphasize key points within the context of my discussion.

I have many people to thank. Professor Anthony Liman of the University of Toronto gave me the early encouragement needed to undertake the study of this complex writer. Hamako Ito Chaplin, retired, Senior Lector of Japanese at Yale University, provided further encouragement throughout the project. Professor Hinotani Teruhiko of Keiō University directed my studies while I was in Japan. Hoga Takashi of Fuji Television and Professor Onuma Tan of Waseda University arranged the necessary introductions culminating in several evenings I was fortunate to spend with Ibuse himself. Professors Robert Leutner of the University of Iowa, Karl Kao of the University of Alberta, and Jay Rubin of the University of Washington read the manuscript and offered many valuable suggestions, as did Marilyn Schiffman.

Most of all, I thank Edwin McClellan, Sumitomo Professor of Japanese Studies at Yale. Professor McClellan originally proposed Ibuse as a dissertation topic and later gave me his valued counsel and support. While the ideas—and errors—are my own, the inspiration behind this book is entirely his.

The Literature
of Ibuse Masuji

Pools
of
Water,
Pillars
of
Fire

Introduction

> In each and every leaf, there is history.
> —"The Pipe"

The place of Ibuse Masuji in the history of modern Japanese literature is both secure and oddly ambiguous. He is considered one of his country's major contemporary writers, yet there is disagreement as to why. One of two distinct characterizations of Ibuse is apt to survive in any single appraisal of his literary significance. The first of these views is entirely appropriate to Ibuse's earliest work—short stories from the 1920s such as "The Salamander." These often delightful and sometimes disturbing tales brought Ibuse a rapid and remarkable success at the outset of his career, building a reputation in his youth which has lasted to the present day. "Only two short years have passed since he began publishing," wrote fellow author Makino Shin'ichi, one of Ibuse's more begrudging admirers, in 1931, "and already his masterpieces illuminate the skies over the literary world."[1] Lyrical, comic, fresh, at times almost childlike, his first stories contrast markedly with the lengthy novel that won him international acclaim in the 1960s, namely, his profound treatment of Hiroshima's nuclear destruction, *Black Rain*. The majority of critics think of Ibuse in terms of his precocious beginnings. The public defines him in terms of this later spectacular achievement. But the author himself has remained much the same man, both in temperament and technique, over the more than half century that separates the first and latest years of his contributions to literature.

Ibuse's writing, through seven mercurial decades, is united in its diverse genres and themes by a constant personal understanding of how the world, or at least his world, works. Not metaphysical, what emerges instead is a closely intimated sense of wholeness most akin to the special pleasure of having touched upon things unexpectedly

3

but intuitively true. This experience culminates a process in which the reader is led from the familiar to the unknown—whether in a dimension of time, space, or sensibility—only to be returned, enriched, to where he or she began. This imaginative trek to a far point and back is precisely the source of the uncanny feeling of asylum that many Ibuse works impart. Ibuse is careful, however, not to become too indulgent of nostalgia lest he risk sentimentality. He is one of the more coolly detached, almost stoic writers of his day. That aura of domestic comfort permeating his stories is thoroughly considered. It is the fortuitous consequence of a choice of themes exploring what binds man to his world—not, as is so often the case in modern fiction, what separates him—coupled with an extraordinarily seductive and soothing gift for simple story telling.

Ibuse has displayed these talents over many years and in many ways. He has published poetry and translations in addition to his stories and novels. Perhaps he has demonstrated his cleverest literary prowess, however, in three genres particularly cultivated throughout the long history of Japanese prose—the diary (*nikki*), the travel journal (*kikōbun*), and the essay (*zuihitsu*). Even Ibuse's purely imaginative fiction shares with these genres their nature as documents of observation and discovery, and their purpose as variously descriptive texts to comprehend and manipulate the world by subjectively delineating it. Insofar as any writer's "world" is subjectively defined by his works, this point may seem tautological. But what Ibuse has achieved by writing so often about writers is a world in which the process of imbuing life with meaning is rendered manifest; it is made as much an object of the reader's attention as the story proper. Ibuse seems, at such moments, a very modern author.

Inseparable from Ibuse's curiosity about the essential and existential powers of literature is his unique command of style. The smooth rhythm of his sentences, obviously polished but pleasantly metered to the cadence of a storyteller's breath, combines with his personal yet never obscure choice of words. His vocabulary borrows not only from the rich lexicon of his native dialect, that of eastern Hiroshima Prefecture, but also from his extensive reading in history as well as from the popular Tokyo parlance of his youth. Above all, Ibuse's words are always deliberate. They mean something distinct. The language, apart from ironic usages, is clear and unambiguous, free from the murky qualifiers or loose concessive clauses apt to obfuscate modern Japanese.

This sturdy style is ideal for Ibuse's writing. His catholic powers of
observation, combined with his dictographic ear for dialogue, perfectly suit his topological themes in mapping the terrain of his special world. This marriage of language and idea may occasionally overwhelm the reader, because Ibuse is thus able to extend his idiosyncratic vision into every corner of the narrative. He insists, even in his apparently straightforward essays, upon fabulizing all characters and incidents. Ibuse subjectivizes, and consequently dominates, the elements of his stories by developing them through an independent and synthesizing point of view. He may tell his tale from a removed first-person perspective, or by means of an even more remote authority, much as Cervantes quotes his knowledgeable Arab historian. Alternatively, the story may be built around a variety of edited, often invented, documents, or more subtly engineered with a viewpoint made distant by the use of irony.

Irony in Ibuse is closely associated with humor, but his works are seldom funny in a hilarious way; rather, motive and meaning in Ibuse are often revealed through his amusing caricature of characters' intentions as well as through his feigned ignorance of their consequences. This irony and its parallel humor, deftly applied, allow Ibuse not only to judge his characters but to invite the reader to concur. Yet however ironic or humorous Ibuse may be, he is never derisive. Eventually, inevitably, Ibuse turns his rhetorical weapons against himself and so avoids arrogance. This ironic relief even suggests a salvation for his many characters left in otherwise dire straits—comedy lurks in the background of Ibuse's often dismal landscapes, and those travelers lost within them are given an unexpected exit.

The world so described within Ibuse's work is made authentic by its ties to traditions often older than those explored by other modern Japanese writers. Ibuse was strongly influenced by the many sad accounts of a harsh and tumultuous peasant past told him in his boyhood by elder villagers who had witnessed rapid change as Japan adopted modern institutions during the Meiji period. Given this valuable if intangible inheritance, enriched by the historical shifts he himself has lived through, Ibuse has shaped a transcendental understanding of historical civilization in his attempts to discern continuity amid change. This basic paradigm of specifically historical circumstances shifting against a background of constant humanist values characterizes Ibuse's best work.

This contrast, the meandering flow of history and the stable virtues of those adrift within it, accounts for that locale in Ibuse's works where such differences are most vivid: the village. Although Ibuse left the countryside for the capital in 1917, his stories regularly travel to small communities, both real and imagined. This does not, however, make Ibuse a rustic writer. "Describe your village," instructed Tolstoy, a favorite author of Ibuse and his generation, "and you will describe the world." Indeed, the idea of "village" in Ibuse is more than physical; it can mean any state of being in which men are fully joined with social and natural surroundings. It is this geography of the mind, and not that of Tokyo, which Ibuse knows in the most detail. The reader who accompanies Ibuse to his figurative mountains and rivers will encounter farmers and fishermen, hermits and charwomen, petty thieves and dunces; will meet them not only today but one hundred, five hundred, a thousand years ago—and in other nations and continents. Yet the landscape of Ibuse's work, for all its heterogeneity, soon seems crisscrossed with roads distinguished by familiar landmarks; for readers native and foreign alike, the work of Ibuse Masuji suggests experiences more quintessentially human than particularly Japanese. Ibuse survives in translation because his writing, being truly individual, is at once universal. When Ibuse looks within himself, and into those many characters who mirror some part of him, he discovers a humanism that razes the differences between men.

Ibuse's stories establish an unspoken covenant between his heroes and their world. This faith affords a firm sense of place and of value which survives the assaults of historical, often catastrophic, change. In understanding the nature of this covenant, we understand how the two divergent interpretations of Ibuse's literary importance come together in a thematic whole, for both the sadly alienated protagonists of his first stories and the tragic victims of his last find themselves searching in common for a secure means of survival. Therefore this study of his career has one special purpose: to understand how and why such a remarkable literary creation as Shizuma Shigematsu, the A-bomb victim and hero of *Black Rain,* was possible and perhaps even necessary. Beyond the borders of Ibuse's archetypal village, and often within, calamitous fate of either a personal or historical nature strikes to undermine the conventions of our institutions; disaster obliterates not only individual lives but also the carefully and arbitrarily construed divisions of history. "In each and every fallen leaf," Ibuse once wrote, "there is history" (4:463).[2] In every symbol of change lies a single pattern of human experience. Fallen leaves are replaced by green ones, and, similarly, the typical Ibuse hero, although he or she suffers great losses, holds to this faith; it is possible to restore the world, even if that means only to understand what it once was like, amid its literal and often literary rubble.

In this faith Ibuse embraces an ancient but persistent view of the world, both organismic and cyclical, which he unhesitatingly applies to our most recent and complex crises. One is tempted to read into Ibuse a convincing mythopoesis inspired by his implicit suprahistorical vision of civilization and by his explicit concrete imagery. Certain extended symbols and figures suggest to the reader the metaphors of medieval science at work; others, the workings of ancient myth. Present in Ibuse are all the elements of the alchemic universe: the earth of his village, the wind that blows his sailors off course, the water that fills his ponds, and the fire that soars high in the sky. Both predatory and Promethean, the pillars of flame that tower over the cities of Ibuse's stories scorch the ground below and at the same time illuminate the night. In an irony typical of Ibuse, the glow of such terrible conflagrations will permit some of his protagonists the light by which to record their experiences.

Like an alchemist, Ibuse manipulates these basic materials of his art for compound ends. He has created a body of work expressing the truths of disparate eras and peoples within a common literary grammar. In a style clear and distinct, and with an approach unarguably modern, Ibuse has nonetheless given us a literature mysterious in its workings. His enduring contribution to twentieth century letters may be that he has reminded us of the power of words, the potential of language to prescribe as well as describe how we see ourselves complete in a fractured world. His friend and fellow writer Kaikō Takeshi has observed in an essay on Ibuse that all literature, "from the caves to the bookstores," is primitive in its fundamental authority.[3] The comment is aptly inspired, for Ibuse's writing begins in fact with the salamander's cave and attains its ultimate expression with the impact of the atomic age. Should Ibuse one day have his stated wish—to be born into the next life as a literary scholar rather than as an author ("My work would be so much simpler," he explained)[4]—let us hope he summons anew, in his role as a critic, the magic he now commands as the creative mind behind some very potent tales.

The
First
Three
Decades:
1898–1929

I threw away any youth I might have had into the gutter.
—"Ushigome Tsurumaki-chō"

Ibuse Masuji has lived more than three-quarters of his life in Tokyo but has never been considered a Tokyo writer, a writer absorbed in the problems of a modern urbanized Japan. This reputation is not necessarily fair, but it is true that when the young Ibuse arrived at Tokyo Station in the summer of 1917, he carried a good deal more than a suitcase: he brought with him a sensibility so thoroughly shaped by his rural upbringing that he would never lose it or, in any move to be fashionable, attempt to conceal it. Indeed, Ibuse would remark in an essay written a quarter of a century later that he still had not grown accustomed to the color of Tokyo soil.[1] Ibuse's first nineteen years of life spent between the mountains and sea in eastern Hiroshima, and his frequent returns home later, have provided both the inspiration and the idiom for much of his mature work. It seems appropriate, therefore, to begin a study of the literature of Ibuse Masuji with a brief look at his birthplace and a few of the people who populated it.

In one sense Ibuse has simplified his biographers' work. Although Ibuse is unusual among modern writers in that he has never made his personal life the stuff of his fiction—as one critic points out, even the jealously private Natsume Sōseki exposed his domestic life to view in *Grass on the Wayside*[2]—his essays and memoirs often speak of certain early experiences. These subjective glimpses of his own life are fragmentary, but his writer's mind has seized upon them as significant to its origins and, thus, to its character. Such insights, however unsystematic, are valuable to any reader seeking the genesis of a creative imagination. As Ibuse leaps from year to year and place to place

in his recollections, at times contradicting himself, his reader at least
learns what is significant to Ibuse, whether it be the factual truth or even part of it.

Everyone would prefer to look back upon youth with nostalgia. Ibuse is no exception, although, like other sensitive people, he can see within his simple longing the less simple source of that part of his nature inherited from the people among whom he matured. His nostalgia, like that of most, is conditional. When Ibuse muses in one essay, "Warming Saké" (*Kandokuri*, 1951), "When I recall my memories as a child they are on the whole not unpleasant, perhaps because they are so faded" (10:380),[3] he is, in fact, telling us that the reality of a difficult childhood still betrays a romantic desire to obscure it. Ibuse has always loved and hated his early years; he has prefaced a memoir of them, "Miscellany" (*Keirokushū*, 1936), with a quoted definition of the Chinese term *chi-le* (Sino-Japanese *keiroku*)—"That which one is ashamed to save yet should regret discarding" (9:244).[4] The reader today is fortunate that Ibuse never did discard his childhood, for his continued ambivalence about it has inspired a major portion of his work.

Kamo

Ibuse was born on February 15, 1898, the thirty-first year of the Meiji period (1868–1912). His birthplace, the hamlet of Awane within the village of Kamo (now part of Fukuyama City), was a small community in mountainous eastern Hiroshima Prefecture, soon to be encroached upon by the changes of the twentieth century. He grew up among people caught between a traditional and a Westernizing society, a circumstance that at least parallels, if not explains, Ibuse's own mixed and conflicting views of his youth. In his memoir *The First Half of My Life* (*Hanseiki*, 1970), Ibuse reflects upon some of the differences in his village, then and now:

> The thirty-first year of Meiji is now seventy-two years behind us. The old-fashioned village customs of that time have disappeared completely. The thirty-first year of Meiji was only thirty-one years after the Edo period [1600–1867]. When I was a child, every household had one or two people who had been born in the Edo period. . . . People then as old as I

am now would have been born in the Bunsei years [1818–1830]. No doubt they were people deeply immersed in the rural customs of Edo. Their language must have reflected that. [13:375]

Almost two decades in this environment have indelibly imprinted Ibuse and his work. The popular cultural legacy of the Edo period is evidenced not only in the preponderance of late Edo settings in his historical fiction, but in the particular dialect spoken by his characters of both past and present times. Many of the adults with whom the young Ibuse associated were born well before the Restoration in 1868, and they told him old stories in an idiom particular to both their locale and era. In fact, Ibuse credits his people with willing him above all else his language as a writer.[5] He describes his diction as "lyrical and sweet," a Japanese "especially sensitive to distinctions of social status."[6] Aside from the "cussing words," which, as he notes in his essay "Country Talk" (Zaisho kotoba, 1954), "are still the same as they were in the old days" (11:81), this nineteenth-century dialect survives only in Ibuse's work. Perhaps in part for this reason, he declares it his most important heritage. It was used eloquently by its original speakers in such a way as to profit Ibuse in his future career. In "Tall Tales" (Usobanashi, 1955) he writes of an annual competition in Kamo which pitted one contestant's fantastic story (usobanashi, literally "lie-stories") against another's. This festival of imaginative story telling delighted Ibuse as a child, and it may well have served as an early apprenticeship in the craft of fiction. Certainly he was exposed at an impressionable age to declamatory exercises in narrative invention.

Kamo and the surrounding region are archaeologically very old and culturally very distinguished. Ibuse's own family, which can trace its origins back to Shimonoseki in Kyūshū, has lived on the same land in Kamo since the middle of the fifteenth century and in the same house since the early nineteenth century.[7] In The First Half of My Life Ibuse describes his family as "farmers" (nōka), but as a boy he was treated with the deference accorded the local gentry. But relative affluence did not guarantee a happy home. Masuji's earliest memory, in one account, is of a funeral,[8] and, in another, of being rammed by a bull on his way to school.[9] These inauspicious beginnings were followed by a chain of infirmities and deaths detailed in several Ibuse works, most notably in "Miscellany."

Even more sad, those in his family who remained well seem to

have offered him exceptionally little comfort. His immediate household consisted of his mother Miya, his father Ikuta, an older brother
Fumio, an older sister Matsuko, and a younger brother Keizō, who
died when Masuji was only five. Neither of Masuji's surviving siblings would appear to have been especially close. Only Fumio figures
significantly in his memoirs, and only because of the authority he
commanded over Masuji, particularly after the death of their father
in 1903. "Miscellany" characterizes Fumio, with typical understatement, as "stern." Fumio was domineering where his father had been
indifferent.

Masuji's father, Ikuta, adopted into his wife's family to serve as an
heir, had always been under the firm control of his father-in-law,
Masuji's grandfather Tamizaemon. Tamizaemon was the undisputed
family patriarch. Ikuta's role was reduced to that of a bystander in
clan affairs, and he naturally grew to resent this peripheral position.
He was finally unable to hide this hurt from his children. Masuji recalls his father as distant and cold, both physically and emotionally.
Owing to the pleural complications that were to kill him, Ikuta eventually had to live apart from the main household in an annex.
Masuji's few memories of his father include times of punishment by
him and, significantly, his face at the hour of his death. In "Piggy-
back" (*Kataguruma*, 1935) Masuji writes not only of that face but
also of a dream in which his father gives him a ride on his shoulders,
a rare treat that fills the boy with simultaneous joy and fear. The
dream epitomizes Masuji's ambiguous feelings for his father, the
twin emotions of attraction and rejection not unlike those he holds
toward the whole of his childhood.

Masuji's earnest wish to admire his father was frustrated by
Ikuta's obvious shortcomings. For instance, Ikuta professed a great
love of literature, and had once published under a pen name a
Chinese poem in *Waseda gakuhō* (*Waseda Gazette*). He had even
named his eldest son Fumio (literally "writing-man"). Yet his will,
shown Ibuse years later by his grandfather, instructed that none of
his children were to pursue writing as a career. Instead, they were to
enter business or commerce—"practical" professions. This posthumous order sought to guarantee for his offspring the respectability he
had never attained; it also tacitly admitted to his own dearth of literary talent. Perhaps the will was effective; both Fumio and Matsuko
did, in fact, abandon their writing ambitions for more secure pursuits.

In an essay entitled "A Tale of the Country" (*Den'enki,* 1933) Ibuse returns one summer to Kamo for a brief visit. He uses the opportunity to peruse his late father's papers. Told that his father had once been an aspiring writer, Ibuse is curious as to what Ikuta had read. Expecting well-worn copies of Shakespeare or Goethe, he discovers trash. When he stumbles upon a collection of letters, Ibuse expects them to be from such literary giants as Ozaki Kōyō or Tsubouchi Shōyō. He is again disappointed. He comes at last upon a notebook filled with poems in his father's hand. But Ibuse soon realizes they are only coarse translations from Chinese and are probably not even his father's own. Ibuse observes, "I had to conclude that father, in matters of literature, had been a young man far behind the times" (9:97). Elsewhere Ibuse disparages his father when he recalls that grandfather Tamizaemon had considered Ikuta's boasts of literary accomplishment to be nothing more than simple vanity.[10]

Ibuse's retrospective assessment of Ikuta's professed strengths and actual weaknesses reveals the contempt he felt for his father. Miya, his mother, fares even less well in her son's published remembrances. She too is described as unaffectionate. In "Miscellany," Ibuse writes, "After father's death mother became strict with us children. She turned into an avid reader of magazines, especially one called *The World of Women's Education*" (9:250). What irreparably damns Ibuse's mother is the total absence in his memoirs of that slight ambiguity in the distaste he felt for his father. Ikuta seems almost tragic, but Miya seems merely stupid. In his essay "Mother" (*Ofukuro,* 1960), Ibuse tells of one of his rare visits to his aging mother. He is irritated, even angered, by her idiotic questions—the sad consequence of advancing senility. He can hardly wait to return to Tokyo, done with his filial duty for another year.

According to Ibuse, his mother never understood or approved of his choice in careers. In "Mother," he tells with spiteful humor of the time a loudspeaker van drove the streets of Kamo announcing the opening of a film based on one of his successful works. His mother became confused and thought the van contained police searching for her fugitive son. Shamed, she retreated into her house and shut all the doors and windows. But his dislike of his mother is not always relieved with such levity. In his poem "One Cold Night I Remember Mother" (*Kan'ya haha o omou,* 1948), Ibuse notes her incessant complaining, calls her a miser, and judges her to be "sad."

These portraits of a carping, ignorant mother and a weak, pathetic father suggest that Ibuse's first years were less than ideal; yet also resident in the family compound were his maternal grandparents, from whom he amply received the love and attention perhaps missing elsewhere. Ibuse's grandparents emerge in his memoirs as great and positive influences upon a character just forming. They were Ibuse's dearest kin, interesting and sensitive people who affected him in ways to be evidenced throughout his life as a writer.

Ibuse has many fond memories of his grandparents. *The First Half of My Life*—in a passage exceptionally vivid for a childhood remembrance written at age seventy-three—recalls that grandmother often placed him in her lap and told stories out of history. He remembers in particular the many tales of peasant famines and uprisings in the Tempō period (1830–1844), an era through which she herself had lived. As a child he listened spellbound to her accounts of brave and ingenious commoners—two virtues that would later mark Ibuse's own *shomin* ("folk") characters. Whether Ibuse borrowed from his grandmother's stories for his own, certainly she must be credited with some part of his remarkable interest in, and knowledge of, Japan's social history.

Ibuse's description of his grandmother's death in 1907 is both poignant and unexpectedly humorous—a clear sign of his affection for her. The news of her death was relayed by a servant to Ibuse, then only in the third grade, as he was on his way home from school. She had fallen ill a short time earlier but had refused to let the doctor examine her because the odor of the horse he had ridden to reach her still attended him. Other recollections include more such examples of a sensitive yet strong-willed woman. In "Miscellany" Ibuse writes, "The death of grandmother was a great blow to my family. The one person who could stand between mother and grandfather to mediate the emotional conflict between them was gone" (9:256).

This remark specifically notes the tension separating his mother from his grandfather. In the context of Ibuse's memoirs, this tension appears inevitable, a necessary clash between two very different people. Grandfather was as warm and supportive as mother was cool and uncaring. Indeed, no one in Ibuse's childhood had a deeper effect than grandfather on Ibuse's character as a man and as a writer. Grandfather Tamizaemon, even more so than grandmother, was the family storyteller. His fantastic tales, most beginning with the familiar "Long, long ago . . . ," transported the young Ibuse to far places and earlier times. On occasion, grandfather led him to the actual scenes of his stories, such as the ruins of Fukuyama Castle dating to the seventeenth century.[11] Perhaps on this excursion Ibuse's fascination with the historical was initially inspired; grandfather's purchase of a castle souvenir for him marked the start of a shared hobby, namely, the collecting of antiques and curios.[12] Ibuse states, in "Antiques" (Kottō, 1953), that his interest in such collections dates from childhood; his story, "A Calamity Befalls the Collection" (Shoga kottō no sainan, 1933), affectionately memorializes his grandfather's mania for amassing things of real or imagined value.

Ibuse has always treasured certain historical or nostalgic possessions, perhaps because he takes after his grandfather, but more likely because their solidity affords him a security. Unlike people, such things neither die nor abandon one. In the essay, "A Desk-Top Landscape" (Kijō fūkei, 1959), Ibuse lists the knickknacks in his study, many given him by family and friends now deceased. Ibuse explains that he must preserve these mementos, for, as with many of the works he has written, they represent men and women whom he has outlived.

Ibuse and his grandfather were apparently close. Their relationship was respectful as well as affectionate, pedagogic as well as familial. Grandfather taught him to keep a diary, just as he had himself since the age of sixteen. The habit was to serve Ibuse in good stead as a writer. Grandfather is remembered as a self-disciplined man, a conservative custodian of traditions, and a believer in the values of self-reliance and persistence. Ibuse writes with admiration in The First Half of My Life:

> When grandfather was sixteen he ran away from home because he wanted to study in Edo. Someone was sent after him to wait at a relative's in Okayama. There he was intercepted and returned home. My grandmother belonged to the Takakusa clan in Bitchū. When grandfather was a young man courting her, he would pay annoying and rather pointless visits to her accompanied by a servant carrying his old-fashioned valise. Finally grandmother succumbed to this test of wills and joined my grandfather's household as his bride.... It was a forward move on my grandfather's part. I do not seem to resemble him in the least. I envy my grandfather his full youth. [13:452]

Yet, as Ibuse has grown older, he realizes how much he has come to resemble his grandfather. Once he considered him old-fashioned, but now Ibuse wears his own hat and coat in his grandfather's style.

The coincidence is inward as well as outward: in *The First Half of*
My Life, Ibuse notes that until late adolescence he chafed under his
grandfather's considerable attentions, but now he looks back upon
him as a source of strength. He likens the old man to the sturdy
eucalyptus tree growing in his yard, and again, in words spoken to a
friend, he describes his grandfather's death as one "as quiet as a tree
withering."[13]

Grandfather's strength was equaled by his sensitivity. He was
often driven to tears reading a sad article in the newspaper. This
combination of strength and sensitivity served Ibuse well when he
was ill as a child, which was often. Grandfather would assume the
bedside responsibilities, nursing him back to health. In his memoir
"Turtles" (*Kame,* 1939), Ibuse recalls how grandfather would cap-
ture turtles, a symbol of longevity in Japan as elsewhere, and write
the name "Masuji" on their shells. Releasing them in a nearby
swamp, he hoped to restore his grandson's vigor in an act of empathic magic. In another essay, "Birthdays" (*Tanjōbi,* 1963), Ibuse
adds that his grandfather's private ritual had embarrassed him as a
child—what if a friend were to stumble across one of the turtles advertising his name?—but now, as a parent himself, he releases carp
(another symbol of health) into a stream when his own child contracts a serious illness.

Another "medicine" grandfather administered was regular vaca-
tioning. Originally prompted by a bout of pleurisy that struck both
Fumio and Masuji when they were small, these trips to the island of
Sensuitō off the coast of the Inland Sea—which included Matsuko,
but neither mother nor grandmother—became an annual event.
Ibuse fell in love with this part of Japan. He once told his friend and
critic, Onuma Tan, that, had the novelist and Ibuse protégé Dazai
Osamu seen the Inland Sea, he would not have killed himself.[14] So
taken was Ibuse with the beauty of this region that he made it the set-
ting for several important works, including his historical novel of
Japan's twelfth-century civil wars, *Waves* (*Sazanami gunki* [literally
A Military Chronicle of Rippling Waves], 1930–1938).

Ibuse's memoirs describe the happiest moments of his childhood
when they speak of these trips down to the sea. Fumio typically
fretted about time lost from school, but his younger brother reveled
in the fond company of their grandfather. Indeed, here Ibuse's grandfather stands out in sharpest relief as an indulgent, eccentric, sometimes serious, but often playful old man. He appears to be the source

and the archetype of the many "old man" characters that populate Ibuse's stories. Strong-willed and old-fashioned, but at the same time eager to display affection, grandfather left Ibuse a valuable legacy: a sense of history manifest in the present, the idea that the past remains significant. He did this not only through his living example but through his story telling, a pastime that probably had more to do with Ibuse's becoming a writer than all of his father's alleged passion for belles lettres. If, as Ibuse has claimed, his village gave him his diction, then his grandfather gave him the measured rhythms of his literary voice. Ibuse's mature style, though thoroughly imbued with erudition, had its genesis in what he heard his grandfather tell. "Miscellany" documents how grandfather read aloud from the newspapers in a distinctive, if somewhat embarrassing, tone. Ibuse has noted ironically that this has affected his writing style:

> I try as hard as I can to avoid giving my words a rhythm when I write, but nonetheless they sound old-fashioned. They read as if I had written them to a beat. The rhythm is similar to that of an old man long ago reading a newspaper aloud; a rhythm that made the reading easier. If I force myself to write when not in the mood, my words very soon take on the tone of my grandfather reading aloud from the papers.[15]

Despite his erstwhile chagrin over his grandfather's foibles, or his annoyance over the insidious influences stubbornly present in his writing, Ibuse admits that the effect of his grandfather upon him has been profound and permanent. Years later, after he had become a professional author in a city hundreds of miles from Kamo, Ibuse would recreate his deceased grandfather even larger than life, shaping characters with values and points of view meant to contrast with those of the typical Tokyoite.

Early Schooling

By 1905 these trips to the shore with grandfather had cured Ibuse's pleurisy. He was enrolled in the local Kamo elementary school, a mile walk from his home. Ibuse does not dwell with any particular affection on his first years of formal education; in *The First Half of My Life,* one reads that the school song was "not bad" and, in "Miscellany," that the principal had a loud voice. Only one of his classmates merits special mention, and then only because of his tragic

death. This young boy was chasing after butterflies when he fell into
a river and drowned. Ibuse, writing of this incident in "Miscellany," says, "The sandals that the child had worn were said to have been found downstream floating around and around in circles" (9:254).

This disturbing scene was destined to be repeated—a haunting central moment in Ibuse's oeuvre. Identical or similar passages have reappeared and evolved in one work after another, from this, its historical origin in "Miscellany," to the like demise of another young boy in "The River" (*Kawa*, 1931–1932), and to those of several A-bomb victims in "The Iris" (*Kakitsubata*, 1951) and *Black Rain*. Even in a story as humorous as "The Salamander," a whirlpool swallows a white flower, spinning faster and faster in ever smaller circles; in the emblematic flower, Ibuse's focus narrows to the poetic image of death itself irrevocably moving in a circle and inscribing the flow of Ibuse's natural world, a world that often carries the seeds of its own obliteration.

Even in his earliest works, death is seldom far from Ibuse's anxious attentions. As a theme, it informs and defines his work as does no other except perhaps that of the loss and recovery of place—through their mutual concern with fearful ends, the themes are naturally related. Ibuse's concept of death and the rituals with which he isolates it will change and grow more complex in his later works. But its personal inspiration and its artistic genesis can be found in the outset of his long life. Recollections of his childhood are marked with the unsettling details of numerous untimely and inappropriate deaths. In addition to his younger brother, his father, and his grandmother, Ibuse lost an aunt and, most notably, all three of the Satō family nurses entrusted with the care of him and his siblings. Two died of madness; a third, the one who accompanied Ibuse to his first funeral, drowned himself in a pond and thus became the model for a series of similar grisly scenes in Ibuse's later fiction. While Ibuse clearly wishes to write about these deaths, and while they may explain why he wrote his memoirs in the first place, his descriptions are so matter-of-fact in style that one wonders whether sheer frequency has not numbed the writer beyond grief. This is not the case, however. Rather, Ibuse is so controlled a writer that what passes for naturalistic alienation is, in truth, a critical distance necessary for the healthy admission of personal loss.

The quick succession of deaths told in Ibuse's two major memoirs, *The First Half of My Life* and "Miscellany," ended with that of his grandmother when he was nine. The next event of note occurred three years later in 1910. Ibuse regards this episode as so amusing, and perhaps meaningful, that he has written of it repeatedly. The most detailed account is in *The First Half of My Life.* One night the family was awakened and startled by thieves who demanded they be let into the locked house. What struck the young Ibuse, however, was not the thieves' demand, but rather their manner—loud shouts of "Akero! To o akero!" ("Open up! Open the door!") marked the first time he had ever heard Tokyo (i.e., standard) Japanese. (Ibuse, who is known to twist the truth if it makes a better story, admits elsewhere that he had, in fact, been exposed to standard Japanese sometime earlier by the neighborhood Kubota sisters.)[16] Ibuse claims that this abrupt introduction to the dominant and literary dialect of Japan caused him to associate it with crime, in particular, and with things awry, in general. Ibuse is joking, of course, but his humor targets the linguistic orthodoxy that he and other writers from rural areas would encounter as insecure young men in Tokyo.

It was in this period that Ibuse first imagined himself as a writer. In his memoir "Practice Period" (*Shūsaku jidai*, 1972), he states he first toyed with the notion because he thought he might prove talented. While confined at home in 1910—this time with a sprained foot—he had ample leisure to read fiction. At first he picked up adventure and mystery stories; later, the serious Romantic works of Kunikida Doppo and the sentimental popular fiction of Yanagawa Shun'yō. His brother Fumio discovered him in tears one day over a book. Mistakenly thinking this a consequence of his reading the latter author (it had in fact been the former), Fumio caustically commented that no one so moved by Shun'yō could ever hope to be a writer.[17]

Adolescence

In 1911 Ibuse failed the entrance exam to a prestigious Hiroshima middle school. The following year, however, he gained admission to Fukuyama Middle School, itself a well-known institution. Before the Restoration, known as the Makoto-no-kan ("Hall of Truth"), it had been the elite academy for the Fukuyama domain and was linked with such eminent classical scholars as Kan Sazan (1748–1827) and Rai San'yō (1780–1833). The older teachers were fond of boasting of their school's pedigree, yet its former mission in training the samurai class struck Ibuse as irrelevant to himself and other students of common origins. Still, the history of the school did record some note of progressive liberality, as Ibuse points out in *The First Half of My Life:*

> Lord Masahiro [Abe Masahiro (1819–1857), ruler of Fukuyama and an important figure in the opening of Japan to the West] was a progressive leader. In accordance with his wishes, the Makoto-no-kan was founded as a school for Western studies, but reputedly it did not emphasize only "Dutch learning," then thought of as the most advanced. If one looks through the library catalogue dating back to those first years, one notices there were English texts as well as those from other nations. Books dealing with pedagogy were numerous. According to Professor Higuchi, who wrote the words to our school song, the calisthenics classes conducted when the academy began were modeled on French military exercises. [13:406]

A relatively modern curriculum, however, did not make the school a welcome experience for Ibuse. Although he was fond of his English teacher, he was on the whole more miserable than he had been in elementary school. In the dormitory, where he did not room for long, students teased him for his thick eyeglasses and even tricked him into believing school regulations prohibited their use. An intimidated Ibuse soon damaged his poor vision further by sheepishly observing this imaginary proscription. Eventually he fled his classmates and commuted first from a relative's home located near the town of Yokoo and later from a house, rented by his mother for the two of them, located behind the ruins of Fukuyama Castle and a shrine to Lord Masahiro.

Ibuse has criticized his middle school for its harsh rules, but never for the quality of the education it provided. Nonetheless, his grandfather objected to what he considered an excessive Western bias in the course of study and arranged for a private tutorial in the Chinese classics. These lessons came to an abrupt halt when Ibuse's tutor, a diehard opponent of his country's Westernization, one day refused to yield the right of way to a bicycle (imported, of course, from the West) and was struck dead.

Ibuse's early interest in literature continued into his adolescence. In this particular field, however, his school's modernity stopped short of allowing such frivolous pastimes as fiction. Students caught reading novels were suspended for a week. The effect of such a rule,

Ibuse writes in his essay "Events Surrounding the [Shiga Naoya] Story 'Tale of a Kidnapping'" ("*Ko o nusumu hanashi*" *no shūhenji*, 1973), was that he knew nothing of writers popular during his middle school years (the first half of the Taishō period). Yet somehow, by the fourth year of his studies, he had read all of Shimazaki Tōson and most of Mori Ōgai. In "A Practical Joke" (*Itazura*, 1931), Ibuse writes that in 1916 he and a classmate had been following the newspaper serialization of Ōgai's biography, *Izawa Ranken*. The classmate, disturbed by Ōgai's treatment of Ranken, who had been physician to Lord Masahiro, cajoled Ibuse into writing a letter of protest. This Ibuse did, though he signed the letter with the pen name "Kuchiki Sansuke." Ibuse received a thoughtful reply from Ōgai, one that he appreciated as much because it bore a Tokyo postmark as because it had come from a famous scholar. Ōgai later quoted from Ibuse's letter (marking, in the absolute sense, Ibuse's debut as a writer). Ōgai commented that he had at first thought the letter to be from a madman or a practical joker, but because it was well written and possibly from an elderly gentleman, he had replied.[18] Ibuse ends "A Practical Joke" by thanking Ōgai for his kindness in granting him his first (if dubious) literary praise.

The irony of this anecdote deepens. While he was still in middle school the first literary work under the name Ibuse Masuji was published, though it was in fact not authored by him. His brother Fumio had wanted to contribute to a literary magazine but had feared disobeying his father's final wishes. He apparently cared little if his younger sibling, under the same interdict, did so, for he had submitted a poem to the Tokyo journal *Shūsai bundan* (*Talented Writers*) under Masuji's name. The poem was published and soon came to the attention of Masuji's middle school principal, a man who decried all literature but the most moralistic poetry. The principal severely reprimanded Masuji for wallowing in such *nambunga-ku,* or "light literature." Masuji was soon consoled, however, when he received two fan letters inspired by the poem—a poem he had not written, but for which he was both damned and praised.

Perhaps because of the trouble a single poem had caused, Ibuse's interest in literature was eclipsed for a short time by the visual arts. Art was well taught at Fukuyama Middle School. Though Ibuse is that institution's only renowned literary figure, several of his fellow alumni have become painters of note. The instructors were professional; their classes, congenial. In one interview Ibuse declared that drawing had been his favorite subject.[19] Ibuse found art fascinating, but not compelling. Several more years would pass before he would commit himself wholeheartedly to a career in writing. In his essay "Kyoto" (*Kyōto*, 1952), Ibuse confesses he once contemplated becoming a painter, not because he believed he had talent, but because he could think of no better alternative. He adds, in *The First Half of My Life:*

> From my third year of middle school I would answer "a painter" whenever asked what I wanted to be. I said that only because I liked pictures. I never meant to imply I would live my entire life as an artist" (13:417).

Art may have been a passing fancy when Ibuse graduated from middle school in 1917, but it was his only interest at the time. He departed in the spring of that year on a two-months' vacation to sketch scenes along the Inland Sea and in and around Kyoto, the first of scores of trips he was to take throughout Japan. He immensely enjoyed this freedom to draw as he pleased, and when a Kyoto innkeeper suggested that he show his work to an established painter, he eagerly agreed. Ibuse hoped that the painter, Hashimoto Kansetsu, would be sufficiently impressed to take him on as a student, but it was a hope unfulfilled, though he has continued to paint as an amateur his whole life. Yasuoka Shōtarō, always an astute critic of Ibuse, offers an interesting theory as to why he flirted with painting as an adolescent and why he eventually became a writer:

> Ibuse may very well have preferred painting to writing because a picture is, more than anything else, an object one can actually grasp and view. Like a farmer looking over his harvest, Ibuse is most satisfied when the fruits of his labor are actual physical things. I sense there exists a mimetic realism at the very root of Ibuse's nature.[20]

Yasuoka proposes a compellingly simple synthesis of several of Ibuse's diverse traits: his manner of careful depiction in writing, his early fascination with drawing, and his constant interest in village life. Ibuse's personality and stories suggest a basic and potent affinity for the concrete. This affinity perhaps first manifested itself in his representational drawing with paint and paper, if not in his even earlier collecting of souvenirs and mementos of historical culture. Eventually the paint brush yielded to the pen, and Ibuse discovered that he could fashion most fully in books his vision of the world before him. Books were tangible "fruits of labor" not solely manual but intellectual as well—a literary "harvest." Critics have long dwelled on Ibuse's concern with rural or folk characters in his fiction, and his basic identification with them as fellow villagers making a living with their hands. Ibuse writes to make books, Yasuoka seems to argue. Indeed, Ibuse's upbringing suggests the hypothesis that he is an author today because his intelligence and sensitivity have joined forces with an acculturated impulse—writer as *homo faber*—to create and manufacture the books that such intelligence and sensitivity have inspired.

Ibuse's urge to create awaited only a specific direction, a direction eventually provided from without. After his rejection in Kyoto, he returned to Kamo to confer with his brother. Both Fumio and one of his friends, Yamane Masakazu, believed that Ibuse should enroll in the literature course of Waseda University in Tokyo, where Yamane was already a student. Ibuse did not instantly leap at the suggestion, but he was inclined to acquiesce. He remembers in *The First Half of My Life:*

> I cannot tell exactly when it was that my brother wanted me to become a writer or a poet. Nor do I know if perhaps any of my middle school teachers had had anything to do with it. I doubt anyone had consulted a fortune-teller about my future. But I do think that Fumio, as my elder brother, wanted me to have every opportunity while I still could. And I was happy to have my brother help me. [13:423]

Masuji's entry into Waseda University was more than just an opportunity for his younger brother, in Fumio's view. It was a vicarious chance for himself. Perhaps this is why Fumio, both at this time and later, countered their mother's objections so that Masuji could continue to study at family expense. Masuji, for his part, did not resent this fraternal guidance. Instead, he proved quite cooperative, and in the fall of 1917 he entered the preparatory course of the Waseda University Literature Department. According to the conventional wisdom of the day, a Waseda degree ensured success. Ibuse Masuji is, however, a writer who has never much profited from what has been deemed the right or obvious course of action.

Tokyo

When Ibuse boarded a train for Tokyo in late August 1917, he was nineteen years of age. That so many of his generation rode similar trains to Tokyo from equally remote corners of the nation should not obscure the significance of this move in his own life. Geographically, he moved from hamlet to one of the world's great cities. Emotionally and psychologically, he traveled even farther. In Japan the dichotomy between rural and urban is deep but imperfect: neither town nor country functions independently of the other. Instead, as symbiotic halves of a national life, they contradict and complement each other; as two imaginative and historical traditions, they revolve about each other and jointly contribute to any individual definition of a Japanese.

Ibuse, like many of his countrymen, is slightly schizoid in this respect. he has boasted of the oldness—"old" implying "legitimate"—of his particular native corner of the archipelago. He cites as proof the ancient excavations, the medieval castles, the continuing fame of Sanyō ceramics, and so on. Yet he also writes in "Tales of Old" (*Mukashibanashi*, 1956) that the old men in his village, influenced by the descriptions in Futabatei Shimei's 1891 novel *Floating Clouds,* all sport moustaches "after the Tokyo fashion." in "Miscellany" Ibuse notes that his father was always quick to adopt whatever was popular in Tokyo; one example he cites was his father's passion for apples, and another the use of dumbbells sent him by a friend. Japanese culture measures and defines itself against its cosmopolitan center.

Ibuse, almost inadvertently, continues to embrace and reject the idea of the urban, a concept with which he was thoroughly familiar from childhood but never experienced for himself until young adulthood. One might have expected thesis and antithesis to produce synthesis, but that is precisely what has not happened. Like the negative and positive poles of a battery, this tension between "home," on the one hand, and the place where one must make one's professional life, on the other, has produced an energy among those writers who, like Ibuse, have found themselves without a stabilizing locale in which to exist as a cultural whole. What arises in lieu of that locale is the imperative to seek it. The force of this contradiction is often tapped to inspire a moment in art.

Ibuse's stories, with those of many other modern writers, imaginatively explore the confines of alienation in our contemporary and changing societies. An essay entitled "Thoughts One February Ninth" (*Nigatsu kokonoka shokan,* 1937) neatly sums up Ibuse's precise, and productive, predicament; "Sometimes I feel that half of me wants to return to the country while the other half would like to cling to Tokyo until the very end" (9:324). This emotional ambiguity has done much to determine the direction of his literature. Ibuse has never voluntarily returned to live in the countryside since he left it in 1917, but he has consistently evoked it in his writing—not as a Romantic ideal, but as a place that is sparse, earthy, complex, and other. He once told a friend how very attached he is to the trees of his hometown, and, on another occasion, how nice Tokyo is now that the trees are again blooming on the streets.[21] Ibuse nurtures a piece of Kamo within himself even while firmly established in Tokyo.

After hearing of Tokyo all his life, Ibuse was understandably impatient to experience it for himself as he rode the train in the summer of 1917. In "Arriving in the Capital" (*Jōkyō chokugo*, 1936), Ibuse recalls his thoughts as he sat in the speeding carriage. Eager to adapt himself to his future home, he tried mimicking the Tokyo dialect he overheard among other passengers. A doctor sitting across from him advised that he must learn each word's pronunciation, word by word. When the train pulled into the station, Ibuse was startled to hear the porters calling out, as thieves once had, in perfectly enunciated standard Japanese. Doctors might be expected to have mastered the nuances of this privileged idiom—but porters?

Ibuse's initial eagerness to greet the challenges of the city was soon replaced with loneliness. In Kamo he had heard that Tokyo was full of "temptations," as much an expression of envy as condemnation. He had naively assumed this to mean attractive and available women. When he was not propositioned immediately upon stepping off the train, he was disappointed. He was even more disappointed when no one, of either gender, paid him the least attention. Moreover, Tokyo seemed somehow imaginary, not a real place at all. In *The First Half of My Life* Ibuse recounts how the city appeared to him as he walked out of the station:

> The streets of Tokyo, which I was seeing for the first time, were not like the streets of Fukuyama. Fukuyama streets were a true earthen color. Tokyo streets were too black, worn and burnished to a thin luster. (Tokyo streets were not paved at that time.) I hesitate to admit it, but I could not accept those dirt streets as real. It did not look as if I would easily grow accustomed to them. [13:401]

Ibuse found lodgings in a student boardinghouse near Waseda. He moved frequently but remained at all times in the vicinity of the university, long after he had quit his studies. Even after he had married and built a house in Ogikubo, then outside the city proper, he would

take an occasional respite from domestic life, returning to one of his
old boardinghouses for a few days. For more than a decade after
coming to Tokyo in 1917, Ibuse led the life of an urban gypsy, regularly switching residences within the neighborhood and frequently
returning home to visit Kamo. In his humorous work *Always Moving (Hikkoshi-yatsure,* 1947), Ibuse describes the many and various
dingy boardinghouses he inhabited during that decade, the decade in
which he resolved to be a writer and in which he scored his first suc-
cesses.

Ibuse's memoirs never account precisely for the restlessness of his
youth, but perhaps it had to do with his inability to settle—in a psychological as well as a physical sense. He "could not accept those dirt
streets as real." Ibuse has referred to his vague feelings of disquiet
and depression as *kuttaku,* a word conveying both anxiety and melancholy. Kuttaku, reiterated not only in his memoirs but throughout
much of his early fiction, fairly characterizes Ibuse's Tokyo youth as
well as his first stories. Behind that anxiety and melancholy loomed
the start of a search for place, not so much for a simple residence as
for an existential state of mind and a satisfactory definition of self.

As a result, Ibuse's years of wandering in Tokyo were also years of
almost random exploration. In the boardinghouses, he associated
with other young men new to the city—men like himself in their relative unsophistication but, as they are remembered in Ibuse's writings,
more eccentric. The years immediately after the First World War had
opened Japan to many new ideas and possibilities, and youth reflected them all. At one boardinghouse, the Takada-kan, Ibuse knew
one aspiring writer who, with a portrait of Lord Byron in hand, went
to a barber and asked for the identical haircut. Later, this same student decided he was really more Verlaine than Byron, so he had his
hair adjusted accordingly. Finally, awake to the fact that his destiny
was Dostoevsky, the student moved to the most squalid of rooms to
lead a life of appropriate hardship. Ibuse's anecdotes tell of a charm-
ing innocence.

Yet these years Ibuse spent around Waseda University are important to him, because there he grew up. Prior to coming to Tokyo, he
had considered himself not much more than a child; after moving out
to his house in Ogikubo, he felt himself adult, even middle-aged.
Ibuse's youth was spent largely in the company of other literary
hopefuls gathered from all parts of Japan in these small rented

rooms. He writes in "Ushigome Tsurumaki-chō" (*Ushigome Tsurumaki-chō,* 1937) that the environs of Waseda were by no means fashionable—not pretty, as were the other student ghettos of Mita, Hongo, or Kanda. But that seems not to have mattered, for he says "I threw away any youth I might have had into the gutter" (9:377). This bitter comment suggests that he had, in fact, no youth; if carefree happiness is a requisite for such, then, indeed, he probably did not. Even taking into account that some measure of anguish is a near sine qua non for modern artists, especially young ones, Ibuse still seems to have exceeded the norm. He graduated into genuine moroseness. Ironically, this distinction contributed to his early success as a writer.

His courses at Waseda began in September, one of that school's most infamous moments. The campus became the battleground between students of differing radical persuasions whose violence exploded into what one historian has called "the most spectacular" university disturbance of that turbulent time.[22] Although he has devoted little of his memoirs to the political vicissitudes that must have colored his entire youth, Ibuse does mention the events surrounding this incident at Waseda in "Arriving in the Capital," but only in enough detail to note with typical humor that he had nothing to do with them.[23] Ibuse was to avoid student politics as carefully as he avoided student politicians. Doctrinaire ideologies never appealed to him, whether they were leftist in the 1920s or reactionary in the 1930s. Ibuse has mentioned encountering the critic Kobayashi Hideo one day on the street. Kobayashi said that he was reading some of Karl Marx and offered to lend Ibuse a volume. Ibuse replied he would borrow it only if Kobayashi would underline the important parts.[24] Although his generation produced many briefly "engaged" writers, Ibuse was not one of them.

Ibuse ignored the student strikes endemic to Waseda in those years, but he also did not attend many classes. In one interview, he states that he grew progressively lazier at Waseda, citing as a cause the "anguish of youth."[25] He confesses in "Ushigome Tsurumaki-chō" that he was so lethargic, he was barely able to summon the energy to go to the public bath or, when he wanted to buy a bicycle, to take on some part-time work. (Unfortunately, his first wages were stolen on his way to, naturally, the public bath.) Instead, he spent the greater part of each day alone in his room. Both ennui and his small stipend discouraged him from venturing out. The one diversion he

and his classmates readily allowed themselves was a table at the
Kaiyōken, the coffee shop favored by Waseda literature students. Although no Café Voltaire, the Kaiyōken was often the scene of heated political and literary arguments as well as impromptu plays and poetry readings. There, rather than in the classroom, Ibuse made many of his acquaintances and acquired an important part of his education. In *The First Half of My Life*, he recounts how, in one night, in the company of a single friend, he was introduced to the triple pleasures of pork cutlets, coffee, and the Kabuki.

Of course, certain professors did inspire him. He never missed any of Tsubouchi Shōyō's Thursday lectures on Shakespeare, any of Yoshida Genjirō's on Bashō, or any of Tatsuno Yutaka's on French fiction and poetry. Studying the masters of literature made Ibuse doubt whether he had what it takes to be a writer. At one point, having read somewhere that the secret to literary inspiration lay in the experience of poverty, he pawned his pocket watch. He did not need the money. He only wanted to live as he thought a writer should. Ibuse's classmates must have been afflicted with similar insecurities. Students entering Waseda his year numbered well over two hundred, most of them aspiring writers or playwrights. Initially Ibuse was intimidated by the presence of students apparently more gifted than he, but fear of his older brother's wrath kept him from dropping out.

Despite misgivings, Ibuse found himself increasingly drawn into the world of Tokyo writers and their circles of admirers. In the fall of 1918, when his depression over his prospects was compounded by a romantic disappointment, he was fortuitously introduced to the naturalist writer Iwano Hōmei. Hōmei was by this time an important figure in literary Tokyo, but earlier he had himself been a melancholy young man. It was well known that he had attempted suicide. Ibuse immediately sensed an affinity. He writes in "A Heart in Mourning" (*Moshō no tsuite iru shinne*, 1934):

> I visited Hōmei at home only twice. Mitsunari Nobuo, a student in political science and economics, took me there the second time. I sat in silence because Mitsunari said everything that I should have said for myself. My first visit was with a group of ten. Hōmei collected five *sen* from each of us and sent the maid to buy rice crackers. We ate them while Hōmei gossiped about other writers and criticized their work. . . .
>
> I sat in one corner of the room and tried to understand what sort of man Hōmei was, but now I remember nothing more than how he

laughed, how he sat—and his smoking. When I laugh aloud even today I believe I can detect some vestige of Hōmei's laughter within my own. If I was influenced this much by him after only one or two visits, then I regret that I did not pick up the more subtle aspects of his character. [1:286]

Ibuse was indeed influenced by Hōmei, who died of natural causes only a year after their meeting. Years after the above lines were written, he wonders again in "My Birdcage" (*Watakushi no torikago*, 1948) if he has not come to resemble him even more. The resemblance, however, is surely personal and not literary, since Ibuse informs us in the same essay that he deliberately refrained from reading any of Hōmei's works until after his death. Hōmei's personality, nonetheless, made the profession of literature more appealing to Ibuse. "My First Famous Writer" (*Hajimete atta bunshi*, 1935) describes how impassioned were Hōmei's remarks on Baudelaire and Tolstoy. In Hōmei, Ibuse may very well have encountered for the first time a man totally absorbed in, and instructed by, literature.

Ibuse was impressed by Hōmei as a man and as a writer, though he qualifies his early admiration when he admits in "My First Famous Writer" that, at this young age, he was in awe of everyone. Ibuse has paid Hōmei his highest compliment in an essay entitled "All About Reporters" (*Kisha no iroiro*, 1956)—"Iwano was what a man should be" (11:212). He has similarly lauded Hōmei's generosity, his humor, and especially his last words, uttered on his deathbed in 1920, when he told a disciple that he surely could have written something good had he been given a little more time. Ibuse, who is convinced he himself will exit this world with considerably less presence of mind, remains impressed.

Aoki Nampachi

After Hōmei's death Ibuse gained the acquaintance of Tanizaki Seiji, Jun'ichirō's younger brother and a scholar of English literature as well as a writer himself. Tanizaki commented on Ibuse's first stories and helped him polish two of the most famous, "The Salamander" and "The Carp" (*Koi*, 1926). But surely Ibuse's most important mentor and friend during his youth was his classmate at Waseda, Aoki Nampachi. They first met in a study group sponsored by the prominent writer and dramatist Yoshida Genjirō around the time Ibuse advanced to the undergraduate literature department, in which Aoki was also enrolled. In this study group, where participants criticized one another's writings, Ibuse was the only one who originally found Aoki's work praiseworthy. As a result, Ibuse began paying Aoki regular visits. A year later, when Aoki entered the French literature course hoping to become a translator, Ibuse tagged along to remain with his friend. The importance of Aoki's companionship would be hard to exaggerate. Ibuse has written often of their friendship, though it lasted only a few years. Ibuse speaks of Aoki at length in *The First Half of My Life:*

Another of my friends was Aoki Nampachi, who commuted to school from his home in the Sakashita-machi neighborhood of Ōtsuka. He, too, wished to be a writer. He liked to study and always attended classes. On odd days, he would go to the university library after school; on even days, to the Ueno Library. He spent his summers translating at a seaside cottage. Extremely nearsighted, he was a refreshingly serious student.

I have written of Aoki Nampachi from time to time. Aside from essays and memoirs, there is my piece "Aoki Nampachi" and the story "The Carp," in which my deep feelings for Nampachi are symbolized in a carp. I have written so much about him that I cannot avoid being redundant. But Nampachi took good care of me in my college years. I think it would be inappropriate to exclude him from *The First Half of My Life.*

Aoki came from a talented family. His oldest brother, Tokuji, excelled at numismatics; his next older brother, Kusuo, achieved remarkable success as a bridge engineer. Kusuo is presently at work on the preparations for the construction of a bridge to link Shikoku with Honshū. It is said that Nampachi, too, exhibited genius. It was because genius and stupidity make good companions that the able Nampachi was kind to someone so dull as myself. . . .

Nampachi encouraged me everyday. He said that the practice of writing was the first obligation of anyone with literary ambitions. He regarded as sacred the practice of writing and its fruits. He was earnest, as men with poetic sensibilities are. When Nampachi would come to my room to wake me, he would sit down and read some of the manuscripts on my desk. I hardly expected Nampachi, with his high critical standards, to like my work. But instead of calling it terrible, he would say such things as "It's all right!" and "You'll make it!" "Make it" was a phrase referring to success and was intended to keep my spirits from falling.

[13:434–36]

Ibuse's respect for Aoki bordered on idolization. Although they were roughly the same age, he looked up to him as a model worthy of imitation. Perhaps Aoki, and not Hōmei or Tanizaki, was most responsible for Ibuse's eventual serious commitment to writing. Aoki offered Ibuse the brotherly intimacy he had craved not only since going to Tokyo but possibly all his life. At the same time, he supplied Ibuse with the discipline and moral support he had needed. As a gift for Aoki, this most important of friends, Ibuse wrote seven short stories, each about a different animal, while at an Inland Sea resort in the summer of 1919. One of these stories was the earliest draft of his debut work, "The Salamander."

That autumn Ibuse returned to Tokyo and his studies at Waseda, but his resolve to attend classes was weaker than ever. He often overslept, deliberately placing books by his pillow so that Aoki would think he had studied throughout the night. Still doubting whether he had sufficient acumen for writing, he began in April 1921 to attend painting classes at an art school once or twice a week. He spent his summer vacation that year sketching rather than writing, and when he returned to the university, he quarreled with two of his professors. Finally, owing to an "unpleasant incident" involving a series of awkward encounters with one of them, the Russian literature scholar Katagami Noburu, Ibuse withdrew from both Waseda and the art school.[26]

At the suggestion of one of his middle school teachers, he left the city to spend some time on Innoshima, an island in the Inland Sea and a prominent setting in his later literature. This repose, spent on the second floor of a doctor's clinic and intended as only a short break from his studies, lasted a full seven months. Innoshima offered more than a site for rest; it became a contemplative retreat where Ibuse pondered the direction of his life. Mired in his bored discomfort and aimless confusion, Ibuse suffered in a prison as psychologically real as that in which he would place his salamander, the protagonist of his first published story.

Ibuse began on Innoshima to explore for paths of escape from his restlessness, hoping to find the freedom that literature in the optimistic Taishō period seemed to offer many of his generation. He tried to relieve his melancholy with revelry. According to "Miscellany," he dallied with geisha and drank a good deal. These diversions were apparently designed to help him "recuperate" from melancholy, as he wrote in an essay appropriately entitled "Samisen Song" (*Samisen uta*, 1952). Presumably, however, not all one's time can be spent at night. Ibuse has stated elsewhere that he used his leisure to read, particularly the Russian authors so popular in Japan at that time.[27]

When he finally returned to Tokyo in March 1922, Ibuse had every intention of resuming his studies. Some, however, now opposed the idea; namely, Fumio and a professor with whom Ibuse had argued. Fumio had no doubt decided his brother had had his chance and wasted it. The professor, called Kataguchi in *The First Half of My Life,* but whose name was in fact Katagami, was an epileptic whom Ibuse had inadvertently embarrassed by witnessing the onset of a seizure. This embarrassment might have been the reason behind the professor's campaign against Ibuse's readmission to the university.

Whatever the true story, Ibuse was made to wait several months while the authorities considered his application. During the interim, in May 1922, Aoki Nampachi contracted a respiratory ailment and died suddenly, the day after Ibuse's older brother Fumio left Tokyo, having come to scold him for the "selfish behavior" leading to the rejection of his application for readmission to Waseda. With so much going on, Ibuse had not suspected his friend was so seriously ill. That inattentive lapse has caused Ibuse endless feelings of guilt. He has written about the shock of Aoki's death a number of times, even fearing that he may have "written about him too much."[28] Only later would Ibuse realize how rare a talented and kind friend like Aoki would be. In "Miscellany" he says:

> The day before he died I bought a cactus at an exhibition in Ueno and went to his home to pay a call. His mother came to meet me at the door, but when she saw my face she broke down in tears, unable to say anything. There were a number of dress shoes left in the entryway by visitors. I realized that Aoki's doctors and relatives had come to be with him at the end. I left the cactus on the edge of the entrance and returned home after signaling a silent farewell to his mother.
>
> Almost all our classmates were at the funeral. We offered incense in his memory. Both the cactus and the square cap he always wore had been placed on his coffin. The third-year students (under the new system) and the most recent graduates (under the old) combined to hold a memorial service for him in the Onshi-kan. Imai Jōkan, a third-year student in French, donned the robes of a priest and read the sutras in a rich, clear voice. Imai was the hereditary chief priest of a temple in Okitsu. Yoshi

Takamatsu and Saijō Yaso gave the eulogy while we sat in hushed silence. [9:264]

Immediately after Aoki's death, Ibuse permanently severed all ties with Waseda University. He insists in *The First Half of My Life* that the two events were unrelated. Nonetheless, at this point, Ibuse threw himself into the very career Aoki had encouraged and might have made his own had he not died so young. Perhaps Ibuse began, after the tragedy of 1922, to live and work for two. In any case upon the death of his best friend, his decision to become a writer was one he has never publicly reconsidered or regretted.

After abandoning plans to finish his formal education, Ibuse at long last became a dedicated student. His days were spent practicing his own prose and reading modern prose masters. He was particularly impressed in these years by Hirotsu Kazuo—a writer whom he once wished he could be like.[29] He also admired Shiga Naoya and Uno Kōji.[30]

In July 1923 Ibuse wrote for the first of the many coterie magazines (*dōjin zasshi*) in which he was to participate. *Seiki* (*The Century*) was published by a small group of Waseda students. Unfortunately it folded after the premier issue when fire destroyed the second. In *The First Half of My Life,* Ibuse surmises he has spent half his life writing for such little magazines. Elsewhere he offers the explanation that "human beings instinctively cluster in herds both large and small."[31] But it is also true that journals such as *Seiki* gave Ibuse his first chance to be read. He could begin to build a reputation among the public.

"Confinement"

Ibuse's contribution to the short-lived *Seiki* was the 1919 "The Salamander," which he had written for Aoki but had renamed "Confinement" (*Yūhei,* 1923) while revising it on Innoshima. "Confinement" was the first published version of his well-known tale of a hapless salamander trapped in an underwater cave. This story was to attain the final stage of its complex evolution in "The Salamander" (1929), the most famous work of Ibuse's early career. Consequently, "Confinement" has been dismissed by most critics as preliminary, tentative, and thus "imperfect." It is seldom read without reference to the changes Ibuse would later make. So fundamental are these changes, however, that "Confinement" deserves to be read as an independent and complete work. Moreover, beyond suggesting the genesis of Ibuse's later and more polished fiction, "Confinement" thematically and structurally represents the archetypal Ibuse short story.

"Confinement," under the title "The Salamander," started its literary life as one of the seven animal tales Ibuse wrote for Aoki Nampachi. Some of these tales have been lost, but those that remain are united by the common motif of isolation leading to depression and finally despair. "Termites" (*Teppōmushi*), for instance, tells of insects imprisoned within wood. Similarly, "Confinement" tells a brief, first-person account of an unfortunate amphibian who has ventured into an underwater cave, has lingered too long, and has grown too large to swim out. "Confinement" conceivably could suggest a children's story, given the choice of an animal as the central character, the comic simplicity of his predicament, and, above all, the style that prompted critic Terada Tōru to remark that Ibuse's works are like "sketches done in crayon."[32] All are elements that suggest a literal reading. yet the absolute and terrifying impossibility of the salamander's escape would render "Confinement" a cruel children's story, indeed. Rather, it seems intended for the same young adult who produced it. As the salamander comes to realize his imprisonment is permanent, and as he falls into a state of anxiety (*kuttaku*), the reader comes to suspect that Ibuse, the author, is perhaps indistinguishable from the story's first-person narrator (*boku*, "I"). "Confinement" is a work without hope.

Ibuse has said that he wrote "Confinement" under the influence of Anton Chekhov's short story "The Bet." But that influence is only casual. The imprisonment of Chekhov's protagonist, a young man, is entirely voluntary—the result of a wager with a friend. The problem is, therefore, ethical, not practical. Ibuse's debt to Chekhov more likely lies in the style of "Confinement," an example of the *hon'yakuchō*, or forced foreign idioms, common in Ibuse's earliest stories and characteristic of those years (never completely over) when many writers were drawing not only their inspiration but their diction from foreign works. For the actual antecedents of "Confinement" it is more profitable to look in Ibuse's youthful memoirs. In

The First Half of My Life Ibuse writes about the world of his salamander among his recollections of Fukuyama Middle School:

> In one corner of the interior garden was a shallow pond the size of one tatami mat. Wire screen was stretched over it with none of the pleasing effect of green moss. Two salamanders had been raised in this pond. One was seventeen inches long; the other, something less than a yard. They were a species of salamander known as the *hanzaki*. The "Lord of Imba Swamp," which I had seen in a side show at a Fukuyama festival, was also a hanzaki. These were just as big. They belonged to Professor Shima, the senior zoology teacher. Professor Shima, who doubled as the head of our dormitory, had a grouchy disposition, but I paid him no heed and fed toads to his salamanders whenever I found some.
>
> It was necessary to obtain Professor Shima's permission to feed his salamanders, but I was not the only one who did so surreptitiously. At first, I would capture toads only after I had stumbled upon them, and I would feed them to the salamanders only because I had captured them. They became sick eating toads, so I substituted frogs. It was fun to watch the salamanders come to the surface of the water and swallow the frogs in one gulp. [13:412]

> Later, when I was a literature student at Waseda and starting to write, I created a story about salamanders. Naturally I wrote it remembering those frogs I and [my roommate] Miyahara had so playfully caught and fed to the salamanders. Known as "living fossils," salamanders can live one or two years without eating. Leeches are also that way. But when salamanders do grow hungry, they will eat their own claws. I wrote my story thinking of that, too. [13:415]

The story Ibuse had wanted Aoki to read in 1919 became the story he wanted everyone to read in 1923. Inspired by his adolescent memory of two imprisoned and self-destructive salamanders ("they will eat their own claws") and by his loneliness upon coming to Tokyo and soon thereafter losing his only friend, "Confinement" provided a tragicomic vehicle for Ibuse's own anxiety. By analogy, the salamander characterized Ibuse's worst despair during the time he felt the most isolated and the most terrified: "Confinement" presented the condition from which Ibuse would have to graduate to become a mature and significant writer.

As the original character who is endangered, forgotten, and, most important, far from home, the salamander of "Confinement" prefigures Ibuse's classic protagonists. This amphibian will appear in other, more anthropoid guises, not only in the early short stories but also throughout Ibuse's long career and in all his best works. Such characters—from young soldiers, to castaways, to victims of the atomic bomb—will become increasingly complex in their alienation and their resolution of it. Nonetheless, they hark back to the simple salamander of "Confinement" and to its author, Ibuse, in his mid-twenties. Alone in Tokyo, no longer the beneficiary of his family's financial largesse, and without his one good friend, Ibuse had many reasons to doubt his chance for literary success. "Confinement" gives expression to these insecurities and is, in this sense, very much the first work of a struggling writer.

Alongside the fear of inadequacy, however, coexists its remedy: humor. The humor in Ibuse's work, certainly that in "Confinement," plays a serious role in affirming, never denying, the presence of essential human hope. E. B. White once said that humor dies under analysis like a frog under dissection. Yasuoka Shōtarō, naturalizing the simile, likens Ibuse's humor (okashisa) to "fine bean curd... impossible to pick up with chopsticks."[33] It may be easier, however, to pinpoint the motivation of humor than its subtle mechanics. The motivation behind Ibuse's humor lies in its power to render a minor protagonist such as the salamander in "Confinement" more universal than could the conventions of tragedy, and consequently more movingly real, even tragic, to the reader. The very absurdity of the salamander's predicament, nearly Kafka-esque in its description, serves to preclude the reader's usual and worn response to pathos, which would otherwise obscure the truer terror of the abject loneliness experienced by the creature. The contradiction, perhaps quintessential to comedy, is that humor can engender the most complete tragedy.

Ibuse has aptly commented that he uses humor to extinguish sentimentality, an emotion conspicuously absent from his work because it obstructs more profound feelings.[34] The humor in "Confinement" makes pity awkward and, instead, focuses the reader's capacity for empathy directly on the salamander. It is an effective device—perhaps Ibuse's best: it is hard to imagine another writer who could have made humor an important part of a serious novel about the atomic bomb. In Black Rain, when Ibuse has fully developed his point of view and powers of characterization, his humor is less absurd and more exacting in its effects. But, as has been observed by

Japanese critics, its source has remained the same since his first stories.[35] Humor consistently functions as a device to limn the protagonist's fate, as a means of rendering the sad not less so but more. Ironically, this is how Ibuse's humor achieves a positive, humanistic affirmation. His characters are offered not only an authenticity but a kind of salvation when Ibuse places them in bizarre circumstances, for against such a foil, their feelings and values become less singular. The salamander, trapped underwater in a cave, becomes any one of us discouraged or even defeated by misfortune: and from experience comes, as we shall subsequently see, the power to survive.

Tanaka Kōtarō

Two months after the publication of "Confinement" and Ibuse's debut into Tokyo literary circles, the city was destroyed by the Great Kantō Earthquake. Amazingly, Ibuse and many other writers survived the fires and riots that swept the capital. Ibuse was, of course, deeply affected. For the first time he had witnessed wide-scale catastrophe, the carnage and destruction wrought not only by tremors but by his fellow man that September 1923. The experience became one source of images for the many disasters treated in Ibuse's works, which are a compendium of earthquakes, volcanic eruptions, floods, fires, and wars unrivaled in modern Japanese literature. These descriptions of catastrophe perhaps suggest a common rhetorical origin in what Ibuse saw at age twenty-five. He writes in *An Ogikubo Almanac (Ogikubo fudoki, 1981–1982)*:

> September 1, 1923. When light broke that day, a terrible rain began to fall. It was a sudden downpour, and I was awakened by the sound. The raindrops were so big they seemed the width of a walking stick, so fat I wondered whether what they call in the South Pacific a "squall" was anything like this.
> The rain stopped unexpectedly, and after the sun had risen the morning sky was pure blue. Later, published accounts reported that the day was perfectly clear, and that it was hot and humid. That is not quite right. After the rain there came a cool and refreshing summer morning. The day grew hot gradually, and at some point huge columns of clouds appeared in the eastern sky. They were strange clouds with delicate folds, something which, like the rain, I had never seen before....

... The earth began to tremble at fifty-eight minutes past eleven in the morning and did so for three minutes.[36]

And then in *The First Half of My Life:*

> Tokyo burned for three days and three nights. When the Shirokiya De-
> partment Store and later the Imperial University caught fire, huge pillars
> of flames shot up. Many refugees were crowded around third base in a
> ball park, about a third of the number who would have been present for a
> Waseda–Keiō match. But unlike the crowd at a baseball game, everyone
> was utterly silent. No one could see the flames of the burning city from
> first base, so on the first, second, and third days there were but a few
> people near it.
>
> The flames were terrible, and so were the cumulonimbus clouds in one
> part of the sky. They were immense. At night they reflected the fires and
> looked like red, inflamed wounds, turning black just before dawn and
> then white once the sun rose. I wondered whether they had not gushed
> out into the sky at the same time the ground had shaken. [13:440–41]

These passages are unmistakably Ibuse. Writing in a careful chronological order, demonstrating his control of prose, Ibuse naturalisti-
cally describes strange quirks in nature, yet he terrifies the reader by
focusing on the calm before disaster strikes, and on that bizarre, abstract beauty that so often attends catastrophe. This earthquake is
only one of the many examples of Ibuse's frightful vision of how,
throughout history and throughout the world, everything seems to
approach annihilation. This vision, here with images first witnessed
during the conflagration of Tokyo's earthquake, is rooted in even
earlier events. Ibuse's fear of death and, paradoxically, his discomfort at surviving the deaths of others, continually resurface in the
various cataclysms catalogued in his literature. A childhood marked
with deaths yields to an adulthood obsessed with how, and to what
end, such deaths occur.

When the earthquake struck Ibuse was at home in his boardinghouse in the Shimo-Totsuka section of the city working on a short
story. After spending his first night on a bench in a baseball park, he
eventually took refuge at a cousin's home located outside of the city
proper. A week after the earthquake he walked along the train tracks
from Ogikubo to Tachikawa where he was able to board a train for
Kamo and the comfort of his family, thus bringing to an end the first
of what Ibuse has called his "refugee experiences."

Soon, however, friends called him back to Tokyo, where he found his fellow writers already back at work and even invigorated by the new construction going on all around them. Ibuse writes in *The First Half of My Life,* "After a month at home I returned to Tokyo. The publishing world was active, even on the verge of a renaissance. But I, wearing the haggard look of a struggling writer, had no hope of success" (13:446). Help appeared at precisely this moment of despair, however. A few weeks after his return to the city, Ibuse was introduced to Tanaka Kōtarō (1880–1941), a writer originally from Shikoku and known for his essays and supernatural stories. Tanaka was to be an important figure in Ibuse's life for the next several years. He was a friend, critic, patron, and inspiration to Ibuse: it was Tanaka who prodded and praised Ibuse in his work; it was Tanaka who gave him a job when he was broke; and it was Tanaka who even found him a wife in 1927. Ibuse once asked Tanaka why he had done him so many favors. Tanaka, who enjoyed liquor to frequent excess, responded in his native country dialect (he and Ibuse shared similar rural roots) that Ibuse was an excellent drinking companion. This anecdote typifies their close and informal relationship, a relationship for which Ibuse was to express gratitude several times in his memoirs.

Tanaka's support was most crucial at the start of their association. "Confinement" had not been well received, and a lack of income forced Ibuse to seek employment. He secured an editing position at Shūhōkaku, a small publishing house, in November 1924, but he quit three months later, citing boredom. Poverty forced him to work there again the following year, but he quit soon again after proving a less than careful editor. Tanaka helped Ibuse by providing him with occasional work proofreading, researching, and tracing the etymologies of words found in Chinese classics, supporting him thus for a full year and a half. This fortuitous friendship repaid Ibuse with more than money. It afforded him the opportunity to learn from a man knowledgeable not only about literary matters but about history, particularly the history of his native region, the important former domain of Tosa. Ibuse's own works, especially his historical fiction, are generously peopled with Tosa characters and feature many Tosa settings. Both Ibuse and Tanaka, writers from areas once historically prominent, were living in a city whose power far eclipsed any place in Japan's past. Thus, perhaps both writers were seeking a modern accommodation of their local heritages within an urban Japanese literature. If so, then Tanaka was well qualified to serve as Ibuse's earliest professional mentor and critic.

"Plum Blossom by Night"

Ibuse wrote two important works while under Tanaka's tutelage. The first, published in 1925, is entitled "Plum Blossom by Night" (*Yofuke to ume no hana*) and marks a crucial development in Ibuse's progress as a writer. This story, like "Confinement" and other early Ibuse works, is told in the first person. The narrator, *watakushi*, who is also the protagonist, resembles Ibuse himself.[37] Watakushi steps out late one night for a bite to eat. He is not only hungry but also vaguely upset (kuttaku). He is accosted by a stuporous drunk who forces a five-yen note upon him, a considerable sum to this young man. For months thereafter, watakushi is periodically seized by the guilty urge to find the drunk and return the money. On the final page of the story, watakushi is himself inebriated. He hallucinates that he is, in fact, the drunk who had accosted him months earlier, a man who, though never to be heard from again, has become a constant obsession.

"Plum Blossom by Night" voices the same mood of ennui and depression found in "Confinement." Rather than a salamander in a cave, however, watakushi is now an impoverished young man in Tokyo. This evolution in character and setting brings Ibuse a step closer to confronting his own uneasiness. In one passage certainly drawn from his own past, Ibuse writes:

> He [Tawa, an old classmate] would come to my place two or three times a month and usually talk about fluctuations in the stock market. He would comment on how I proofread for various printers with remarks like "You can't go on living like someone's handyman. It doesn't matter what you do for a profession, but you mustn't go to seed. You have to think of the future. Be more positive! Positive!"
> ... But he never did succeed in making me more positive [1:24]

Such were Ibuse's own worries in 1925. His concerns over his fate were to persist and even deepen at times, but in "Plum Blossom by Night" the reader can detect Ibuse's first moves to free himself. First, in an important admission, Ibuse identifies the protagonist closely with himself. Then he has watakushi momentarily imagine himself as someone else, the drunk who had given him the five-yen bill. Wata-kushi is not only made cognizant of another person, but he even visualizes himself in that person's body and is, thus, temporarily permitted an escape from his own anxieties. This illusion, though brief, had not been possible in "Confinement." There the protagonist had been absolutely, irrefutably alone.

"The Carp"

Ibuse's next short story, one of his best known, is a brilliant portrait of a young man (again referred to as watakushi) who, as before, finds bizarre companionship in the midst of gloom. "The Carp" was published initially in Tanaka's own journal, *Kagetsu (Beautiful Moon)*, in September 1926, and revised for the February 1928 issue of *Mita bungaku (Mita Literature)*. A very short story, "The Carp" demonstrates that brevity serves poignancy. It is perhaps the most moving of Ibuse's early works, especially if the reader understands the story as a confession.

"The Carp" appeared in *Kagetsu* not as a work of fiction but as an essay. At times Ibuse refers to it as a story (see p. 29, above) and at times as his first essay.[38] Such genre distinctions mean less to Ibuse than to others. As he once explained, when he is low on funds, he submits what he has written as "fiction" because it pays better than "essays."[39] At first glance, "The Carp" may indeed appear to be an essay. Upon close examination, however, some of its most important points are entirely fictive. Ibuse writes in "Tanaka Kōtarō, My Teacher" (*Tanaka Kōtarō-sensei no koto*, 1972) that he has always felt compelled to change the names of characters from real life in his fiction, so when one notes in "The Carp" that true names are used—Aoki Nampachi is mentioned in the first paragraph—one naturally assumes the work is an essay. This is an incorrect assumption. "The Carp" has features of both fiction and nonfiction because Ibuse is writing both about himself and about Aoki. He allows himself liberties with the former while maintaining strict veracity regarding the latter. Ibuse elucidates the relationship between his stories and his essays in "Random Jottings" (*Oriori sōshi*, 1955);

> Must an essay speak of things exactly as they are? Such an attempt often results in nothing more than the barest skeleton of a work. Is it not permissible, without indulging in creative writing, to proceed in a manner

distinct from simple description and put our trust in the accidental effects
of fiction? ... When I write of other people I put the question of the finished product out of my mind and usually write the actual truth; but
when I write of myself, I do use some elements of fiction. [11:138–39]

"The Carp" combines accidental effects with the actual truth.
Aoki's role in "The Carp" is the drunk's in "Plum Blossom by
Night"; both are psychological foils to Ibuse's melancholy. Pure invention and the memory of a dead friend interact to create a truth
that is not necessarily factual.

"The Carp" relates that Aoki, motivated by "whole-hearted kindness," gives Ibuse a gift of a white carp. Ibuse promises him that he
will care for the carp forever, and he releases it in a small pond located behind his boardinghouse.

When Ibuse moves to different quarters, he must find a new place
to keep the carp. He consults with Aoki and decides to place it in the
pond behind the home of Aoki's girl friend.

> Before releasing the carp in the pond, I insisted that even though I was
> placing the fish in a pond that belonged to his girl friend, I still possessed
> all rights to it. . . . I had pledged to Aoki that I would care for this fish, no
> matter what. [1:13]

Six years later, Aoki is dying. Ibuse means to call on his best friend
on the eve of his death, bringing a cactus as a present. But he notices
the shoes of Aoki's girl friend in the entryway. Without entering,
Ibuse returns home. He leaves the cactus in the entryway. At Aoki's
funeral, Ibuse spots his friend's favorite cap and the cactus on top of
the coffin. He restrains himself from a sudden urge to run and fetch
the carp and place it, too, on the coffin.

A few days later Ibuse resolves to fish the carp out of the girl
friend's pond. He obtains permission by letter. While retrieving it, he
helps himself to a number of the loquats that dangle over the water.
After catching the carp and transferring it to a pool on the Waseda
University campus, he makes a point of going back to the pool every
day to see his pet swimming around "like a king." He frequents the
pool, even in winter, hoping each time to spy his big white fish. The
story ends:

> One morning a thin snow fell onto the ice. I picked up a long bamboo
> pole and drew a picture on its surface. It was a picture of a fish over eigh-
> teen feet long. I imagined it to be my white carp.

When I finished the drawing I thought of writing some words by the carp's mouth, but gave up the idea. Instead I drew beside it a large number of roach and killifish. They were chasing after the carp, trying not to fall behind. But how foolish and pitiful they looked! They had neither fins nor eyes nor mouths. I was utterly content. [1:17]

This testament to Ibuse's loneliness, and to Aoki's welcome, if brief, intrusion into it, is already familiar to any reader of "Miscellany." Yet much is new in "The Carp." These are the "elements of fiction" mentioned in "Random Jottings." Neither the carp nor the girl friend is mentioned elsewhere in Ibuse's writings, and the reader may provisionally assume that therein lies the story. There were no girl friend's shoes when Ibuse actually paid his aborted visit to Aoki; there was no urge to place a white carp on the coffin. Both moments were created to represent the twin emotions of jealousy and love that characterized Ibuse's friendship with Aoki.

Ibuse has alluded in *The First Half of My Life* to the "deep feelings" (*kangai*) for Aoki which the carp symbolized.[40] The carp is large, white, and, like Melville's whale, a sign of virility and love. The carp is a natural symbol of those "deep feelings" Ibuse pledges to preserve, nurture, and always "care for." The true importance of these emotions is demonstrated when they are threatened. Ibuse defensively insists the carp is his as he places it in the pond belonging to his rival for Aoki's affections. Covetous of the carp and jealous of Aoki, Ibuse resents the meddlesome existence of the girl friend. He will not enter his friend's home while she is there. Finally, when he retrieves the carp from her pond—both decline to meet each other face to face—Ibuse feasts on fruit as if to suggest that only his relationship with Aoki was fertile.

There are strong suggestions of eroticism here, although one that Ibuse can enjoy solely through the proxy of the carp. That is why he is so eager to move the carp out of the girl friend's pond. The university pool, its new home, is equally significant. Pools (*pūru*) in Japanese literature connote an image of the modern, the urban: that, combined with the fact that this pool is surrounded by young men as happy as Ibuse and Aoki once were themselves, makes the transfer of the carp a leap into a world where only their friendship was allowed, the world of their classmates, the world of their ambitions, and a world without the presence of women.

The final image of the story is also its most striking—the huge outline of the carp drawn in the snow. The gargantuan carp is tailed by "foolish" and ignoble fish, just as Ibuse believed Aoki's genius dwarfed his own meager talents ("It was because genius and stupidity make good companions...."). Ibuse is "utterly content"; with this drawing he has restored his relationship with his deceased friend to its proper, if unequal, proportions. The drawing of the carp takes on further significance when one remembers Yasuoka's words about Ibuse being most satisfied when the fruits of his labor were actual physical things. With an etching in the snow, Ibuse has made secure the memory of Aoki. He has made Aoki the giant in death that he had been in his admirer's eyes while alive.

The conclusion of "The Carp" addresses not only the reader but Aoki himself. Twice in this short story, Ibuse mentions Aoki's spirit (*tama*). Once he even speaks to it directly. Ibuse apparently believes his friend's soul not only survives but judges, for he asks its understanding. "The Carp" can be read as an apology, a confession of feelings perhaps never articulated when Aoki was alive to hear them. "The Carp" is an important work in the history of Ibuse's writings, not only because it so succinctly expresses profound personal emotion, but because it is the first of his many stories honoring deceased friends, family, and countrymen by ensuring their continued existence within his words.

Yet while "The Carp" is new, it is also familiar: the story of an estranged young man in the city who would establish ties with the greater world he sees all about him, much as the salamander in the cave would wish. This passage from "The Carp" links it thematically with "Confinement" and "Plum Blossom by Night":

> I released the carp in the pool at Waseda University.
>
> When summer came, the students began to swim in the pool. I would come to watch every afternoon. As I peered through the chain link fence surrounding the pool, I thought their skillful swimming was wonderful. I was already out of work by that time, and it seemed appropriate that I should be looking on from the sideline.
>
> When the sun began to set, the students would come out of the water and lie naked under the trees to smoke cigarettes and joke among themselves. I would gaze upon their healthy physiques and happy swimming and heave many deep sighs. [1:15–16]

When Ibuse peers longingly through the metal fence at the students swimming in a pool, he remembers Fukuyama Middle School and Professor Shima's salamanders, kept captive by the metal grid suspended over their pond. In "The Carp" Ibuse, too, is held captive, like the salamander of "Confinement," restricted to gazing through at the normal "healthy" world. Both are forced eventually to confront that world. The cave, whether literal or figurative, is the principal setting of Ibuse's early works, isolating him from the outside world where everyone else appears to function without despair. But in "Plum Blossom by Night," Ibuse makes increasing room for others to join him in his melancholy. In "The Carp" his company consists of a fish: later it becomes more anthropoidal. The final line of "The Carp"—"I was utterly content"—suggests an ironic reading. But it also portends a consolation that the carp, a living symbol of "deep feelings," can offer to Ibuse even after the human object of these feelings is gone.

The carp is one of Ibuse's finest characters. It joins the image of a simple and common creature with the anguish of Ibuse's youth and his hope for an integration with the natural world. This integration is achieved by such late Ibuse characters as *Black Rain's* Shigematsu when as a bomb victim in poor health, he turns to nurturing baby carp to nurture himself. But when Ibuse was writing "The Carp," he was alone in the Ushigome section of Tokyo, in a room with a view of a pond within the grounds of the First Waseda Secondary School. He describes the panorama in his essay "The Woods of Toyama School" (*Toyama gakkō no mori*, 1936). From his window he could see a cemetery that included yawning graves, fallen tombstones, and even exposed bones: the sight suited well his state of mind, one that Ibuse himself has characterized as "dark . . . because I had no hope for my future."[41] Between the view of a pond and that of graves, Ibuse placed his carp in a tale meant similarly to oppose the promise of a full life with a limited reality, a reality that continued for several years without great improvement.

The melancholy voiced in "The Carp" seemed confirmed by the work's unremarkable reception among the public. Nor was "The Carp" the critical success Ibuse and Tanaka had hoped it would be, although Kobayashi Hideo recognized its merit in a review appearing in the journal *Bungei shunjū* (*Literary Chronicles*).[42] Ibuse and his mentor became increasingly concerned over his future. In "Tanaka Kōtarō, My Teacher" Ibuse recounts an important favor Tanaka rendered him at this doubtful time, the autumn of 1926:

> Just after Tanaka had moved to Himon'ya, we were sitting in his parlor having a drink when he looked me straight in the eye and said, "I wonder

why you can't make it to the top?" Later he added, "I don't know anything about real fiction myself. I'll introduce you to someone who does."

He went into his study and wrote a letter of introduction addressed to
Satō Haruo.[43]

Ibuse took a copy of "The Carp" with him on his initial visit to
Satō, the first of many visits to come. In "Miscellany" Ibuse writes
that Satō, one of the leading writers of the day, greeted him
brusquely and immediately began to read the story. The room remained still except for an occasional grunt from Satō. Then he
handed it back to Ibuse and declared it merited a passing grade: but
this was apparently good enough, for Satō, a powerful figure in the
literary establishment known as the *bundan* ("literary elite"), chose
to help Ibuse by critiquing his subsequent work and introducing him
to other important writers, editors, and publishers. Yet it would be
misleading to consider Ibuse a disciple, or even a student, of Satō's.
Their relationship was beneficial to Ibuse but hardly close. Ibuse has
written little of Satō (although in one unforgettable piece, he un-
favorably compares his famously unattractive face to a gas mask).[44]
Also, as in his association with Hōmei, he confesses to having read
none of his patron's work so as to avoid undue influence on his own
style. Tanizaki Seiji considers Ibuse truly remarkable in that no one
writer or thinker has colored his prose detectably: his words as well
as his themes are quite his own.[45] But Ibuse's silence on the relationship he enjoyed with one of the giants of Japanese literature does not
deny its timely value to his budding career.

1927

The following year, 1927, ranks with 1941—the year he was
drafted and sent to war—as one of the crucial turning points of
Ibuse's life. In February, when his grandfather died, Ibuse lost not
only his most loved relative but his only affectionate tie to his
hometown. Suddenly he was truly alone in Tokyo. That same month
marked another milestone: "An Elliptical Design" (*Ibitsu na zuan*)
was published in *Fudōchō* (*Off-key*) magazine, and Ibuse received
his first payment for a work of fiction. He and his fiancée Akimoto
Setsuyo, to whom he was engaged through the continuing good offices of Tanaka Kōtarō, promptly spent it on the practical purchase

of a brazier for his new house in Ogikubo. Ibuse had built the house with funds in part granted from his brother Fumio and in part borrowed in Tokyo. Ogikubo is today not considered far from the center of Tokyo, but at the time, as Ibuse recalls in *An Ogikubo Almanac,* Ogikubo and other "remote" stops along the suburban Chūō rail line were still mostly rice paddies. Ogikubo was strictly for third-rate writers, Ōmori was for popular writers, and Setagaya, adds Ibuse, was for the leftists.

If so, then Setagaya must have been quite crowded in 1927. The proletarian-literature movement was nearing its zenith, and its adherents fairly dominated the bundan. The early Shōwa period (1926–   ) ushered in a time of considerable political and social turmoil, turmoil that was bound to affect not only literature generally, but Ibuse Masuji personally.

Whether as a university student or an emerging writer, Ibuse did not join the radical drift of his generation. In 1927 he was a participant in the coterie journal *Jintsū jidai (Birth of the Age),* formed the previous year by many of his associates from *Seiki,* when all its members, save him, enlisted en masse in the All-Japan Proletarian Art League (Zen-Nihon Musansha Geijutsu Remmei), a Socialist writers organization. Ibuse has declared that he was simply "lazy" (*kibushō*) but surely the lazy person would have gone along with the crowd.[46] The true reasons behind the refusal were not only his aversion to any sort of ideology dictating literature but also his sincere doubt that he was capable of politically committed writing. He did make a weak attempt in a few stories to address popular social issues, but even the best of these, "Mining-Town Clinic" (*Tankōjitai byōin,* 1929)—published in the same year as proletarian novelists Kobayashi Takiji's *The Cannery Ship (Kani Kōsen)* and Tokunaga Sunao's *City Without Sun (Taiyō no nai machi)*—seems finally more about Ibuse's ever-present melancholy than about class conflict. His talent, and his heart, did not lie in protest. In "Lingering Flavors" (*Atoaji no yosa,* 1974) he tells of encountering the established writer Tokuda Shūsei one day on the Ginza in these early years. Tokuda admonished him to write not from any popular creed but from what he had naturally "within himself" (*mune no sanzunshihō*).[47] But what Ibuse may modestly credit to the advice of others was, of course, already dictated by his own character. Ibuse was, in fact, unable to rally with his friends under the banner of proletarian literature because his struggle was not in the streets, but within himself as he sought to understand his potential as a writer.

As a result, Ibuse stood increasingly alone professionally as well as personally. While his peers were busy with their causes, Ibuse must have felt, with no little irony, to be his own salamander in a dark crevice peeking out into the world of light. This deliberate separation from his colleagues was, along with the death of Aoki Nampachi, one of the crucial and definitive events of his youth. It is hard to imagine from our present perspective, when the proletarian movement in Japanese literature appears to have been so feeble, how Ibuse must have suffered from his decision not to take part in the great calling of his day. His friends, convinced they were doing the historically necessary and humanely correct thing, did so with an assurance that made Ibuse feel old-fashioned, foolish, or even cowardly. Ibuse continued to enjoy the company of older writers and editors who had also repudiated the role of politics in literature, but one must remember the importance of belonging to one's own generation—certainly for many Japanese, and perhaps for writers in particular. With the apparent revocation of that membership in 1927, Ibuse became increasingly isolated and depressed.

In 1928 Ibuse turned thirty. He made a new start with other young writers who were indifferent or antagonistic to the proletarian-literature movement, such as Funabashi Seiichi, Asami Fukashi, Kon Hidemi, and Kajii Motojirō. Together they published a brief-lived magazine, *Bungei toshi* (*Literary City*), which nonetheless provided a vehicle for much of Ibuse's early work and also an opportunity for him to make new friends. These were friends he would keep in the difficult years ahead.

This new association proved productive for Ibuse. In 1929 he published eight new works, among which are some of his best. The writing is more plentiful and skilled, but its themes are familiar. Three of the eight—"Sawan on the Roof" (*Yane no ue no Sawan*), "Kuchisuke's Valley" (*Kuchisuke no iru tanima*), and "The Salamander"—are works that bring the literature of Ibuse's youth to its technical and substantive fruition.

"Sawan on the Roof"

"Sawan on the Roof" was published in *Bungaku* (*Literature*), a journal founded by such writers as Yokomitsu Riichi and Kawabata Yasunari. Like *Bungei toshi,* it was a major outlet for those writers not affiliated with the proletarian movement. As with most of Ibuse's finer work, "Sawan" is based on a true story.[48] Adapted from an incident heard at second hand from a Waseda classmate, the first-person narrative is told by a young man who discovers a wounded wild goose. He names it Sawan (a word Ibuse elsewhere reports to mean "season" in one of the languages of India).[49] After nursing it back to health, he finds one day that it has flown off to rejoin its flock.

As early as the story's second paragraph, the mood is familiar. "My hands felt the warmth of the feathers and flesh of this wandering fowl, and its unexpected weight consoled my troubled heart [*omoikusshita kokoro*]" (1:72). This protagonist watakushi is indistinguishable from watakushis encountered earlier. Moreover, like the fish in "The Carp," the goose helps watakushi overcome his loneliness by becoming a valued companion, a metaphor for human affection. Unlike the carp, however, the goose is restless and wants to escape from watakushi's stifling attentions. Watakushi will not grant his companion freedom, of course, since the presence of the bird drives away his "worrisome thoughts" (*kuttaku shita shisō*) (1:75).

Eventually watakushi realizes that he and Sawan share a common isolation: alone and apart from their species, they are each trapped in their respective caves, watching their fellow creatures pass by. Ibuse describes Sawan perched on watakushi's roof: "He looked like some old philosopher who had been shipwrecked on a distant island, catching sight of the first ship in ten years to sail by on the horizon" (1:77).

Yet even after watakushi realizes the plight of his pet, he remains unable to release the goose, for in so doing he would leave himself once more wholly alienated. When Sawan's cries finally drive watakushi to do what he must, it is already too late to demonstrate the love in that decision: the goose has broken free of its fetters and has flown off into the sky.

The critic Hasegawa Izumi considers "Sawan" to be the major representative work of Ibuse's youth. Hasegawa, an authority on the works of Kawabata Yasunari, points out that Ibuse's many animal characters do not mean that he is misanthropic, as he believes Kawabata to be.[50] Hasegawa's reading is astute: Ibuse's animals function as other egos meant to contrast with and complement the protagonist's own, and, to the extent that Ibuse identifies with his characters, his ego is seeking an understanding among the amphibians and mammals and birds.

The use of animals in his early fiction was an efficient device for Ibuse, allowing him first to describe and divest his own depression, then to transfer it to his fictional characters. While Ibuse was working on these animal stories, he was gradually developing a new point of view. Perhaps, then, instead of perceiving "Sawan" as the representative story of Ibuse's youth, one is tempted to concur with critic Kamei Katsuichirō, who terms it "a work of the last day of Ibuse's youth."[51] In "Sawan," Ibuse achieves maturity by recognizing the parallel existence of another ego at exactly that moment when watakushi goes to free the goose. Ibuse, in this achievement, begins to ease himself out of the narrative center stage and to direct a fiction there in his place. Ibuse becomes thenceforward the observer of his predicaments rather than the disguised participant. In "Sawan," the process of this shifting identification is not yet complete. Ibuse is still very much present in the middle of his fictions, as morose and lonely as ever; but now he has a friend who, unlike the utterly passive carp, feels and acts precisely as does he. "Sawan" represents, in hindsight, an evolutionary step in Ibuse's metamorphosis from a confessional writer to a creative one.

"Kuchisuke's Valley"

Ibuse's next step was greater still. "Kuchisuke's Valley," a longer and structurally more complex work that "Sawan," was published in Sōsaku gekkan (Creative Writing Monthly) in May 1929. If "Sawan" is one of Ibuse's most representative pieces, then Kuchisuke is certainly one of his most representative characters. Kuchisuke (a pseudonym inspired from the name used by the adolescent Ibuse in writing to Ōgai) is the first of many old men—he is well into his seventies—who will appear prominently in Ibuse's writing for the next half century. Kuchisuke is one of the most memorable; he is described in such detail and with such subtle affection that one suspects his model was Ibuse's grandfather. Kuchisuke himself becomes the model for the other elderly male characters populating Ibuse's fiction—each eccentric, and each apparently made that way by the passing of time and the changing of the world. These men and the rural lives they lead stand in opposition to all that is signified by Tokyo, the modern city. Ibuse's old men are heirs to tradition; his cities detach us from our pasts. Perhaps the dichotomy between his old men and the urbanity they eschew is similar to the split Ibuse felt within himself. The conflict between the city and the country that he once knew as a young man at Waseda is, with "Kuchisuke," played out within the confines of a story—not in Ibuse's own emotional life.

The voice of old age is a sage voice for Ibuse. Increasingly he refers to himself as "old" from these years onward, not because he is sensitive to aging, but because such an attitude neatly dovetails with his increasingly detached narrative perspective. One has the impression that Ibuse is eager to grow old for its cathartic potential, since youth is recalled as having been so uniformly dismal. These likely connections between Ibuse's own emotional evolution and his evolving narrative strategy are seen most clearly in "Kuchisuke," among his early stories.

Taniki ("valley-tree") Kuchisuke is the watchman of a mountain, a resident caretaker whose work is closely tied with the natural world. Before he had assumed these duties, however, Kuchisuke had worked as a male nurse for the narrator of the story (watakushi, once more) and his siblings. The setting and the characters are reminiscent of Ibuse and his own male nurse described in "Miscellany." Events in the story, too, seem to parallel those of Ibuse's childhood. When watakushi recalls those early years, he remembers Kuchisuke teaching him Pidgin English—a patois the old man had mastered as a laborer in Hawaii—as well as words from his peculiar dialect of Japanese. This linguistic education seems much like the one Ibuse received as a child in his village of Kamo. Most of Ibuse's old men, in fact, speak in highlighted dialects, a literary maneuver indicating that they speak from the privileged vantage of truth, as distinct from standard Japanese (i.e., the language of Tokyo) with its implied values of modernity. Kuchisuke's rural idiom, when contrasted with watakushi's recently acquired Tokyo speech, becomes embedded in a tension between age and youth, country and city, and finally, even authenticity and inauthenticity. This opposition in "Kuchisuke" not only of parlance but of principles is most skillfully established. Ibuse has begun to understand himself, both as a man and as a writer, and might now surpass as well as encompass his experiences in literature.

In this story, although watakushi no longer needs a nurse, his ties with Kuchisuke remain. Once a week, watakushi goes to Kuchisuke's home for English lessons. Kuchisuke takes these lessons very seriously, donning the formal kimono that watakushi's grandfather had once presented him and conducting the tutorial with strict, almost comical, discipline. At the close of each lesson, he warns watakushi not to dawdle while crossing the bridge on his way home, lest he fall into the whirlpool below—the terrifying watery vortex of Ibuse's childhood and his adult fiction.

Twenty years pass, and now watakushi lives in Tokyo as an aspiring writer. He has never told Kuchisuke of this ambition, because he is certain the old man would disapprove. Both the dichotomy and the proof of common roots between watakushi and Kuchisuke appear here—shame is entailed in living in the city and pursuing a profession thought less than respectable elsewhere. Watakushi has allowed Kuchisuke to gather the impression that he is a dentist, and later, a lawyer.

This charade is destined to end the day watakushi receives a letter from Kuchisuke's granddaughter Taeto. The legacy of Kuchisuke's stay in Hawaii, Taeto is a young, half-Japanese woman who has recently come to Japan to live with her grandfather. She writes watakushi that a dam has been built in the valley where she and Kuchisuke make their home. Soon the sluice gates will be closed and the low land, including their house, will be submerged under water. There is no chance of reversing the government's decision to proceed with the project, but still Kuchisuke refuses to budge from his home. Taeto pleads with watakushi—whom she too supposes to be a lawyer—to write her grandfather and persuade him to relocate.

Watakushi leaves Tokyo immediately to talk to Kuchisuke in person, arriving in the valley after nightfall. He is struck by its natural beauty, only to encounter something that will destroy it: the dam. He searches to find a way past it to Kuchisuke's home:

> Finally, not in the stone wall itself but in the hill of rock, I discovered a large tunnel. Using my matches for light, I entered. A cool breeze swept through the tunnel, which was about as high and wide as a railroad underpass. Water dripped from the ceiling that had been carved out in an arch through the thickest section of the hill. Bats dwelled in the crevices. [1:41]

As watakushi passes through the tunnel, he might seem to be entering another of Ibuse's existential caves. But though the imagery recalls such earlier works as "Confinement," that previous perspective is reversed: watakushi is entering the cave from the outside, only to discover within it (in a valley cut off from the world by a dam, a product of the civilization that watakushi represents) not himself but

Kuchisuke, a man who (for the first time in an Ibuse story) is content to remain there and watch with little concern the rest of the world go by.

"Kuchisuke" completes the process of disengagement begun in earlier stories. Step by step, the population of Ibuse's cave has shifted from Ibuse alone, to Ibuse with some friends, to, finally, no Ibuse at all. "Kuchisuke" marks Ibuse's release from writing of entrapment in his own anxious melancholy (kuttaku), and his turn towards writing of how others might cope with their own. In this instance the subject is Kuchisuke, whom the reader meets when watakushi awakens in his valley home the following morning. Watakushi hears Kuchisuke chopping wood outdoors and goes to talk to him. He is surprised to learn that Kuchisuke has given in and decided to move after all. The government will build him a new home and will even appoint him watchman of the dam. Nonetheless Kuchisuke would like to hear watakushi defend his right to stay, having never heard him deliver an oratory.

Later the two men take a bath together outdoors. Kuchisuke jokes that watakushi is even uglier with his glasses off than on. When watakushi obligingly puts his glasses back on, he notes that the valley around them looks "just like a scene painted on a wall in a Tokyo bathhouse." In this comment, watakushi not only pokes fun at himself but significantly widens the gap between him and Kuchisuke. For this valley, all of Kuchisuke's world, is reduced in watakashi's view to nothing more than a reflection of a mural, which, because it is in Tokyo, represents the more familiar world. Watakushi appears more and more an outsider, unable to comprehend life in the valley (read "cave") as it really exists.

That night, after they have retired, Kuchisuke muses aloud to himself, debating and pondering which variety of fowl is tastiest. He advances to the speculation that all the birds in the valley will have to find new homes. In their place will come fish. He also reflects that, although the artificial lake will destroy this one valley, its inlets will, in effect, create many more. These allied observations suddenly supply Kuchisuke with a measure of solace. Kuchisuke's logic accepts the changes to be wrought by the dam by regarding them as a fair exchange. This view of historical change as an equal displacement of one mode of life for another, maintaining a measured and comforting equilibrium, is a view that Ibuse will elaborate in later works. It will be a source of personal comfort when his own life is dramatically altered.

Kuchisuke concludes his rambling chatter with a vow to release one hundred baby carp into the lake once it is created. He may prefer birds personally, but birds cannot be raised by humans. (Ibuse has himself confessed to inadvertently killing birds in captivity, a lesson that watakushi in "Sawan" nearly learns as well.)[52] One notes, however, that the raising of the animal, not necessarily the animal itself, is paramount to Kuchisuke. He will console himself for the loss of his home by aligning his activities with a natural cycle, the life of the carp.

The day soon arrives when Kuchisuke and Taeto must move. Watakushi assists. But Kuchisuke is not entirely pleased with his new house and insists on sleeping one more night in the old place. Later that same night, watakushi attempts to bring him back; but when he visits the old home, Kuchisuke is fully awake, deep in thought. Watakushi's footsteps destroy Kuchisuke's concentration, and so they talk:

> "It's bad for your health to try to sleep in a place like that by the window."
> "I don't feel like sleeping. I'm just worried and upset about things."
> "It's late. Let's go home."
> "I like this house so much more. It should be up to me what roof I want to live under. . . . "
> There was nothing I could do to dissuade him. I started home but then stopped to glance back. Assuming I was gone, Kuchisuke had put his chin back on his arms and had resumed his thoughts. That is how I left him. [1:54]

The next day Kuchisuke returns to his new home. It is raining, but they can hear the sound of trees being felled in the valley below. Workmen are clearing the land and are floating the logs out of the valley down a river. Kuchisuke's valley is being dismantled by degrees with each passing day.

This work continues for nearly a week. Finally, one day brings silence. Soon thereafter, the sluice gates close and the valley begins its transformation into a lake—one from which Kuchisuke, in a moment of panic, fears "a demon will arise."

As the water level reaches his old home, Kuchisuke grows visibly distraught. He fantasizes that a tidal wave will drown them all. A bird circles high above because, as he had predicted, it no longer has a place to alight. Kuchisuke declares the lake cruel. His repeated sighs cause watakushi to suspect that he is physically trying to dispel his *kuttaku shita shisō*—the same expression for "worrisome thoughts" found in "Sawan." Here the story ends.

"Kuchisuke" is a pivotal text in understanding Ibuse's artistic, thematic, and personal progression during the last year of his youth. More than any other work of these early years, it carries within it his promise of success as a mature writer. "Kuchisuke" introduces several of the themes that will later become Ibuse's hallmarks: the loss and recovery of place (Kuchisuke's displacement), the violent nature of change (explosives, triggering a landslide, are detonated in preparing the valley for its new use), and the distinct perspectives of urban and rural life (the interaction of Kuchisuke with watakushi). In addition, the single viewpoint is introduced in the narrator's new role as a bystander in the action (watakushi's presence is necessary only for telling the story, not for its plot). In retrospect, this marks the beginning of Ibuse's objective authorial voice, for, having once detached himself from the forces of his stories, he is saved from the fate of telling the same tale over and over—the fate of many minor writers in Ibuse's intensely introspective day. Ibuse, escaping his cave and assuming a new persona in "Kuchisuke," frees himself to break the cycle of self-absorption. He brings his years of apprenticeship to a close and moves on to conceive his ambitious and worldly works.

"The Salamander"

Only "The Salamander" remains between these early years and Ibuse's sophisticated fiction of the 1930s. "The Salamander," ironically, is often considered the work most characteristic of Ibuse in his youth. Yet after such stories as "The Carp," "Sawan," and "Kuchisuke," it reads more convincingly as a postscript to the first ten years of his career. Perhaps Ibuse, intending deliberately to conclude this first phase of his professional life by tying together all loose ends, returned to "Confinement," restored its original 1919 title, and rewrote it from his new perspective. The unhappy student who wrote "Confinement" was now a confident writer—thanks to the intervention of a carp, a goose, and an old man. "The Salamander" is surely not the last work of Ibuse's early years but, instead, the first of his middle ones.

"The Salamander" published in the May 1929 issue of *Bungei toshi* is still only one version of a work in progress. The definitive version, begun ten years earlier, would require yet another decade. The standard text included in Ibuse's collected works was not to be published until March 1941. The 1929 story, however, marks the most radical revision of "Confinement." It begins with Ibuse's most famous line: "The salamander was sad" (*Sanshōuo wa kanashinda*).[53] His critic and friend Kawakami Tetsutarō has claimed that this three-word sentence typifies all of Ibuse's work: "Ibuse, beginning in his debut story, has written a literature of sadness."[54] Yet more significant in this first line than its melancholy—surely no surprise to the reader—is that the "I" (*boku*) of "Confinement" has become the "he" (*sanshōuo*, subsequently *kare*) of "The Salamander." Gloom colors both works, "Confinement" especially so, but with "The Salamander" comes proof of that basic shift in Ibuse's narrative perspective seen first in "Kuchisuke." The point of view is no longer that of the trapped creature itself, but of an omniscient and outside observer: Ibuse Masuji. The author now distances himself from the pathos of the story in a process the reader has monitored in the preceding works. To the aware reader, Ibuse announces in "The Salamander" not his sadness but his freedom.

Yet Ibuse still wishes to write about isolation and depression, even if it is not any longer his own. The salamander is again stuck in a small cave without a means of escape. Trapped permanently, the poor creature's only diversion is gazing out of the small opening at the greater world beyond. But as the omniscient narrator states, "The best way to see a lot of things is through a small window" (1:4). Never in "Confinement" could there have been a line with such potential.

Among the things the salamander watches are the killifish swimming in schools through the grasses growing in the backwaters of the fast-flowing stream. The salamander sneers at these little fish, because "the entire group of them would veer this way and that. Should just one of them turn left by mistake, then so would most of the others, afraid of falling behind. . . . For that reason, it seemed exceedingly difficult for any single fish freely to leave the pack" (1:5).

This likely allusion to the politics of his generation, personally noted by Ibuse in the years since his first draft of "The Salamander," is followed by a warning: above these tiny killifish swirls a deadly whirlpool. As the salamander watches, "a petal of a white flower traveled in circles in the backwater, gradually enscribing smaller and smaller circumferences. . . . Finally, describing the minutest of circles, it was swallowed into the very center of the whirlpool" (1:5). Perhaps Ibuse wishes to suggest that his cave was, after all, safest of places in which to spend his youth.

Some time later the salamander thinks that he is "worrying and getting wrapped up in his own thoughts" (*kuttaku suru mono'omoi ni fukeru*; nearly the same words as Kuchisuke's). Deciding that he must act positively, he tries to force his way through the entrance of the cave only to become stuck in it like a cork. He tries again and fails again. The only avenue of escape left him is fantasy. Closing his eyes, the walls of his confinement recede and are replaced by a limitless darkness. He knows he can open his eyes at any time and return to reality, but he chooses not to. It is enough to know that he can. This refuge taken in the powers of a creative imagination parallels Ibuse's, who took sanctuary from his own dark thoughts when he became a writer and, specifically, when he created characters to host a melancholy once his.

In "Confinement" the salamander sees others only at a distance: a silent shrimp laying it eggs leaves him feeling so lonely that he is physically chilled. In "The Salamander," however, he is given a more equal companion when one day a hapless frog swims into his cave. The salamander blocks his egress and refuses to let him leave. The two insult and taunt each other but eventually lapse into a silence that lasts a full year until the bickering begins anew. Then another year of silence passes. "The Salamander" concludes with the conversation that terminates this second mute interim:

> It was not the salamander but his companion in the hollow of the rock who was first careless enough to breath a deep sigh, a murmur like the softest of breezes. As the year before, it was the sight of the hair moss busy releasing its pollen that had prompted the sigh.
>
> The salamander could not ignore the sound. He looked up and asked with eyes filled with friendship, "You sighed just now, didn't you?"
>
> "And what if I did?" answered the frog with bravura.
>
> "You don't have to reply like that. It's all right if you want to come down from there."
>
> "I'm so hungry I can't move."

"You mean, it's all over?"

"It does seem that way."

Some time passed before the salamander asked the frog what he was thinking about.

The frog responded with the utmost reserve. "Even now I'm not particularly angry with you." [1:10–11]

This passage features a friendship akin to watakushi's for a carp and a goose, and an acceptance of fate not unlike Kuchisuke's. The cave will never grant its prisoners freedom, but perhaps companionship transcends that end: though "The Salamander" is longer, reworded, and rearranged when compared with "Confinement," the truer distinction is its bittersweet retelling of Ibuse's youth, gone by the time he wrote of it. Ibuse, characteristically hard on himself, considers "The Salamander" a failure, a bit "stiff."[55] But it can claim great success as an illustration of his growth from alienation to affirmation, and as an illustration of the depth of perspective present in his early works. Unsure of what he was and where he belonged when he first came to Tokyo, Ibuse finally found his definitions in the profession of literature, a career that, in the words of "The Salamander," gave him "control of the immense darkness." Had Ibuse attempted simply to ignore the existence of his dark cave, he would also have forsaken that distance between himself and the light which permitted him to write of the world outside that confinement. "The Salamander" is a confession of how Ibuse learned to write in the years from "Confinement" to "Kuchisuke"; as with any confession, its author could write it only after he had finished with the emotions and events involved.

One might reasonably argue that Ibuse was hardly unique in this regard, that melancholy was the seemingly unavoidable baggage of being a Japanese writer in the 1920s. Akutagawa Ryūnosuke cited a "vague ill-ease" when he killed himself in 1927. Earlier, Kajii Motojirō, a writer unlike Ibuse in other respects, used a fruit in his famous story "The Lemon" to "explode" a depression and effect a catharsis similar to Ibuse's more pacific results with animals. Yet even if there did exist some sort of a generational malaise, Ibuse still appears special. In "Recess" (Kyūkei jikan, 1930), written just when his memory should have been the sharpest, Ibuse declared the idea of youth absurd, "the sequel to a one-act comedy," and termed his own youth unhappy.[56] The critic Tōgō Katsumi has perceptively noted that it is hard to imagine Ibuse at twenty;[57] indeed, Ibuse fled into middle age as quickly as he could, leaving scant trace of his younger years. He found it easier, perhaps, to reflect on the pain of his youth rather than confront it. Whatever his discomfort, however, the lessons of that pain brought Ibuse in 1929 to the threshold of acclaim as an important writer. With "The Salamander," Ibuse became a mature author; with the works that followed, an ambitious one.

Rivers, the Sea, an Island: The 1930s

The 1930s began happily for Ibuse. In April 1930 he was present at the founding of the New Artists Club (Shinkō Geijutsuha Kurabu), a loose association of well-known writers unsympathetic to left-wing literature. With the rapid collapse of such literature after the Manchurian Incident the following year, the association—its raison d'être gone—soon dissipated, but Ibuse retained many of the friends he had made through his participation. Moreover, in May 1930 Nagai Tatsuo and Nakamura Masatsune sponsored him for membership in the new and prestigious coterie journal *Sakuhin* (*Literary Work*), an event confirming his elevation to the higher ranks of young writers. There, in the company of Sakaguchi Ango, Ōoka Shōhei, Yoshida Ken'ichi, and others, Ibuse was provided with the companionship of colleagues who were to remain his friends in the decades to come.[1]

Nineteen-thirty was also the year in which Ibuse suddenly found himself the teacher rather than the pupil; a shy young man from the provinces, later known as Dazai Osamu and destined to be a major force in fiction, especially in the first postwar years, approached Ibuse for literary advice. Thus was initiated one of the most famous —and most controversial—friendships in the annals of modern Japanese literature.

At age thirty-two, however, Ibuse had not entirely graduated from his melancholy youth. He continued to create sad and lonely characters, even if he himself was no longer quite so. The plaintive tone of "The Carp" and "The Salamander" continued into such later works as "A Delicate Canary" (*Hoso-kanariya*, 1930), the tale of a bird kept captive alone in a cage. This and similarly somber stories that followed, however, no longer addressed Ibuse's own youthful depression and anxiety, the most common stance of his earliest writings. More confident now, Ibuse found his vision outside the cave and in the light, free and unobstructed. He commenced exploring and mapping the world with which he was to establish his reputation as a major writer.

Two works written by Ibuse in his thirties illustrate his extension of themes: "The River," a short story published in four parts in 1931 and 1932, and *Waves,* a full-length novel on which Ibuse worked intermittently from 1930 to 1938. These two projects were Ibuse's apprenticeship in sustained and structured prose, and both are of interest primarily for that reason. Ibuse, like many other Japanese writers, has been accused of a disconcerting laxity in his story telling: but narrative rigor is not restricted to simple plots. Although Ibuse's stories often meander among diverse situations or ideas, what remains consistent is the authorial voice governing their disclosure. His writing, in fact, may seem the least organized when that voice is most like his own, when he allows his pen to pursue the same tangents as would his curiosity in a conversation.

This pursuit, however, has its own principles. Ibuse plots his longer works in one or more of three simple ways, each derived from a notion of contiguous association. The most common and conventional of these methods is the ordering of narrative in a strict chronological sequence, often as mechanically as a diary—which, in fact, many of his works appear to be. Even as early and as short a piece as "Confinement" resembles a diary in that it moves steadily forward in time without complex references either to past events or those to come. Another method is the free association of ideas or memories, most often used in Ibuse's essays or autobiographical writings: one passage is linked to the next through an almost accidental coincidence of often minor circumstances. A third technique involves a progression of setting from one proximate point to the next, as in travel writing. The underlying commonality of these three approaches to organizing a story is identified in a Japanese literary term applied to Ibuse's literature—*renzoku shōsetsu* or "linked fiction," that is, fiction organized as cumulative yet autonomous vignettes. "The River" and *Waves* are, in fact, two works that unfold not by the means of any sophisticated scheme, but by simple geography in the first instance, and by the lunar calendar in the second.

Furthermore, locale and chronology are not only their organizing principles but also, ultimately, their themes. In this regard, these two texts exemplify the "topography" of Ibuse's natural world.

"Natural world" is used here in two senses interchangeably, one specific and the other general. In the first sense, the natural world can be synonymous with nature, the physical environment: Japanese *shizen*. Ibuse is clearly at home among flora and fauna. Stories such as "Kuchisuke's Valley" and "The Salamander" show how fond he is of mountains, trees, and animals. This natural world has provided Ibuse with a rich source of detail and imagery. But in its larger sense, encompassing not only the material environment but the temporal, i.e., historical, Ibuse's natural world is decidedly less physical and more metaphysical, a universe not only of matter but of causal principles and processes. This expanded natural world contains Ibuse's complete system of cosmology, teleology, and ethics; it is broad enough, in fact, to be synonymous with his vision as an author.

Ibuse's natural world is informed by the complex interaction of forces from both nature and history. "The River" and *Waves* are his first ambitious attempts to establish a vocabulary of words and themes for this interaction. Indeed, the reader can sense Ibuse groping his way, gingerly testing the ground ahead as he marks a trail through his most important literary terrain. Ibuse's collection of characters may have originated in his earliest stories, and his most masterful realization of them will come much later, but it is in these works of the 1930s that he gives them a time and a place in which to dwell.

"The River"

The first part of "The River" was published in the September 1931 issue of *Bungei shunjū* under the title, "Actual Scenes from along the River" (*Kawazoi no jissha fūkei*). Later installments followed in the December issue of *Chūō kōron (Central Review)*, the January 1932 issue of *Shinchō (New Current)*, and the May issue of *Bungei shunjū*. Although "The River" is now considered Ibuse's first longer work of fiction, at the time all of its constituent parts were read separately as complete short short-stories. This was neatly allowed, of course, by their nature as loosely "linked" sections of an open-ended whole, but since they also read smoothly as a single novella, they attest to Ibuse's consistent and controlled style.

The final and complete version of "The River," published in October 1932, is an unusual work of fiction. Its protagonist—the agent advancing the action—is the river itself. Rivers, no less than mountains, trees, or animals, are important to Ibuse and his imagery. Rivers have figured importantly in many Ibuse works, from "The Salamander" on: they symbolize the confluence, as in a body of water and its tributaries, of the dynamic forces of Ibuse's natural world. In "The Waseda Woods" (*Waseda no mori*, 1971), Ibuse writes of the Bashōgawa River, which once flowed near Waseda University: "The trees have all disappeared, but the river still survives underground." This river, while specific, is emblematic of Ibuse's general belief, a belief in the continuity and inevitability of the natural and historical world chronicled in his literature.

Of Ibuse's many rivers, however, that of "The River" remains his best known. Here the river is not simply an occasional metaphor or leitmotif. It constitutes the core of the story. Ibuse refuses the temptation, however, to personify the river. On the contrary, human beings are "naturalized" in this novella insofar as they reflect the river's characteristics. The river's existence seems most real—certainly more substantial than that of the people who happen to spend their short lifespans on its banks. The river is not an expedient device for structuring the work. Far from being an excuse for a story, it is the story itself.

"The River," as befits a work establishing the foundation of Ibuse's natural world, opens at the moment of creation—the birth of the river. Far from the sea that will ultimately absorb it, the river is traced to its origin high in a distant mountain. A large rock—a "huge black moon" *(kuroi iro no ōinaru tsuki)*—juts out from the side of the mountain. Its blackness suggests foreboding; its shape, disaster. Teetering on a fragile balance, it might fall at any moment and crush whomever might be below. From under the rock issues a small spring, a rivulet whose waters mark the source of the river. This rock signifies a menaced beginning, perhaps even the original curse of birth and the start of a cycle that will see the life of the river through one ominous phase to the next. The dark and inauspicious infancy of the river sets the stage for the story—the world to be described will be powerful and precarious, dangerous and damning.

Ibuse's literary eye retreats to view the rock from a wider perspective. It stands among a forest of conifers (*shin'yōju:* Ibuse, attentive to details, would never say simply "trees"), and small pines grow out of its fissures. These parasitic pines look as if they are about to wither and die. Their contorted figurations suggest that they are scrounging in vain for the sustenance of the soil: they appear to have "fled in confusion." This dark image complements that of the black and unsteady rock, intimating a poverty in nature that steers life in all its manifestations, whether the lowly vegetation here or the higher orders to follow. The river is still small; properly speaking, it is not a river at all, but its character is already implicated in its inhospitable surroundings.

The spring water drips from under the rock and, as it collects and flows, dampens the flora below. It is described in a calmly precise and, at times, even technical language—"The volume of water appears to flow at a rate of approximately one liter every ten minutes" (1:182). The water from this spring—introduced with as much care as one might introduce a human hero—is portrayed in terms suggestive of a dispassionate and deliberate objectivity. Yet Ibuse is preparing the reader to accept his most subjective views, views that hold nature to be brutally cruel in its detached coldness. High above the valley and mountains flies an eagle, surveying from its aerial viewpoint the expanse of all that ranges below, from the spring out to the sea. Suddenly a bolt of lightning illuminates the terrain with an awesome brilliance. The birth of the river, which should have inspired only anticipation, now suggests impending doom. This connection of life with the threat of death implied by a burst of energy will prove to be a cornerstone of the ontology of Ibuse's natural world.

The water that has collected beneath the rock begins to flow down the side of the mountain past "species of moss" and "species of ferns" until it reaches the valley:

At the foot of the mountain flourish small trees and vines. Creeping vines, durmast, deutzia, boxwood, arrowroot, akebia, silk trees, rhododendrons, bamboo, bamboo grasses, wisteria, and more. Beneath this luxuriant growth flows the water, never revealing itself. [1:182–83]

Ibuse is always specific about the details of his natural world, especially the names of its flora. The list of plants (written phonetically, as if to focus the reader's attention on the names themselves rather than on the spurious associations of their Chinese glosses) is precise in its terminology. But Ibuse's precision here reflects more than a

typical taxonomical conscientiousness: botanical exactitude is demanded by the theme of "The River," the topology of Ibuse's natural
world. For instance, trees figure prominently not only in "The River"
but throughout Ibuse's literature. In addition to their endless variety
of species, what fascinates Ibuse, as he notes in an essay appropriately entitled "Arbor" (*Jumoku*, 1936), is their longevity. They stand
witness to the passage of time and can serve as repositories of history. Although the waters of "The River," like those of the
Bashōgawa near Waseda, pass unseen by man, their flow through
both time and space is scrutinized by their silent observers in nature.
Ibuse would seem to imply that some special wisdom thereby accrues
to these trees, a wisdom borne of their long life, their rooted immo-
bility, and their patience—characteristics that Ibuse also attributes to
his hardy human elders, such as Kuchisuke.

Human witnesses are also present in "The River." As the shallow
stream pours into the valley and swells into a true river, it passes
fragile earthen banks that threaten to crumble and slide. It winds its
way past a man-made dwelling. An old man sits by the window of his
hovel and stares out, observing the river as silently as the trees. He
observes, but not in the usual sense, for the old man is blind. His eyes
have rolled back up into his head, an affliction for which the local
children tease him cruelly. His sole pleasure is to sit by his window,
listening to the sounds of the river below:

> All the sounds of the water as it struck the rocks and cascaded down-
> wards combined in a single noise. The old man, however, was able to
> select each sound from the orchestration and to identify its name and
> source. The lowest of them, *don-don,* was a booming roar created in a
> gourd-shaped area where the river cut across the foot of the moun-
> tain. . . . Close by, the highest sound was that of water plummeting onto a
> bed of stones. [1:185]

This sightless man observes the water with his ears as precisely as
the omniscient narrator has earlier observed the trees and bushes;
and, as with the trees and bushes, each sound is defined or named. In
fact, the old man's act of "naming" serves to introduce a major
theme: man's relationship to Ibuse's natural world. As the blind man
identifies and regulates the confused cacophony of the river into an
orchestration of distinct sounds, he brings his own life into syn-
chrony with nature by creating a culture—in this instance, a range of
musical signs. This active process of organizing the world in human

terms sustains the old man through his otherwise sad existence. It also anticipates similar processes utilized by a host of later Ibuse characters.

"The River" continually points to symbiotic correspondences between the natural world and the human. The old man, for instance, dwells in a poverty that recalls the pines searching for life in the crevices of a rock. Once he owned a rice field, but it was repossessed when he fell behind in his payments. Nor is he the only one found destitute in "The River"; everyone suffers the same harsh life. The course of the river passes a tiny hamlet of six households. Ibuse details each of the six, listing them as he has the plants and the sounds. In the first dwell a woodcutter and his wife; he is a victim of trachoma and their two children have drowned in the river. One of the children had tumbled from a bridge on which he had been chasing butterflies—an accident, noted earlier, that actually befell one of Ibuse's childhood playmates. Nor have any of the other five households fared much better. All are families made miserable by deprivation and misfortune. Life remains as cruel, dark, and foreboding as the rock about to fall, the pines about to wither, and the river banks about to crumble.

Farther down the river lies another disturbing scene, one which, like the death of the child chasing butterflies, evokes Ibuse's early years and charges "The River" with a private terror. The whirlpool described here was also described in Ibuse's memoirs, in "Kuchi-suke's Valley," and in "The Salamander"; but here it penetrates deepest into the fearful dynamics of Ibuse's natural world:

In this deep water too an uneven number of whirlpools swirled endlessly. Various vortexes, both large and small, appeared on the surface in similar configurations. At times they chased others about and at times, as fate dictated, they suddenly disappeared. A trio of small ones was apt to veer off in a wild direction before it started to collapse, while at the same moment a single large whirlpool would form where the others had been. This big whirlpool would move about impetuously as whirlpools do, but soon it too showed signs of decay, and the small trio would again surface on the water. [1:190]

The language is spare and analytical in its description of this natural phenomenon. Nouns predominate. Adjectives and adverbs are relatively few. One interesting and distinguishing characteristic of "The River" is the marked paucity of onomatopoeic expressions so common in Japanese discussions of water. Perhaps Ibuse avoids them because such expressions, which are often idiolectal in Japanese, would imply an individualized narrator at work in the story. Ibuse perhaps eschews such presence in "The River" because he remains sensitive to the excess of ego in his early work and the work of his peers. "The River" represents, however, an extreme attempt to depersonalize his writing, an attempt from which he soon retreats, later readmitting a first-person voice—significantly, no longer his own. Still, "The River" shares with the work to follow an accented distancing of narrative subject with object, which isolates and emphasizes the pure elements of story. In this instance the separation is accomplished, stylistically as well as formally, by the neutral and occasionally even pseudoscientific tone of the prose. The description of the whirlpools, for instance, which mirrors the fluid and cyclical nature of Ibuse's world, also uses the coolly detached power of its language to highlight in stark outline the tragic and gripping tale to follow.

Tada Otaki

This is a tale of death, the thematic centerpin of "The River" and, indeed, of Ibuse's literary world. In hindsight, the whirlpool passage of this novella stands as a crucial key in understanding the close interrelation for Ibuse of life and death. An odd number—in itself an inauspicious sign—of vortexes forever appear and vanish, the brevity or length of their existence determined only by fate (*shukumei*). "Fate" is the first explicit mention of a very powerful principle. Everyone "both large and small" will one day "veer off in a wild direction" and disappear, only to be replaced by others. This simple calculus, condensed in a few sentences, affords the plainest diagram of Ibuse's material and historical values.

The whirlpools of "The River" are bordered by a river bank lush with a grove of jujube trees, a verdant image that again contrasts with and complements the idea of mortality proclaimed in the cycle of vortexes. Among those trees there suddenly appears one day a stone *jizō*, the statue of a Buddhist deity believed patron not only of children but of pregnant women and, by extension, of fertility. The local villagers suppose that the statue has found its way to the river from the "city" some hundreds of miles away. They suspect it has followed Tada Otaki, a young woman who left the village twelve years ago to live in the city and who has only recently returned. But she has changed: her Japanese, for instance, is now full of *shareta kotoba* ("fancy words"), a phrase suggesting both envy and derision. The villagers believe the statue is as fascinated as they are by her new accent, and for that reason it has pursued her to her birthplace.

Unfortunately, not only the jizō but also a certain young man is drawn to Otaki. One day he forces himself upon her. Otaki, rather than resist with inferior force, tries to discourage him with words:

> Please don't hurt me. I'm exhausted both mentally and physically. They made me work so hard at the factory, I've nothing but bitter memories left. They used me up until I was nothing but skin and bones. I've known nothing but misfortune, and there's no one to help me. [1:192]

Such abuse can lead to despair and, as it often will in Ibuse's world, to death:

> Tada Otaki had killed herself in a very ordinary fashion. Her corpse was discovered on the surface of the deep water two days after death had occurred. The corpse had its limbs casually outstretched as if to signify an intention to float forever gazing upward. But the many whirlpools in the water would not allow her to rest. The large whirlpool made the stiff corpse rotate, first pivoting about the head and then the buttocks. When the corpse turned about the head, the length of the body described a circumference, but, as a consequence, the center of the large whirlpool would try to drag the head of the corpse down to the bottom of the pool. When the large whirlpool metamorphosed into a trio of three small ones, the corpse would be freed from its revolutions; only Otaki's hair and loose clothing would be tugged towards the bottom of the water. [1:195]

This postmortem account, chilling without resorting to emotive language, exemplifies Ibuse's mature style and subject. In a historical sense it marks his evolution from being a writer who had described himself in such affected terms as "worried," "melancholy," and "anxious," to one capable of the most disinterested objectivity. The language of "The River" categorizes everything, from the flow of water to a suicide, in a style that unites all phenomena in the natural world with itself as a common denominator—a vast and comprehensive principle activated in the rational discourse of the narrative. This language has the further effect of rendering all events and people subject not only to the flow of narrative but to the inexorable hand of fate. This fate, like the whirlpool, makes not only Otaki's lifeless body revolve but, indeed, all the world.

The development of Ibuse's view of nature and its dynamic principles thus parallels the development of his voice as a writer. The style of his prose shifts in the direction of a careful objectivity, from the time he first moves to free his salamander from the cave, allowing him full vision. As Ibuse fashions a point of view apart from and transcendent over events, much as the eagle in "The River" views the earth, he simultaneously posits an active axiom equally apart from and transcendent over those events. This results in passages like that of Otaki's death—where description is in no way changed or reduced by the intervening emotional filter of a narrator. The irony of this technical removal of a narrative presence is that rhetorically it pushes the reader into a "direct" confrontation with the events, as if one were at the water oneself and were alone in discovering Otaki's corpse. At the same time, language that permits the reader such an immediate encounter also suggests the possibility of accurately gauging reality: whirlpools tugging at the cranium and then the buttocks, hair and clothing sucked into the deep hole of swirling water, all signify the precise action of absolute forces at work. These forces, explored in "The River" as deadly, will, in later works, prove also efficacious for good; the naturalistic power of these invisible energies transcends what men judge as moral or immoral, advantageous or disastrous, peaceable or violent.

Paralleling the carefully objectified language in the description of Otaki's death is the villagers' strangely unperturbed response to her death. Their stoicism affirms the passive and peripheral status of people in Ibuse's world, and it is a stoicism in some part his own. In "Miscellany" Ibuse tells of a young nanny, Okichi, who drowns herself after rumors have spread that she will soon be married to a man she does not want: the villagers who find Otaki in "The River" are Ibuse's own townspeople finding Okichi:

> The people standing on the cliff looking down upon the unhappy sight all seemed to be absorbed in the same thoughts. . . . One man on the very edge of the precipice spoke in a voice so quiet it was difficult to catch.
>
> "I've been looking down into the water for a while, thinking there was something awfully gaudy there. Now that I know what it is, it's so pitiable I can't look anymore."

Yet, though it would have been easy, no one on the cliff made any move to leave. [1:195–96]

The villagers are loitering not near the water but some distance away, atop a high cliff. This physical distance corresponds to an emotional alienation. No crying or insensitive chatter is heard. The distance that looms between the tragic event and its cognition—be it physical in the instance of Otaki and the villagers, or emotional in the instance of catastrophe and Ibuse—is not so much interpretive as technical, for only after an estrangement from the immediate proximity of the experience can it be seen in its entirety; again, Ibuse's metaphor is that of the eagle and the earth. The death of Tada Otaki is an event outside the cave. Her suicide, the tragic end to a tragic life, is witnessed but not internalized, because it belongs in another world, a world *extra muros*.

Five months later Yoshioka, the man who has assaulted and later harangued Otaki, commits suicide himself. He is found dead in the same waters and in the same ghastly position as was Otaki: congruent with Ibuse's simple laws, fate has extracted a punishment befitting the crime. Shortly thereafter Yoshioka's younger sister also kills herself, again in the same grotesque fashion. But a string connects her corpse with the stone jizō which still maintains a silent watch over the deep water. This linking of a fertility symbol with a dead woman suggests an economy of birth and decay central to Ibuse's natural world.

As the river flows on it passes more old men, two of whom (the "bald-headed" old man and the "white-haired" old man) feud over an obscure insult dating back to their grandfathers' generation. For Ibuse this is proof that the house of the bald-headed man carries an "old history." The river traverses this history, yet while it is given this chronological dimension it is also given a physical, human dimension when likened to "the veins of a human body." Tributaries wind through fields and paddies until "they return to their mother." Just as fluminous offspring come home, so do those of men: the river passes through another community so indigent that the possession of two cows deems one family rich. A day-laborer who is forced for lack of shelter to sleep under other people's eaves receives the happy news that his errant son is returning to the village from prison. Unfortunately his return coincides with a flood that forces the villagers onto their roofs—if they are lucky enough to have roofs. When the high waters recede and the river is calm again, the old man and his son are discovered dead in each other's embrace.

As the river pushes on it grows wider, and its currents have slowed to create two sandbars in its middle. These two small islands have been ravaged by the same flood that killed the old man and his son, but the six people in two households who inhabit the islands immediately set about to rebuild their devastated homes. The islands renew themselves: the population increases by a birth to seven, the number of horses by one, and the vegetation blooms. A persimmon tree that had not flowered before the flood now blossoms, and the house that had earlier looked as if it might topple is repainted.

This sudden shift from the previous gloom provides a glimpse of the regenerative forces of Ibuse's natural world, forces that will figure more prominently in his later work. In "The River," however, these renascent powers are mentioned only briefly, and soon the narrative slips back, as if Ibuse were reiterating the ceaselessly cyclical nature of his world, into its familiar litany of pathos and death. Downriver from the island, an old man has been shamed and frustrated by a false charge of theft leveled against him by the authorities. He puts an end to his troubles by leaping into the powerful vortex of the river:

> The drowned corpse seems to have drifted until it caught on an obstacle. On the morning of the third day it was discovered by a passerby at the end of a drainage pipe. When it appeared that the body might free itself and flow out the pipe, the passerby closed the downspout in alarm.
>
> The doctor who came to examine the corpse ordered that it be carried to the top of the dike and stretched out facing upward. He forced the deceased's eyelids open with his fingertips and, after doing nothing more than probing the stomach, declared that death had occurred two days earlier. He had guessed remarkably well. [1:216–17]

"Stretched out and facing upward"—as was Otaki in the whirlpool—the old man's corpse is described in the same deliberately objective, clinical style. Moreover, witnessing this scene is another crowd of spectators indifferent to the tragedy. A busy young man on a bicycle has his day only slightly disrupted by the discovery of a cadaver; children and birds continue to play and flock without care near the sluice gate where the body has drifted.

Death never seems far from the ordinary in "The River." Yet the river continues to flow, and in that ceaseless motion is found the active principle of Ibuse's world, in the restless and natural waters that circulate like blood through the lives and deaths of the river's people. Ibuse documents the impoverished and demoralized existences of several more communities before the river so broadens that it is indistinguishable from the ocean. Sea gulls soar above, and finally, in the last paragraph of the novella, Ibuse returns to the beginning and completes the cycle. A lone gray bird ascends high into the sky and flies upstream. Climbing to greater heights, the bird gazes down towards the earth. Like the eagle, this bird can see everything in its entirety and its logic. His view is our own, and at the conclusion of Ibuse's "The River," the course of the world appears vast, eternal, and inevitable.

The Natural World

Ironically, this lofty vision traces its origin to a small hometown. "The River," Ibuse's first extended piece of fiction and, thus, the first to articulate a complete thematic macrocosm, seems heavily indebted to the village of Kamo. The river that expresses the darkly cyclical movement of his universe is inspired by the tributary of the Ashidagawa River that flows near Kamo, a tributary for which, as Ibuse writes in "A Town Under the River" (*Kawazoko no machi*, 1970), he has always felt an affinity. To this source of imagery borrowed from childhood, however, he has added a host of beliefs realized in adulthood:

> I intended in this work to express the powerful feeling of a river flowing leisurely and far. I had imagined it would engender an image of eternity, of a river that rolls and never ceases. I had hoped to be able to construct an image of living and constant change.[2]

Ibuse neatly confirms the interpretation of "The River" as a diagram of his natural world: powerful, leisurely, eternal, living, and changing. For most of history, men have thought their universe timeless and transcendental, ordinate yet obscure, but Ibuse's particular vision of the fateful forces that govern in "The River" seems terribly dark and ominous. The disasters both man-made and natural which plague the villagers alongside the river, and the ideology they imply, make this story the most morose of his major works. Ibuse's beleaguered victims of fate's seeming caprice do not struggle against the terms of their natural world but instead accommodate themselves to its omnipotence. "The River" reads pessimistically if one insists on the capacity of the human will, through its simple exercise, to effect change. Yet from another perspective, the conclusions of "The River" are strangely comforting, because its world is so absolutely seamless in its unity as a closed system of fate. Perhaps Ibuse, melancholy himself at the time of "The River," projected onto its pages his own sorrow over personal loss and his own sense of foreboding. Simultaneously, perhaps he sought to transcend these by denying any means of altering destiny. Ibuse may have chosen to sacrifice human conation to an imperative of natural and historical forces in order to minimize his own regrets and lingering guilt.

Of all the ways Ibuse expresses the terror that fate promises, none is more common than catastrophe. In "The River" floods level the occasional evidences of human civilization found along a river's banks and sandbars. Although later works will emphasize affirmative responses of men and institutions to disasters, the destructive inevitability not only of inundations but of volcanic eruptions, earthquakes, fires, and droughts will continually reaffirm Ibuse's basic tenet that nature challenges us not to conquer but simply to survive. As Ibuse's own personal experiences in the years ahead will corroborate, men are defenseless against the superior force of fate and can hope for an accommodation only by synchronizing themselves with it; this theme will increasingly occupy his attentions in the years ahead as he explores, as a writer and a man, such a coexistence with the pernicious aspects of the natural world.

"The River" might conceivably be read not as a story of nature's transgressions against man, but of man's cruelty to his own kind—several of its tragedies are induced by man rather than nature. Such an interpretation, however, makes a distinction where Ibuse does not. Ibuse is careful to apply the same descriptive phraseology to men and women as he does to flora and fauna, suggesting that both the human and natural worlds are subject to the same rules. The differences between men and their surroundings disappear in "The River" because the configuration of destructive forces operating in nature is the same configuration found in the society men have built for themselves. The suicide of Tada Otaki, for example, is as "natural" as those of the laborer and his son, because all are the result of a blind and belligerent necessity dictating the course of every life.

This fundamental unity of diverse experience under a single principle of fate does, however, dissemble a duality hinted at throughout
Ibuse's work in the 1930s. The destructive phase of the natural cycle
coincides with a regenerative one. In "The River," for instance, the
survivors of the flood rebuild their homes. In "The Persimmon Tree
of Nakajima" (Nakajima no kaki no ki, 1938) some inhabitants of a
village drown in a flood, but others are saved by climbing into the
limbs of a persimmon tree tall enough to tower over the rising
waters. Like its sister persimmon tree in "The River," it embodies the
powers of life inherent in nature. Nearly an entire village clinging to
the branches of a fruit tree under siege by a deluge seems a perfect
image of Ibuse's world, one which bespeaks a common ground for
both life's tragedies and its miracles. "The Carp" tells of a living carp
given by a dead friend; "The River" conversely tells of a living
landscape littered with dead victims. The natural world reflects the
synergic relationships between men, their surroundings, and their
fate as extensions of an equation in which any addition requires a
counterbalancing subtraction.

Ibuse's growing interest in this natural world led him to explore
the countryside. From the 1930s on he began traveling frequently in
eastern Japan and beyond in search of interesting rivers, roads,
mountains, and valleys. These trips often provided Ibuse with the
material for his stories and essays. Perhaps the preeminent example
of his early travel literature is his humorous novel, The Traveling
Debt Collectors (Shūkin ryokō, 1935–1937), in which two mis-
matched Tokyoites—a young writer and a beautiful woman with a
history of various lovers—travel the length of Japan, including
Ibuse's home village of Kamo, in search of money owed to a friend of
the writer's and to the beautiful woman herself. Most of Ibuse's
travel writings, however, have been serious, even scholarly. The rural
excursions of both his life and literature also led him into the past records of the places he visited, and thus into the study of history itself.
Eventually Ibuse turned to the writing of historical fiction, some of
which now accounts for his most valued work. In fact, it is not coin-
cidental that Ibuse in the 1930s focused on both the natural world
and history, for as Ibuse continued to distance himself from the cave
in which he had been imprisoned, he found his field of vision en-
larged chronologically as well as spatially. The principles he discovered in the terrain of Japan, he also found in its past.

Waves

Ibuse's first historical work is also his first that can properly be called a novel, that is, an extended prose narrative written from a modern (i.e., self-aware) point of view. Interestingly, however, the textual history of *Waves* reveals it to be the consolidated series of many novellas and short stories published sporadically throughout the 1930s. Its constituent parts are written in the form of excerpts lifted from a diary supposedly kept by a young Taira aristocrat, forced to flee Kyoto during the twelfth-century civil war fought by his clan with the rival Minamoto. This ambitious undertaking occupied Ibuse on and off for the greater part of his first decade as a mature writer. Consequently, *Waves* reads as a textual barometer of how Ibuse himself changed during those years. Ibuse himself has stated in the preface, "This tale is like an album in which my feelings over ten years are pasted here and there."[3]

The assembled order in which the reader today receives the novel is, as with "The River," not necessarily that of its original and rather scattered publication. The final and complete version covers the rich slice of history from the seventh month of the second year of the Juei imperial reign period (1183) to the third month of the following year. The first part of the novel, from the introduction through the twenty-eighth day of the seventh month, was published under the title "A Record of Escape" (*Nigete iku kiroku*) in the 1930 collection of Ibuse's early stories *Fond Realities* (*Natsukashiki genjitsu*). Some have argued, however, that this first part was perhaps written as early as 1927, the year in which Ibuse's grandfather died and his friends turned to politics.[4] Supporting this theory is Ibuse's remark that he first thought of writing *Waves* before he joined *Bungei toshi* in 1928.[5] Perhaps he gained the impetus for a historical novel from the contemporary events of his youth that had left him alone and abandoned. Certainly Ibuse's youth did play some part in the development of the novel:

> It was my plan from the very start to write it this way [over a long period of time]. I thought this would be one means to write about a youth, the hero of the tale, maturing rapidly into an adult, owing to the turmoil of war.[6]

Ibuse required a decade to finish *Waves*, perhaps because he was living the story as he wrote it. The very nature of its theme, a young person's disillusionment and consequent maturity, demanded that Ibuse himself complete this process in order to create a character with authenticity. Different parts of the novel, occasionally even out of chronological order, were published in different places and at different times, but, as in "The River," a single point of view unites the work convincingly.

In *Waves* Ibuse continued his experiments with longer forms of fiction, finally fixing upon a method nascent in his early short stories and destined to be a trademark of much of later and best work: the diary. The introduction to *Waves* reads:

> In the seventh month of the second year of the Juei period, a military revolt forced the entire Taira clan to flee the imperial capital. The following is an account of their flight kept by one of their young men, one part of which I have translated into the modern vernacular. [1:370]

This short preface says much. Ibuse states that he will tell (or as he would pretend, retell)[7] the past from the present position of the diary's translator. Ibuse's fiction often exploits this technique of "doubling" any reading of history. He explains that he has discovered old documents that, after judicious editing, he now presents to the modern reader. The conceit enables Ibuse to keep himself both in and out of the text. Acting as if he were not the author but merely his latter-day and removed assistant, Ibuse selects and interprets (translating "one part") from the work to create his own work while preserving the original's privileged status as factual documentary. Free to reorganize and reword one closed text (closed in the sense that a diary limits itself from one point in time to another) into a new and open one, Ibuse forces the diarist to make room for a modern consciousness that rereads his entries and thus imposes a second, and competing, structure onto the work. A parallel can be drawn with Ibuse's method in "The River," where an unspecified narrative voice leaps from one river locale to another, disrupting the natural and continual flow of the waters themselves to construct a story reflective of that voice's interests and understanding. In *Waves,* that spatial continuum of the river's course is replaced by a chronological sequence of events, but Ibuse's manipulation of his readers' expectations and attentions remains the same.

This is not a new technique, of course. Storytellers and novelists have for a very long time substantiated narrative through invoking imaginary, extratextual historical sources. The reader understands such invention as a command to read ironically, to juggle constantly every "objective" and "subjective" statement. Ibuse consequently succeeds in firmly establishing a critical and structural distance between the story of his works and his own persona within them. This distance is required if Ibuse is to remain an observer outside the cave. *Waves* reads at least two ways; as a historical document that Ibuse merely passes on to the reader, and as a subjectivized original, creatively fashioned through means of omission and translation. Ibuse's writing up to this point has involved a steady process of removing himself as much as possible from the story. With *Waves* he is able to maintain his hard-earned aloofness and yet reenter the narrative in a new and powerful role, that of an extratextual arbiter of its interpretation. By inventing the presence of a diarist, Ibuse intends to minimize himself as an authorial force; but by prefacing the diary with a paragraph establishing it as simply an extended quotation following a watakushi's comments, Ibuse again emerges as a major force in the work. The three short sentences introducing *Waves* tell the reader the novel will be as much about the writing of history as about history itself.

The potential for ironic readings is made even clearer when the first entry of the diary throws its own writing into the midst of rapidly shifting and historically momentous events. Dated the fifteenth day of the seventh month, the diarist (watakushi, identified by a reference early in the novel as the historical figure Taira Tomoakira)[8] reports that an expeditionary force numbering in the thousands has returned to the clan headquarters in the capital, Rokuhara, after successfully quelling a rebellion. The leaders of this force look magnificent in the light of the fires in the courtyard, yet the diarist cannot help feeling sad at the sight of the battleworn clothing. This subjective reaction of the diarist immediately pulls the reader into an ironic confrontation with the (historical) past and the (narrative) present. Ibuse assumes of his Japanese readers a knowledge of the thirteenth-century classic *Heike monogatari* (*The Tale of the Heike*) and its chronicle of the downfall of the entire Taira clan.[9] The *Heike*—according to Ibuse, the only classic he has read cover to cover[10]—remains as centrally present in the reading of *Waves* as Ibuse himself, thus suggesting an interpretation of the novel as the interplay between several potent and ironic narratives wholly anterior to itself. The *Heike* acts as a "past" to the "present" of the novel to create an impression of inevitable destiny, an impression not only deliberate but very much related to Ibuse's purposes in "The River."

ahead quickly. News reaches the capital that the Taira have suffered
a crushing defeat in Etchū to the north. Advance units of the
Minamoto's allies, the Kiso, are about to enter the city itself. Plans
are made for the possible evacuation of Rokuhara. The last paragraph reads:

> Today was very hot. I thought the leaves of the *bashō* tree in the garden
> had grown no larger than in other years, but when I glanced at them just
> a moment ago I noticed they were twice as big as they had been last year.
> Under the shade of this *bashō* bloomed hardy flowers. [1:372]

The exaggerated growth of the persimmon tree after the flood in
"The River" suggests a resurgence of the natural world after disaster;
but in *Waves* the *bashō*, or plantain, seems an unusual and ominous
departure from the expected, an omen of catastrophe ahead. That
the same phenomenon of sudden vegetation could signal rebirth in
one context and portend tragedy in another indicates that the
dynamics of Ibuse's world are diverse in their application and significance. The alert reader is again asked to consider any event in the
novel against events elsewhere, not only in the *Heike* but in those
Ibuse works contributing to the same portrait of the world as *Waves*.

The entry for the seventeenth tells of a larger warrior on horseback
who approaches the Rokuhara gates to taunt the Taira within. He
challenges the clan to send someone out to fight him, and though the
diarist's father Tomomori, who holds the superior rank of general,
should defend the Taira honor himself, he instead places a dull-
witted retainer on his horse and sends him out in a cruel masquerade.
The retainer cuts a dashing figure even as he rides out to certain
death, and the diarist is moved to record his battle dress so as to
memorialize (*kinen suru*) the man's courage. This, the first of many
references in *Waves* to the acts of recording and commemoration, establishes a link between one's real and one's textual existences. Like
the relationship between the eulogy of "The Carp" and the dead
friend for whom it was written, the diarist's description of the hapless soldier is a *kinen*, literally a "record-thought," of an existence
soon to end. The diarist describes how this man, through his own father's cowardice, is killed in a most bloody duel, utterly outclassed
by his opponent. Confused, forgetful of words he meant to exclaim
to his enemy, the retainer announced himself only as "Tomomori,
the equal of a thousand horsemen." He is summarily killed when the

enemy decapitates him with tremendous brute strength. The retainer's loss of words is met with the diarist's command of them: understandably upset at what he has seen, he declares it an "atrocity" and claims to "detest" all military violence in unmistakably clear language. *Waves* thematically commences here, when Tomoakira the diarist first experiences the disillusionment that will become the principal theme of the novel.

On the eighteenth day the situation for the Taira and their Rokuhara leaders worsens. Even were we to take the tonsure and defect from the clan's standard, argues the diarist, priests are no more than a "perversion" (*hentai*) of our own "class" (*kaikyū*). Disillusionment in this cynical observation borders on the political, and words such as "class" seem oddly anachronistic in this ostensibly twelfth-century story. Ibuse has conceded in an interview that the proletarian-literature movement was a factor in his writing of *Waves*.[11] Perhaps such modern terms were prominent in his vocabulary at the time. Some critics have gone so far as to suggest that leftist politics stood behind the entire conception of the novel: Ōoka Shōkei argues that although the proletarian movement was in a state of decline in the 1930s, writers still felt they could not surpass political literature until they had encompassed it, implying that Ibuse was, in fact, attempting to write a work critical of the left in *Waves*.[12] The evidence seems less than convincing. Rather, allusions in the novel to modern notions of class—and "perversion"—serve as yet another means of restating the familiar dilemma of Ibuse's protagonists. The diarist, like the salamander, finds himself alone and alienated within the small world around him.

Constricted by his membership in the privileged aristocracy during a time of tremendous change, the diarist finds his condition suddenly aggravated when, according to the entry for the nineteenth, Rokuhara begins to be evacuated. Plans call for burning everything before their departure. His past now literally about to be destroyed, the diarist is in typical Ibuse fashion rendered a castaway, severed from the place that once defined him. By the twenty-fifth, the day on which the clan finally leaves Kyoto, the diarist senses the drastic changes ahead. He writes that no one seems to know where they are headed. Burning buildings illuminate the evening sky. Yet while he acknowledges turmoil, he also carefully notes it, ending his entry for the day with the identification "I record this in our field camp this evening" (1:380). In this second reference to the actual writing of the

diary, the narrative turns on the verb "record," or Japanese
shitatameru, a word with the added sense of "drawing up" and
"preparing." The diarist is beginning to move beyond passive description into an active textual organization of his jarring experiences.
From this day forward his conventional existence ceases and only un-
certainty lies ahead. The diary is henceforth required to guide in its
author's understanding, assimilation, and mastery of each new day
at war.

This new task of writing is emphasized in the next entry. Unsure of
the date, the diarist hesitates to ask anyone because "dates are necessary only to those who embrace home" (1:380). Yet dates are also
necessary to those who, like Tomoakira, keep diaries, and so his
journal becomes closely associated with the preservation of hopes
and, by extension, of survival. In this sense *Waves* is a book about
the power of books, arguing that the act of narration can enable
psychic continuity through a reflexivity of the author in his words.
Like Scheherazade, the watakushi of *Waves* must keep telling tales or
die.

The entry for the twenty-eighth, which movingly details the
Taira's incineration of their former capital of Fukuhara and their
subsequent flight from the main island of Honshū, completes the first
published section of the novel. The next installment, which resumes
on the sixteenth day of the eighth month and ends on the twenty-
first, was published in two parts in June and July 1930 under the
title, "A Chronicle of Exile" (*Bōmeiki*). It was later revised to include
the entry for the twenty-second and was issued in a book of the same
title in 1934. These entries describe the deteriorating military position of the Taira as they are stricken with desertions and supply
problems. The references to class and social stratification persist.
Some are subtle, as when Ibuse carefully distinguishes between the
newer and older ranks of samurai. Others are pointed. On the seventeenth, a country samurai is honored with a nonsense title in order to
placate him, and the diarist wryly observes that, after all, such privi-
leges allow "his" class to retain power over "them." On the nineteenth, they seek refuge in a harbor where the villagers welcome
them warmly. Had they not, notes the diarist, their homes would
have been burned to the ground. In fact, *Waves* is full of the mention
of atrocities not just threatened but perpetrated. Its record of excessive or inappropriate violence in the twelfth century will pale in
comparison with what Ibuse will write of, and live through, in the

twentieth. Nonetheless, it demonstrates what he considered at this early stage of his career to be one of the distinguishing characteristics of history.

While in this village the young Taira aristocrat takes an important step towards adulthood when he meets a charmingly unsophisticated local girl and realizes he is strongly attracted to her. He concludes his entry for the evening of the nineteenth with an introspective comment on his new feelings: "I want now to be shown kindnesses by someone outside our class" (1:390). His emotions belie an anxious insecurity, inspired by the yearning to share his sense of loneliness and social isolation as an aristocrat cast among a rural populace who fear him and his power. Like the erstwhile salamander seeking the companionship of a frog, the diarist of *Waves* looks to the attentions of a woman to help him escape from a figurative prison in part of his own making.

History, however, conspires against his hopes. In the entry for the twentieth, watakushi reports that he has been ordered to burn the homes of thirty-six villagers because they assisted the desertion of twenty Taira soldiers. He regrets the order but executes it, admitting his true feelings only to his diary: "I am the one who wishes to desert. I would flee first from my own men" (1:392). The brutality of the fighting has discouraged and disillusioned the diarist, but he also realizes he can do nothing but resign himself to his fate and that of his clan. The historical world of *Waves* has become as ominously dark as the natural world of "The River."

Kotarō and Kakutan

On the twenty-first, now on yet another island somewhere in the Inland Sea, the diarist reports he has been joined in his guard duty by a local samurai, Miyaji Kotarō, who is rustic but mannered, unlettered but loyal. Ibuse's sensitive portrait of this major figure exemplifies his skill in defining literary character with great economy. Kotarō holds thematic importance in *Waves*. His role throughout the remainder of the work is suggested at the outset. The diarist writes in the evening of the day they met, "Earlier Kotarō came by and watched with awe as I wrote in the diary. He stoked the fire for me and spoke of news in the camp" (1:402). Hereafter Kotarō serves not only as an assistant in war but as an accomplice in recording it. He provides the information from which the diarist writes and the very light that enables him to do so. The writing of the diary begins to assume the character of a ritual, a regularly enacted and sympathetic activity done to affect and control its performers' environment. Around the campfire in *Waves,* the performers are the diarist and Kotarō, and the environment is a nation at war.

On the following day the diarist is joined by another samurai who develops into a crucial character in the novel—this is Kakutan, a tonsured soldier from a temple, a monk with incredible bravery and strategic acumen. Kakutan, the diarist, and Kotarō form an intriguing trio at the center of the novel. Each has his own reasons for, and perspective on, his role in the civil war—yet all three share a common fate. On the twenty-second, they lead a scouting party back to the island where the diarist had met his young woman—but after learning that the inhabitants' sympathies are largely with their enemies, and that even some of their own clan's women have deserted, only to become prostitutes, the daring exploits of Kotarō and Kakutan as they destroy Minamoto armories do little to raise the diarist's spirits. Indeed, he would like to confess his own thoughts of desertion to Kakutan. Ibuse has created three characters and a situation ripe for the greatest irony of the novel—the diarist's most profound disillusionment still lies in the future.

Six years in Ibuse's life passed between this entry, the twenty-second of the seventh month, and the next, the twenty-fourth day of the ninth month. Ibuse published no further installments of the novel until 1937, by which time much had changed. The proletarian movement in literature had run its course. Japan had plunged into its misadventures in China and, as if life were imitating art, had posed a contemporary war alongside *Waves'* historical account. Literature dealing with conflict would be read differently in the latter half of the 1930s than in the first. Ibuse had also changed. By any criterion he was now an established writer, the winner of prizes. Increasingly he would write from the reflective stance of middle age. The tone of the latter half (actually, closer to two-thirds) of *Waves* seems altered. Gone are the diarist's youthful doubts and insecurities, as were Ibuse's own. No longer an aspiring writer but a successful one, Ibuse resumed work on *Waves* with a new perspective and sharpened talents in 1937. He wrote its conclusion with a new purpose in 1938.

Ibuse published the rest of *Waves,* under various titles, from June 1937 through October 1938 in the magazine *Bungakukai (Literary*

World). The entry for the twenty-fourth day of the ninth month, however, resumes precisely where Ibuse had left his readers six years earlier. The diarist, Kotarō, and Kakutan are still conducting reconnaissance on the movements of the Minamoto. Life, even in flight, has settled into a routine:

> On our ship the soldiers stood along the bulwarks and silently observed the coastline. Now and then one would shift his footing and make his armor creak. It was a most unpleasant sound, reminding me of how I had hated the clash of metal as a child. Apparently I had changed at some point, however, for now that sound gave me strength. When young, I could not stand such noises as the sharpening of swords, but this morning I woke to the pleasant music of Kotarō honing my own blade. [1:414–15]

The diarist has left his childhood forever behind him. In its place now looms the precarious life of a young adult entrusted with important responsibilities. That precariousness is heightened when Kakutan reports the devastating news that the Kiso forces now completely control the capital and its government, that a prince sympathetic to the Minamoto cause has been named emperor, and that the Taira have been declared enemies of the court. At this moment, when his clan's fortunes have never seemed lower, the diarist again chooses to write about writing itself, to return to the refuge he has secured for himself within the pages of his journal:

> Miyaji Kotarō sat stiffly beside Kakutan until he and I had finished our conversation. Then, as he does whenever I write, Kotarō built the campfire for me. This evening, like all others, I kept my diary by the light of the fire. [1:416]

In the following entry, the twenty-sixth, the diarist and his men leave on a long and dangerous voyage to northern Kyūshū, where some of the Taira are reputedly regrouping. Before departing, however, he pays a final call on the young girl he had met months earlier, again noting in his diary that "what makes me most happy is to be shown love by someone outside our class." But he is disappointed to find her home abandoned, his gentle friend perhaps in flight from the fighting. The diarist's last chance for solace is denied him; he is left with no affectionate ties to the world that his clan hopes to regain.

Deserted by his love, the diarist soon discovers that he has also been abandoned by the main Taira forces, who have already sailed on to their next strategic stronghold. Shuddering at this turn of events, he dispatches Kotarō to investigate the truth of these reports. Kotarō and Kakutan sail for Innoshima Island, Kotarō's home and the site of Ibuse's 1921 summer retreat. The diarist remains behind, bereft of his comrades' companionship. When his favorite horse, emaciated and dying, is thrown overboard, he retreats into his diary to forget his loneliness and to muse of the happier days spent within Rokuhara.

On the twenty-ninth, Kotarō and Kakutan return from their mission with a ship bearing provisions and many new recruits. But they also bring disturbing intelligence. Kakutan relays reports confirmed on Innoshima that allies in Kyūshū have revolted due to Minamoto machinations, that an important Taira general has committed suicide, and that the Taira command has now fled to Yashima on the island of Shikoku.

The next several entries describe a demoralized and exhausted band of men fighting their way to Yashima. Progress is slow, as they must travel in stealth from one island to the next. Against these deteriorating conditions, the diarist's response is to rely increasingly on his journal as a ritual activity that not only parallels but supplants some functions of his life. Kotarō continues to assist in the execution of the ritual, while the diarist asks its power to grant him an ever greater control over reality:

The Thirtieth Day of the First Month

Today is the thirtieth day of the first month in the first year of the so-called Genryaku reign period. But I would record it for all time as the thirtieth day of the first month of the third year of Juei.

The Thirtieth Day of the First Month, Juei Three [1:438]

The diarist, since he does not recognize the ascendancy of Emperor Gotoku over former Emperor Antoku, also refuses to recognize the new reign appellation promulgated by the court. Consequently, the dates in his diary continue to follow the chronology of the old calendar. The implication is that no date is real other than the one he chooses to record. In effect, the diarist attributes to his diary the authority to refute external reality and to assert instead an interior, textual one. The reader knows, of course, that history will decide this the first year of Genryaku, but this irony only underscores the diarist's reflexive reality and emphasizes the process by which he constructs it. The diarist does intuitively what patients undergoing analysis are sometimes told to do by their doctors: in analysis, psychic disequilibrium, as it is transferred to the pages of a journal, is first organized as it is composed; then it is assimilated and understood. Ibuse's diarists—Tomoakira in *Waves* is only his first—go one step further when they seem to shift some aspects of their identity onto their texts.

In the last lines of this entry for the thirtieth day of the first month, the diarist gives his usual thanks: "Tonight, too, Kotarō keeps the fire bright" (1:441). To this rote mention of the light by which he writes, however, he unexpectedly adds another paragraph:

> Kakutan draws and erases characters in the ashes with a tree branch. He looks tired but remains absorbed in tracing out a sutra with his stick. No doubt he is thinking back to his younger days when he was a gifted student at the academy. [1:441]

The diarist is no longer the sole writer in *Waves*. Kakutan, scribbling in the very ashes of the fire that supplies light for his lord's text, "remains absorbed" in invoking a special power inherent in sacred writing as he scratches with a stick—recalling the most primitive literary technology—a Buddhist scripture learned in his youth. In doing so he not only returns to a nostalgic time but enacts a ritual associated with holy revelation and supernatural truth. This ritual complements the diarist's. The function of both is to imbue their lives with contexts, one a Buddhist and metaphysical world invoked by the mention of sutras, and the other a world of writing empowered with such words as "draws," "erases," and "tracing."

Kakutan's participation in the literary rituals of *Waves* broadens to involve even Kotarō, an illiterate. The diarist writes in his entry for the first day of the second month:

> When I returned to camp I found Kakutan warming himself by the fire and reading a manual of military strategies to Miyaji Kotarō. No doubt he had succumbed to Kotarō's earnest requests and had finally taken it out for him. When he had been at Yashima, Kakutan never unrolled the scroll unless Kotarō had begged him three or four times. His reason was that Kotarō already knew the military classics by heart. But Kotarō wanted to hear the strong voice of his respected hero recite those very tomes that he had fondly committed to memory.
>
> Kotarō sat most formally and listened to Kakutan recite. Kakutan, his

back to the fire, had the open scroll before him and read the same section over and over. [1:444]

Kakutan has memorized a sutra; Kotarō a work on military theory. Both have internalized texts that impose significance upon their lives. The diarist, who notes this in his own book, creates a circle in which writing is both determinant of and determined by historical events. As these three central characters of the novel sit around the campfire, they are neatly linked in interdependent "literary" acts furnishing them with a past (the sutra), a present (the military manual), and a future (the diary), effectively closing off their world (their circle) to forces they choose not to admit.

The structure of Waves has thus grown powerfully complex. As the diary organizes personal experience, the military manual dictates the conduct of soldiers, and the sutra predicts the course of the entire universe. Writing exerts an ever growing hegemony over the lives of the characters, doubling and reversing the authority of words, readers, and writers. But Ibuse himself, acting anteriorly as author, establishes a hierarchy within the circle. Like the Chinese puzzle that hides one box within another, Ibuse embeds one text within the next. The outermost text is his introduction, written in the present day ("The following is an account. . . ."). Within that lies the second text, Tomoakira's diary placed in historical time (during the Juei reign period). Within the diary lie sutras etched in ashes and classics rolled into scrolls which, as they proceed along supernatural or abstract lines, are essentially ahistorical—identified with neither past nor present. Seen this way, narrative progression in Waves moves from one time framework to another, with its final stage not properly "time" at all, but its denial. In this penultimate phase of the novel, the characters perceive an escape from their predicament. By turning evermore inward toward their textual existences, they simultaneously turn away from their historical ones. They remain safe on the written page. The role of "text" in Waves is akin to that of "river" in "The River," a nurturing undercurrent of life, a separate reality that flows unseen beneath the surface.

In the last entries of Waves, the story acquires another text, and so acquires another layer of meaning. The Taira have decided to make their stand at Ichinotani. The diarist thinks the plan ill advised but accepts his orders. Just as the clan is busy with its preparations for this upcoming and decisive battle, he receives astounding news, which he notes at the head of his entry for the fifth day of the second month. "The unexpected development of Kakutan's desertion from camp yesterday is a great and shocking event both for myself and his student, Miyaji Kotarō" (1:449).

Although they had been plagued by frequent desertions ever since fleeing the capital, the Taira had not until now suffered the loss of such a renowned warrior. Described in the diary not only as a skillful fighter but as a wise man with a knowledge of the principles of the universe, Kakutan is believed to possess insights into the "course of the world" (sejō no dōkō). This phrase, in a novel informed by the Heike monogatari, can mean nothing but inexorable decline. Thus, Kakutan's desertion is interpreted by the diarist not as an individual act of cowardice but as an informed prediction of the future. The Taira are done for. The irony of the diarist's earlier inner thoughts expressing his own desire to desert is now allowed its fullest impact.

A Journal of the Juei Period

Kakutan is not absent for long. He is soon found and led back to camp. His return incites in the diarist mixed feelings of relief and disgust. Informed that Kakutan, when captured, was on his way back to the Taira because he had thought of a weakness in the clan's fortifications about which he wanted to warn his former comrades, the diarist finds his desertion stranger still. It seems the act not so much of a traitor but of a seer with a frightening but sure vision of how history will inevitably unfold.

Although the Taira are thus alerted to the vulnerability of their defenses, there is no time to strengthen them. Attack by the Minamoto is imminent. Rather than executing or even incarcerating Kakutan, however, the diarist allows him to stay in their shared quarters and to begin work on a special project:

> Kakutan now began work on an account of us since the flight from the capital which he previously had said he wanted to write. This document, entitled A Journal of the Juei Period, will probably be quite voluminous, and Kakutan says he does not want to die in battle until he has finished it. Once done, however, Kakutan has said he would be happy to use the opportunity his return has provided to get a taste of the famed Minamoto no Yoshitsune's skill in battle.

As usual I am writing this in my diary by the light of the fire. Miyaji Kotarō sits formally on the other side and makes sure the flames do not die. Kakutan sits cross-legged, thinking of nothing but his *Journal*. It seems an evening spent in a peaceful family far from the reality of war. [1:452]

The trio of central characters is again jointly engaged in the ritual of writing. In the light of the fire, the diarist, assisted by Kotarō, continues in his journal while Kakutan initiates his own, parallel historical document. The reader is told that Kakutan "previously had said he wanted to write" such a chronicle, but we learn this only now, when Kakutan's life is suddenly tied directly to its existence. On the one hand, the *Journal* preserves its author's life by recording its details. On the other hand, it extends his life by postponing its author's eventual confrontation with his enemy on the battlefield. Seen as the "textual" climax of the novel, this *Journal* (literally "A Record of Long Life") epitomizes Ibuse's vital usage of writing. When Kakutan completes his history, he too will be completed. The connection between literature and human survival is made explicit in an amplification of the more subtle relationship between the diarist and his own journal. If each page of the *Journal* represents another day of life for Kakutan, then each entry in Tomoakira's diary represents another day in which he is still functioning as a whole human being capable of remarking the events of his life.

What Kakutan, the oracle of *Waves,* writes in his final testament is revealed in the diarist's entry for the twentieth day of the second month. The Taira have been routed at Ichinotani. Miyaji Kotarō has died bravely in battle. Erroneous rumors also claim Tomoakira as dead.[13] The truth, however, is that he, with Kakutan and a small band of men, has made it to safety and is preparing to fight again:

To cheer myself I took out the manuscript on which Kakutan is working. It is written in an elegant hand suggesting the flow of the Fujiwara style of calligraphy. The first chapter begins with the Chinese poem: "Nations fall, but mountains and rivers remain / Where the capital once stood, now trees and grasses grow in the spring / Even the scent of nameless flowers speaks of the sadness that the mighty must fall." This first chapter tells of how our clan fled from Fukuhara, and it includes details of how the Rokuhara and Komatsu palaces, and the estates on West Eighth Avenue, were engulfed in flames. "The black smoke obscured the sun in the heavens, and although it was day it seemed like night. The Phoenix

Palace left only its foundations; the imperial carriage, only debris."
Kakutan sees the destruction of our clan as the consequence of the inevitable flow of time. He calls the tyranny of our own Kiyomori simply
an earlier form of rule by the military class, a form to be perfected in the
future by Minamoto no Yoshitsune. He further suggests that he was himself dragged along by the currents of time and joined in our clan's cause
to follow this flow of nature and eventually to depart the world. I suddenly felt I was reading a work of total despair, and I stopped halfway
into the first chapter. I returned the *Journal* to Kakutan's chest. [1:472]

Kakutan's *Journal* reads as a precursor of the *Heike monogatari*,
with its view of the decline of the Taira as a natural cosmological
movement. The *Journal* straddles two time frames, that of 1184, the
year of its composition, and that of the present day, when the modern and ironic interpretation of its events determines our reading.
Consequently the *Journal* stands in no single time frame. Unlike the
earlier sutra and military manual, it attains not to an ahistorical but a
suprahistorical nature, one that expresses a general and transcendent
principle of history. His *Journal* further consolidates in a single
theory "the currents of time" and the "flow of nature," a con-
currence that demonstrates how Ibuse's historical and natural worlds
are not distinct but are in fact reflective of each other. This excerpt
from the *Journal* is the *locus classicus* of Ibuse's historical vision of
time, as the whirlpool description in "The River" is of his equally
cyclical vision of nature. The *Journal* is the reader's confirmation,
and the diarist's revelation, of the inevitable direction of history towards the destruction of one earthly age and the birth of another.
Kakutan serves as Ibuse's omniscient voice of fate because he sees, as
does the protagonist of "The Priest of Fumon'in Temple" (*Fumon'in-
san*, 1949), "history and the present day mesh together." That voice
remains metahistorical because it stands outside any particular sequence of chronological events and so constructs Ibuse's fundamental paradigm. As the water of "The River" flows through varying terrain but unchanging human life, so history in *Waves* winds through
the years like a spiral, never repeating itself precisely but always covering the same ground. The whirlpool that traps Otaki in its watery
revolution is the same vortex that traps the diarist in the political revolution of the twelfth century.

The military situation for the survivors of Ichinotani worsens
steadily. The diarist and Kakutan, however, manage to continue

their writing. Neither journal is a distraction easily dispensed with. Each is now a central activity, and although one may be personal and the other epic, they converge as works that keep their authors alive:

> The sun sets over the sea at Awaji. I cannot imagine being able to sleep tonight. Kakutan is working calmly on his *Journal,* and so I am writing in my diary aboard ship, too. But Miyaji Kotarō, who always looked after the fire for me, is no longer with us in this world. [1:464]

The Minamoto and their allies are rapidly closing in. The diarist's entry for the twenty-seventh day of the second month includes the nearly casual speculation that the home of his young woman friend has undoubtedly been burned to the ground. The truce between the two sides in the civil war has been violated, and the Taira can put no further trust in diplomacy than they can in their diminished troops. *Waves* concludes without epic suspense but rather with historically informed pathos:

Fourth Day of the Third Month

> Today we occupied a place on Shiraishijima called Kitahama. Our booty was twelve enemy vessels and three hundred sacks of grain. But in the middle of the fighting I was hit in my right arm by an arrow. I can no longer hold a writing brush, and so I am dictating this to Fukasu no Kurō. Since I left the capital last year I have made no mistakes in any of our many battles, but today, on some remote island, an anonymous common soldier has wounded me. It was my own fault. Kakutan today, as always, distinguished himself.

The following is recorded respectfully by Fukasu no Kurō:

> Our lord is resting peacefully. His wound is shallow, and there is no cause for worry. He is quite weak from having bled so. Lord Kakutan sits in a corner of the room placidly writing his *Journal.* We are in one room of a commoner's home in Kitahama on Shiraishijima. In the garden stands a huge tree which, though past its prime, still retains its beauty. One stray arrow has found a mark in its trunk. It is evening now, and the mountains on the fair island are dyed violet. [1:480]

A reader might complain that *Waves* is a novel without satisfying closure. One might suspect that Ibuse stopped here arbitrarily, or only because the book had, as he did admit, "gone on too long." [14] But to say the ending is abrupt is not to say it is meaningless or ineffective. The action of *Waves* concludes before the last stand of the Taira at Dannoura but after the diarist is wounded and no longer able to write, that is, to further prolong his surrogate life within the text. His power to control experience becomes a casualty of the arrow that cripples his writing arm. The diarist can no longer exercise the ritual and literary direction that once he could. The story is over.

The postscript to this final entry, however, suggests that the writing of the *Journal* continues after that of the diary has ceased. "Lord Kakutan sits in a corner of the room placidly writing." The *Journal*, already established in the novel as the vehicle for Ibuse's expression of suprahistorical principles of fate, is not subject to the same historical constraints as other texts. It alone survives after other works terminate, because it alone articulates a law to which all else submits.

This notion of omnipotent fate is as absolute in its tyranny as it was in "The River." Ōoka Shōhei, himself the veteran of the Second World War and the author of works cataloguing its atrocities, was unable to read all of *Waves* for just this reason.[15] The cruelty of the world into which the diarist flees is exacerbated by the naïveté of his earlier life within Rokuhara. His precarious exile in an inhospitable countryside, much like Ōoka's own terrifying wanderings in the wartime Philippines, results in a disillusionment all the greater for its utter discontinuity with prior experience. The diarist's ingenious response to this crisis, first anticipated by the blind old man who names the sounds of the river in "The River," is found in the creative work of writing. Ibuse's response was the same: by becoming a writer he successfully circumvented a debilitating melancholy in the 1920s. Ibuse's remedy for challenges posed to the psychic integrity of either himself or his characters would seem to be: writing on the walls of the cave to scribble one's way out.

The Historical World

The literary historian Nakamura Mitsuo no doubt was thinking of *Waves* when he compared Ibuse's historical fiction to confessional writing (*shi-shōsetsu*). He has termed the diarist "an idealized portrait" of Ibuse himself, recognizing the correlation between the protagonist's dilemma and Ibuse's own.[16] While Nakamura's attempt to include *Waves* within this most egocentric of Japanese literary genres overlooks Ibuse's careful efforts to distinguish himself from his narratives, Ibuse's personal concerns are indeed crucial in his vision of the historical and natural world. Although *Waves* takes as its textual antecedent the *Heike monogatari*, a classic that inspired Ibuse to write about people and events from "historical fact,"[17] he has also admitted that it is a novel "mostly imagined."[18] But here, "imagined" means not "fictitious" but "inspired." Both *Waves* and the *Heike*, for example, are set along the Inland Sea. This is a historical fact of the Gempei civil war. At the same time, Yasuoka Shōtarō suspects that in many of the novel's descriptions of the coast Ibuse was remembering scenes of his own youth.[19] This mixture of national with personal history is, furthermore, an extension and development of a system of symbols and themes used in earlier stories. Water—whether of a pond, a pool, a river, or the ocean—is omnipresent in Ibuse's works as a natural sign of the powerful forces of life and death. Just as his river ("The River") flows past the vicissitudinous lives of modern people, his sea (*Waves*) stands witness to the rise and fall of those who struggled nearly a millennium ago.

Ibuse's selection of the historical figure Tomoakira as his diarist also reveals the clever interaction of fact, autobiography, and literary imagination in the novel. Tomoakira and his father Tomomori personify the force of fate—*Heike*'s principal theme—more than any other characters in the classic.[20] The historical Tomoakira and Ibuse's version of him as the diarist share a common inability to control their own destinies, destinies that, in the former, lead to death in battle and, in the latter, to death as an authorial presence. Ibuse often regards the lives of his characters from the vantage points of their demises. One of his first memories of himself, after all, is his attendance at a funeral. *Waves* is, in this sense, a logical and consistent development in Ibuse's literature, a sophisticated instance of an increasingly diverse cast of characters and settings organized about an invariably dark theme. "The Salamander" initially phrases the dialogue between the human condition and the environment that shapes it, "The River" maps in detail its geography, and *Waves* explores its precedents.

That exploration accounts for the novel's nature as "historical fiction." An ancient setting is not a sufficient or even necessary condition for a work to be thought historical in the sense that it gauges historical forces. Ibuse himself does not refer to his historical writings by the usual appellation *rekishi-shōsetsu* ("history-fiction"), but prefers instead the rather recherché term *magemono*, literally "topknot stories," alluding to the hair styles of the Edo period, but perhaps best translated as "period pieces." In fact, as "period piece" suggests, some of Ibuse's works considered historical fiction are nothing more than essentially modern stories set in the past for exotic effect. The exceptions, such as *Waves*, are truly historical fiction by virtue of the active presence of a concept of history that shapes the narrative. Historical fiction is necessarily about history, but that is not to say all or any of its narrative events must transpire in the "past." *Waves*, for instance, is a novel very much in, and dependent upon, the present. None of the work's pathos or irony could exist without the implicit context of the twentieth century.

Ōoka Shōhei has noted that Japanese historical fiction vacillates conspicuously between two understandings of itself—as a re-creation of the past following the lines of history but using modern techniques of realism, and as a borrowing of improbable situations from the past to indulge readers' Romanesque appetites.[21] His distinction is between the "historically historical" and the simply melodramatic. Only the former can be historical fiction, then, because only there does history truly matter. History figures prominently in a surprising number of Ibuse's works, some of which have nothing to do with clear evocations of the past: "The River" could be thought one example. Even in those works that do unfold in former times, some characters seem obviously modern. Most of Ibuse's historical writing is heavily indebted to his own experience. The majority of such stories are set in the Edo period, particularly the late Edo (in this, *Waves* is the notable exception), and in either the Kōshū or Bingo regions (several are placed in the remote Bingo village of Kobatake, made most famous by *Black Rain*, itself a work of historical fiction in this extended sense). Both era and locale would suggest Ibuse is retelling tales originally heard on his grandparents' laps. His heroes resemble the collective personalities common in oral traditions. Their identities are submerged, their names generalized, their lives made unexceptional in every way—except that they happen to be present when a great historical or natural event (war or a volcanic eruption) occurs to disrupt and test them. Like Kuchisuke, these historical characters stand as stubborn symbols of the strengths upon which ordinary people depend to survive. As such, they serve as passive reflections of the historical and natural forces acting upon them and their era.

In this, Ibuse's characters differ considerably from those of other
historical novelists, who most commonly turn to history to recreate distinct political figures who dominated their times. Ibuse attempts the opposite. Unlike those novelists who have adapted their techniques from traditional historiography—the study of great men— Ibuse is inspired by the parable, a narrative without a potently specific antagonist but imbued with a powerful inevitability. Ibuse comes from a background rich in this sort of story telling and believes, perhaps as a result, that forces such as fate, and not individual initiative, determine the course of world events. For this reason Ibuse's early historical fiction studies not character, but how the abstract dynamics of his world act upon its most minor actors. His heroes realize in themselves the tensions and direction of history; they lead existences that epitomize processes of change and continuity through time. That is why *Waves* is about a relatively obscure sixteen year old and not a Taira or Minamoto general. Such exceptional figures may be compelling, but they belong only in historical fiction predicated on the idea that they changed the past. Ibuse is interested solely in how it was typified.

In his story "Tajinko Village" (*Tajinko-mura*, 1939), the central character, a country constable named Kōda, is told a story by the widow of the local shrine's priest. Long ago there was an assault upon the castle in their town, an assault at the end of which the defenders' women and children threw themselves into a pond rather than be captured. This further example of perhaps the most common demise found in Ibuse's literature additionally provides him an opportunity to elaborate his concept of history. Speaking through the widow he writes:

> When my husband was alive you could hear the women and children crying at the pond every autumn. But when my son took over as priest at the shrine, he insisted it was all foolishness. Now you never hear their cries. That is how the history of long ago gradually disappears. [2:321]

Although not ordinarily included in the canon of Ibuse's historical fiction, "Tajinko Village" articulates a cardinal principle of his historical world. History consists of traditions, faiths, and beliefs, and especially beliefs in those who have tragically died. Ibuse increasingly turns to historical fiction to keep alive the memory of those who died before him, just as the old priest in Tajinko keeps the brave defenders of their castle alive even in death. The diarist of *Waves* writes to stay alive; Ibuse writes to resuscitate others.

The narrator of "An Old Man Speaks of the Mountain" (*Yama o mite rōjin no kataru,* 1939) is an old man who, pointing out a mountain in Kōshū, recalls a battle fought there in 1868 between the forces of the Tokugawa government and the Royalists. His father Kanjirō, once a gambler, joined the shogun's army as an artilleryman not to support a cause he thought just, but to earn money "for each shot of the cannon he fired." Having recently lost his wife, Kanjirō strapped his seven-year-old son (the narrator) onto his back and brought him into battle because "he thought war must not allow parents and children to be separated." The old man still clearly recalls the sounds of the guns.

Fighting on the mountain began sooner than expected, and Kanjirō's side was unprepared. When the artillerymen, largely inexperienced, fail to halt the enemy, Kanjirō, with his son, deserts and flees into the hills. "Later my father and I roved from place to place. Since the search for deserters was intense he threw his sword away into the river" (2:235). Kanjirō is an example of Ibuse's typically anonymous heroes dogged by historical forces they neither comprehend nor control. He, like the diarist of *Waves,* is caught in a war that, while it does not interest him, threatens him.

The possibility of sudden and indiscriminate death is present in nearly all of Ibuse's historical stories. The actual deaths of those close to Ibuse in his youth, an obsessive theme in his literature, leads him to explore other such encounters with fate, elsewhere and earlier. Yet these encounters remain enigmatic. Just as he had no idea that his friend's illness was terminal, he is at a similar loss to explain why history takes the precise turns it does. In his essay "Takachiho in Hyūga" (*Hyūga Takachiho,* 1939), Ibuse argues that history—here specifically the divine cosmological myths of Japan associated with Hyūga—must and should be respected as a mystery men cannot penetrate. Ibuse will never know why Aoki Nampachi had to die before him, and the diarist of *Waves* will never totally understand why his clan had to fall; both puzzles bring the reader to a theory of history readily yielded by Ibuse's tales of common people buffeted about in past times. To borrow an image from "The River," Ibuse and his characters are swept up in a a fast stream that moves them irrevocably and inexplicably. Only birds that soar high, or men with exceptional gifts, like Kakutan, can perceive the whole and its dynamic workings.

Ibuse aspires to such panoramic vision. The irresistible force of history, which in his own life separated him prematurely from family and friends, is through his literature transformed into a source of comfort as it lessens guilt and insecurity by eliminating any consideration of human will as a factor in his world. In an essay entitled "Gyokusenji Temple" (*Gyokusenji*, 1937), Ibuse states that men are desirous of "the past that they do not see" (*mienai kako*). The word *mienai* ("unseen") is the same used to describe the waters that flow underground near Waseda in "The Waseda Woods" and beneath the growth on a mountain in "The River." Now it is used to describe history. Ibuse begins in his historical works of the 1930s to fathom that unseen past, to leave his dark cave and stand in the light.

Ibuse is not striking out in a new and radical direction when he turns to historical fiction. He continues rather to progress in lines already established in his earlier literature, lines roughly parallel to those in the works that defined his natural world. A unity of themes emerges in the 1930s as it did in the 1920s. A similarly structured world view can be discovered in places as different as the geography of "The River" and the chronology of *Waves*. Even within a single work Ibuse moves with ease from past to present, travelogue to chronicle, biography to fiction; such shifts in genre and subject matter not as much to Ibuse as do underlying principles of change and continuity. He posits in both time and nature, the two axes of his writer's world, a mutual set of powerful rules, prompting critic Tōgō Katsumi to observe, "For Ibuse, history is ultimately something quite close to nature."[22]

This is very true in, for instance, "An Old Man Speaks of the Mountain," where the description of a historical battle is intertwined with a description of a mountain. A river in the story also flows through both time and space, much like its sister river in "The River" and the ever-present sea in *Waves*. These are examples of how arbitrary, and finally misleading, can be the division of Ibuse's works into "natural" and "historical" pieces. In his literature such terms cannot be genres but only interchangeable and allied approaches to describing any phenomenon in detail. In "Mother" Ibuse tells his mother that he writes his works from "the various scenes and rivers and mountains I see, the history books I read, my own ideas and

what I have seen for myself in the world." All possible sources of inspiration often, in fact, come together in a single work. "Stories of
Kōshū" (*Kōshū no hanashi,* 1935) combines both Ibuse's diverse resources and his varied narratives. Ibuse traces the tributaries of the
Fujikawa River, taking advantage of interesting places along the way
to make extended detours into history.

Put another way, Ibuse pursues alternately the temporal and physical flow of the river. Most of his historical inquiries lead him to the
harsh and cruel natural and social conditions under which peasants
have suffered. *Seven Roads* (*Nanatsu no kaidō,* 1952–1957), a collection of travel essays on seven famous old highways, takes Ibuse
back into the many and exceptionally violent peasant uprisings that
arose in the late Edo period. Images of the natural world are consistently linked with those of the historical, such as that of an old
man and a mountain in "A Watch in a Mountain Hut" (*Yamagoya
no bannin,* 1933) and that of a carp and a castle in "The Story of a
Moat" (*Ohori ni kan suru hanashi,* 1939). One of the best examples
of the imagery of Ibuse's natural and historical worlds, combined to
express a common truth, is "A Town Under the River." The story begins, as mentioned earlier, with an admission of the fondness Ibuse
has always felt for a tributary of the Ashidagawa River flowing near
his hometown of Kamo. Ibuse goes on to explain that in the early
1920s archaeologists discovered artifacts buried in successive layers
under the sand of a small island in the middle of the river. Rumors
afoot at the time suggested that an entire village—soon dubbed a
"phantom" village—lay interred below.

In fact, a flood of some years before happened to uncover a number of jugs dating from the thirteenth century. Later, while Ibuse was
evacuated to his hometown at the end of the Second World War, he
would occasionally fish near this river island. After the war it was
found that, indeed, a whole community hundreds of years old was
buried in the sand, and, beneath that, yet another and even older one.
Ibuse describes how layers of sand, changing in color from white to
green and finally to black, are successively removed to reveal the
heretofore "unseen" past. Unfortunately, Ibuse writes, the island and
the villages it once hid will soon be buried again when a large reser-
voir for a nearby steel plant is completed and the waters (like those of
Kuchisuke's valley) rise to submerge them. "The town at the bottom
of the island will again become a phantom village" (14:284). Within
a few pages the reader is presented the complete dimensions of

Ibuse's world. The river in which he fishes and which flows through
his own personal past in Kamo also contains the past of his entire
culture. Yet it is only accidentally and momentarily revealed. Ibuse's
world in general is very much a "town at the bottom of a river."
There the forces of nature mingle with those of history, joining
strengths to become one powerful current in the lives, and deaths, of
all things temporal and terrestrial.

"A General Account of Aogashima"

The most fascinating example of Ibuse's double inquiry into the
physical breadth and chronological depth of this world in the 1930s
is the story "A General Account of Aogashima" (*Aogashima taigaiki*,
1934). Based on actual records, "Aogashima" borrows the form of a
document: its structure is that of a lengthy letter written by the inhabitants of Aogashima to the authorities, thanking them for their
help during the calamity that has befallen their island and reporting
on efforts to rebuild it. Like the diary of *Waves*, the epistolary discourse of "Aogashima" reads as a history granted the special authenticity of a contemporary account. Ibuse again intends to exploit the
ironic potential of writing that is simultaneously fictive and real.

The story begins with an outline of the island's mythological origins. Created by a deity "sometime in the distant past," Aogashima
was first home for a bizarre race of creatures who neither groomed
themselves in the accustomed fashion nor spoke any recognizable
language, choosing rather to "cry like birds." Civilization came to
the island only much later, when a ship carrying rice to the province
of Ise drifted ashore. A divination rite established that rice was indeed edible, and the islanders conceived a plan to steal all of it off the
ship. Unfortunately for the islanders, the ship's crew discovered the
conspiracy and killed nearly all the inhabitants, after which the island was colonized by real human beings from neighboring Hachijōjima Island.

For a time all went well. The population grew over the years to
more than three hundred and forty. Suddenly, however, disaster
struck in the late eighteenth century, forcing those who survived
back to Hachijōjima. An old man—Ibuse's favorite source of history—relates exactly what happened.

On the seventeenth day of the sixth month of 1780, the ground be-

gan to tremble and continued to do so for a week. The terrified islanders would not venture into their fields. On the twenty-sixth day
the tremors subsided, but a rain began which grew into a deluge.
When the water in a lake commenced boiling, the villagers chanted
prayers for their salvation.

The boiling water flooded their fields. Lava began to ooze out of a
number of spots in the earth. The islanders petitioned officials on
Hachijōjima for help, and an inspector sent by those officials re-
ported that "ashes fall onto the hills like a strange rain" and that
"even years from now the land will not be easily cultivated," each an
observation eerily foreshadowing Ibuse's atomic-bomb literature.
The report of this inspector, worded in the same precise, objective
language encountered in "The River," makes meaningful reference
to the fact that the current disaster was preceded by a series of
strange distortions in nature. For instance, two men had suddenly
been swept out to sea from the shore. Another had been buried alive
with his family beneath a landslide. In the most characteristic of
Ibuse's litany of ill omens, the potatoes planted on the mountainside
a year earlier had rotted in the ground for some unfathomed reason.
Such quirks in the natural world have been common in Ibuse's fiction, from the *bashō* tree that suddenly bloomed in the Rokuhara
garden to the irradiated vegetation of twentieth-century Hiroshima.
Also common, however, has been the dual nature of these unusual
occurrences which allows a single phenomenon to be interpreted
both as a sign of hope and of destruction. When eruptions began a
second time on Aogashima, fourteen people were killed along with
all the plant life of the island save for one camellia tree and the scant
grass surrounding it. The islanders looked upon this tree and, encouraged by its survival, were consoled.

Food and water became scarce on the island just as an old official
from Hachijōjima arrived to estimate the extent of the damage. His
name was Asanuma. (He will appear in several other of Ibuse's catastrophe stories in the multiple roles of record keeper, historian, and
observer. In "Aogashima," as elsewhere, his function is quite like
Ibuse's own; exterior to the main action of the narrative, he measures
and evaluates changes that occur within. When he makes his debut in
"Aogashima" as an aged bureaucrat, the shock at what he sees
moves him to distribute stored grain among the island's survivors,
but otherwise, like his fellow historians elsewhere in the literature of

Ibuse Masuji, he is there simply to describe and not to determine the course of actual events.)

The eruptions continued. The volcano spewed white smoke, then black. In the words of yet another Hachijōjima functionary, conditions on the island were "truly frightening." Hachijōjima was finally forced to send three ships to evacuate the beleaguered population, but they could board only one hundred thirty, leaving another one hundred and forty people behind on the shore shouting for help. The eruptions worsened, burying everything and everyone on the island until it could only be called "an island of death." Miraculously, one living thing survived the endless hail of ashes: an old cow, standing high on a ledge, remained as hardy a sign of the power of life as the camellia tree before her.

The human survivors assembled on Hachijōjima were not welcomed with much enthusiasm by the native population of an already overcrowded island. The Aogashima refugees could not hope to return home as long as ashes continued to rain down over the fields and villages that had supported them. Occasionally a few of them made short excursions back to survey conditions. One noted how the flora had begun to revive in certain areas amid the devastation. He catalogued as Ibuse had in "The River," the varieties of trees in evidence:

> Species: mulberry, *katsura*, cherry, box, willow, privet, cycad, alder, *tami*, *matami*, *shidaki*, *atsukai*, ilex, rattan, *shidoko*, *saima*. Fauna, with the exception of snakes, is practically no different from that of the mainland. [1:306]

Although the plant and animal life of Ibuse's natural world began to revive, this vigor was not initially matched by that of the island's people. Still apprehensive of further eruptions, they hesitated to return. Years passed. A decade later, the former populace of Aogashima was still living a makeshift existence on Hachijōjima. Their numbers, in fact, only grew as they bore children who were shunned by the natives as *hinin* ("outcasts"), the same term used to denigrate the Taira after their fall from power in the *Heike monogatari*. They and their parents had come to be a "ruined people," castaways and exiles forced onto an island no longer their own and harassed by unsympathetic officials. Their predicament recalls that of Ibuse's salamander, Kuchisuke, Tomoakira, and even of Ibuse himself in his

100
Rivers,
the Sea,
an Island:
The
1930s

youth. Displaced and alienated, Ibuse's characters face their fates alone.

Finally, pressure exerted by the authorities left the refugees no choice but to return to Aogashima. The resettlement began with a small group of young men and grew to several dozen households; livestock was imported, and the planting of new crops was resumed. The regeneration of the island, in spite of both natural and man-made obstacles, at last seemed guaranteed, thus ensuring the presence of Ibuse's fullest range of images and themes. The reader has been led through withering plants, through volcanic pillars of fire, through the black rain of pumiceous ash and deluges to castaways, the hardy survivors of catastrophe and oppressive officialdom. Finally the trees have bloomed and a new generation peoples anew the land.

The Aogashima Islanders are forlorn and insignificant peasants who are alternately ignored and hounded by bureaucrats as they struggle to survive the fury of an active volcano. In other words, the islanders fight both historical and natural forces. The fate of these people—Ibuse's theme throughout the 1930s—is the result of their historical position in society and their geographical position atop a violent chain of mountains, isolated in a small cluster of islands hundreds of miles south of the government that rules them. Ibuse has dramatically joined his historical and natural world in this one short story. The chain of tragedies inflicted upon Aogashima reflects the combined intensity of these worlds, but the promise of rebirth offered at the story's conclusion establishes that intensity as twofold, beneficent as well as brutal.

"Aogashima" and its characters are a microcosm of Ibuse's vision as a writer, a vision darkened by gloom ultimately derived from the sullen perspective of his own life magnified through his selective reading of history. That vision will be further oppressed by Japan's growing belligerence in the 1930s, and a world war in the 1940s, which, like the whirlpool of "The River," draws Ibuse personally into its vortex. But beyond that discouraged vision looms a world that will become progressively brighter as Ibuse deepens his understanding of how human beings endure to survive even the worst adversities. As time passes, both in Ibuse's life and his work, fate will recede as the sole force motivating his universe and will allow room for more humanist values. In the 1930s, however, Ibuse and his writing had not yet really been put to the test. What he did firmly establish in this decade were the basic themes and the symbolic vocabulary that he would continue to use even as he amended and refined his work as a writer in the years to come. "The River" and *Waves,* though surpassed in many artistic respects by the works to follow, remain the two fundamental definitions of a personal vision that flows strongly and broadly in every major story Ibuse has written since. Rivers, the sea, and islands upon which men make their lives and encounter their deaths will be the terrain of Ibuse's imagination for the rest of his long career.

Beautiful Endings: The Second World War

Nations fall,
but rivers and mountains remain.
—*Waves*

When, upon reading *Waves,* Yasuoka Shōtarō remarked that Ibuse must have had a premonition of the coming defeat of Japan in the Second World War, he was referring to the novel's foreboding motif of impending peril and doom.[1] It is a mood present not only in that novel but in a host of other works written between 1931, when Japan's misadventures on the Asian continent assumed the character of a full-scale conflict, and 1941, when Ibuse was drafted and Japan's conflict became worldwide. This was the decade that saw Ibuse and his country dragged, as Kakutan wrote of the Taira, "by the currents of time" towards a rout as inevitable, in hindsight, as that of his character's clan. In fact, Ibuse has said that he realized Japan would lose the war long before most of his countrymen did, at a time when the Empire was still scoring victory after victory. Present at Japan's proudest moment, when Percival surrendered Singapore in early 1942, Ibuse understood that his country's war machine was propelled by a fanatical zeal that could not be long sustained.[2] Yet even earlier, as Yasuoka notes, Ibuse was writing as if his audience were a defeated people. His stories from the 1930s often read as ones written much later, so strong is their sense of irony, regret, or acrimony.

Before his own personal involvement as an army draftee, as well as afterwards, the war was of crucial concern to Ibuse and his literature. As years have passed, he has devoted more and more of his literary attentions to its events. Indeed, his most recent reminiscences invariably return to those days spent and those comrades lost during turbulent years that, more for Japan than any other nation, divide into halves the history of this century. In the essay "A Story in

102

103
Beautiful
Endings:
The
Second
World
War

Pieces" (*Kataware sōshi*, 1963), Ibuse writes that he often recalls the war, frequently rereading his wartime diaries (of which there are many) and, when drunk, making his wife remember with him. The need to relive the war is no doubt common to many of its veterans, but Ibuse has his own reasons—nostalgia is not among them—for wanting constantly to reexperience and recreate that period of his life. The Second World War, even as it distorted and perverted the lives of his countrymen, seemed to test, confirm, and advance the delicate, tentative hypothesis of the historical and natural world of his literature, formulated in an earlier and more peaceful time.

The experience of national catastrophe on a hitherto unimagined scale has challenged all men's understanding. The stories of "The River" and *Waves,* inspired in part by Ibuse's private calamities, have become thematic models for comprehending the scale of violence between modern nations. One effect of the war has been to transform the literature of Ibuse into a literature of the twentieth century, a time in which the contradictions of civilization, now armed with powerful weapons, has made survival—long Ibuse's personal concern—the paramount question for everyone.

Ibuse was not, however, an outspoken opponent of the Second World War. He eschewed politics in his youth and proved to be no different in middle age. He did not, however much he regretted the war, ever truly protest it. If he is to be judged cowardly in this regard, then he at least enjoys the company of nearly all his generation, especially his peers in literature. Ibuse's name appears in literary histories as one of the first writers to work for the army's official propaganda service, but only because of the caprice of the Japanese draft, which eventually took all ablebodied men of letters and put them to work advertising the nationalist ideology. Reference to his early participation in the military creates as misleading an impression as do his defenders who claim he did decry the war, "but in his own way."[3] A disinterested reading of Ibuse suggests he was indifferent to the political aims of the war, but was concerned from the outset with the physical and psychological carnage wreaked among his friends and countrymen in the implementation of those aims. His humanist concern, sincere and amply evident in his work from the early 1930s onward, was politically innocent, permitting him surprising freedom to publish without interference. Throughout the war Ibuse remained a "good" Japanese, but one sensitive to the subtle as well as obvious havoc created in the lives around him.

104
Beautiful
Endings:
The
Second
World
War

The Verge of War

Ibuse emerged from the war with a relatively untarnished reputation, in part because there existed no bona fide protest literature and thus no politicized heroes to cast others in dubious light. But he wrote a number of strong works, all of them embodying disquiet at the ominous changes in everyday Japanese life, that are at times irreverently humorous, at times bitter. These pieces predate those final years of the war when perhaps none other than a disillusioned attitude was possible. These are works that are not tragic but troubled—stories that hint prophetically at darker times, which did indeed follow.

One of the earliest is "The Chinese Ink Stick" (*Seimakkan*, 1932), in which Ibuse notes that since the Shanghai Incident in the first months of 1932, nearly all the Chinese students in Japan have returned home, probably never to set foot in his country again. These returnees include several whom Ibuse knows personally. One owns a noodle shop; another is a Waseda University alumnus; a third has been studying at a women's college. The closest of Ibuse's acquaintances, however, is a poet by the name of Huang Ying.

Huang Ying writes his poetry in Japanese. Ibuse's favorite, not surprisingly, is a poem recalling Huang's hometown of Tientsin. Even after Huang is repatriated and the Nineteenth Army is meeting the Japanese with stiff resistance, Huang is still corresponding with Japanese magazines, requesting that his submissions be returned to him. Ibuse wonders whether Huang writes his letters in the trenches. He is certain they imply he will not be coming back to Japan.

Ibuse pays a call on the Chinese noodle-shop owner shortly before hostilities break out between Japan and China, something the restaurateur has predicted will happen. Ibuse apologizes when he off-handedly remarks to a friend that war appears imminent; the Chinese responds with a silent and deep bow in Ibuse's direction. The concluding paragraphs of "The Chinese Ink Stick" are a postscript meant to update the reader: Huang is safely encamped outside Nanking and invites Ibuse to visit him there. Ibuse writes that he must decline, and so ends the story.

"The Chinese Ink Stick" is a depressing piece to read today, when history has charged the word "Nanking"—site of the most infamous Japanese atrocity of the war—with terror akin to "Auschwitz" or "Hiroshima." The work may have come back to haunt Ibuse a decade later as he, too, was "safely" removed to rural areas pummeled by B-29 raids. "The Chinese Ink Stick" expresses grief and a sense of loss when the war was not yet full scale but was instead a series of incidents. Yet stories such as this will note and thus memorialize the often anonymous—save for Ibuse's mention—victims of the war. They constitute the major thematic thrust of Ibuse's wartime literature, a voluminous assortment of works arguably among his best.

At the same time Ibuse was writing such sad and serious pieces, however, he was also having great fun at the expense of the Japanese establishment by satirizing the xenophobic tendencies of politicians and scholars alike. It is, for instance, in this lighter vein that Ibuse belittles the pseudoacademic attempts of the day to create a myth of a divine Japanese race. In "A Genealogy of Fantastic Creatures" (*Kakū dōbutsu fu*, 1933), Ibuse compares mermaids in Western literature with those of the Orient. Of course they are not the same, the chief difference being that Japanese mermaids (*ningyo*) actually exist. No less an authority than the great writer Izumi Kyōka says they can even fly. Surely Europe cannot boast of such wonders. Nor does the West have dragons. But if it did, rest assured an Oriental dragon would still emerge victorious in battle.

Ibuse's sarcasm might have raised a few eyebrows (more likely a few chuckles), but rather than desist, he began to blaspheme still more sacred ground. In 1934 he ridiculed a symbol far dearer to the militarist heart than mermaids. In an essay entitled "The Flag" (*Kokki*), Ibuse confesses that in the seven years he has been a resident of Ogikubo, he has never flown the flag at New Year's. He prefers to leave the front of his house looking crude and inhospitable; it keeps the beggars and salesmen away. At one time he did own a flag, and although flying it outside his door made him uncomfortable ("*Kimari ga warui kokochi ga shita*"), at least he was "a solid citizen" (*chakujitsu na shimin no hitori*). With endearing humor, Ibuse adds that the flag had cost so much he was unable to pay the rice man when he came to collect. To avoid a scene with the understandably upset rice man, Ibuse allowed him to take a desk lamp and the new flag in lieu of cash. "The Flag" describes the rice man riding off awkwardly on his bicycle with the lamp and flag—a bizarre sight "unequaled as a symbol of peace."

Such pointed and even subversive humor, however, could not continue for long. Japan in the 1930s was rapidly becoming a nation disinclined to laugh at itself. The occasional battle on the continent was

106
Beautiful
Endings:
The
Second
World
War

now a full-fledged war, and casualties began to mount. Parody made room for pathos, and even Ibuse's world of writers, editors, and publishers did not long remain untouched. In 1938 Ibuse takes alarming note of how ordinary life is being distorted. In a piece entitled, after his home address, "Suginami-ku Shimizu-chō," Ibuse is at his neighborhood bathhouse when he overhears two men talking about a local restaurant owner who has been sent recently to the front. Ibuse, who knows this man well, is taken aback. The man had always come by each vernal equinox to take an order for sushi, but, come to think of it, this year he had not. Now Ibuse knows why.

This restaurateur is the first resident of Ibuse's neighborhood to go to war, but he is soon joined by many others: the butcher, the noodle-shop proprietor, the fish-store owner, the stationer, and then, one day, the father of a child who often plays in Ibuse's yard. Later, when other children sing a war song, this man's son alone stands silently apart. Ibuse tries, without success, to imagine what the child must feel.

In "Hunting Sights" (*Kari mimono*, 1939) Ibuse talks to a soldier recently returned from the front. He has wanted to speak with such a man for some time, perhaps curious of life for his many neighbors now at war. Ibuse spends over a month at the veteran's mountaintop inn. They speak mostly of hunting, a sport the man cannot presently enjoy for lack of a license. At the front, he says, he used to chase after cranes. "Could you catch them?" Ibuse asks. "No, not me. But I did get some pigs."

These stories of the late 1930s already possess an irony in contrasting a naive and innocent narrator—Ibuse—with a wartime reality disabused of naïveté and innocence. Ibuse surely knows that his acquaintances will have to fight, and that life at the front will be harsh; but in his literature he chooses to be surprised by such facts, as if to elicit the same surprise from his readers. This is a narrative perspective soon abandoned, however, and these early war stories will contrast starkly with later ones in which the narrator—again Ibuse—will be as disillusioned as his predecessor was wondrous. Yet Ibuse's wartime writing reveals consistency as well as change, for all of it tells about the common and unexceptional people on both sides of the conflict. Thus far he has written of Huang, the neighborhood restaurateur, and a mountain innkeeper: they and their heirs in the works to follow are the persons through whom Ibuse will chronicle his personal history of the Second World War. Like the characters of his historical fiction, those in his war literature will be the passive victims and not the active perpetrators of this century's own disastrous history.

Examples abound of Ibuse's critically "popular" approach to the Second World War. In the 1939 essay "Takachiho in Hyūga," Ibuse visits the site of the imperial family's descent to earth twenty-six hundred years ago. He finds that the nationalist ideology derived from its myths has been undermined by local disputes regarding the legitimacy of certain hereditary claims among the villagers. The implication is that even in as sacred a place as Hyūga, ordinary people behave as always, thus contrasting ideological precept (the origin of the state) with human truth (the fundamentally factious nature of man). For Ibuse it is invariably the latter that is historically constant; he takes a certain measure of comfort from this. Opposed to the delightfully contentious villagers of Ibuse's literature stand the hypocritical figures of authority. In the short work of historical fiction "Enshin's Conduct" (*Enshin no gyōjō,* 1940), a seventeenth-century Buddhist monk, who converts (*tenkō,* a word used to describe the recantation of leftist writers in Ibuse's own day) to Confucianism to escape persecution, falls into thievery; similarly, the intellectual high priests of Japan in the 1930s and 1940s indulged in their own demoralized behavior under the overwhelming pressure of politics.

The war and the domestic changes it wrought were affecting a wide range of themes in Ibuse's writing. In "The Notions Shop" (*Komamonoya,* 1941), one friend has been killed in the fighting and another wounded. Still, Ibuse is able to treat the war as "news," for he is not yet personally involved. The killing is tragic, the militarists silly, yet all this contemporary history stands outside the main concerns of Ibuse's literature. Imagination is still more powerful than experience. The war has deflected Ibuse's stories but has not yet tested his assumptions.

Until the end of 1941 Ibuse's writing was colored by approaching dark clouds but was not directly beneath them. The last of his prefatory pieces, the last before Ibuse was drafted and his work changed forever, was published in September 1941 and was entitled "Morikichi from Beppu Village on Oki Island" (*Oki Beppu-mura no Morikichi*). The story of a late Edo peasant-soldier who is declared a hero for inadvertently saving his village from being pillaged by a Russian ship, "Morikichi" was written, according to an afterword published in 1946, because Ibuse preferred to tell of "a simple peasant at the

108
Beautiful
Endings:
The
Second
World
War

time of national crisis" instead of "men with brave characters."[4] Morikichi is no exceptional hero, but rather an unexceptional neighbor who embodies for Ibuse the deeper strengths of the Japanese people. In this he is a character descended from Kuchisuke, another personification of the idealized bucolic ethos that pervades so much of Ibuse's work.

For Ibuse, this ethos is the source of an anchored stability in life, impervious to the emotional and historical vicissitudes of first his urban, and now his wartime, existence. Later, this ethos will assume a more vital function (literally as well as figuratively) when that existence, radically challenged as Ibuse goes to war and the war comes home to Japan, requires the sustaining social matrix such as an ethos inspires. On the eve of his induction in late 1941, Ibuse could still create characters under wartime duress who were not himself, or at least part of himself: in the months and years to follow, the careful dichotomy between his own and his characters' existences would collapse under the heavier weight of a dichotomy between life and death. The contrast between his prewar and postwar writing is made clear by a comparison of his last major story before induction, "Tajinko Village," with what followed.

"Tajinko Village"

One critic has called "Tajinko Village" and its sequel "Tajinko Village Continued" (*Tajinko-mura hoi*, 1940) the most representative work of Ibuse's middle period, those years in which Japan was waging, and then recovering from, war.[5] It was a great success. Another critic considers it Ibuse's most famous story,[6] and Ibuse himself has declared it his favorite (but for the typically unserious reason that it earned him enough royalties to live on).[7] Written in the form of a diary kept by a country constable, this story is Ibuse's last vehicle for his prewar and romanticized vision of agrarian life. For this reason — as well as for its literary structure as a diary and its contribution to Ibuse's concept of the natural and historical worlds — it is an important work in his oeuvre. But it is most germane to a discussion of the 1940s, because it depicts a world that Ibuse will never be able to create again in quite the same way. War is about to destroy his ability to fantasize with such detachment.

Although Ibuse credits his original inspiration for the story to

diaries sent him by a policemen in a small and isolated town, he confesses in the same breath that the story became progressively more
his own invention.[8] These diaries, when retold by Ibuse, reveal the
life of a community almost archetypally plebian and very much in
the Ibuse tradition of pastoral literature. In the first entry, December
eighth in a recent but unspecified year, the diarist-constable, Kōda,
describes his efforts to control the crowds seeing off troops headed
for the front. He mentions that this is a duty he has had to perform
previously: the reader is instantly placed in the midst of a nation at
war. At the close of the entry, however, the reader is forced to with-
draw somewhat from that nation when Kōda, the wry and gentle
bungler, notes he is unable to execute the proper salute as the troop
train pulls out of the local station. The mood is much the same as
when Ibuse once tried to become a good citizen by buying a flag.

The people of Tajinko village, while Japanese, exist in their own
fantastic limbo where not all the disagreeable demands and opinions
of their government hold equal sway. This strangely detached and
isolated community is defined in the second entry—Kōda asks a
friend what will happen to all the carp in a pond soon to be filled in
to make way for an airfield. "They say that even if the carp are
buried underground, they can survive the winter as long as the dirt
remains damp" (2:238). The carp, of course, are the villagers, and
the winter they will survive is the war: Ibuse believed that one could,
in fact, hide from what was coming, that it might be possible to survive intact. The whole of "Tajinko Village" develops the theme that,
come what may, whatever the ravages of history, the villagers of
Tajinko will continue to lead unperturbed, if rather eccentric, lives,
exhibiting a patience and wisdom peculiarly and romantically their
own.

This is a theme never totally repudiated by Ibuse, even after the
events of the Second World War so fundamentally challenged the
bases of ordinary life everywhere in Japan. Yet Ibuse's descriptions
of villages and their inhabitants would never again be so simplistic or
facile. His narrative stance would never again be quite so confident
nor so removed: in one sense the catastrophic events of the 1940s
forced Ibuse back into a cave. To poke fun, as "Tajinko Village"
does, at sloganeers and jingoists while celebrating the communal and
ritual character of rural life is to confirm Ibuse's essentially prewar
concept of the model pastoral, a rural equilibrium where all joys and
sadnesses finally seem balanced. Such a concept is rendered useless

110
Beautiful
Endings:
The
Second
World
War

once society, both urban and rural, has confronted its possible annihilation, once the humiliation of defeat has made Japanese everywhere, and in all walks of life, the same.

But in "Tajinko Village," before such a fate was foreseen, Ibuse
was still busy postulating an idealized community indefatigable in its
human resources. That is why so many Japanese readers enjoyed it at
the time, and why now it perhaps seems so dated. As Constable Kōda
makes his rounds, the reader learns of the villagers' marital difficulties, their business intrigues, and their sexual mores. While it
would be inaccurate to say everyone in Tajinko is happy, if they are
unhappy, they are so in a picaresque or half-comical way. The novella makes a near fetish of endearing human foibles. The drunks are
all lovable; the thieves are all misunderstood; the prostitutes are all
kind-hearted; and the constable is always able to mediate every dis-
pute.

Critics mislead when they laud "Tajinko Village" as representative
of Ibuse's middle period, a period dominated by the Second World
War, because, in fact, the story refuses to yield to any tragic reality,
including that of a war that was, even at the time of "Tajinko Village"'s publication, killing the sons of just such villagers. "Tajinko
Village" was written by a writer still personally uninvolved in the
war but already, prematurely, imaging a response to it. It lacks the
gravity any reader today would expect from a work of fiction placed
during those violent years. What it does offer, instead, is the most
complete picture of Ibuse's prewar ideal of a settled life, an ideal
made to seem ridiculous after the dislocation of Japanese society in
the 1940s. Indeed, it is impossible today to read "Tajinko Village"
without ironic reference to what followed in history soon afterwards.
What follows in Ibuse's works will of course reflect that history:
some of Ibuse's assumptions, conceived in a more comfortable time,
will be undermined by his experiences in a conflict whose ferocity he
scarcely could have imagined. After "Tajinko Village" Ibuse will
again be present in his writing, as he had been in that of the 1920s,
but this time as a man more challenged by his experiences than imprisoned by them.

1941

With the traumatic events of 1941, Ibuse's life and literature took
a new and tumultuous direction. First, his mentor and friend Tanaka

Kōtarō died at the beginning of the year after a painful illness. Ibuse
writes in "Reminiscences" (*Tsuikai no ki,* 1952) of Tanaka's last
days and his funeral, noting with irony that the cemetery in which he
was buried would be converted into a military facility with the start
of the Pacific War. This desecration foretold the changes that would
transform Japan that year as the nation prepared for the imminent
war, changes that would affect even the dead in their graves.

November 1941 was the turning point for Ibuse. In the essay "Inns
and Barracks" (*Ryokan —heisha,* 1943), Ibuse writes that he and fellow writer Oda Takeo were on a fishing trip in Kōfu when he learned
from his wife that he had received his draft notice. He had only three
days before he must report to duty. He chose to spend them leisurely
with Oda, who soon heard that he too had been conscripted. In fact,
writers all over the country had received similar orders, destined to
be part of the first wave of drafted propagandists assigned to the nations Japan had decided to occupy. Of course, neither Ibuse nor the
conscripts knew this at the time. Indeed, Ibuse knew nothing of what
lay ahead, and that ignorance fueled his apprehension. As he writes
in his memoir *An Ogikubo Almanac,* "Oda and I exchanged not a
word with each other as we rode the train from Kōfu to Shinjuku
Station."[9]

The year in military service upon which Ibuse embarked with that
quiet train ride into Shinjuku was one that he would remember in
astounding detail and write about steadily for the rest of his career,
beginning with the diary he kept from the day of his induction and
including his full-length memoir of life as a soldier, *Under Arms*
(*Chōyōchū no koto,* 1977–1980). There were compelling reasons
for this obsession, beyond the memorable and dramatic effects of
combat. For the first time in his life Ibuse actually inhabited the fantastic world of his writings. He lived the lives of his characters—the
life of a salamander trapped in the dark, of a man exiled from his
home, of a person ripped out of the conventional pattern of a comfortable existence and suddenly cast into alien and inhospitable circumstances.

The initial group of writers inducted into the Imperial Army comprised a bizarre collection of men of many ages and artistic tempera-
ments. In "Inns and Barracks," Ibuse recalls the day they first assembled:

We were inducted on a very cold November 22. Although we became military personnel upon completing the swearing-in ceremony, we had no

112
Beautiful
Endings:
The
Second
World
War

way of knowing what we were to do or where we were to go. Such secrecy was a defense against espionage. What kept me silent more than anything else, however, was the fact that I was already old for a soldier. That was embarrassing to me. [10:96]

The authorities were equally at a loss, baffled by these literary notables whom they now had to fashion into soldiers. The writers were thought to be less than keen on the militarist ideology (apparently a correct assumption) and were treated by the officers with an ill-concealed contempt. After orientation in Osaka, Ibuse was put aboard a troop transport named the *Afurika-maru* on December 2. Ibuse had not the least idea where he was headed. In this "cramped" and "cold" ship, Ibuse perhaps felt like the diarist of *Waves* when he left the capital for parts unknown. Or perhaps he felt like the protagonist of "The Salamander" constricted in the dark, damp hold of a ship and surrounded by water. Certainly he felt genuinely terrified. Compounding the general tension of the moment was a specific bewilderment. Ibuse writes in *Under Arms:*

> When I was first drafted and assigned to a camp in Osaka, I worried how I should best and most quickly learn how things worked in the army. As the first wave of draftees to be sent to Southeast Asia as propaganda corpsmen, we were divided into four units, one to go to the Philippines (120 men), one to Malaya (120), one to Burma (80), and another to Java (120). It was said that we had been modeled after the German writers units, but many of the officials already stationed in these countries had no idea how to deal with conscripts and no idea what a propaganda corps was supposed to do. We draftees ourselves had not the least inkling. In fact, I believe that even our commanding officer aboard the transport did not know.[10]

Ibuse and his fellow draftees—men like Nakamura Chihei and Kaionji Chōgorō—some of whom were, with Ibuse, prominent in literary society, were suddenly dropped into unfamiliar and even hostile territory. And that hostility issued from their own side as well as the enemy's. No longer treated with deferential respect, Ibuse and his fellow corpsmen were naturally intimidated. The commanding officer aboard the *Afurika-maru* immediately announced he wanted as little to do with the draftees as possible. He emerged from his quarters only to summon his men periodically onto the deck to bow towards Tokyo in obeisance to the Emperor. This officer, later the model for a famous character in Ibuse's postwar fiction, frightened Ibuse. Indeed, everything frightened him. He would confess more than once, for example in "The Flashlight" (*Kaichū dentō,* 1949), that he was cowardly, and, in "Inns and Barracks," that he felt some reserve (*enryo*) not only towards the officers but his fellow conscripts—the result, perhaps, of embarrassment over his fears.

113
"An
Account
of My
Voyage
South"

The response Ibuse formulated to cope with his terror was entirely consistent with those solutions sought by his literary characters caught in similar straits. Like the diarist of *Waves,* Ibuse began to write a journal. Like Tomoakira, who was told to light no fires lest their position be detected, but did, Ibuse was commanded on the day of his induction to keep no diaries for security reasons, but did. He disobeyed and wrote, even copiously. Ibuse sought solace through writing and attempted to assert a measure of control over his life, a life now largely in the hands of superiors who disliked him. By defining his experiences within the literary limits of a journal, Ibuse made writing as cathartic an exercise for himself as it had been for his fictional characters of the 1930s, and, in another way, as it had been for himself as a young man in the 1920s. Even after the war had ended, the writing continued because the war's scars remained. Writing thus became a means of assimilating past experience as well as memorializing the lives of those who did not return home to write themselves. Ibuse says in his Preface to the collection of recent works, *Up From the Sea* (*Umi-agari,* 1981):

> This is an extremely limited and partial record of a huge war, but each time I think back to it I want to write something down on paper. I keep saying the same things over and over, always repeating my stories.[11]

"An Account of My Voyage South"

This imperative to write about the war, still strong even in the Ibuse of the 1980s, was first evidenced in a diary published relatively soon after it was written. "An Account of My Voyage South" (*Nankō taigaiki,* 1943) covers the events in Ibuse's life from the day of his induction, November 22, 1941, through March 19 of the following year. Ibuse has said in *The First Half of My Life* that this work constitutes the record of his one year in the military. A critic has praised it as one of the most dispassionate accounts of wartime

114
Beautiful
Endings:
The
Second
World
War

service written by any Japanese.[12] Like *Waves*, "Voyage South" begins with a prefatory comment on the personal value of the text itself:

> For over ten years I had not kept a diary for even a single day, but upon entering the service I decided to write one for a while. At first I was quite diligent, but gradually I grew lazy and finally I stopped—it was that sort of diary. While in the service I caught no serious disease, nor was I ever hit by enemy fire. As a member of the propaganda corps I made no extraordinary contributions. But now I would like to think of this diary as a memorial of the time I spent as a military journalist. [10:10]

This preface gives the diary a context and an explicit purpose, namely, to recreate a crucial year of its author's life. Ibuse, a survivor of the war, published his diary upon returning to Japan as one means of comprehending, and perhaps atoning for, his good fortune. "Voyage South" describes a few of the months he lived in Southeast Asia, but those months constitute, like the entries in *Waves*, only one of the two chronologies operative in the work. The other is the psychological time of the present, when Ibuse reread and reproduced the "memorial." The preface clearly refers to both the original act of recording memories and to their later retrieval. Through retrieval, Ibuse gives the reader, and himself, one reliquary of this difficult period of his life. The preface to "Voyage South" makes explicit the purpose of most of the diaries that appear throughout Ibuse's writings. They are meant not only to recall the past but to absorb and justify it. The fact of his survival has moved the author to examine repeatedly ("I keep saying the same things over and over") the circumstances of his fate in order to accept them.

From the very start, "Voyage South" expresses Ibuse's terrors. The day he is drafted he feels as if he is catching a cold and cannot sleep. When he boards the *Afurika-maru* he admits to a gnawing fear, a fear described in "My Fountain Pen" (*Watakushi no mannenhitsu*, 1948) as an anxiety about possible submarine attacks, manifesting itself in stomach aches and a fever. Ibuse soon imagines his eyesight is failing and his hair graying. He wonders if the fanatical commanding officer who makes him bow to the Emperor every day is not also responsible for the mysterious disappearance of one of the more outspoken draftees. Ibuse feels he is trapped with no exit. He has become, now more than he ever was as a student in Tokyo, a salamander in a cave.

The entry for December eighth confirms Ibuse's fears when he records that Japan has declared war against the Allies. "Voyage South"
makes only a short, almost telegraphically understated reference to
the official declaration. The severe style is representative of the entire
work. Elsewhere, however, Ibuse elaborates on the events of that
day. In *Under Arms* he writes:

115
"An
Account
of My
Voyage
South"

> We learned of the outbreak of war at six in the morning on December
> eighth while our ship was sailing south off the coast of Hong Kong. I was
> told that an ordinary vessel would have proceeded two hundred nautical
> miles off of Hong Kong, but because we were on guard for American sub-
> marines from the Philippines we were fifty miles closer to shore. Then
> again, there were others who claimed that though the norm was one hun-
> dred fifty miles offshore, it seemed we were sailing at a distance of two
> hundred miles, throwing the compass bearing into doubt.
>
> "Hostilities between Japanese and American–British forces have com-
> menced in the Pacific," announced the radio and telegraph. The com-
> manding officer ordered that we bow on deck in respect [*yōhai*]. The men
> who had been assigned to the artillery gathered by the big guns at the bow
> of the ship and began to practice. Our transport was of the ten-thousand-
> ton class, so it was outfitted with real guns. (The small cargo vessels I had
> seen pass by had been equipped with guns made of wood painted black.)
> The newspaper we published on board, the *South-Sailing News*, con-
> ducted a survey of opinions on the outbreak of war. "What was coming
> has finally come, there was no stopping it" was the view of between sixty
> and seventy percent of those interviewed. (This did not seem to please the
> commanding officer. Later, in an incident that even now I do not wish to
> recall, the C.O. issued orders that the *South-Sailing News* cease publica-
> tion.)[13]

The distressing incident is explained in "My Fountain Pen." Terazaki
Hiroshi, a fellow draftee-writer aboard the *Afurika-maru*, is taken
away in the middle of the night for an abusive interrogation after the
South-Sailing News has published an anonymous story poking fun at
certain of the ship's officers. Although Terazaki has in fact had nothing to do with the story, he finds himself under constant suspicion
thereafter. The mood aboard ship remains tense and uncomfortable
until they finally debark. The December fifteenth entry in "Voyage
South" notes Ibuse's arrival in Indo-China at the mouth of the
Mekong River, the first time he has ever been in a foreign country.
Unfortunately the circumstances of his visit are less than pleasant.

116

Beautiful
Endings:
The
Second
World
War

Writing of Saigon, Ibuse's reaction to an alien culture is one of curiosity, much as he had shown towards the remote regions of Japan he had earlier visited. His approach to organizing his impressions is the same: systematic, nearly scientific. He makes notes in his journal of the various flora, especially the species of trees. He is interested in the Indo-Chinese population and the dialects they speak. His writer's eye does not veer far from what is immediately before him. He appears in as much control of himself and his words as he had been in more familiar terrain back home. His writing remains neutral in tone and meticulous in detail. So much so, in fact, that "Voyage South" at times hardly seems a journal of wartime. Indeed, it is just that dispassionate quality of the writing that has struck critics as remarkable. Ibuse refrains from political or emotional judgments in describing Southeast Asia at war.

Ibuse's journal of his first ocean crossing during the violent final weeks of 1941 suggests the travelogue of a natural or social scientist. The work supplies the reader with the tonnage of ships, local phone numbers, names of obscure plants, and the peculiarities of strange languages. The effect, quite deliberate, is to create within the work an impression of a solid reality, a world in which the diarist has constructed, and thus controls, his otherwise tenuous environment. Common sense would seem to dictate that the experience of being a Japanese soldier in Indo-China (a colony ceded to Japan as a "protectorate" only six months earlier) could not have been as cordial as it would seem from the diary. Ibuse, a particularly sensitive person under any circumstances, must have been profoundly uncomfortable as one of the new colonialists, however transient. The text reflects none of that discomfort because the diary functions as a reflexive control on Ibuse's actual experiences. The reader can gather the impression that Ibuse quite enjoys his Saigon stay—he likes the food and is fascinated by the trees. But this impression belongs to "Voyage South" and not necessarily to the real events beyond it. As with the diarist and his journal in *Waves,* Ibuse and "Voyage South" share a convenient fiction that, in one sense, enables survival.

On the evening of December twenty-second Ibuse and his comrades are moved to a new ship, and five days later they are delivered to the Thai port city of Songkhla. The next morning he rides in the back of a truck into Malaya, the site of fierce fighting between the British and the Japanese. Although Ibuse is edging ever closer to the front, the tone of his diary remains unconcerned with the details of battle. He speaks not of war but of trees, especially the rubber trees he sees growing on the ubiquitous plantations. The apparent calm of his diary, however, hides what most certainly is growing consternation.

Ibuse's ability to control his life through his literature is being challenged as it has not been since the early 1920s. Problems once solved reemerge. His youthful ambivalence about where he belonged has returned to plague him. In the January seventh entry, a civilian employee tries to give Ibuse a decorated plate found in the Malayan home they have commandeered. Ibuse says of his comrade, "His own conscience did not allow him to keep it for himself. Yet at the same time he would have regretted leaving it behind" (10:36–37). Such sentiment echoes Ibuse's own feelings over his twin attachment to town and country told earlier in "Thoughts One February Ninth." And it recalls his quoted definition of the term *keiroku* in the Japanese title of "Miscellany"—something "one is ashamed to save yet should regret discarding." The ambivalence Ibuse once felt towards his youth, his hometown, and Tokyo is now an ambivalence towards the moral conduct of war.

Ibuse is waging his own private battle to keep a lid of words on his fears and doubts amidst the Malayan campaign, a particularly savage chapter of the Second World War. With each passing day he is taken closer and closer to the clashing armies of two empires and to the sort of cataclysm that, only a few years earlier, he had invented for his fictional or historical characters. "Voyage South" notes that on January eleventh Ibuse has entered Kuala Lumpur, a city still not securely in Japanese hands but, in Ibuse's words, already a "city of death" (for different and ultimately more unsettling reasons, Aogashima had been an "island of death"). There, and then farther down the peninsula, Ibuse and his fellow propaganda corpsmen would await the fall of Singapore, their final destination. In the last days of this historic battle, which pitted one hundred thousand Japanese troops against sixty thousand British, Indian, and Australian soldiers, Ibuse would stand on a hill on the north side of the Johor Strait—a hill given prominent mention in Ibuse's writings—and would watch the metropolis below burn as Japanese planes bombarded and ignited oil tanks that shot up huge pillars of flame and smoke, forming clouds like the one soon to rise over the city of Hiroshima.

As Ibuse stood on that hill his thoughts were surely with the people

118

Beautiful
Endings:
The
Second
World
War

below. Perhaps he was putting himself in their places, imagining and thus experiencing their fiery deaths. Atop that knoll he was moved to regard the war as an instance of a universal history, a history he had begun to chronicle before the 1940s but which from this point on would almost exclusively occupy him. One critic has said that "Voyage South" reads much like a version of *Waves* in which Ibuse plays the protagonist.[14] Ibuse's perspective as a soldier in an army that, in Singapore at least, was ultimately victorious is quite different from that of a defeated Taira nobleman. In fact, to write about the experience of defeat, Ibuse was inspired to conceive another work, parallel to yet opposite from "Voyage South." While Ibuse stood on that hill he might very well have decided to write that work, which is in several ways the most interesting of all his wartime literature.

"A Young Girl's Wartime Diary"

"A Young Girl's Wartime Diary" (*Aru shōjo no senji nikki,* 1943), though entitled a diary, is in fact a story organized as a journal documenting the Japanese siege of Singapore. As a journal, it covers the same slice of time as "Voyage South," but from the opposing vantage point of the Singaporean enemy; not the victorious, but the vanquished. "Wartime Diary" constitutes an alternate but parallel history of Ibuse's participation in war; as such it forms, with "Voyage South," a complete reading of how his personal vision and worldly experiences meshed so neatly, so tragically, in the 1940s.

As is his frequent custom, Ibuse introduces the diary of "Wartime Diary" with a brief note explaining how he has happened to obtain it—though the reader can be sure, once again, that there is more of Ibuse himself in its pages than anyone else. He claims while stationed in Singapore to have asked a number of local journalists if any of them has kept a diary of the battle for their city. Ibuse wishes to borrow one. Naturally enough under the circumstances, everyone invents an excuse why he could not lend Ibuse such a document. Ibuse persists, however, and claims to have acquired such a diary written by a fourteen-year-old girl of European and Asian ancestry, a diarist whom Ibuse terms "a Eurasian without a motherland." Mixed lineage accomplishes several things for Ibuse's narrative point of view, because the diarist is thereby neither friend nor foe. Like Ibuse himself in some of his earlier stories, she is in one sense the disinterested observer of interaction between two peoples, neither her own. Moreover, as an outsider she becomes a person without place, a castaway, an anonymous figure conceived and caught between the clash of alien cultures and thus even more isolated than the other people besieged in Singapore. The image of this adolescent living on an island, "without a motherland" and increasingly hemmed in by the approaching Japanese army, recalls that of a salamander trapped in a cave. The individual trapped in the dark history of the twentieth century is a theme Ibuse would have had ample opportunity to contemplate while traveling himself to the antipodes in the dark hold of the *Afurika-maru.*

Ibuse, characteristically exercising his editorial prerogative, quotes from the diary selectively. The young girl's entries (she remains nameless) date from the outbreak of war on December eighth through the surrender of the colony of February fifteenth. The diary is pared down to an essential account of the gradual yet steady deterioration of life in a city facing defeat. On December eighth the young girl and her fellow nursing students are awakened in their dormitory by an air raid warning. The hospital soon begins to receive casualties incurred in the predawn bombardment of the Singapore airfield. Although actual fighting is still far from the city, on the ninth the diarist reports rumors that the Japanese have succeeded in making a landing in Malaya, rumors apparently confirmed when the government orders a black-out that night. She admits to her diary, "I am unhappy at being restricted" (10:100), a comment echoing the sigh of a salamander twenty years earlier.

Some semblance of normal life continues in Singapore for a short while. On December twelfth she writes that most people believe the danger to have passed. The next day a neighbor ventures out to do some Christmas shopping. The indefatigable desire to maintain convention, even at the cost of fatal self-deception, is, as prefigured in *Waves,* a theme common in Ibuse's catastrophe literature. Through minor but vital rites of everyday life—such as shopping—Ibuse's people defend the integrity of their social and emotional existences.

On December fifteenth, however, events are recorded that strain any pretense of normalcy. The *Prince of Wales* and the *Repulse* are sunk, Kelantan falls, and evacuation of the British residents of Singapore is begun. The island's food supply is being threatened: on the seventeenth the citizenry is ordered to grow vegetables at home. In "Wartime Diary" as in *Waves,* each passing day brings worsening

120

Beautiful
Endings:
The
Second
World
War

news. On December eighteenth the public park is closed. On the nineteenth the diarist is in a movie theater when another air raid cuts her excursion short. Her vaunted courage is turning into a depressed fatalism. She notes on December twenty-first that not only has Penang been captured but that the animals in the Singapore Zoo have been killed. "It is terribly sad that this had to be their fate. But on the other hand, I am glad. I mean, they are not going to suffer anymore." As air raid after air raid punishes the island, she observes that only "the monkeys and small birds were set free" (10:103). Animals, once so important in Ibuse's early short stories, are now called upon again as allegorical figures. Some, like Sawan, embody freedom through an escape denied human beings; others embody peace attained only through death.

Christmas—the day Hong Kong falls—passes without the usual festivities. The diarist notes that everyone is saying death is imminent. On the twenty-sixth Kuala Lumpur is bombed for the first time, and on the twenty-ninth Singapore itself is subjected to five hours of continuous air raids. Ibuse's young diarist, whose style and diction now increasingly resemble his own, writes in the safety of her shelter that night one of the central passages of the work:

> A great many people stood in the streets to watch the searchlights following the planes and the explosions of the antiaircraft shells. Whenever the authorities came along with their whips to disperse the crowds, the people would simply return to their homes through one door and promptly exit by another. Bombs fell on the encampments of troops who had retreated to Singapore. When the crude oil tanks on Alexandra Road were bombed, they burst into huge pillars of fire. They were beautiful to look at. I heard someone shout, "I'm worried about my family too, but I can't help looking at these pillars of fire." [10:104]

These burning oil tanks on Alexandra Road are apparently the ones seen by Ibuse from the opposite side of the Johor Strait in "Voyage South," but they are also recurring instances of the pillars of fire he and other homeless victims of the 1923 Great Kantō Earthquake had watched from a baseball park. Flames illuminating the sky recur with significant frequency in Ibuse's work. A city on fire represents his vision of the end: awesome, beautiful, compelling. Ibuse's eschatological insight, in which his imagination fixes his relationship to death, forms a cornerstone of his literature. The people of Singapore must stare at their island on fire just as Tada Otaki's neighbors must stare at her corpse revolving endlessly in a whirlpool. Both are terrifying yet awe inspiring, particular yet universal. Singapore 1941 is a cataclysm of which Ibuse, unknowingly, has written before.

"Wartime Diary" relates how the young diarist and the whole of her city are soon irrefutably isolated and emotionally numbed by the war finally brought to the shores of their own island. On the assumption that any attack must come from the sea, Singapore's defenses had been installed on the southern coast of the island; now, Japanese forces led by one of the most capable generals of the war, Yamashita Tomoyuki, are racing down the peninsula towards the city. Hope is impossible. Those who have not obtained passage out, or fled to villages in the countryside, have been forced to resign themselves, like Ibuse's salamander, to the inevitable. The diarist notes in her entry for January first—no celebrations on that holiday, either—that nighttime air raids have obscured the distinction between dreams and reality. The light of the exploding bombs, she writes, is "a beautiful spectacle."

At this juncture in the narrative, Ibuse interrupts the diary to tell his own story within an extended parenthetical note. He has been billeted in a small town near Singapore from January twenty-ninth to February eleventh, waiting for the besieged city to surrender. Here, as well as in "Voyage South," Ibuse says he "could see the sky beyond the rubber plantations glowing red. It was the light of the crude oil tanks burning at the Seletar Naval Base" (10:107). This personal note by the author, placed *in medias res,* serves to situate Ibuse, never far from the diarist's life, in her same historical moment. The young girl's entry for New Year's Day and Ibuse's sudden interjection share a similar fascination with the horror and beauty of a city in flames. "Wartime Diary" is no longer a work simply about the victory of the Japanese over the British in Singapore. It is expanded through its inclusion of two points of view into a story about the fundamental unity of experience and history, and about the common world shared by both the victor and the defeated.

When the diary resumes, after Ibuse's note, with an entry for February seventh, it is wholly occupied with recording the details of the final strangulation of the city. Rumors fly; casualties mount; the population is ordered to remain indoors. According to her entry for the fourteenth, the diarist has promised to go to the shelter as little as possible, so accustomed is she now to the boom of artillery. "There is

122
Beautiful
Endings:
The
Second
World
War

no solace or honor in doing otherwise" (10:114). Yet life continues to be meaningful and worthwhile as long as people insist on observing the small rituals of everyday existence. The diarist writes:

Tonight one woman's younger sister and a third-year student at Raffles College held their wedding ceremony in the shelter. Since no minister was present, Mr. Burrough, as the oldest person there, undertook to perform the service. They say it was the third time Mr. Burrough had acted as a minister within the shelter. [10:114–15]

In *Black Rain* Shigematsu, an office worker without religious credentials, will enact the role of a Buddhist priest and read the sutras in order to give victims of the Hiroshima atomic bomb the semblance of a funeral. In "Wartime Diary" another layman, one on the opposing side of the war, performs what is in one sense the opposing ritual, a marriage ceremony. But in another sense both men and both rituals are akin: Shigematsu and Burrough demonstrate the preservation of social and ritual structure even in the midst of the most wanton destruction, and funerals and marriages are each rites of passage and of rebirth. The exigencies of crisis assert the most important function of social organization for Ibuse, the maintenance of communion with tradition, the natural cycle, and the future. Closely allied with such rituals and their performers in the literature of Ibuse Masuji are, of course, diaries and their authors: the young Eurasian, never before a historian, is called upon to preserve the continuity of life as much as is Shigematsu or Burrough. Her endeavor is to describe and record this continuity under the most inhospitable of circumstances.

Ibuse's excerpts from the young girl's diary end on the following day, February fifteenth. She writes that she has not seen the sun for three days. There are no longer any newspapers, and the telegraph office was destroyed almost a week earlier. Reliable information being unobtainable, rumors rule the city. The diarist's response, appropriate to her new role as a defender of continuity, is to declare in her diary: "I thought I would verify for myself what events happened today" (10:115). She becomes the objective reporter, the detailed observer, the heir of history: she becomes Ibuse himself in his favorite role of scribe placed among historic events, yet separated from them by reifying their progress within a narrative. Returning from the shelter to the second floor of her own home, the diarist writes the last lines of her journal: "The sky is illuminated red by various blazes in a number of locations"; and finally, "Everyone among us remarked that he felt as if he had left something important behind" (10:115). The final moments of a British Singapore are both deadly and cathartic, both an end and a beginning.

This poignant conclusion to Ibuse's selected translations from a young girl's diary is not, however, the conclusion to "Wartime Diary." Again Ibuse addresses the reader directly in a postscript, reiterating and linking the diarist's experiences with his own. February fifteenth, the last entry in the young girl's diary, also marks Ibuse's forty-fourth birthday. Ibuse, quartered in an abandoned house in the town of Johor Baharu, is watching the assault on the city:

> Smoke from the burning crude oil tanks rose from three different places on the opposite side of the Johor Strait. The smoke from the tanks in the Seletar Naval Base to the left was the most spectacular. The huge tower of smoke pierced through the black clouds above to soar even higher. It seemed to loom even higher than Mount Fuji does above its clouds. Undisturbed by any winds, the smoke ascended and spread out broadly in all directions to form the shape of an umbrella. Once night fell, pillars of flame leaping up from the source of the smoke became visible. Sometimes, when there was the sharp sound of an explosion, new pillars of fire would shoot up and create a swiftly swirling whirlpool of smoke. The next day, the morning of the sixteenth, we crossed over a makeshift bridge and entered Singapore. [10:116]

This panoramic description of the fiery destruction of a city not only complements the young girl's depiction of the same scene, from another angle, but more closely focuses Ibuse's earlier yet equally comprehensive imaginings of the world on fire. The obscure whirlpools and blazing pillars of fire, which so often herald the violent demise of people and places just on the horizon, comprise the central images of Ibuse's beautiful end—that particular experience of witnessing with both fear and fascination the destruction wrought by history or nature. Ibuse and his characters always observe, and always survive, the chaos: their seemingly contradictory emotions reflect, on the one hand, a disengagement from the violence and, on the other, a guilt at the safety such disengagement ensures. The concept of a beautiful end links two opposing notions—the handsome and the horrific. Death, for Ibuse, simultaneously attracts and repulses, incorporating the ambivalence found elsewhere in his litera-

124
Beautiful
Endings:
The
Second
World
War

ture and, like the charged poles of a battery, energizing his words with the contradiction it poses: some live while most die.

In wartime Singapore, as in Tokyo of 1923 and eighteenth-century Aogashima, the beautiful end is enveloped in flame and smoke; it is also, as it was for the victims of "The River," "a swiftly swirling whirlpool." The power vortex is fundamental to the import of Ibuse's beautiful endings because it represents the irresistible action of his universe, a metaphor for historical and natural dynamics that attract and consume whatever approaches. This system of omnipotent imagery was germinated in the events of Ibuse's childhood and was encouraged by those of his young adulthood. It was first expressed in his early short stories and was developed in his works from the 1930s as a basis for metaphysics. Finally, in the years of war with the rest of the world, it was given a specific historical reference as he recalled standing alone on a hill far from home watching a city burn. From this point on, Ibuse's vision of a beautiful end was ever less his alone and ever more ours: the Second World War rendered his private experience of a compelling encounter with mass violence the distinguishing characteristic of perhaps an entire century.

"Wartime Diary" is in retrospect one of Ibuse's more important works, a pivotal development in his growth as a writer who unites personal and universal concerns. Written under the least hospitable conditions, both physically and politically, the story advances the whole of his writings' thematic structure. Using one motif of his earlier writing, that of the isolated victim trapped in a catastrophic historical moment, Ibuse finds, in the epic tragedy of the Second World War, victims everywhere. "Wartime Diary" merges Ibuse's autobiographical and essay genres with his imaginative fiction to engender a work embracing all three; broadly stated, the effect of the war's diverse hardships on Ibuse and his literature was to amalgamate the particular and invented literary experience with the general and authentic historical reality.

This coincidence of prewar sensibilities and wartime facts which makes Ibuse's writing from this period onwards so convincingly powerful began with "Wartime Diary" but did not end for nearly a decade, with the last of Ibuse's postwar works in the early 1950s. ("Postwar" in the sense that these stories deal directly with the experience of defeat. More broadly interpreted, of course, any work after 1945 can be termed postwar, insofar as Ibuse's experiences of that time might direct any reading—or writing—of them.) Part of this continuing transformation took place immediately, however, once Ibuse climbed down from his hilltop and lived in occupied Singapore, renamed Shōnan by the Japanese.

Singapore

As the final sentence of "Wartime Diary" indicates, Ibuse was among the first Japanese to enter the city after Percival's surrender and Japan's greatest victory of the war. Ibuse's entry for February fifteenth in "Voyage South" reads simply: "This auspicious day should be commemorated. Singapore has fallen. At 7:15 in the evening the enemy surrendered unconditionally" (10:50). The very next day, one somewhat less auspicious in hindsight, Ibuse and other members of the propaganda corps assigned to Malaya crossed into the still smoldering city. Ibuse, a man so nervous that he will not fail to run out into his garden at the least tremor, or to whimper at lightning,[15] must have been fairly petrified with fear as he walked the streets of Singapore for the first time. He describes the scene in an essay entitled "When We Published the *Shōnan Times*" (Shōnan taimuzu *hakkan no koro*, 1943):

> The restaurants and shops were still closed at the time. Singapore fell on February fifteenth, and we of the propaganda corps entered the city on the sixteenth. On the eighteenth [our interpreter] Furuyama and I were taken by Hara, a civilian employee of the military, to the offices of the *Shōnan Times* newspaper to conduct an investigation. Japanese were still forbidden to enter the city proper. We did so only after obtaining special military permits. Here and there stood military police at barricades erected on street corners. They stopped us frequently, but when we showed them our permits, they thanked us for our efforts ["*Gokurō-sama desu*"] and we replied in kind. Scattered on the pavement everywhere were helmets and rifles discarded by the enemy. Malay and Indian laborers would explode bullets that had been swept up into piles by stamping on them with their feet. The bullets would go off with a big bang, but none of the men looked as if what they were doing was the least bit dangerous. Rather, as they casually folded their arms, the only stern thing about them was the way they looked at us. [10:88]

Ibuse's assigned duties in Singapore were principally editorial tasks in the offices of the city's English-language daily, the *Strait*

126

Beautiful
Endings:
The
Second
World
War

Times (renamed the *Shōnan Times* under the Japanese administration). Later Ibuse also lectured on history at a Japanese language and culture school established for the benefit of the local population. At the paper, Ibuse worked not only with other military journalists but with a largely Singaporean staff, that is, a mix of Indians, Malays, Chinese, and one Burmese. All the English staff had either fled or had been interned in Changi prison. Life was not entirely unpleasant, if the reader accepts at face value what Ibuse wrote of his tour of duty. Much later, and in private conversations, Ibuse has painted a very different picture of a brutal colonial administration.[16] But in contemporary written accounts, Ibuse tended to document only his leisure activities, his free time to explore the island, to make friends of some of its inhabitants, and, certainly, to write. His writing, like Kakutan's history of the *Taira,* was voluminous; literature served to buffer and sustain him.

Ibuse's essays and stories written about Singapore while he was there—as opposed to some written afterwards—maintain the fiction begun in "Voyage South" of an apparently sanitized and almost innocuous war. His many such works hardly touch upon the violence of the war, and they lack entirely in rhetoric. If "Voyage South" can be likened to *Waves,* but with Ibuse as its protagonist, then *City of Flowers* (*Hana no machi,* 1942), which characterizes the relations between the Japanese occupiers and the Singaporeans with humor and even an ironic warmth, can be likened to "Tajinko Village" and its idealized portrait of everyday life in one community, but with Ibuse, not Kōda, as its likable constable.

Ibuse creates joviality and pleasantries where they could hardly have been representative of the mood. He invents a fragile normalcy where conventional existences could only have been distorted. In literature Ibuse found such fictions seductively possible, and no doubt these were fictions his readership enjoyed sharing with him. He exploited autonomy of writing to its fullest extent, for in Singapore Ibuse was in fact experiencing fear and depression. In *Under Arms,* written almost forty years later, he candidly admits what his life in Singapore had really been. He explains why "Voyage South" ends abruptly on March nineteenth, only a month after he had assumed his duties at the *Shōnan Times:*

This diary ended on March nineteenth. I stopped because a diary kept with military censorship in mind seemed idiotic. I clearly realized more

and more that though Singapore had fallen, the war would not be over. In
the soldiers' song "Carrying Your Comrade's Ashes," a line says "Singapore falls, but still we advance." Within that line is the unspoken but earnest hope of the ordinary private that he himself will not be ordered to advance. All of us were aware of that hope. That is why all of us choked with emotion when we sang that song."[17]

"Voyage South" ceases in March, but other Ibuse writings pick up where it leaves off. There seems to be another diary, elsewhere referred to simply as his "service diary" (*jūgun nikki*), which was kept throughout his entire year in uniform. It is perhaps the master diary from which "Voyage South" is only an excerpt. Parts of this master diary appear here and there to flesh out other works. Some of these excerpts, more often than those found in "Voyage South," reveal their cathartic purpose as terror is displaced by trivia. In "Singapore Diary" (*Shōnan nikki*, 1942), which details events of 1942 from June seventeenth to July ninth, and in "Late July of 1942" (*Jūshichinen shichigatsu gejungoro*, 1943), which adds the three days from July twenty-first through the twenty-third, Ibuse writes of nearly everything but the war. Instead, the reader is treated to anecdotes about a Chinese who writes haiku, the mother of one of the newspaper's reporters, shopping, a woman in labor, news from home, and the grades earned by Ibuse's pupils at the Japanese language school. Perhaps Ibuse was trying to convince himself that life is no more difficult than as it is remembered. *Crede quod habes et habes:* Believe that you have something, and you do. He was therein reserving for himself a benign if perhaps fantastic literary space where he could safely dwell for the duration of his service.

The fruits of this retreat were works that "domesticated" the unlikely trio of Tomoakira, Kakutan, and Miyaji in *Waves,* describing the harmonious existence of that most basic social unit, the family: in *City of Flowers,* a work praised as the "sturdiest" (*kengo*) of any Japanese work written during the war,[18] the family is the Chinese Liangs. In "A Talk with Abu Bakr" (*Abubaka to no hanashi,* 1942), the family is Moslem and Malayan. Detailed descriptions of domestic life create an illusion of decorum; humor masks the guilt of the occupier (everyone is always trying to put something over on the Japanese). Such exaggerated accounts of tranquil oases among turmoil required constant reinforcement, constant re-creation through further acts of writing to weather the assaults made upon

128
Beautiful
Endings:
The
Second
World
War

Ibuse's convenient fictions by the obvious savagery of the war—
savagery of which Ibuse must have been aware as an editor for the
principal newspaper of the Southeast Asian theater.

Ibuse's prolificacy as a writer, even while he was fully engaged as a
corpsman, is as plausible as it is amazing. No matter how relatively
comfortable Ibuse's assignment might have been—and the reader
cannot fully trust Ibuse's claims—the conditions under which he
wrote his novels, diaries, stories, and essays were certainly trying. In
the essay "From Gemas to Keluang" (*Gemasu kara Kuruan e,* 1943)
Ibuse recalls how he penned his manuscripts atop a trunk borrowed
from a fellow corpsman, who further obliged Ibuse by doing his K.P.
for him in exchange for a reading of his works. Nor was Ibuse alone
in his dedication to writing of the war, despite strict military orders
prohibiting such activity. In a more recent memoir, Ibuse has described the efforts of his comrade Nakamura Chōjirō to keep his
own diary:

> Wherever encamped, whether in a foxhole, an air raid shelter dug in the
> ground, or an iron pipe, he wrote by the light of a flashlight. The flash-
> lights left behind by the English troops were capable of shedding a little
> light, so it was best that they shed it for keeping diaries.[19]

Ten years after the fictional Tomoakira, Kakutan, and Miyaji had
gathered around a campfire in a diary-writing ritual, Ibuse's actual
wartime comrade must do the same with his modern equivalent of
the campfire—a flashlight. The ironies of history, the sense of life imitating art, must have struck Ibuse full force. The experiences of war
had confirmed imagination, proving that life and literature are indeed implicated in the same commandment that words be written,
"whether in a foxhole, an air raid shelter dug in the ground, or an
iron pipe." Much of Ibuse's wartime writing can be read as an am-
bitiously therapeutic exercise in the potential of imagination, for it
was within that infinitely resourceful faculty of the mind that Ibuse
dwelled for much of the time he was "under arms."

Fortunately that time was not to be long. For most of his stay in
Singapore, the days passed without notable event. The essay "Trips
While in the Service" (*Chōyōchū no ryokō,* 1957) mentions several
excursions, principally one to Malacca, but none seem to have been
particularly distracting. Never wounded or seriously taken ill, as he
notes in his preface to "Voyage South," his life as a soldier distinctly

lacked for drama. Boredom soon allowed him to feel acutely homesick. In "Scents" (*Nioi*, 1961) Ibuse writes that he felt most strongly
nostalgic whenever he caught a whiff of boiling rice or simmering
miso soup, or the scent of a hearth. Unlike most of his comrades
similarly homesick, however, Ibuse did not long suffer. In November
1942 Ibuse's tour of duty was abruptly ended and he was returned to
Japan.

Return to Japan

In "Papaya" (*Papaia*, 1949), a story providing a key to much of his
postwar literature, Ibuse reveals why he was prematurely repatriated. The commander of the propaganda corps in Singapore is a
temperamental officer by the name of Ōkubo. One day Ibuse is summoned to Ōkubo's office and told their meeting is to be kept strictly
confidential. Ōkubo has been instructed to send three of his men
home immediately, for what reason he does not know. Furthermore,
since a ship would take too long, he must dispatch the three lucky
men by plane. He asks Ibuse who, in his opinion, these three should
be. Without hesitation Ibuse responds that he has no idea whatso-
ever. Ōkubo rephrases his question: who does Ibuse think most
wants to return? Ibuse replies everyone does—equally. He is dismissed after again being admonished to keep this conversation
secret.

On the way to his quarters Ibuse reflects that, in effect, he has just
been asked if he personally would wish to be one of the three repatriated. He further reflects that of course he would, especially since
planes were a much safer means of transportation than ships: in late
1942, Ibuse notes, hardly one ship in three was reaching its destination intact. Once in his quarters Ibuse forgets his orders and tells the
poet and fellow journalist Jimbo Kōtarō all that has happened.
Jimbo, sympathizing with his friend's embarrassment, offers to take
him to an old schoolmate, now a doctor, who can issue a certificate
conveniently prohibiting Ibuse from air travel for health reasons. The
doctor, however, counters with the logical observation that any such
certificate might also prevent Ibuse from later boarding a ship if he
should so wish. He advises Ibuse to follow orders, whatever they
may be.

130
Beautiful
Endings:
The
Second
World
War

In fact, Ibuse is one of the three named. Two days later he is aboard an aircraft headed for Saigon, the first leg of the trip back to Tokyo and civilian life.

These circumstances elucidated in "Papaya" take on special significance when considered against the many stories Ibuse was to write about friends and fellow soldiers left dead on the soon-forgotten battlefields of Asia and the Pacific. Ibuse, who returned home not only healthy but early, must have felt somewhat ashamed. When Aoki Nampachi died, Ibuse had experienced the guilt of being a survivor: in the war, when many more young men died, perhaps Ibuse experienced that earlier guilt but on a considerably larger scale. In "Papaya" he begins to confess this guilt, but he cannot exhaust, much less expiate, it. Indeed today, forty years later, his shame seems hardly lessened. Ibuse continues to wonder—through what workings of fate has he remained alive? And what does that obligate him to do as a writer?

In late 1942, however, his obligations were clear enough. The government had ordered some writers repatriated, Ibuse soon learned, to bolster morale among the Japanese citizenry. He was sent on a lecture tour to talk about the progress of the war and to visit certain families with husbands and sons at the front. He was to write patriotic broadsides celebrating these model families' brave sacrifices. Ibuse did not find the assignment inspiring. In the 1959 essay "The Fisherman's Field of Nanaura" (*Nanaura no ryōshi hara*), Ibuse writes with obvious irony about one such heroine, a beautiful woman who harvests seaweed from the ocean to assist in food production. Ibuse had visited her in a small hamlet northwest of Matsue. The essay begins: "It was over ten years ago, when the shadow of defeat was darkening" (12:13); it ends with an anecdote of how Ibuse's friend and fellow propagandist Kamei Katsuichirō, also on assignment to write of a model wife, could not interview his subject because she had just run off with another man.

Even more ironically, Ibuse was serving as a celebrity apologist for the war effort when he wrote what is considered his most antiwar story.[20] "The Day of a Memorial Service for a Bell" (*Kane kuyō no hi*, 1943), published in a military journal (which seemingly would call its protest into question), tells of a temple that has been ordered to contribute its bell to the war effort, metal being in short supply. The temple does its duty and surrenders the bell, but not without regret. A service is held to mark the passage of its "soul." As in so much of Japan's supposed protest literature, there is no militancy in this story but only *mono no aware,* a heightened sensitivity to intrinsic "evanescence."

While "Service for a Bell" can hardly be thought an antiwar piece in any serious sense, it is important for another reason. It marks the last work of fiction that Ibuse was to publish for the next two years, until well after the end of the war. For Ibuse, by nature a prolific writer, this would be the longest hiatus in all of his career. What special circumstances might explain this? In several ways, the two years spent in Japan (1944, 1945) were far more difficult for Ibuse than the one year in Southeast Asia. Japan had changed considerably in Ibuse's absence, and not in ways conducive to writing. He remembers in his essay "About Abe Shinnosuke" (*Abe Shinnosuke no koto,* 1964): "My first impression upon returning to Tokyo was that, in the short period of one year, great shortages of goods had developed and free speech had been repressed far more in the home islands than in the colonies" (14:450).

Conceivably, Ibuse joined such other writers as Tanizaki Jun'ichirō and Nagai Kafū in remaining silent for the duration of the war out of political considerations; much more likely, however, is the dramatic effect on his disposition of evacuation into the countryside, once Japanese cities were targets for American raids. These years of silence were also years of exile.

Many Japanese were ordered to rural areas or smaller cities in 1944, but Ibuse was affected differently than most. To him, his life had suddenly become as nomadic and unstable as it had been when he was a student at Waseda. In his poem "On the Road Relocating Again" (*Saisokai tojō,* 1961) he describes himself and his family spending a night in a train station while moving from one refuge to another, just as he had himself after the Great Kantō Earthquake in 1923. From May 1944 until July 1945 he moved from village to village in Kōfu, when finally the bombs drove him to his hometown of Kamo. Although the war ended scarcely a month later, Tokyo was in ruins, and the Ibuse family remained in Kamo until July 1947.

These three years, the longest time Ibuse would ever spend away from the home he had built in Ogikubo in 1927, were especially disruptive and disturbing for him. Throughout most of the 1940s, in fact, Ibuse was robbed of his hard-earned sense of place, that critical identity that had made writing possible for him. In other words, Ibuse was silent so long not because he did not want to write, but be-

132

Beautiful
Endings:
The
Second
World
War

cause temporarily he could not. Like so many of his characters, Ibuse had been set adrift. Ibuse, like the salamander, Kuchisuke, and Tomoakira, was trapped in an isolated time and place not his own. True, many writers were forced to roam as was Ibuse, but perhaps none felt quite so keenly the world of their literature now mirroring the present day. Ibuse's extended period of evacuation seems a sequel to his year in Singapore, for upon return to a devastated Japan, his life continued to recall the mood of his earlier dark stories and to confirm their inexorable force of fate.

Ibuse might have been expected to write furiously during his evacuation, and towards the end of it, he did. The first two of his three years in the countryside—when the exile was involuntary, not self-imposed— were a time when Ibuse's activities and thoughts did not translate into writing. He certainly had the opportunity, for he says in "The Experiences of a Go-Between" (Nakōdo no keiken, 1955) that he "had no work to do and so went stream fishing every day." But the fact that these years were silent does not mean that they were not important, for in fact they were crucial in light of the works that did eventually follow, such as his memoirs of this exile "Evacuation Diary" (Sokai nikki, 1949), and "Careless Talk" (Ukatsu na hanashi, 1950). More interesting, however, and equally demonstrative of his own experiences, are those fictionalized novels and stories that deal with the loss of place, such as Always Moving or Room for Rent (Kashima ari, 1948), the story of various people who inhabited a boardinghouse immediately after the war. The theme of restlessness, already a major note in Ibuse's prewar writing, is granted new status, with added personal emphasis, in the postwar period after Ibuse returned from his prolonged rural residence. History and the inner life again coincide in his literature, for, in one sense, stories of his sokai ("evacuation") are also very much stories of his sogai ("alienation"). Both experiences, one physical and the other psychological, are forms of dislocation that simultaneously obscure and clarify Ibuse's vision as a writer: the confusion of these years also throws his most important literary themes into bold outline.

Unlike many of his colleagues, Ibuse maintained his silence for the better part of a year after the surrender in August 1945. Although the immediate postwar period witnessed an explosion of literary activity, Ibuse remained silent in Kamo—waiting, watching, thinking. When Ibuse did resume publication the results reveal how worthwhile his solitary sabbatical had been. The influence of the war, his evacuation, and Japan's defeat had slowly refined to inspire a literature now revised to speak of national history as well as personal experience. Ibuse's long wait had given him the perspective to see contemporary events in the context of the past. Suddenly Ibuse's style and message seemed almost urgently sincere to postwar readers: he was writing of a time and an ordeal painfully common to them all.

The First Postwar Stories

The first of Ibuse's postwar stories deals with the experience that dramatically marked the start of that era, the official announcement of defeat. "The Sutra Case" (*Kyōzutsu*, 1946) is set in Ibuse's hometown during his evacuation there. An old man, Ryūsaburō, finds something resembling a tea canister while working in the fields. He takes it to Ibuse, who is able to identify it as a sutra case dating from the eleventh century. Ryūsaburō and Ibuse become friends. Soon thereafter, they are together on the day their country declares its surrender:

> The morning of the day of the announcement of defeat, Ryūsaburō had come to my home and asked permission to gather some *sakaki* wood, once used to adorn graves during the summer observances of the dead. Of course I had no objections. The old man was cutting *sakaki* branches on the hill behind my house when he heard the radio come on at noon. He descended the hill and stood in my garden, listening to the announcement, with all the branches still strapped to his back. Unfortunately my radio was not working well at the time, and the more impatiently I tried to adjust it, the worse it became. We did not understand what the Emperor's words had meant.
>
> "Ryūsa', did you get it? What the radio just said."
>
> "No, none of it. With all due respect, I wonder what he was talking about."
>
> Just then a fellow named Kuji, who had previously belonged to the Agricultural Association, came over to my place in a state of excitement.
>
> "How was your radio? Ours is no good. But while I've been running around the neighborhood, at least I've found out that the fighting has stopped. Japan has lost!"
>
> "Don't make things up," said Ryūsaburō with a frown.

134

Beautiful
Endings:
The
Second
World
War

"What do you mean? If you think I'm lying, go ask Tarō down the hill. Tarō's radio got it in clear. We've surrendered."

"Well, is that so? Is that what it's all about? I'll be damned. . . . "

With that comment, Ryūsaburō lowered his bundle of branches from his back onto the ground. [3:255]

With this powerfully understated story of how he greeted defeat, Ibuse begins his postwar career. "The Sutra Case" uses a subtlety typical of Ibuse in its treatment of these historic events. Ryūsaburō is later haunted by the suspicion that, because he has unearthed the sutra case and has thus disturbed the peaceful sleep of history, his nation has now had the bad fortune to lose the war. Ibuse's ironic humor is present even here, but as usual he is only partly in jest. Ryūsaburō is gathering *sakaki*—the tree of Shintoism that stands on the border of heaven and earth—when the most august of Shintoists proclaims the Empire's defeat. With Ibuse to hear this news is a characteristically earthy pair of villagers; just down the road they are joined by a neighbor, representatively named "Tarō." Not too sure of how they should respond to this news, they probably are not really much affected. Ryūsaburō, like the rest of his countrymen, merely puts his burden down. The men of "The Sutra Case" inhabit Ibuse's rediscovered world, the rural corners of Japan where, as an evacuee he has been forced to live, and where, as a writer, he is newly aware of the insurmountable power of history, speaking his first words on the defeat. Ibuse reemerges as an author in 1946 with new company in his stories—in a nation numbed after fifteen years of catastrophic violence yet still capable of survival.

An example of Ibuse's postwar perspective, enriched by his experiences among rural people, can be found in "Tales of Thieves" (*Oihagi no hanashi*, 1946), a delightfully humorous story recording the deliberations of a village committee formed to combat a rise in local crime. Ibuse states in his essay "Letters" (*Tegami no koto*, 1947) that he has attempted in this story to describe "the world after war" (*shūsengo no sejō*). In that world a variety of men and women thrive and everyone is charmingly individual in his or her views. The reader suspects that the garrulous villagers of "Tales of Thieves" are characters inspired by their real-life counterparts in Japan's postwar intellectual circles; but at the same time they are genuine figures drawn from Ibuse's own observations among them. "Tales of Thieves" is one of Ibuse's first steps in the postwar period towards building a redemptive theory of human resilience in the aftermath of catastrophe. The practice of that theory is found in the sturdy and proud common characters who, more than ever before, dominate his writing.

"Wabisuke"

These ordinary men and women and the world they inhabit, a world profoundly informed by Ibuse's experience of the Second World War, are the principal theme of a long short-story published immediately after "The Sutra Case," "Wabisuke" (*Wabisuke,* 1946) is a unique work, perhaps the most important fictional piece of his postwar years. Ibuse wrote in his preface to it:

> I published only a single five-page essay in 1945, the year Japan lost the war. The only writing I did regularly was in my diary. At the time I believed that an actual record of the experiences of one peasant [*shomin*] would have infinitely more worth than any story constructed from my barren imagination.[21]

Like the Eurasian diarist of "Wartime Diary," who, in the last days of Singapore's British rule, wanted only to "verify . . . events," Ibuse's ability to imagine, in a year of the unimaginable, was also impaired. The only writing possible was a literal record (*kiroku*)—either in a diary or a historical novella. To resolve the quandary put to him by contemporary history, he turned to past history. This source of stories Ibuse had always found rich, but in the immediate postwar years, it seemed particularly attractive—and stable—when compared to current events. "Wabisuke" was thus not only a retreat into history but also an advance into an individualized truth, an attempt to establish a metonymical equivalence between "the experiences of one peasant" and those of an entire nation, perhaps even the world. Beginning with "Wabisuke," Ibuse's historical fiction makes increasingly frequent connections between his own present and others' pasts.

As in *Waves,* and in nearly all of his historical fiction, Ibuse's conceit of an "actual record" is belied by imaginative themes and a distinctive style undoubtedly his own. In "Wabisuke," once again Ibuse interjects himself early and forcefully into a narrative supposedly not his own. He begins the story, again characteristically, in the present

136
Beautiful
Endings:
The
Second
World
War

moment. He carefully guides the reader back into the past by first describing seven hamlets along the Fujikawa River in Yamanashi Prefecture. One of the hamlets, Hadakajima ("Waves-Are-High Island"), is not far from where Ibuse was first evacuated in May 1944. This circumstance not only links the novella's historical narrative with Ibuse's recent experiences but establishes for the reader three distinct, but ironically intertwined, times within the story: the past, the present, and "wartime."

Ibuse had been familiar with Hadakajima for a number of years. His essay "A Tributary of the Fujikawa River" (*Fujikawa shiryū*, 1934) explains that he first visited this obscure community only because he was intrigued by its name—an "island" not an island. As Ibuse explores the geography in this part of the former province of Kai, he concurrently researches its curious history; after describing the lay of the land in the controlled topological terms his readers know will prefigure tragedy, he does indeed discover that the Fujikawa, like the river in "A Town Under the River," conceals much beneath its waters. As in "The River," a sad history parallels a sullen landscape.

The first paragraph of "Wabisuke" explains that before a violent earthquake had destroyed it in 1707, a real island, Hadakajima, had stood in the middle of the river. Hadakajima is now the name of a later settlement on the shore. For the five years prior to its cataclysmic destruction, Hadakajima Island had served as a penal colony for criminal exiles (*ryūnin*) found guilty of violating the Shogun Tsunayoshi's infamous 1687 edict banning the killing of any living creature—the Law of Compassion for Fellow Creatures (*Shōrui awaremi no rei*). So many people were convicted of breaking this law that, in addition to local prisoners, Hadakajima had had to accommodate the overflow from the city of Edo, because there was no room on Edo's other exile islands of Hachijōjima and Miyakejima (both the subject and setting of other Ibuse stories). The geological tragedy of Hadakajima thus coincides with the absurd judicial excesses of a political regime: the parallels of the natural and human worlds of the past suggest similar affinities in the present. Ibuse himself, after all, had just lived through a time when his country had been shattered both physically and morally.

One of Hadakajima's exiles is a bird catcher by the name of Wabisuke, a man whose very name suggests the misery (*wabi*) of his life.

His profession almost guarantees that he will be in constant violation of the Buddhist precept made secular law, an offense doubly ironic since he often procures fowl in secret for high officials with carnivorous appetites. Caught red-handed one day delivering ducks to a wealthy customer, Wabisuke is sent to Miyakejima for three years' hard labor. He serves his time only to be caught again for the same offence. He discovers in his second place of exile, Hadakajima, that many of his fellow prisoners are there for equally cruel or just plain unlucky reasons. "It was terrifying. Over eight thousand people in just one year!" exclaims Wabisuke when he recalls how many people were convicted in Edo alone. One of the prisoners, a woman called Omon, tells Wabisuke of her sentencing for the crime of fishing:

> The official told me, " . . . That is a violation of the law. It is for the good of the nation that everyone must obey. For the sake of your country you must give it your all." He spoke in earnest, but of things which I could not fathom. [3:294–95]

What comes under implicit criticism here and elsewhere in "Wabisuke" is not so much the law itself, but the authorities' often absurd applications of it. This excess, repeated in Ibuse's own day under the wartime militarists, would be immediately recalled by any contemporary Japanese reader of the above passage. In this century as well as the eighteenth, one's efforts were all "for the good of the nation." Yet Wabisuke, and the muzzled writers of the 1940s, were hardly dangerous subversives. In fact, of all the prisoners on Hadakajima, the exile of Wabisuke appears the most ludicrous in light of his tenderly benevolent attitude towards life. In one important passage, Ibuse describes in sensitive detail how Wabisuke gingerly, respectfully, captures his prey: the imprisoned man imprisons others with care, suggesting, along with so many of Ibuse's characters from "The Carp" onwards, the presence of a sympathetic, sustaining bond between man and creature. Both exiles in a forsaken place, these captives share a similar fate. But only to a certain point: perhaps most cruelly, it is finally better to be an animal than a man on Hadakajima (or, the reader recalls, in Singapore). "There are no naughty children to tease the birds, or evil snakes to steal their eggs" (3:291–92). Indeed, the existence of any lowly animal on Hadakajima is infinitely more pleasant than that of a human exile:

138
Beautiful
Endings:
The
Second
World
War

There was no peasant who did not envy the lot of dogs and birds. The exiles of Hadakajima had a song about that: "We have ourselves no great ambition to become dogs or such, but we should like to be blessed in the next life with the good fortune to be reborn as birds. If you wish to know why, it is because birds, unlike men, need not worry about stepping on their eggs and being whipped for it. If this wish is not possible, then let us become the tail feathers of a white heron. If you wish to know why, it is because there at least we might fit into place." [3:292]

The human characters of "Wabisuke" live in a time and place where animals are afforded more protection than are people. They envy creatures their secure sense of belonging ("we might fit into place"), a comfort denied them as exiles. Once Ibuse has established in his story this social alienation of an entire community, he is ready to confirm its radical and historical implications with a radical and historical event. As is inevitable in Ibuse's catastrophe fiction, there are early warnings. Prisoners who slip away to fish report that their lures move in the water in strange ways. "They say it is as if they fled into the riverbed like bolts of lightning" (3:293). Disaster is preceded by disruptive occurrences in nature which no one (but the reader) interprets correctly, creating the ironic effect fundamental to Ibuse's power as a writer. Yet the disappearance of mere fishing lures leads to an eventual cataclysm that no one in Ibuse's audience could fully have anticipated:

The calamity of Hadakajima occurred in the autumn of that year, in the tenth month of the old lunar calendar. The sudden catastrophe was of heretofore unknown proportions. An outline of what happened was recorded in the report of the Office of the Magistrate: " . . . On the fourth day of the tenth month, early in the morning at the Hour of the Hare, an earthquake shook the ground. Heaven and earth trembled. Three aftershocks followed. On the fifth day two more small tremors were followed by a very great earthquake. Mount Fuji burst into flames and spewed ashes. Although it was exceedingly difficult to tell from our vantage point, it appeared that rocks fell from the sky for several miles around the mountain. The biggest rocks were bigger than temple bells or braziers; the smallest, about the size of beans or chestnuts. These rocks were surprisingly light in weight. According to the exiles of Hadakajima, it was at the time of this great earthquake, on the fifth day, that the banks at the mouth of the Shimobe tributary of the Fujikawa River collapsed. Hadakajima began its horrible slide towards the bottom. It disappeared beneath the waters in the blink of an eye. Huge waves arose, a waterspout formed, and the winds blew to dump the water as far as the exiles' earthen building sites. Where the island is now remembered to have been, blue water in boundless quantities flowed deep and without end. As it slid towards the bottom of the river, all vestiges of Hadakajima completely vanished. The inmates report that their island was thus spirited away by the gods. . . . "

This catastrophe occurred at four in the afternoon. The exiles, who were at that hour clearing land at the base of a hill on the shore, saw Mount Fuji cloud over with water spray. They stood erect, speechless, to watch. Only by accident did Wabisuke catch a glimpse of Hadakajima sliding into the river. The waters seemed to flow backwards. At the same time, within his view the entire island changed into a large pure-white waterspout. As this beautiful waterspout drew itself up by sucking what seemed to be the entire river, the island utterly vanished. The water turned into a tidal wave that washed the shores. A moment passed. All that remained in Wabisuke's inward eye was some sort of red flower in wild unseasonal bloom that he had seen among the fields of the is-land—the island that he had just seen disappear. [3:308–09]

Suddenly, compressed in a few lines, is one of the most spectacular endings found anywhere in Ibuse's writings. All at once the small world of Wabisuke and his peers is visited by earthquakes, volcanic eruptions, landslides, waterspouts, winds, and tidal waves. More graphically than in any previous work, Ibuse has described here an-other vision of his beautiful end—the violent yet compelling con-frontation of his characters with the destruction of their surround-ings. As did Ibuse in Johor Baharu, Wabisuke stands on a distant hill and witnesses the death of an island. Magnificent pillars of fire in Singapore; beautiful waterspouts in Hadakajima: these nearly mythi-cal symbols of Ibuse's dark universe are balanced, however, with small reminders of their complementary converse. In "Wabisuke" the last image is that of a red flower "in wild unseasonal bloom" (*kuruizaki*), a distortion of nature that recalls precedents in "The River" and *Waves* and that further suggests, like a red rising sun against a background of white, the recent defeat of Japan, in particu-lar, and the recurring imperative of historical change, in general. Japan as well as Hadakajima had been an island cut off from the rest of the world; its exiles, as well, stood "speechless" (*iu beki kotoba mo shirazu*) before the calamities that befell them. Though ostensibly

140

Beautiful
Endings:
The
Second
World
War

historical fiction, "Wabisuke" reads as a remarkable allegory of the Second World War. It successfully unites Ibuse's trauma as an exile in wartime with the tale of a penal colony suffering the twin terrors inflicted by man and nature.

The theme of "Wabisuke" and its cataclysmic conclusion is rewritten again and again in Ibuse's literature, in historical as well as contemporary works written after the war. Ibuse was writing about history at a time when history, since its truths and purposes had been so abused by prewar jingoists, was scorned in intellectual circles. Ibuse's writing was not fashionable. Yet he found it personally necessary, and artistically fruitful, to extend his experiences beyond the immediate, to universalize them in time so as to reconcile himself to recent events.

His prewar work supplied ample formal and thematic precedents. The river in "Wabisuke" that rises up to engulf Hadakajima represents as much the inexorable flow of time and natural fate as did the river in "The River." Furthermore, as in "The River," the dynamics of the natural world precisely parallel those of the historical, a purposeful coincidence that Ibuse's own experiences demonstrated (as when, for instance, Hiroshima suffered terrible floods soon after the atomic bombing). At the same time "Wabisuke" gives sharpened expression to the theme of loneliness and isolation found in Ibuse's earliest short stories. Although the critics are correct when they claim one can sense the "wounds of the war" in "Wabisuke,"[22] one also is aware of a return to a time before the war. This story stands in relation to "The River," *Waves,* and "A General Account of Aogashima" in much the same way "The Salamander" does to "Confinement" and "Sawan on the Roof." In a sense, it rewrites those works that preceded it, deepening the reader's scope of interpretation while simultaneously elaborating their shared significance.

"Wabisuke" is also a forerunner of Ibuse's best postwar works, stories that similarly link the personal circumstances of an individual with the theme of catastrophic experience and its import. One of Ibuse's critics suggests that "Wabisuke" is a pivotal work in global, not just Japanese, literary history because it prefigures the genre of concentration-camp literature.[23] More modestly, the story certainly seems an appropriate example of twentieth-century literature of atrocity, as a work dealing allegorically with mass destruction in a world where suddenly that is an ever-present possibility.

Ibuse's fresh appreciation of the violence of history inspired, after "Wabisuke," a new series of works expressing the force of that awareness. That awareness was born, however, not solely from the national experience of the Second World War, but from a personal crisis Ibuse suffered in the postwar period, namely, the death of his disciple and friend, Dazai Osamu. In June 1948, the double suicide of Dazai and his mistress by drowning was, in retrospect, as shocking and disorienting, and nearly as influential on Ibuse's writing, as was the war itself. The troubling circumstances attending the demise of this talented writer, Ibuse's closest friend since Aoki Nampachi, would serve to compound and confirm Ibuse's similarly tragic experiences as a soldier and then an evacuee. In other words, the death of Dazai once again rendered Ibuse the close observer of death, the immediate survivor of a tragedy.

Ibuse was thirty-two and Dazai twenty-one when they first met. An aspiring writer, newly arrived in Tokyo, Dazai had been impressed with Ibuse ever since reading "Confinement" as a middle school student in Aomori in northern Japan. It was precisely the sort of story that would have appealed to Dazai's own feelings of loneliness and isolation as a youth with artistic potential, trapped both by his position as the son of a prominent family and by his domicile in a far province. Nearly as soon as he freed himself by entering the French Literature Department at Tokyo Imperial University in 1930, he wrote Ibuse a desperate letter demanding that he consent to meet with him or he would kill himself. In one of Ibuse's many memoirs of Dazai, he recalls that such an ultimatum left him no choice but to see the fellow.[24] Had it not been for this unusual first encounter, after which Dazai apprenticed himself to Ibuse for many years, Tōgō Katsumi speculates that the reading public would never have known quite the same Dazai, and that, indeed, without Ibuse's frequent intercessions, of which this was only the first, Dazai would have ended his life even earlier.[25]

At first their relationship was the traditional pedagogic one of an established writer with a neophyte. Ibuse advised Dazai to read Chinese poetry and modern Western classics, especially those of Proust, Pushkin, and Chekhov. Each read the other's stories and acted as critic and editor. Ibuse has stated several times that Dazai helped him write the eruption scene in "A General Account of

142
Beautiful
Endings:
The
Second
World
War

Aogashima." And he revealed after Dazai's death that "Yōnosuke's Boasts" (*Yōnosuke no kien*, 1934), though published under Ibuse's name, had in fact been a joint effort. For his part, Dazai seemed to have inherited something of Ibuse's flair for characterization. Gradually, however, their association grew less literary and more personal, eventually becoming like that of a father and son, involving not only the affection but the rivalry and frustration that so often accompanies such a bond in real life.

What Dazai might very well have been seeking from Ibuse was, in fact, a mentor whom he could respect, a role his actual father did not fulfill. In an essay appended to an edition of Ibuse's works, written on the eve of his suicide, Dazai said of Ibuse:

> Reflecting upon this collection of short stories, I experienced a strong sensation, something like a mystical revelation yet somehow one still very physical. Everything seemed "all right" [*daijōbu*]. . . . I had the feeling that this writer is "all right," and the feeling made me happy.[26]

Ibuse did little to discourage Dazai's deepening dependency upon him. He interceded with his family whenever there was trouble, which was often and which usually involved women. He acted as the go-between for Dazai's last marriage, looked after him in the hospital, sought to cure him of the drug addiction he developed there, and continued as his patron in Tokyo literary circles. They were as close as men of nearly different generations could be.

Eventually, however, they drifted apart. Dazai's career was as dissolute as Ibuse's was upright. They were evacuated to the same village in Kōfu in 1944, by which time, according to Ibuse in "Fishermen" (*Tsuriudo*, 1970), Dazai already seemed prepared to die. One might wonder, of course, if this was true or simply an observation, after the fact, to assuage guilt; but it does seem that Dazai's tendencies towards self-destruction were accelerating. The men were separated later when Ibuse was evacuated to Kamo and Dazai to Aomori; but even after the war, back in Tokyo, the two met only a few times, and then only in the protective company of Dazai's circle of self-proclaimed decadents.

No matter how prepared Ibuse might have been for Dazai's death, it still came as a great shock to him. He writes in "The Ways of Women" (*Onnagokoro*, 1949) about the loss of his best friend in much the same fashion he had written decades earlier about Tada Otaki:

The police officer told his story. A writer by the name of Dazai had thrown himself into the water. When the corpse was found he went to the scene as the investigating detective. The results of his examination revealed bruises on Mr. Dazai's neck and throat caused by a cord or rope. It was called an involuntary double suicide [*muri shinjū*]. In deference to the position of the deceased, however, this was not announced to the public. [10:306]

What is interesting here is not only that Ibuse speaks through a calm observer, the policeman, to recount the details of his friend's death—that technique is familiar—but that Ibuse subtly suggests that the circumstances of that death are open to varying interpretations. So shortly after the tragedy, Ibuse perhaps wished to believe anything but that Dazai was actually to blame for what had happened to him. Dazai's absolution would be Ibuse's own: he died leaving the world a suicide note which, among other things, decried Ibuse as an "evil man" (*akunin*).

This unexpected accusation became something of a literary scandal at the time. A number of theories were offered to explain, or discount, this evidence of a surprising enmity harbored by the disciple for his teacher. Some claimed that it was his mistress and fellow suicide, Yamazaki Tomie, who in fact wrote the note,[27] a supposition built on the knowledge that she disliked Ibuse.[28] Satō Haruo, however, proposed the far more likely hypothesis that this note, like all of Dazai's literature, was cryptic. Satō exculpates his own disciple, Ibuse, by insisting that Dazai was only decrying his efforts to make him respectable, efforts that had included marriage to a good woman and the subsequent birth of children, whose existence no doubt had made the decision to kill himself in the spring of 1948 a difficult, torturous one.[29]

Yet whatever excuses might be offered, the combination of Dazai's death and his personal rebuke first upset and then obsessed Ibuse. Although he had written of Dazai long before his suicide (he is first mentioned in 1932)[30] and had even kept a special "Dazai diary" on five separate occasions, after his death Ibuse was to publish over thirty works specifically about Dazai, at least half a dozen in 1948 alone. Dazai Osamu holds the record as Ibuse's most written-of figure, a fact that should establish him as one of the principal themes of Ibuse's literature.[31]

The first pieces Ibuse wrote about Dazai after his suicide are alter-

144
Beautiful
Endings:
The
Second
World
War

nately confused and bitter, as if he felt betrayed by his friend's death. In "Parting Regrets" (*Sekibetsu,* 1948), along with a protest that he really did like Dazai, Ibuse insists that his friend had died abruptly, without explanation and without "leaving behind anything written for me." It seems as if Ibuse wishes to deny the existence, or at least the direct import, of the note. In "Dazai" (*Dazai-kun no koto,* 1948) Ibuse begins with the defensive disclaimer: "I have no idea why Dazai died" (10:192). Perhaps it is easier for Ibuse to accept Dazai's death if he views him and his final act as an enigma. In *An Ogikubo Almanac* Ibuse remembers his first encounter with Dazai and his impression at the time that "I did not know how this youth reacted to me in his heart."[32] This attempt to anticipate, and thus deny, a later embarrassment (resulting not only from the suicide note, but from the fact that Ibuse, an older man, had survived a younger) parallels similar attempts elsewhere.

Ibuse had tried to mitigate similar feelings about survival after the death of Aoki Nampachi, and, on a broader scale, in the immediate postwar years after the loss of so many young men. Dazai's death fueled and intensified these feelings. In "Ten Years Ago" (*Jūnenmae-goro,* 1948) Ibuse confesses some measure of his imagined culpability when he recounts how Dazai always needed someone to watch over him. Once he had even asked Ibuse to become his legal guardian. Ibuse had refused. Later, writing in guilty hindsight, Ibuse states, "Looking back over the time we spent together, it cannot be said I was one of his inner circle, or even a good friend" (10:238). Ibuse claims Dazai deliberately avoided him in his last years, citing this as proof that he must somehow have failed him. These masochistic sentiments persist for years in Ibuse's writing, found in such works as "Sociability" (*Shakōsei,* 1956) in the 1950s, "The Tale of the Koto" (*Koto no ki,* 1960) in the 1960s, and "Someone I Miss" (*Oshii hito,* 1974) in the 1970s.

But the repercussions of Dazai's death went far beyond those stories specifically about him; Ibuse's emotions of loss and abandonment were compounded by similar emotions generated in the wake of the Second World War. With the death of Dazai Ibuse began to write about the friends and comrades he had lost during the war years. The coincidence of Japan's tragedy as a nation and with Ibuse's as an individual represents a critical confluence in Ibuse's postwar literature. Death seemed again to be pursuing Ibuse whichever way he turned. Ibuse was forced to struggle with his condition as a survivor among the dead, a witness to history racing past.

145
"A
Guide
to the
Ravine"

"A Guide to the Ravine"

In this crucial year of 1948 Ibuse wrote a story that combines his familiar natural and historical worlds with the most recent events of the war and, in a brief reference, even Dazai. The resulting work expresses Ibuse's bewilderment at the quirks of fate and his confusion as to why he alone should have survived. "A Guide to the Ravine" (*Sankyō fūbutsu shi*) begins with Ibuse's lament that he has had little opportunity to know "mountain men" (*yama no hito*), that is, men who are born in and spend their entire lives among the hills. The mention of Dazai comes early in the story when Ibuse notes that once, while on a trip with Dazai, he did meet such a mountain man, an old man in his eighties (there are, needless to say, no young mountain men in Ibuse's writings). But since that trip, Ibuse has come to know another mountain man, a doctor named Yoneyama. Immediately after the war, Ibuse was researching a work that would describe Yoneyama's mountainous region of Yamanashi Prefecture. He returned to Yoneyama's valley to interview him. The greater part of "A Guide to the Ravine" transcribes Yoneyama's rambling monologue on his birthplace. He becomes, like so many of Ibuse's old men, the voice of folk history with its powerfully wise perspective.

Yoneyama explains to Ibuse that while he was living with his son during the war—like Ibuse, he was a displaced person during those years—he made the acquaintance of another old man, named Jinsaku. Jinsaku and he shared a common interest in the wild monkeys that inhabit their valley. An especially fierce species, these simians have been responsible not only for destroyed crops but even the deaths of adult men. They are only one factor among many, however, which render life in this valley particularly harsh. Indeed, this valley is called a *senkyō* by outsiders, a term ordinarily denoting a magic land where *sennin* (hermits with the power of immortality) dwell. In this particular usage, however, senkyō seems to refer to a land where it is so exceedingly hard to survive that its inhabitants are assumed to have mastered some part of the sennin's powers. Jinsaku's own life would seem to warrant this assumption and its

146
Beautiful
Endings:
The
Second
World
War

nomenclature: all three of his sons have died in the war, one inten-
tionally after hearing rumors that his wife back home was involved
in a scandalous incident of infidelity.

This daughter-in-law of Jinsaku, named Miyo, her reputation
ruined, has taken up with yet another man, who has left her pregnant. At this point her path has crossed with that of Yoneyama who,
as a doctor, finds himself beseeched to perform an abortion on the
woman. This request to terminate the life of a child moves
Yoneyama to share his own story with Ibuse. Not that long ago, he
reminds him, unwanted children were simply thrown into a river.
Moreover, children thought at birth to show any signs of mental
deficiency were similarly disposed of; interestingly, adults who de-
velop such handicaps are known in this area as the magical sennin,
perhaps an ironic suggestion that idiots are suited for survival in a
senkyō.

Yoneyama himself, he reveals, was judged an idiot at birth and
was ordered murdered by the attending midwife. Only the cowardice
of a servant told to carry out the act, and then the compassion of his
grandmother, had saved him. "Though presently alive and well, I
was once a human being destined to die upon birth" (4:28).
Yoneyama credits fate for his survival. Still, his survival is contingent
upon his constant awareness of that fate: "I am a man no different
from those who have died" (4:30). "A Guide to the Ravine" concludes with Yoneyama's final thoughts on Miyo's request for the ter-
mination of her pregnancy:

> I got myself off the hook right away, using one of our old sayings in my
> typically jaded way. There's an old tradition in this valley. The saying
> goes that if it's under three months, it's like something growing in the
> ground. I'm sure you saw our terraced fields on your way here. You must
> have noticed tea shrubs planted here and there about some of those fields.
> Occasional rows of three or four, some large and some small, growing in
> one place or another. That's an old custom of ours, to plant a tea shrub
> where we've buried what we've aborted. Their rough arrangement is a
> relic bespeaking that custom. They're the same as graves. The fact that
> people here prize and even revere the tea shrubs is proof that they didn't
> despise what they killed, even if you say the shrubs only exist because
> they did have the abortions. I really believe it's true. [4:30]

This powerful tale that begins so innocently, even humorously,
and ends so movingly, suggests a great many of Ibuse's own troubled

feelings at the time. The harsh mountains and their valley, which sustains so little life, seem a clear metaphor for the equally inhospitable landscape of Ibuse's existence in the midst of an exceptionally violent century. The story's characters, all old men, evacuees, and fellow survivors of lost families and friends, reflect the author's own plight. Most important, their combined marvel and resignation at the working of individual destiny fairly parallel Ibuse's continuing and disturbing search for a reconciliation of his life with those of his dead comrades. In the largest sense Ibuse, together with Yoneyama and Jinsaku, inhabits a senkyō, a place that not only challenges him to survive but to justify that survival. Like the sennin, he seems immortal; but like the poor idiots similarly labeled, that fate inspires little joy.

Yoneyama, the miraculous survivor, remains in his monkey-ravaged valley because he has a duty to do so, a duty dictated by the fact that it is there he has survived. Similarly, Ibuse has a duty to write, furiously, about those whom he has outlived, to commemorate with words much as the inhabitants of "A Guide to the Ravine" commemorate with tea bushes. This story elaborates a theme of survival guilt looming large in Ibuse's life, both recent and past, beginning with the deaths of his relatives, intensifying with that of Aoki Nampachi, and leading up to the tragedy of Dazai Osamu. "A Guide to the Ravine" is also a work that could not have been written had Ibuse not personally experienced a world war. The war had forced him to consider on an immense scale the capriciously cruel calculus of living and dying.

Remembering such works as "The Carp," this story takes its place in a long tradition of Ibuse pieces seeking to memorialize, and at times apologize to, the dead. Together, such works comprise Ibuse's hallmark genre of *chinkon bungaku,* "requiem literature," a series of recorded dialogues with the dead conducted by one of the repentant living. Since the war, this genre has been predominantly concerned with the friends Ibuse lost to its violence.

For decades Ibuse has written frequently about his dead comrades, and with increasing sadness and intensity as the years pass. The number of his friends killed in Southeast Asia, for example, was not especially great, but each of them is written about repeatedly, suggesting that Ibuse is attempting to construct a depth, a "body" of words about the victims to give them a literary existence replacing their corporeal one. The reader receives the impression of a cycle, a chant, a

148
Beautiful
Endings:
The
Second
World
War

liturgy; the empathic magic so implied is the basis of Ibuse's, perhaps of all, chinkon bungaku. On a recent anniversary of Japan's surrender, Ibuse wrote:

While I was in the service there were a number of victims [*giseisha*] among my comrades (120 draftees). One died in battle. Named Yanagi Shigenori, he had been an honest reporter for the *Tōkyō Nichi-Nichi Shimbun*. Another of my comrades succumbed to the violence of the war and tried to kill himself by putting a blade to his throat. Another went insane, overwhelmed by the war's cruelty. After he formed a partisan unit and began to ravage Malay and Chinese homes, the Japanese military police killed him in an assault. Yet another was reassigned to Sumatra and was shot dead by an enemy soldier who had not heard the news that the war was won and hostilities were over. It was sad for all of them. I came back alive, and I am still alive. For some reason or another, Yanagi comes back to mind. It must be because my memories, too, constantly return.[33]

Not only the gloom but the guilt intimated in this passage ("I came back alive, and I am still alive") is present in the very first of Ibuse's works dealing with the war dead. This story of demobilized soldiers returning to their home village—the village to which both Ibuse and Dazai had been evacuated—was in fact published the month Dazai killed himself. It may, like others of these stories, speak of that event as well. "Talk of the Returnees" (*Fukuinsha no uwasa*, 1948) tells that a total of thirty-one men were drafted from the village after the Manchurian Incident of 1931. Eventually twelve died in battle and two died of disease; another two were crippled. The rest returned home intact. Two were luckier still; they were drafted after the war had ended. Their conscription orders were in the mail when Japan surrendered, and they did not know what to do once they received them. The village headman insisted they follow orders and even gave them a patriotic send-off. The very next day the men returned home after finding the Imperial Army indifferent to their arrival. Yet the men were welcomed by their families as enthusiastically as they had been sent off. This is characteristic of Ibuse's wry humor. It captivates, not so much because it is funny but because it is insightfully ironic, a humor that destabilizes as it derides, poking fun at attitudes and institutions in such a way as to challenge and entertain the reader. In many of Ibuse's stories about the war dead, the reader submits to such challenges, albeit they are derived not always from humor but from an infectious guilt. In "Talk of the Returnees" that guilt is embodied in the character of the village's first returning demobilized soldier, Sakuda Naokichi:

> He rode in from town on a charcoal-fueled bus. The other passengers did not hesitate to talk to him, but he just hung his head low and responded to none of their questions. He somehow had the look of a man who knew a great deal. He later confessed that he had been intimidated by the fact that he was returning home so early and had feared that the families of others who had died would resent him. [4:33–34]

Ibuse, like Sakuda, had been an early returnee from the war and must have shared his character's apprehensions and fears. Ibuse has articulated these embarrassed feelings time and again, as if he believes that to confess them is to diminish them. In "Death in the Field, Death in the Field Hospital" (*Senshi—sembyōshi*, 1963) Ibuse not only retells the stories of his comrades' deaths but goes on to protest, after noting how safe he had been behind a desk in Singapore, that he in fact feels no guilty remorse (*nezame no warui omoi*) at surviving, because "it would be intolerable to be so hard on oneself" (8:287). Yet in the decades since the war, Ibuse has indeed been hard on himself, stopping short of admitting it in so many words only because he fears what this would do to him. The guilt is nearly inexhaustible, since it dates not just from the first half of the 1940s but indeed from his entire life, spanning the century and regularly punctuated with untimely, inappropriate deaths. The war years and their accelerated occurrence of such deaths have become a trope in Ibuse's writing, epitomizing his experiences. As time passes, the tragedies of the war merge with tragedy in general, taking their place in the long conundrum of history. This process of thematic synthesis is evident in the 1970 story "Hirano Naomi, A Wartime Draftee" (*Sensōchū no chōin—Hirano Naomi*) and again in the 1978 "Yanagi Shigenori and the Three-Forked Road at Bukit Timah" (*Bukitema sansaro to Yanagi Shigenori no koto*). In the latter Ibuse writes that Yanagi, one of his aforementioned "victims," died because he was "caught in a whirlpool . . . a whirlpool he unwittingly entered."[34] Like Tada Otaki and the characters that followed (including, at times, Ibuse himself), Yanagi was dragged down into powerful waters never to surface again. In the final stage of his career, Ibuse has been able to accommodate even the dead of the Second World War in his vision of the natural and historical world.

150
Beautiful
Endings:
The
Second
World
War

These dead, or rather the memories of them, pursue Ibuse like unforgiving ghosts into even the most unlikely corners of his literature. No small number of stories and essays make a casual, and therein often devastating, reference to the dead. At the conclusion of some otherwise entertaining anecdote, Ibuse will suddenly state, as if reminding the reader, that the butt of the joke died in Malaya, or Java, or the Philippines. The effect is to charge the entire story with an ironic gravity that actually renders Ibuse's biographical quip a relic of his association with the deceased. "Hops" (*Karahanagusa*, 1956), for instance, begins, unexpectedly didactic, with an explanation of the difference between male and female hops; then advances to the topic of beer in general. Ibuse knows more than most on this subject, for he once had a friend who told him much about it. That friend, the reader learns in the essay's last line, died in northern China during the war: the force of such a sentence transforms all that precedes it into a memorial. More than a decade after the war, even the sight of a field of grain compels Ibuse to recall how much he has lost to the vortex of history.

"Lieutenant Lookeast"

Such stories, both direct and oblique, are joined by several longer works that subsume the theme of death and its attendant guilt within the greater context of Ibuse's transcendental theory of continuity and change. One of these, "Lieutenant Lookeast" (*Yōhai taichō*, 1950), is considered by the critic Usui Yoshimi to be the tragic masterpiece of the Second World War.[35] This lengthy story successfully encompasses military and civilian, wartime and postwar Japan in the single portrait of one of its equally schizoid citizens.

"Lieutenant Lookeast" draws on many sources, but principally on Ibuse's experiences in Southeast Asia, the people he met there, and the stories he heard from them. In an interview, Ibuse has revealed that the original inspiration was an anecdote told him by a friend about a disturbed former sergeant major who lived in the town where she maintained a summer home.[36] Yet Ibuse's fictional Lieutenant Okazaki seems at one point surprisingly like Yamashita Tomoyuki, the famous general and architect of Japan's Malay campaign, who once severely reprimanded Ibuse in Singapore for his lack of soldierly discipline.[37] Lieutenant Lookeast is, however, most like the commander of the *Afurika-maru*. Ibuse recalls this fanatical officer aboard his troop ship in *The First Half of My Life:*

> The officer in command of the transport lectured us on morality. He began by announcing that from now on our lives were in his hands. We felt as if we had been jolted. One could hear people clearing their throats and whispering to one another, but the C.O. continued, raising his voice until he was shouting in anger that he would kill any of us who complained. "Just try it!" dared Kaionji Chōgorō in a loud voice. Someone else said something in a quieter voice. The C.O., perhaps intimidated, became defiant and continued to expound upon the soldier's spirit. One might say he screamed about it. Finally he told us, "Subversives like you are dangerous, there's no helping that. Once you're on the ship you won't find me anywhere near you." Later I would borrow the simpler side of this transport C.O. when I was writing "Lieutenant Lookeast." [13:451]

The "simpler side" that Ibuse borrowed from an actual acquaintance can be seen in the caricatured ultrazealousness of Okazaki, the central character in "Lieutenant Lookeast." Okazaki is a war veteran from one of the villages to which Ibuse had been evacuated. In his youth, according to a lengthy flashback, he was honored with a place at the army college and was sent after graduation to Southeast Asia. In a passage that might as readily be found in the memoirs of the *Afurika-maru*, Ibuse writes of how Okazaki was nicknamed "Lieutenant Lookeast":

> Lieutenant Lookeast had long been fond of bowing east as a sign of respect towards the Emperor. Even on the ship he would assemble his men on deck to bow eastward and shout "Long live the Emperor!" whenever the radio reported good news. [4:317]

Ibuse himself had been forced to do likewise on December 8, 1941, when the "good news" of open hostilities was announced. This experience, as with so many during his one year of service, has remained vivid. Okazaki is Ibuse's composite portrait of a personality warped by the exigencies of history: he, too, shouts that he will kill anyone who dares complain. The absurdity—or so it seems today—of such a character is not allowed to degenerate into snide ridicule, for one day Okazaki's manic zeal for discipline and obedience results in some sobering complications. A lance-corporal named Tomomura, serving in Malaya under Okazaki, is heard to grumble rather innocently that war is "a waste. An absolute waste. To start with, it sure must cost a

152

Beautiful
Endings:
The
Second
World
War

lot of money" (4:308). Okazaki becomes incensed at what he thinks treasonous talk and strikes Tomomura across the face, inadvertently causing both of them to fall off the bridge upon which they have been standing. The accident kills Tomomura and critically injures Okazaki.

While recuperating in a field hospital, the lieutenant becomes delirious and often shouts militarist slogans. Another patient speculates that Okazaki is being tormented by Tomomura's spirit. If true, then Okazaki is to be haunted thus forever, for although he survives bodily, with only a limp to show, his mind is permanently distorted. He eventually returns to his home village after a discharge from a mental institution, but he continues to suffer occasional fits when he imagines he is still an active officer at war. With no warning, he is apt to accost his fellow villagers and berate them for lapses of vigilance. At first these hallucinations are mild and infrequent. His behavior is thought only "strange" as Japan's defeat approaches. But "it was a few days after the surrender that he began to show signs of being truly mad" (4:302).

This change in the villagers' perception of Okazaki forms the very crux of the story, for it is not so much that he is insane—throughout the war, after all, everyone was mouthing such slogans—as that after August 15, 1945, this once-sanctioned behavior suddenly becomes "abnormal." The lieutenant acts no differently in his hometown than he had on the battlefield. But the end of the war reverses everything, and conduct once demanded is now decried. It is even thought insane. In "Lieutenant Lookeast" Ibuse suggests how easily history and one's reading of its lessons can change; he provides a clever demonstration of effortlessly exchanged ideologies. Two villagers confront Okazaki, and then each other, over his crazed, jingoistic ravings:

> "Hey, what does he mean, he'll 'butcher' me? That's the sort of thing those fascist types say. Just hearing it makes me mad all over again."
>
> "Now don't go saying things like that. If it were still wartime we'd have to put up with it, wouldn't we? That's the sort of stuff we heard all the time during the war. Haven't both of us gone through listening to talk like that?"
>
> "Hold on, Matsumura Munejirō. What do you mean, 'still wartime'? I can't let you get away with such scandalous talk. We're a nation that has renounced war. If you're going to say things like that, I'll just return all the charcoal I bought from you." [4:300]

Within this characteristically ironic and humorous exchange, Ibuse not only emphasizes how mercurial any standard of behavior can be, but he reasserts his belief that while certain superstructural manifestations may change (Taira/Minamoto, militarism/democracy), those manifestations are finally as inconsequential as they are inevitable. Fate, as a powerful principle in the lives of both individuals and nations, was firmly established in Ibuse's prewar works. But it is called upon again to assist Ibuse in the assimilation of epochal events otherwise beyond his control. His cyclical view of the natural, historical world had indeed seemed confirmed as one era so easily gave way to another. There is, of course, comfort in this. Inevitability precludes responsibility. The deranged lieutenant represents an anomaly only because he is temporally out of step with his countrymen, caught in a warp that leaves him "unhistorical." An injury to the head accidentally pardons him from the forward movement of history (or, in the idiom of *Waves*, from "the currents of time"), thereby throwing that movement into bold relief.

Ibuse generously peoples his postwar literature with such illustrative characters, men whose erratic behavior at first reads as parody but later provides the key for an ironic dismantling of the opposition of "normal" and "abnormal." "The Hashimoto Inn" (*Hashimotoya*, 1946) is the story of an old innkeeper named Isomatsu whom Ibuse has come to know over the course of his many fishing trips. The war and its aftermath have not been kind to Isomatsu: his son, at one time listed as killed in action, has returned home only to leave again immediately without a single word for his father; his son's wife has borne a child by a local villain. Perhaps as a result, Isomatsu contracts a "strange illness," which initially causes him to ride the train past his inn every day, tossing fruit, which he purchases at an exorbitant cost, out the train window to his waiting granddaughters. This same "illness" later causes him to waste his dwindling cash just as extravagantly.

Isomatsu's disease, like Okazaki's, is an affliction of the times, a syndrome of irrational acts perhaps no more deranged than the tragic circumstances that inspire them. In "The Hashimoto Inn," as in "Lieutenant Lookeast," codes of accepted behavior clash to render one another meaningless, creating a confusion out of which emerges a clearer principle: the surrender of human precepts to an abstract history, of human prerogatives to the coercive dynamics of the natural world. "Lieutenant Lookeast" necessarily moves back and forth

154
Beautiful
Endings:
The
Second
World
War

between the past (of the war) and the present (of a postwar Japan) in order to blur any distinction between the two. This attack upon the notion of progress, that is, the cumulative acquisition of ever-improved institutions, seems the consequence not only of Ibuse's long-held views on the nature of history and the destructive, "retrogressive" experience of the Second World War, but of Dazai's suicide, an event that similarly discouraged Ibuse from drawing any satisfaction from his own survival.

Ibuse's developing philosophy, his system of validating beliefs, derives directly from his personal struggle to accommodate both living and dying within a single, synthetic moral calculus. So many of his various stories return to this basic and problematic theme. Like Wabisuke who stood on the shore and watched as Hadakajima—his world—ended, Ibuse as well found himself "speechless." Words failed him completely for the two long years marking the end of the war; later, they still seemed inadequate. Ibuse's immediate postwar works can be read like a map, tracing tracks as he found his way, literally, out from among the dead. The thematic and idiomatic framework of his earlier writing could provide compass points, as it were, but those same themes and idioms had to be revised in the face of historic destruction unimaginable at the time he wrote "The River" and *Waves*. Ibuse's attempt to forge his prewar themes and his recent experiences is perhaps most explicit in an essay that might claim to effect closure upon his postwar writing—though of course this has never come to an end. "Sacrifices" (*Gisei*, 1951) typifies much literature after the violence of the Second World War, literature that has been undermined by history as well as informed by it. "Sacrifices" is yet another Ibuse work memorializing the five men among his comrades in Southeast Asia who died, but for the first time he admits to a paradox of words and silence:

> "Do not speak of the trenches." There are some who say this commandment is the armor of men who have known war. They are words that define war as a tragedy. Behind them stands the further imperative, "Say nothing more!" The power of these words is great. There is something ominous here. I will keep them in mind while I try to tell of what happened when I was in the service. In other words, I fear I must make a long story short. [5:81]

Having thus warned the reader that he embarks upon the difficult project of balancing the need to both remember and forget, Ibuse

proceeds to discuss the fates of such now-familiar casualties as
Terazaki and Yanagi, men made victims by the war Ibuse himself
survived. But of all his works commemorating these friends, perhaps
"Sacrifices" remembers them best: Ibuse seems to be standing on his
hill again, watching a beautiful ending, immersing his perceptive
powers but not his physical self in the experience of death. The true
story told in "Sacrifices" is the attempt to convey that experience.
Two months before "Sacrifices" appeared, Ibuse published the first
of his works to deal with the atomic bombing of Hiroshima; such
catastrophic experiences, be they in Malaya or Japan, challenged
Ibuse as a survivor and a writer to justify his existence as either. He
has been successful, if for no other reason than because his audience,
too, shares so many of the same doubts. From the 1940s came an
Ibuse with a surer, albeit more terrible, tale to tell; namely,
his—everyone's—struggle to remain whole in a world now faced
with the possibility of total destruction; a world in which all people
now stand transfixed by beautiful endings.

The Castaways: Usaburō and the 1950s

I was put aboard a steamship called the *Afurika-maru* and carried away from Osaka harbor to the tropics.
—"My Fountain Pen"

As if to bury his earlier years of silence under a mountain of words, Ibuse wrote copiously throughout the 1950s. His works in this decade were many and lengthy and were, furthermore, distinguished by a conservative style and an unfashionable insistence upon atopical themes. Ibuse nonetheless attracted much critical attention: his story "No Consultations Today" (*Honjitsu kyūshin*, 1949–1950) won the first Yomiuri Prize in 1950. This same work, in a more commercial tribute, was made into a successful motion picture, as were the later novels *The Station Hotel* (*Ekimae ryokan*, 1956–1957) and *The Curio-Shop Proprietor* (*Chimpindō shujin*, 1959). Owing not only to the broad appeal of the cinema but to his popular translations of Hugh Lofting's *Doctor Dolittle* books (a series whose entertaining tales of a man and his encounters with animals echoed one of his own literary themes), the name of Ibuse Masuji was now familiar to people who had never read any of his fiction.[1]

Yet in fact Ibuse was steadily clarifying the themes of his own writing during this decade. With a vigor characteristic of creative people in late middle age, he was continually at work on stories that increasingly emphasized those historical conflicts most recently evidenced in the course of his own life. His writing in the 1950s, becoming not only longer but more prosaic, completed the turn initiated in the 1930s from the lyrical short story to complex novels exploring a range of serious problems. Surely this evolutionary change had been accelerated by Ibuse's disturbing experiences during the Second World War, when he was forcibly confronted by the distortion of human societies in its calamitous wake. No other reading can account for the frequent coincidence of his personal history with that of

Japan's in his work after 1945, beginning with "Wabisuke" and culminating in such studies of modern men under the duress of this century as "Lieutenant Lookeast." Throughout the 1950s Ibuse was advancing towards the final definition of his writer's vision, preparing to place a human figure in his world of mountains and rivers, whirlpools and fires, a figure who, in surviving Hiroshima, might stand for all survivors.

157
The
Castaways:
Usaburō
and
the
1950s

But that ultimate incarnation of Ibuse's most important themes would be prefigured by several intermediary heroes. And perhaps the most important among these is found in *Castaway Usaburō* (*Hyōmin Usaburō*, 1954–1955), the novelization of the story of an Edo period sailor for which, in part, Ibuse was awarded the 1955 Art Academy Prize (*Geijutsuin-shō*). Although heralded as a new kind of literature, *Castaway Usaburō* was in one sense a return to an older genre of Japanese letters, the *hyōryūki*, or "castaway accounts." These often dry but on occasion surprisingly literary, records of Japanese seamen once lost in the open waters of the Pacific were of interest chiefly to historians until Ibuse used them, and his imagination, as the materials for a series of essays, stories, and novels culminating in *Castaway Usaburō*. In a decade when established prewar writers as well as recent postwar talents were crowding the bookstores with "new" writing, Ibuse's historical, old-fashioned tale of a nineteenth-century shipwrecked sailor still attracted many readers. Perhaps in Ibuse's use of the past as an allegory of the present, readers of his *hyōryūmono* ("castaway stories," modern interpretations of the historical *hyōryūki*) saw something of themselves and found this work contemporary.

Ibuse's unique adaptations of the records of Japan's castaways revived a critical interest in these neglected official reports. Collectively they read almost as a counterhistory of an Edo period Japan in not-so-total isolation from the outside world. The *hyōryūki* tell of foreign lands at a time when such knowledge, much less actual travel, was regarded with the utmost suspicion by the authorities. Consequently they are implicitly political, potentially subversive. Like the roughly contemporaneous slave narratives of North America, the *hyōryūki* exist only because an oppressive state controlled the free movement of its citizens. Both speak of escape and punishment, both document strange lands and places that the reading public otherwise visited only via imagination. When Tokugawa Iemitsu, the third shogun of the Edo period, prohibited nearly all contacts be-

158

The
Castaways:
Usaburō
and
the
1950s

tween his country and others in 1639, the effects of his policies went well beyond the commercial and diplomatic. Japan's literary life was forced in on itself for the next two hundred years—with the exception of those records transcribing the testimony of sailors who, through no fault of their own, had become castaways in alien places prohibited the rest of their countrymen. Fickle weather compounded by primitive navigational techniques stranded a surprising number of Japanese crews. Occasionally, gracious hosts made it possible for such castaways to return home, but only after they had been exposed to the languages, religions, and customs of cultures not their own. Upon their repatriation they were regarded very warily by xenophobic Japanese officials.

The returned castaways, technically guilty of a crime, were interrogated as any criminals might be. As a result, the transcribed statements of these unintentional emissaries—sailors who had drifted east, west, north, and south to civilizations both more and less developed than Japan—kept a steady stream of information coming into an ostensibly sequestered nation. At the time, such information was sometimes prized, more often scorned. To read these accounts now, however, as Ibuse did, is to be impressed not by talk of steam engines or Russian Orthodox rituals, but by the amazing luck and courageous persistence of the castaways themselves. Considering the geographical, and then legal, obstacles returning castaways had to surmount, their stories are testaments to the human spirit.

In his essay "A Watch and the Naoki Prize" (*Tokei to Naoki-shō*, 1963), Ibuse quotes a historian who notes that Japanese castaways made it to North American and Southeast Asian shores in every year of the Edo period. One result of Iemitsu's policy of national seclusion was the growth of domestic commerce and, with it, of maritime shipping between Japanese ports. Japanese merchant vessels, simple one-mast crafts that sailed by following the shore line, were often blown off course by the notoriously unpredictable winds of both Japan's coasts. Only a small fraction could have encountered either land or fellow travelers in the huge and nearly empty Pacific Ocean. Furthermore, only a fraction of that fraction could have returned to Japan, a country seldom visited by others and which, in any case, did not welcome the repatriation of its errant nationals. In addition, not all those allowed to return would have had their stories recorded in detail. In fact, castaways were strictly forbidden to speak to anyone of their adventures abroad once they had filed the required affidavit (*kuchigaki*) with both the Edo officials and those of the castaway's own local domain. Only if the very highest levels of government had found a castaway's story especially interesting would he be summoned for an exhaustive interview, from which a scholar (usually one versed in *rangaku*, "Dutch learning") would compile a detailed record of the subject's experiences. Again, according to Ibuse's historian in "A Watch and the Naoki Prize," some twelve hundred of these Edo texts, now known as hyōryūki, have been catalogued in libraries and archives throughout the country. Staggering in number, they bear witness of the power of men to survive all manner of natural and human obstacles.

That the hyōryūki would stir the imagination of Ibuse Masuji, himself a twentieth-century survivor, is no surprise. In his own castaway stories Ibuse preserves not only the essential details of the historical records but his own historical cynicism. The castaways themselves, Ibuse's portraits of them, and the heroes of so many of his other works, are caught between conflicting natural and political forces they can not control. Some of the original hyōryūki, compiled by domains unfriendly to the central government, were used as intelligence in their struggle against it; that government itself, when finally faced with hostile American and European powers at their door, executed a neat about-face and made the once-criminal castaways their interpreters and advisers. Survivors first of the seas, and then of the political vicissitudes of their age, Japanese castaways are prototypes of the ideal Ibuse hero: common man, the victim of circumstance, who survives through an intuitive reliance upon innate individual and cultural strengths.

The central figures of Ibuse's castaway stories are referred to as charmed in their fortunes, brave in their souls, resourceful in their imaginations, and nearly epic in their adventures. They might indeed be called epic characters, for they embody the national identity of the Japanese people from whom they are separated as castaways. That identity is sharply delineated within the castaway stories; once the sailors are among alien peoples and territories, they become obsessed with the problem of retaining their Japanese sense of self, apparently a fragile consensus that does not transplant easily. As in Defoe's *Robinson Crusoe*—which was translated into Japanese by Ibuse[2]—there is something profoundly expressive of national identity in Ibuse's castaway works as well as something allegorically autobiographical. Ibuse takes the original hyōryūki, retains their exotic

159
The
Castaways:
Usaburō
and
the
1950s

160

The
Castaways:
Usaburō
and
the
1950s

romanticism (men with such plebeian names as Ichirō and Dembei riding railroads, walking the streets of cosmopolitan cities, marrying foreign women, and so on) and adds, often between the lines, a new story of his own. *Castaway Usaburō* in particular is transformed into a historical and personal parable, the apologue of earlier Japanese who, like those of Ibuse's own time, found themselves lost and without the familiar cultural conventions upon which they had customarily relied. In the eighteenth and nineteenth centuries, this alienation was the result of a geographical dislocation; in the twentieth, of a psychological or technological one. The experiences may in some sense be contiguous, but in Ibuse's versions of the historical castaways for modern readers, attention is riveted on the reverse side of the lesson. Edo period audiences valued the hyōryūki, which they obtained only through privilege or stealth, for what they revealed of peoples who were *not* Japanese; for modern readers, Ibuse retells the same adventures for what they reveal of those who *are*. He supplies the hyōryūki with a wholly new gloss, a modern relevance, and a moving significance as the work of a man who has survived some difficult times himself.

This very significance has inspired Yasuoka Shōtarō to proclaim Ibuse's castaway stories as "a pillar of his literature."[3] Such works—and they are not limited to those which speak specifically of shipwrecked sailors—epitomize the central theme in much of Ibuse's best writing. "Ibuse's works are born from vagabondage," writes Kamei Katsuichirō,[4] echoing Yasuoka but going one crucial step further in universalizing the exceptional experience of the castaway, making it synonymous with being rootless, alone, even criminal. There are many criminals, exiles, and abandoned low-lifers in Ibuse's fiction. Theirs is a castaway experience brought about not by the power of the ocean but by the power of men. Wabisuke, for instance, knew that well. Kamei's term "vagabondage" (*hōrōreki*) finally points to that condition of an imposed alienation present in much of Ibuse's world, be it geographical, political, historical, or literary. Among Ibuse's hyōryūmono are included "Confinement," the story of a salamander trapped in a watery cave; "Sawan on the Roof," with its bird separated from the flock; and *Waves*, a panoramic sweep of history that casts its young hero into a life of sailing from one island of refuge to another. Perhaps much of Ibuse's wartime and postwar work should also be included, for the years

"Japanese Castaways"

Ibuse's interest in historical castaways dates from relatively early in his career. One source quotes him to the effect that his casual reading of a castaway account—A Report of Siberia (Hokusa bunryaku) —originally inspired him to study the subject.[5] It seems probable he read it in 1933, for in that year Ibuse published an important essay, "Japanese Castaways" (Nihon hyōmin). In this essay Ibuse states that he has just read two hyōryūki, Strange Tales of the Seas (Kankai ibun) as well as A Report of Siberia.[6] Both concern Japanese sailors marooned in Russia during the latter part of the eighteenth century. These two castaway reports are examples of those compiled secretly—A Report of Siberia by the Tokugawa shogunate and Strange Tales of the Seas by the Sendai domain—but later copied and widely read. Ibuse's encounter with these historical records excites his imagination. He wonders aloud in "Japanese Castaways" whether he might not write a work about such men and their troubles. Even in 1933 this topic is clearly compatible with much of his earlier work describing men and animals abandoned, isolated, and eventually restored. In fact, though images of the solitary survivor permeate Ibuse's literature, those of the castaway are the most starkly drawn. A frequent idiom in Ibuse's work, zekkai no kotō, is awkwardly rendered into English as "an isolated island on the far seas." On such desolate scraps of dry land are found, "a select few . . . surrounded by fortune in the midst of catastrophe,"[7] to quote historian Arakawa Hidetoshi, who considers the stories of castaways as one chapter in the long "history of Japanese calamities" (saigaishi).[8] Ibuse would agree. Those "select few" are some of Ibuse's most memorable and typical characters, average Japanese chosen by circumstances to be challenged in extraordinary ways. An even more select few will become Ibuse's typical heroes, for they will respond to the test by summoning special strengths that life under more hospitable conditions had obscured.

"Japanese Castaways" is an essay compiled from Ibuse's notes while reading A Report of Siberia and Strange Tales of the Seas. The

162
The
Castaways:
Usaburō
and
the
1950s

particular historical castaways on whom Ibuse focuses suggest what sort of shipwrecked protagonists will appear in his later fiction. For example, among those mentioned in *Strange Tales of the Seas,* Ibuse is most interested in the youngest of the four sailors, out of an original crew of sixteen, to return safely to Japan in 1804 after over ten years abroad. This fellow, known as Tajūrō, does not get along with either his fellow castaways or the Russians among whom he lives. The Russians treat the Japanese as a "stupid race" (*gumai na jinshu*) and have in fact rescued them for other than humanitarian reasons. The castaways are to be pawns in Russia's struggle to win concessions from the shogunate. First abused by the elements, then by the Russians, and finally by the Japanese officials who await them upon their repatriation, the sailors in *Strange Tales of the Seas* inspire Ibuse's sympathy as much as any other of his exploited historical characters.

Since these castaways are to be a gift from the Russians to the Japanese, they are given an audience before Czar Alexander I, if only to ensure a favorable report upon their return. The Czar's personal interpreter, a naturalized Japanese by the name of Nikolai Shinzō, had been shipwrecked himself years earlier in the then-Russian Aleutian Islands. He is a talented man, obviously a remarkable survivor who has risen to a high position in the Russian court. He is living proof, writes Ibuse, that "one cannot say that Japanese castaways of that time were necessarily stupid" (9:57). Nikolai is the only one of his crew to have remained in Russia. He had become a teacher at the Japanese language school in Irkutsk, a school in the tradition of the first such academy founded by Peter the Great, who had been an enthusiastic student of things Japanese, in St. Petersburg in 1705. Ibuse seems greatly interested in these schools—in another ironic twist of history, he was to teach in one himself while in Singapore—and he will write of them in detail in *Castaway Usaburō.* In "Japanese Castaways," however, his attention quickly returns to Tajūrō, his fellow castaways, and their rather different fate. For eight long years they wait in Irkutsk for passage home, working as common laborers and trusting in Russian good intentions. "Japanese Castaways" concludes:

> While they continued working as laborers in Irkutsk, one of their number, Kichirōji of Kotakehama, died of illness. He was not entitled to a church funeral since he died without having been baptized. The cast-

aways placed his body in a coffin and buried him in a plot they had pur-
chased on the edge of the cemetery. No one had money to buy a
gravestone, but later they contributed enough, little by little, to erect a
Japanese-style monument in his memory. On it they inscribed: "Kichirōji
of Kotakehama, Oga County, Sendai Domain, The Region of Mutsu,
Japan—The Twenty-eighth Day of the Second Month, The Eleventh Year
of the Kansei Period, Seventy-Three Years of Age." Tajūrō did the carving.

Among the graves of the Russians in this cemetery were the markers of
other Japanese who had been shipwrecked. There was one with the name
"Takeuchi Tokubei" carved on it, another so worn that only the words
"Tenth Year of the Kyōhō Period" were legible, and one grave identified
only as that of "Kyūhei of Matsumoto Village." [9:63]

Ibuse's first work about Japanese castaways ends where his personal memoirs begin—with a funeral. Not only does this passage
evoke past history, with its references to castaways who lived and
died in a distant, inhospitable Russia centuries ago, but it also evokes
a modern time when soldiers as well as sailors have continued to die
equally obscure deaths on equally ·distant, inhospitable battlefields.
Death plays as important a role in Ibuse's castaway literature as elsewhere. Indeed, the prominence of death in these stories points to the
crucial yet problematic significance of this theme in all his writing.
In the final paragraphs of "Japanese Castaways," death in Ibuse's
world must somehow be rendered appropriate, which is to say accepted within a religious, social, or cultural context. The castaways
in Irkutsk bring their comrade's life to a satisfactory conclusion
through the symbolism and ritual of erecting a Japanese stone monument in his memory. Ibuse drew a picture in the snow for his dead
friend Aoki Nampachi in "The Carp"; in "Japanese Castaways"
"Tajūrō did the carving." Ibuse's career spans a tumultuous seven
decades, but his thoughts about death and the need to insulate it with
ceremonies remains constant, perhaps because of that very tumult.
An obsession with death is assuaged with rituals, and this theme is
linked to the power of specifically cultural rituals: the funeral of
Kichirōji is one of the last means for his survivors to remain Japanese. Simultaneously, coincidentally, such rites rationalize the life of
the deceased. For that reason, they are rites that all of Ibuse's survivors, from himself in "The Carp" to the citizens of Hiroshima in
Black Rain, will cling to dearly.

164

The
Castaways:
Usaburō
and
the
1950s

Chōhei

Rituals of many sorts played a vital role in the first of Ibuse's fictionalized castaway works.[9] "Chōhei on an Uninhabited Island" (*Mujintō Chōhei*), and its sequel, "Chōhei's Grave" (*Chōhei no haka*), were both published in 1936.

The true story of Chōhei is told in such hyōryūki as *Depositions of the Returnees from an Uninhabited Island (Mujintō yori kikoku no mono gochōsho)*[10] and *Castaway Account of an Uninhabited Island (Mujintō hyōryūki)*.[11] These were the source for Ibuse's stories of five Tosa domain sailors marooned on a small island in 1785. This island, Torishima (also known as Marcus Island), is 590 kilometers south of Tokyo. Though it is now administratively part of that city, it is still uninhabited. In the eighteenth century, it must have seemed the antipodes to its castaways. Not until thirteen years later did Chōhei succeed in returning to Tosa, the only one of his crew to do so.

In some ways Ibuse's first castaway is his most interesting, for Chōhei is the only one placed in total solitude. This radical isolation allows Ibuse the freest hand in exploring how men behave when released from one environment and endangered by another. Arakawa, the hyōryūki historian, has attributed to such castaways "a great vital force."[12] This vitality makes men like Chōhei some of Ibuse's most compelling heroes. Tomoakira, Wabisuke, and other remarkable survivors not only demonstrate Ibuse's concept of the heroic, they define it. Perhaps none do so better than Chōhei, for in no other Ibuse work is the challenge of survival—staying alive marooned on a small and barren island—so starkly articulated. Chōhei has no choice but to build his world anew. None other exists. He is a man suddenly cast into a primitive past, but left with a sophisticated cultural memory. The historical and social legacy bequeathed Chōhei as a Japanese will manifest itself in his behavior on Torishima. In theory once shipwrecked he will be free to affirm or reject any of the conventions he had been coerced to follow in Tosa. Indeed, what Chōhei "keeps" and what he "discards" will lie at the core of Ibuse's stories about him, and at the root of Ibuse's interest in the whole of the castaway experience.

The first Chōhei story begins as if an essay. While touring Shikoku to see the ruins of the old Tosa domain, Ibuse has learned that along a stretch of the coast called Uda-no-Matsubara lies a grave marked

"Chōhei of the Uninhabited Island." Ibuse thus begins his first castaway story where his first castaway essay had concluded—in a cemetery. Although the Chōhei stories tell of one man's miraculous survival, Ibuse rather typically develops the narrative against the back drop of his demise. Uda-no-Matsubara is described as an impoverished place, its destitution epitomized in the humbleness of Chōhei's grave, a simple marker hardly recognizable among the pines. Ibuse notes with understatement, "Chōhei's life after returning from the deserted island was not, one may imagine, blessed in its last years" (9:198). With this one remark Ibuse establishes tension between Chōhei's historical uniqueness as a castaway and his historical anonymity as an indigent peasant.

Ibuse recounts Chōhei's life from the first month of 1785 when, at the age of twenty-four, he is hired to serve aboard a ship transporting rice between two Tosa coastal towns. While on his maiden voyage, however, a strong westerly wind blows the vessel off course southeast towards the open sea. Soon the crew realizes it has been caught in the midst of a typhoon, in a part of the ocean where typhoons are notoriously violent. (Ibuse notes that he himself saw on his sightseeing trip homes still damaged from a typhoon the previous year.) Chōhei and his fellow sailors drift for two weeks until they at last spy land—a small distant island. Unfortunately their broken rudder and sails makes navigation impossible. Only after praying fervently to the "gods and Buddhas" do they eventually drift towards the island, arriving the evening of the fourteenth day of the second month. Still, the rocky coast affords no natural harbor; the men are forced to anchor offshore and wait for daybreak. The following day they swim to shore, exhausted and having "narrowly escaped death."

This island, harboring no sign of humankind, is termed a *zekkai no kotō*, the most remote of terrains. The castaways are reduced to subsisting on weeds, raw shellfish, and the flesh of large gulls that, being ignorant of carnivorous species, do not flee when approached. Small indentations in rocks, and a barrel salvaged from the ship before it broke up on the shoals, provide their only means for collecting fresh water on the island. By the middle of the fifth month, when the gulls have migrated from the island, the four remaining castaways have devised a crude method of fishing. By using shellfish as bait on hooks made of nails and line twisted from bark, they are able to secure a source of protein to replace that of the departed birds. This first part of "Chōhei on an Uninhabited Island" reads as an adven-

166

The
Castaways:
Usaburō
and
the
1950s

ture of ingenuity and improvisation. When the birds return in the ninth month, the castaways prudently dry the meat of those they can still catch as a hedge against the day they will again fly off.

The focus of the story now shifts and becomes more interesting, more quintessentially Ibuse. None of the castaways' extraordinary measures to ensure their survival prevents one of their number from eventually succumbing to what Ibuse reservedly calls their "straitened existence" (*funyoi na kurashi*). The sailor dies on the twenty-ninth day of the ninth month of the first year of the castaways' self-appointed "Desert Island reign period" (*Mujintō kigen gannen*). Like Tomoakira in *Waves*, and like the survivors of Hiroshima who date their experiences not "August 6" or "August 7," but the "first day" and "second day," the castaways of Torishima construct abstract as well as practical systems of survival. They reorganize the course of their lives, and their comrade's death, about a new postcataclysmic chronology. They create this not because the previous reign period (*Temmei*) has been terminated, but because it is now, to a group of isolated survivors, wholly inappropriate. In inventing the term *Mujintō kigen gannen,* the castaways invent a new beginning for themselves, taking an important step towards dominating a world that had heretofore dominated them. Chōhei and his cohorts, both on Torishima and elsewhere in Ibuse's literature, find that time has no meaning beyond what they assign it. Suddenly, with the intervention of a calendar, the confines of their imprisonment are that much less narrow for being measured.

When Chōhei's remaining two companions on Torishima die, Chōhei is isolated not only from Japan but from any contact with human society. "Chōhei was left utterly alone on the small and distant island [*zekkai no kotō*] to be its sole exile" (9:201). In the fourth year of his Desert Island reign period (1788), however, Chōhei's absolute loneliness is mitigated when yet another Japanese ship drifts to Torishima. Suddenly he has the company of eleven new castaways, whose ship, unfortunately, is destroyed on the rocks. Marooned with Chōhei, their first project as a community of survivors is the dedication of a makeshift shrine to the sun goddess Amaterasu, which they have erected atop a knoll with a full view of the horizon. About this shrine the castaways quickly establish a pattern of ritual behavior:

> They agreed to make the fifteenth of the first, fifth, and ninth months major holy days on which all would pray together throughout the night.

Thus, the castaways intuitively extend the physical structure of the shrine with a liturgical presence. The shrine and the services of prayer they perform before it impose a social and mythic matrix, (i.e., an orderly arrangement that simultaneously regularizes time, behavior, and belief) upon their otherwise precarious existences. Such a powerful matrix, wherever it appears in Ibuse's work, marks a response when human beings, located either physically or culturally *in extremis,* are challenged by catastrophe. The mechanism of the matrix proves sturdy: Chōhei and his companions live within the provisional culture that they have built about their faith in the sun goddess for two years, until it is altered by the arrival of yet a third ship on Torishima's shores in 1790.

The story of this third ship, and with it Chōhei's eventual rescue, is told in the sequel, "Chōhei's Grave." Much remains to be explained, as Ibuse notes in the first line of this second account. Still to be explored is the continued and validating importance of rituals in the lives of Torishima's castaways, now numbering well over a dozen. These six new citizens bring more to the expanding community than simply themselves. They carry the tools that will enable them to build the vessel that takes them back to Japan:

> All the men on the island gathered together before the shrine to Amaterasu and pledged to build a ship capable of carrying them home. Amaterasu was the goddess to whom Chōhei and the rest prayed each day. They worshipped at this small shrine in a cave atop the same rocky hill from which they scouted the horizon. The shrine was made of little more than simple Shinto offerings of paper, but the castaways prayed there daily out of deep faith in its spirit. They begged that they be allowed to return to their homes soon. On the holy day of each month they devoted themselves exclusively to prayer. [9:204]

As in "Chōhei on an Uninhabited Island," life on Torishima as described in "Chōhei's Grave" is regulated by the small but original ceremonies of its transient population. The castaways elect no leader to direct them, nor do they abandon their devotion to Amaterasu once they have secured the means of their salvation, the tools: their system of faith is amply represented by a few strips of paper hung in a cave. The ritual life of the island flourishes, because their need to

168
The
Castaways:
Usaburō
and
the
1950s

make an overt expression of their hopes is not born of desperation. It is born, instead, of the ritual's practical use as a device for both psychic and social organization: psychic, because faith functions as an inner dynamic, placing the believer in a sustained and sustaining network of beliefs; and social, because faith is also an external dynamic, uniting the castaways into a community through the rites they celebrate.

At the same time they construct a faith, the castaways are busy building a boat. The project takes many arduous years. Finally, provisioned with rainwater and dried meat, Chōhei, thirteen years after he first swam ashore, departs with thirteen other survivors on the eighth day of the sixth month of 1797. They set forth in their homemade ark for wherever it may take them.

After only a few days at sea, they sight land, but it is only another island. Fortunately there are signs of human habitation. The castaways swim ashore and search for the natives. Here "Chōhei's Grave" momentarily dovetails with another of Ibuse's works written in the 1930s. The tragedy of the castaway marooned on the desert island merges with the tragedy of the exile on the destroyed island, for Chōhei finds himself on Aogashima at the time of the calamity described by Ibuse in "A General Account of Aogashima":

> The island was Aogashima, one of the Hachijōjima chain. There were nine households on it. Earlier the island had exploded and its whole population, more than two hundred and eighty people, had fled to Hachijōjima. One hundred and forty of them were lost at sea. The nine households on the island belonged to those few who had returned. Hot springs bubbled up from a number of spots on the island, and boiling water spewed forth from the bottom of a big lake more than two miles around. [9:205–06]

The Torishima castaways are soon taken from disaster-stricken Aogashima to Hachijōjima for interrogation. Although the official inquiries are tiresome, the local population more than compensates with food and other kindnesses, prompting the lucky returnees to thank "the gods and the Buddhas" for their good fortune.

Until the investigation is completed, however, the castaways are suspected criminals in the eyes of the law. One liberty upon which they insist, nonetheless, is the right to carry back to the Japanese mainland the remains of their comrades who died on Torishima.

They must fulfill their duty to the relatives of the deceased. The authorities refuse to permit even this, leaving the castaways no recourse but to inter their fellow sailors' bones within the grounds of a Hachijōjima temple. They request the services of a priest and order grave markers to be carved. Ibuse again returns the reader to his commemorative scene, that of the living honoring the dead. Graves naturally abound throughout his literature—the sites of his morbid obsession and a source of his writing's disturbingly powerful effect. Indeed, Chōhei's adventures are not to end until he attends yet another funeral rite, this time his own. Chōhei is the first of Ibuse's characters to be granted the unusual privilege of being memorialized in ceremonies conducted by relatives who assume him dead. In early 1798, his lengthy detainment by officialdom in Hachijōjima, Uraga, Edo, and Tosa at last over, Chōhei returns to his native village just in time to witness the scene of annual prayers offered for the repose of his soul:

> It was the twenty-ninth day of the first month, and the thirteenth memorial service of Chōhei's death was underway in his vacant house. The people gathered for this religious service imagined that it was Chōhei's spirit which now appeared before them. They rose to their feet in great agitation. Chōhei stood in his garden and calmly spoke of his remarkable adventures over the previous thirteen years in the smooth speech he had learned in Edo.
>
> Chōhei's grave remains in Matsubara in Tosa's Kishimoto Bay. It is marked by a humble gravestone one foot high and seven inches wide. [9:207]

Although such an antemortem consecration might be a unique personal experience, such moments are encountered elsewhere in Ibuse's works. This reversal of what might be thought the natural order of events occurs figuratively whenever Ibuse or his characters have stood on the high ground and watched flames soar high, or have felt the ground beneath them tremble; it occurs whenever the human imagination is allowed to contemplate both man's extraordinary talent for survival and his inevitable demise. This inversion of death and life is not always portrayed as "beautiful," as it is in "A Young Girl's Wartime Diary" and "Wabisuke"; sometimes the end is private and not spectacular. It may even be humble, like Chōhei's grave. Yet, in each instance, the creative task of an Ibuse story is to envision successfully either a death or a life otherwise thought inappropriate

170
The
Castaways:
Usaburō
and
the
1950s

within the context of history or nature. Chōhei never seems more a child of Ibuse's fancy than when he walks into his garden and glimpses the ritual end of his life.

Once in conversation, Ibuse remarked that the least earth tremor sends him fleeing into his own garden: in real life as in fiction, there are special places from which Ibuse imagines the experience of his own death, an experience he believes himself constantly spared.[13] The funeral represents the human counterpart of the pillar of fire and the whirlpool, a symbol of the social matrix insulating death to complement the natural. While Ibuse was writing of Chōhei—the mid-1930s—he was also busy constructing his social and natural worlds of death in other works, specifically in "The River" and *Waves*. The personal inspiration of Ibuse's castaway works must be sought where all his literature is found, in the curious terror of an apparently saturnine world. His biographical account of Chōhei both commences and concludes with a reference to his gravestone, itself an enduring text that functions much as does Ibuse's journal, "Voyage South," namely, as a memento (*kinen*) of life under extraordinary adversity. The Chōhei stories reveal the same thematization of Ibuse's evolving natural and historical worlds as do "The River" or *Waves*, the same emphasis upon the centrality of death as does "The Carp," the same account of the historical oppression of the common man as do "Lieutenant Lookeast" or "Wabisuke," and the same creative and formal use of ritual as do his most recent works. Ibuse's early interest in the potential of hyōryūki for extending the metaphors of themes seems entirely appropriate, for in those first years as well as the later, he has been a writer concerned with what sets a man adrift from, and conversely anchors him to, his self and his culture.

The Castaway Account of John Manjirō

Ibuse's next work based on Japan's historical castaways remains his best known. Indeed, until *Black Rain* made the name Shigematsu nearly synonymous with Ibuse's own, the hero of *The Castaway Account of John Manjirō* (*Jon Manjirō hyōryūki*, 1937), Nakahama Manjirō (known in some Western accounts as John Mung), was arguably Ibuse's most famous and popular character. Manjirō's life story—that of a humble sailor who by dint of his own talents as well as extraordinary good fortune rose to great prominence—has become one of several familiar rags-to-riches legends typical of the pioneering Meiji period. Ibuse chose to write of Manjirō perhaps because he was the most spectacular of Japan's many castaways—he had become a genuine folk hero.[14] Or perhaps because his story was guaranteed to excite the adventuresome Japanese imagination much as the inspirational stories of Horatio Alger had intrigued American dreamers.

Reduced to their simplest, the plots are attractively similar: small-town boy goes away and makes good. "When John Manjirō left Tosa," writes Ibuse in "A Watch and the Naoki Prize," " . . . he was an uneducated, illiterate youth, yet he possessed a very great sense of curiosity. That is what I was writing about" (14:461). Just as with watakushi in *Waves*, Ibuse writes of a maturing youth in this first castaway novel. Unlike watakushi, however, Manjirō meets not a tragic end but an illustrious one, for Ibuse's "uneducated, illiterate youth" was destined to become a *hatamoto*, a personal retainer of the shogun. In 1860 he was further honored by his inclusion in Japan's first diplomatic mission dispatched to the United States. No doubt it was this remarkable tale of adversity met with able ambition that made *John Manjirō* such a popular success. This novel, and not the inescapably somber *Waves*, won for Ibuse the 1938 Naoki Prize.

Yet *John Manjirō*, still regarded as one of his more important works, remains something of an anomaly within Ibuse's oeuvre. Closely, almost indistinguishably, drawn from historical sources, *John Manjirō* deliberately suppresses obvious artistic invention. Ibuse intended a modern version of an original *hyōryūki* which would lay claim to the same degree of authenticity. Although Ibuse frequently resorts to the use of historical records, even in his most imaginative enterprises, nowhere but in *John Manjirō* do these documents so dominate both structure and style that they exclude the typical Ibuse narrative voice—that detached and omniscient first-person perspective perfected by the time he began work on his castaway stories. When Ibuse claimed he "translated" and edited a twelfth-century diary in *Waves*, he was, in fact, making fiction; in *John Manjirō* his heavy reliance on actual historical texts has nearly an opposite effect, "de-fictionalizing" a novel that employs all the elements of imaginative writing.

Ibuse drew his material from two hyōryūki, *Castaway Adventures* (*Hyōkaku kidan*)[15] and *Castaway Manjirō Returns to Japan* (*Hyōryū Manjirō kichō ki*),[16] as well as from Nakahama Tōichirō's later

172

The
Castaways:
Usaburō
and
the
1950s

biography of his father, *The Life of Nakahama Manjirō* (*Nakahama Manjirō den*).[17] He is hardly troubled by the largely derivative nature of his efforts. Indeed, Ibuse boasts in "A Watch and the Naoki Prize" that *John Manjirō* is the only one of his works included in a multi-volumed anthology of *kiroku bungaku,* or "documentary literature."[18] In the same essay Ibuse somewhat defensively maintains that since there have been so many accounts told of Manjirō, including an enactment of his life on the Kabuki stage by Danjūrō IX in the Meiji period, his story now belongs in the public domain, available for use by any writer. Perhaps Ibuse undertook the project not to elaborate on an already well-known plot, but to experiment with the peculiar powers and limits of historiographic writing. In retrospect *John Manjirō* seems not only a treatment of a favored Ibuse theme, that of the castaway, but an extreme instance of his search for narrative authenticity. "This is not fiction. I simply put together the documents [that had been lent me]. It was written precisely to be documentary literature," states Ibuse of *John Manjirō.*[19]

An author's analysis of his own means and objectives is not, however, necessarily exhaustive. The question of *John Manjirō*'s relationship to the notions of fiction (*shōsetsu*) and fact (*kiroku*) cannot rest solely on the basis of Ibuse's intent, but must take into consideration the readers' response. Even granted that the distinction between the original and the derivative has been traditionally murky in Japan, few writers in the modern period have been as free as Ibuse in borrowing from documents (including diaries and memoirs) for inclusion in their fiction. Always, however, Ibuse is careful to preserve the sense of such texts as historical artifacts. They consequently lend a substantiating weight to his writing, imbuing the stories with a powerful, often ironic, intertextuality—and no more so than when the documents are wholly fanciful. Sincerity and insincerity, in the sense of what a reader trusts and what he must pretend to trust, cohabit in the text—much to Ibuse's success. The combination provides the critically aware audience with an additional level of discourse, namely, the intriguing dialogue that Ibuse conducts with his documents.

Ibuse is not a writer who cares to explain his works—he once disparaged interviews, calling them police interrogations[20]—but he is unusually introspective in an essay written just when he had begun *John Manjirō*. In "'But,' 'Then,' 'However'" ("*Ga,*" "*soshite,*" "*shi-*

173
The
Castaway
Account
of John
Manjirō

kashi," 1936) Ibuse declares that he desires for himself not a "perfect" style but one "in accord with the material I wish to write."[21] There is no confusion here of a work and its sources, but instead a sophisticated dialectic of his stylistic autonomy as an author and his insistence upon an equal and distinct autonomy for his work. Ibuse controls his materials and is controlled by them; the game becomes complicated, and a work such as *John Manjirō*, based on actual records, demonstrates that a structural as well as a thematic tension has always been incumbent within Ibuse's method. This tension will be exploited more fully in *Black Rain,* where it takes on moral as well as literary implications. But, like that much later novel, *John Manjirō* is also a work in which, due to its careful correspondence with historical fact, the reader feels the power of a taboo on the flight of literary imagination.

Ibuse published, and apparently wrote, *John Manjirō* quickly. It appeared as a book without prior serialization in November 1937. The novel's nine chapters traverse the historically hectic Japanese nineteenth century. As a result, it is Ibuse's most rapidly paced major work. His authorial attentions seldom meander or digress, one sure sign that he is following the dry and elliptic histories rather than the usual whims of his fanciful mind. Another such sign is the explanatory title he gives each of the chapters—old fashioned epithets suggesting the hyōryūki from which the novel derives. The first of these is "Manjirō and Four Other Fishermen Are Set Adrift upon the Waves." Ibuse delves immediately into his material without the usual preface explaining his stance vis-à-vis the work; the reader is meant to accept the narrative with total naïveté.

Manjirō was born sometime in 1827 in the Tosa coastal village of Nakanohama. He lived an early life of poverty that allowed no such luxuries as education. From a tender age he worked on fishing boats, and so on the fifth day of the first month of his fifteenth year, 1841, he went out to sea for the traditional first catch of the year. Manjirō was accompanied by four other hands: the thirty-eight-year-old Denzō, Denzō's twenty-five-year-old brother Jūsuke, Denzō's fifteen-year-old son Goemon, and the twenty-seven-year-old Toraemon. They had little luck in catching any sea bass, the auspicious symbol of the New Year. This portent bode them ill. Soon a strong wind rose to make the sea so rough they could not haul in their nets. Rain fell to obscure visibility.

174

The
Castaways:
Usaburō
and
the
1950s

They put themselves in the hands of fate. While they lay prostrate on the deck of their ship, the five men prayed to the gods and the Buddhas. The ship seemed to be drifting towards the southeast. [2:69]

The storm continued for days. Soon their meager store of rice was gone. Then, as the temperature turned bitterly cold, hunger and exposure took their toll on Goemon:

> Denzō, his father, took a slip of paper with words written on it from his bag of amulets. In lieu of real medicine he placed it in Goemon's mouth. To all appearances this seemed to bring his fever down by half. [2:70]

The ritual of prayer was supplemented with the ritual of magic writing: Denzō trusted in the power of his amulet-text to cure his son's affliction. Such sorcery has a history. When Ibuse himself was ill as a child, his grandfather, as noted earlier, would write his name on the back of a turtle hoping to heal him. Just as Ibuse indeed survived, perhaps due to the empathic efficacy of their prayers and ceremonies, the castaways soon thereafter sighted land. After anchoring nearby, Toraemon persuasively argued that since they were all so close to death, they had no choice but to attempt a landing. The next day they scaled the rocky shores and successfully made it to dry land.

In the second chapter, "The Castaways Look for Rescue on a Distant Isle," the fishermen scouted their new home and discovered it to be a small uninhabited island. Manjirō, like Chōhei and other castaways before him, had drifted to Torishima. Its latest guests were at once relieved and frightened to find this refuge. "Perhaps even the barren Mountain of Swords [*tsurugi no yama*] depicted in Buddhist paintings of hell had been inspired by what they saw here" (2:73).

Closer inspection of the island revealed evidence of sailors shipwrecked long before themselves. Manjirō and the others soon learned, like their predecessors, to survive on whatever rare fish or fowl was available. The men of *John Manjirō*, no different from Ibuse's other castaways or many of his characters in general, had been suddenly transported into a vacuum and had thereby been deprived of the references to an identifiable geography, culture, and political society by which they would customarily have defined themselves. They soon, however, set about shaping such references anew. Toraemon, fearing that they had drifted perilously far north, wondered aloud whether they had, in fact, come to the very edge of the world. Denzō's response intitiated the castaways' task of reconstruction:

> "The edge of the world can be reached in any direction—north, south, east or west—if only you go far enough. But even if we're nowhere near the edge, I can't in my wildest dreams imagine that any ship that could save us would be sailing this far out. When we set foot on this island, it was to stay until we all rot. Yet, in another way, we could think of our arrival here as the beginning of a new world [*ame-tsuchi no hajime*]. Are we that brave?"

The four others replied affirmatively, and so it was decided. In other words, when they declared that day the first in their Year One of the Desert Island reign period, they chose to affirm themselves as men who treasure their own lives. [2:75]

This is a crucial passage in Ibuse's castaway literature, for it articulates the fundamental attitude of the victim towards his condition of victimization. First, the stranded fishermen accepted their fate ("we all rot"). Then they mitigated it by agreeing to share a myth, namely, that they had returned to the most sacred site of their cosmology, the place where the world began. In effect, they would replace their loss of a geographical certainty with a religious one. Denzō offered no rationale for his creative interpretation of their predicament, nor was one needed. Subsequently the castaways adopted a new chronology, in a move similar to watakushi's insistence upon observing the old calendar (*Waves*) and identical to Chōhei's declaration of a *Mujintō kigen gannen*. All time henceforth was dated from the establishment of this chronology marked from the "original" year of their shipwrecked arrival on Torishima. The castaways neatly had provided themselves with both a mythological past and a measurable future.

In this remote corner of the world—perhaps mortally close to its edge—the castaways began, with the assistance of both a cosmology and a calendar, to restructure a cultural context within which to dwell. This context enabled them "to affirm themselves as men who treasure their own lives." Much of the work in imposing such a context upon their new home was linguistic: recognizing the authority of words, they named everything, not only their island as *ame-tsuchi no hajime* (literally "the beginning of heaven and earth"), but all the vital accessories of their existence. The three barrels in which they col-

176

The
Castaways:
Usaburō
and
the
1950s

lected precious rainwater were dubbed "The Well of Life," "The Well of Pure Water," and "The Reserve Well." Where no culture, no abstract sustenance, previously existed, the castaways improvised with simple words behind which loomed powerful ideas.

However necessary such ideological or social artifices were for survival, they were not sufficient. The physical well-being of the castaways deteriorated steadily over the ensuing several months. Eventually only Manjirō remained relatively healthy. Thus it was he who, then in the sixth month, caught sight of a ship sailing on the horizon. This ship, the American whaler *John Howland,* dispatched a dinghy close to shore and beckoned the Japanese to swim out to it. But the castaways were frightened by this sudden appearance of non-Japanese. Only Manjirō—by this point in the novel obviously the most intelligent, capable, and daring of the lot—was brave enough to do so. When it was clear that the Americans' intentions were benign, the rest allowed themselves to be rescued.

The third chapter, "The Castaways Evermore Distant from Their Homeland," describes life aboard the *John Howland,* a whaler out of New Bedford under the command of a Captain Whitfield. The Japanese, bewildered by the exotic and unexpectedly comfortable way of life on the big ship, were soon nursed back to health. Manjirō developed a passionate interest in whaling and in no time was assisting the crew. Six months later—it was now late November 1841—the *John Howland* sailed into Honolulu, capital of the Sandwich Islands and at the time the largest whaling port in the world. The local authorities granted the castaways landed-immigrant status, but Captain Whitfield, who had grown quite fond of Manjirō over their months at sea together, proposed to take him back to New England for a "proper" education. This posed a serious dilemma for the castaways. Should they allow themselves to be separated in a strange land? Finally Manjirō's own ambition to see the world prevailed, and his comrades acquiesced to Whitfield's plans.

With this turn of the plot, *John Manjirō* becomes the exclusive story of Manjirō and his odyssey around the globe. Now known as "John," after the name of the ship that saved him, he sailed with Whitfield around Cape Horn to reach New Bedford in 1844. Whitfield left him in the care of a local family and set sail once more. John, however, heard the call of the sea himself and in 1846 joined a whaling crew. His travels took him around Africa to Australia, Java, and then the Ryūkyū Islands. There John, now the ship's first mate, boarded a launch and rowed out to a group of native fishermen. He attempted to communicate with them, clumsily, in his Tosa Japanese. The locals, of course, were bewildered by this sailor in Western garb trying to speak some distant cousin of their language. They refused even to acknowledge his shouted greetings. John returned to his ship without success.

Later, while calling in Honolulu, John was briefly reunited with his fellow castaways. In his absence they had fashioned new lives for themselves. Toraemon was a carpenter's apprentice, while Denzō and his son were farming after an ill-fated attempt to return to Japan. Only Jūsuke was gone, having succumbed to illness.

John continued in his new career as a whaler until he heard of the gold rush in California. He left the seas for the hills and, he hoped, his fortune. He was soon cheated by a Dutch prospector and was forced to book passage on a ship to Honolulu. There, possibly discouraged by his experiences in California, John intended to make plans with the three other surviving castaways to repatriate. He discovered, however, that he may have waited too long for this change of heart. Goemon had not only converted to Christianity but had married a local girl. Should he have returned to Japan, he might have been able to hide his conversion from the authorities, but never a wife. Moreover, Denzō would not return home if it meant leaving his son behind. Finally, however, under considerable pressure, Goemon relented and agreed to desert his wife.

> They spoke in Japanese to keep their conversation private.
>
> "I don't know if it's a good thing or bad," said Denzō, "but in Tosa there's an old saying—'The heart is a demon.'" He looked for a reaction on his son's face.
>
> Goemon turned pale. Denzō continued.
>
> "Tora', listen to me. You too, Manjirō. I have lived to this day only to return to Japan."
>
> John and Toraemon nodded deeply but remained silent. Goemon thought for a while and finally said, "I'll return with you."
>
> They agreed not to let his wife know of their plans and to board a ship in secret. [2:111–12]

First, however, they had to find a ship. John persuaded the captain of a trader headed for Shanghai, the *Sarah Boyd*, to let them come along in the hope that the ship might pass close enough to Japan to enable them to row to shore. Their plans were set, but Toraemon had

178
The
Castaways:
Usaburō
and
the
1950s

a change of heart: he protested that the venture was too risky, but in fact he had lost his desire to return to Japan. Hawaii was now his home.

John prepared the dinghy, christened the *Adventure,* that would carry him and his countrymen from the *Sarah Boyd* to the shores of their native Japan. In the seventh chapter, "All Goes Well and the Castaways Row to the Ryūkyūs to Return to the Villages of Their Births," the Japanese found themselves in early 1851 close enough to row ashore in the *Adventure.* They were not near to Satsuma proper in southern Kyūshū but rather to Okinawa. Their arrival frightened off the local villagers. Even Denzō, whose Japanese had remained the most intact over the past decade, was unable to make himself understood. "Nothing gets across," he complained. "Perhaps I have forgotten Japanese in the long time I was abroad" (2:119).

This interesting phenomenon—Japanese "forgetting" their language—is exploited by Ibuse in this novel to raise in one more way the entire question of self-definition. Indeed, the officials' problem in determining the nationality of these castaways takes up some pages in *John Manjirō.* "The locals thought these three were castaways from a foreign country" (2:120) and not Japanese at all. This, of course, accounts for some part of the great interest Japanese have taken in their castaways—men simultaneously foreign and native. Such an idea is patently impossible, given the rules of Japanese society, and yet highly desirable. In this sense John Manjirō epitomizes the Japanese castaway, for none was ever so outlandishly barbarian as he. He seemed the most bizarre of the three, and he made the officials who received them exceedingly nervous. None of the castaways, in fact, was really believed to be Japanese until they were caught observing a convention adjudged to be quintessentially and exclusively native:

> The officials testified that the castaways must be Japanese because they ate rice with chopsticks. The officials still could not say, however, just to what extent these castaways had been made dangerous, or civilized. [2:121]

Significantly, a social custom was used to define the castaways in *John Manjirō*—much as other such ritualized acts have been used by Ibuse characters elsewhere to define themselves. Satisfied that they were indeed dealing with their own kind, the officials began their interrogation in earnest. The interviews in Okinawa lasted seven

months. All the while, however, the castaways were well treated, for 179
*The
Castaway
Account
of John
Manjirō* the Satsuma officials in charge in Okinawa were careful to keep their sudden windfalls—men with knowledge of the outside world— cooperative.

The questioning continued after the castaways were moved to the Satsuma capital, Kagoshima. They were asked repeatedly not only about their personal experiences, but about the state of American politics, education, and armaments. Only John—known again as Manjirō—was brave enough to answer all the questions. The information gained was, naturally, for the benefit of Satsuma and not the shogunate; the central government in Edo was apprised of only the barest facts. Not until the latter part of 1851 were the castaways transferred, as the law dictated, to the Edo government authorities in Nagasaki.

Once in Nagasaki, the principal center for the disposition of re- turned castaways, the cycle of interrogations began again. In addi- tion to endless questioning, the castaways were required to trample a crucifix to prove they were not Christians. Goemon complied with- out the least hint of a troubled conscience. More questioning fol- lowed the castaways' return to Tosa in the summer of 1852. Finally Manjirō was freed that autumn, twelve years after a storm had blown him off course. He went home to his mother in Nakanohama and resumed his life as an ordinary, if somewhat stigmatized, peas- ant.

Here most castaway tales would end. History, however, conspired to prolong Manjirō's story. The following year, 1853, Commodore Perry sailed into Uraga, thus ending not only Japan's isolation but also Manjirō's. Suddenly Manjirō was summoned to Edo by the highest levels of the government—Lord Abe Masahiro, in fact, the progressive ruler of the Fukuyama domain mentioned in Ibuse's memoirs—to share his knowledge of the United States. As befitted one with such responsibilities, Manjirō was awarded an appropriate status:

> This social outcast, forbidden to live outside of Tosa, was made a per- sonal retainer of the shogun in one fell swoop. It might be said that he rode upon the wave of the times [*jisei no nami*]. In the official circles of the day it was a startling appointment. [2:131]

At his own suggestion, Manjirō's long experience at sea was put to use in the establishment of a shipbuilding program. Then, in 1860,

180
The
Castaways:
Usaburō
and
the
1950s

he was ordered to accompany the Japanese mission sailing to the United States to conclude commercial treaties. One of ninety diplomats headed by Shimmi Masaoki and Muragaki Norimasa and including Fukuzawa Yukichi, Manjirō was of considerable assistance as an interpreter and adviser. Upon his return to Japan he again threw himself into projects for Japan's modernization. The civil war put an end to the government's shipbuilding enterprises, but Manjirō's star continued to rise after the Restoration under the new Meiji oligarchy. After having represented Tosa interests in Edo, after leading a military delegation to Europe, and after having served as a vice-principal of the Kaisei Gakkō (at one time the government's department for Western studies, and later a school eventually incorporated into the Tokyo Imperial University), Manjirō of Nakahama died, a distinguished public figure, in 1898, the year of Ibuse's birth.

Manjirō's final eminence makes him an unusual Ibuse character. This is, in part, a distinction dictated by historical fact and not by any authorial intention. Yet Ibuse's deliberate choice of Manjirō as the hero of his first castaway novel should suggest some consistency of purpose. Indeed, Manjirō is a typical Ibuse hero insofar as all are, without exception, uncanny survivors. Some are survivors who, like Manjirō, surmount great physical and practical adversities through the exercise of will or sheer vigor; others, like Ibuse himself, survive in the sense that they outlive those especially close to them. This challenge simply to remain intact over time takes place within a broad context of vague discomfort—one recalls what Ibuse felt as a young man—and it is a challenge to live without succumbing to that despair.

In this, Manjirō was a success. He, perhaps more than any other Ibuse character, adapted the most readily to everchanging circumstances. "Manjirō" became "John" who became "Manjirō" again. The evolution seemed effortless. Manjirō might be called an ultimate survivor, a winner in New Bedford as well as Edo. His career was far more illustrious, certainly more celebrated, than that of any other Ibuse character, and it was strikingly different from any of the obscure anonymous lives told of in "The River" or *Waves*. But all were united by the common assault of natural and historical forces upon them and their times, and by their common reaction of assimilation. The victims of the river synthesized the vicissitudes of a violent natural world into their life cycle: the victims of a civil war turned their experiences into written accounts; and the victim of a wayward fishing boat put his innate talents to work in both foreign and elite cultures.

Castaway Usaburō

Ibuse's next castaway novel was not written until two decades after *John Manjirō*, not until Ibuse himself had been a castaway. The Second World War and its radical dislocation of Ibuse, in both a literal physical and abstract psychic sense, inspired a great range of diverse writing that might well be considered twentieth-century hyōryūmono; "Voyage South" is the obvious example; "Wabisuke," perhaps the more interesting one. But the war did more than broaden and deepen Ibuse's understanding of how the "shipwrecked" experience had moved to the center of contemporary cultural discourse. The war fundamentally changed that understanding.

Although Manjirō may have prefigured Usaburō, insofar as both were men suddenly and existentially challenged by an alien world, Usaburō more significantly prefigured the hero of Ibuse's novel of Hiroshima. Usaburō and Shigematsu are both "postwar" protagonists, men who have survived yet still remain profoundly alienated from their own eras and societies. For Ibuse, the simplicity of Manjirō's success was displaced by the complexity of Usaburō's failure. Critical opinion concurs that *Castaway Usaburō* is the pinnacle of Ibuse's castaway literature because of this sophisticated modernity implicit in a historical work. One critic has termed it as great a masterpiece as *Black Rain*.[22] Both are novels in which the post-1945 Ibuse insists upon remaining personally present in the narrative.

Unlike his oblique absence from the telling of *John Manjirō*, Ibuse is conspicuous in *Castaway Usaburō* as a narrator entering and leaving the story. At times he identifies with Usaburō, as he never does with Manjirō. In fact, a close look reveals that *Castaway Usaburō* is a novel as dependent upon Ibuse's own recent castaway experiences in Southeast Asia and the Japanese countryside as it is on historical hyōryūki. *Castaway Usaburō* cannot be the heroic work *John Manjirō* was, for wars in the twentieth-century have had a way of rendering heroism absurd. The novel is frankly antiheroic. Usaburō rejects the values that Manjirō embraced; the result, perhaps, of Ibuse's and his culture's postwar disillusionment and his subsequent use of the

182
The
Castaways:
Usaburō
and
the
1950s

castaway as a metaphor for that process. In *John Manjirō* the marooned condition is an agent permitting a character the full scope of his abilities; in *Castaway Usaburō* that same condition is the very heart of the work. This shift in emphasis is attributable to the author's own changed perspective in their interim.

However much Ibuse may have made Usaburō a character reflective of his own experiences, he is presented as an actual historical figure. The factual background in *Castaway Usaburō* is drawn from four hyōryūki, according to the novel: two extant accounts, *Tales of the Barbarians (Bandan)*[23] and *The Tale of the Clock (Tokei monogatari)*,[24] and two others possibly of Ibuse's own invention, *Report of the Castaways (Hyōmin bunsho)*[25] and *Tales of Foreign Lands (Ikoku monogatari)*.[26] All four sources tell of the crew of the Etchū rice ship *Chōja-maru* and their adventures after they drifted off course on their way to Edo in 1838. Only *Tales of Foreign Lands*, however, records in any detail the story of the galley hand Usaburō. Like Toraemon in *John Manjirō*, Usaburō, once rescued, chose to remain abroad rather than return to Japan. On account of such outlaw conduct, any mention of him was scrupulously avoided in the official records compiled upon his fellow crewmen's repatriation. Had Ibuse been so inclined, he could have chosen as the main character in his novel not Usaburō but Jirokichi, a quick-witted sailor in the mold of Manjirō. But the exceptional no longer interested Ibuse. Rather, he focused on a youth of average abilities who, like all of Ibuse's postwar protagonists, was the passive object and not the active subject of historical and social forces.

Castaway Usaburō is complex in plot as well as characterization. The story races across continents and through numerous dramatic situations. It reads as a novel should, with a richness of descriptive detail and psychological insight lacking in *John Manjirō*. *Castaway Usaburō* opens with a lengthy preface, including a plot précis told in Ibuse's own voice. He tells us that in the Tempō era, in a small Echigo village, there lived a sailor by the name of Kinroku. Kinroku had a younger brother, Usaburō, who, unlike Kinroku himself, was timid by nature. Already the reader may assume that here is a character who is not apt to become a personal retainer of the shogun. Kinroku was dependable (*shikkarimono*); Usaburō, lazy (*guzu*). Yet once Ibuse observes that the historical records reveal little of Usaburō,[27] he takes upon himself as author the task of retrieving

Usaburō from historical obscurity. In "Sacrifices" Ibuse did much the same for his fallen comrades in the Second World War, and *Castaway Usaburō* only contributes to the impression that his most earnest intent in the postwar years was to act as a literary caretaker for obscured or forgotten graves.

At length, Ibuse begins the story in detail. Unlike Manjirō, Usaburō has no love of the sea. He becomes a mess hand on the *Chōja-maru* only because he has no other opportunities. Thus, at age eighteen, he and the rest of the crew—Kinroku, the captain Heishirō, first mate Hachizaemon, hands Tasaburō, Yoshiemon, Rokubei, Shichizaemon, Jirokichi, Isaburō, and Kinzō—leave Matsumae for Edo on the tenth day of the tenth month of the year 1838. But this is an "inauspicious" (*engi no warui*) moment to begin their voyage, for the *Chōja-maru* collides with another vessel on its way out of the harbor and has to lay in for repairs.

As is the custom, the crew commissions the reading of sutras and other propitious ceremonies for the success of their journey. The faith of these eleven sailors in the power of ritual sets the tone early in the novel, in which such scenes are frequent. Unfortunately, the value of these religious precautions is placed in doubt when a priestess, employed to purify the ship, warns that they will encounter trouble near the end of the following month. The crew, normally devout, react to her doomsaying with laughter and derision.

The priestess' prophecy is fulfilled. Once back at sea, the *Chōja-maru* encounters bad weather. They are blown off course. Soon they discover their provisions to be unexpectedly low; Heishirō had secretly sold most of their rice before they left land. Yoshiemon shows signs of hysteria and then true insanity. The rest of the hungry crew struggles for five days to save their ship from the raging storms, after which time, defeated and exhausted, "they surrendered to fate and slept."

Unfavorable weather continues for several weeks. The *Chōja-maru* drifts far from Japan. In desperation its crew, like *Ibuse*'s earlier castaways, turn to simple expressions of religious belief to save themselves. They pray not for rescue but for the salvation of their souls. Death does indeed appear certain. By the middle of the twelfth month it is clear that they have drifted very far north. The weather grows wintry. The rice has almost entirely been consumed. Tempers flare. "As the rice gradually disappeared, the mood of the crew grad-

184

The
Castaways:
Usaburō
and
the
1950s

ually grew violent" (6:81). At the conclusion of the novel's first of twenty-one chapters, however, Usaburō makes an interesting discovery within his own diminishing rations:

> "A fertile kernel! I'll plant it. Even one is enough. I'll start a rice nursery with it."
> Usaburō suddenly shouted out the news of his find, frightening Hachizaemon who had been lying nearby.
> Hachizaemon got up. "But Usa'," he said, "There's no soil."
> All he needed was a little. There was a big planter with a plum tree in it on deck. As for water, he could make do with squeezing water from a cloth into a box whenever it rained. [6:82]

This minuscule rice kernel suddenly gives Usaburō added reason to live. Much like those flood victims of "The River" who rebuild their lives by adapting to, and identifying with, the natural cycle of the river and its seasons, Usaburō sees his whole future foretold in the potential of a seed. Wabisuke enjoys a special and sustaining communion with his birds; Usaburō will nurture himself through nurturing a plant.

Just when Usaburō contemplates the initiation of one life cycle with his kernel of rice, another comes to its conclusion with the death of Isaburō from deprivation. Ironically, his death is followed by a "merciful rain," which his survivors collect and offer to his lifeless corpse as a posthumous sacrament. Water remains a symbol continually accompanying and contrasting with death; in *Castaway Usaburō*, water both threatens and succors the castaways. The hull of the *Chōja-maru* springs a leak that requires the crew to bail out the hold daily. Throughout these increasingly dark days, however, Usaburō does not forget the promise of life foretold in his discovery of the fertile rice kernel:

> Today was the seventh-day observance of Isaburō's death. Usaburō was resting in a corner after bailing out the hold when Hachizaemon, who had been close by, chewing on grains of rice one at a time, spoke.
> "Say, Usa', the other day you told me you were going to make a rice nursery in the dirt from the tree pot. You've given up already?"
> "Oh, that. There's not enough water. There's nothing I can do. I'll plant the kernel once we reach land."
> By now even drinking water had to be conserved carefully. Usaburō's new idea was to make his rice paddy when, fate willing, they drifted to

land. He had put his one kernel of unhulled rice in an envelope and stored it in a drawer underneath the Shinto altar. There Usaburō did not fear its becoming wet from the ocean brine.

"Usa', what do you make of this?"

Hachizaemon rose to show Usaburō something on the palm of his hand. It was another kernel of unhulled rice.

"'Hey, that's a kernel of nonglutinous rice."

"Right. I found it among the regular rice. As long as you won't eat it, I'll give it to you as a present." [6:88–89]

The discovery of still another seed makes Usaburō's ambition more feasible in theory, but the continuing scarcity of water precludes it in practice. The problem of water soon becomes one of life and death for the crew itself. "No one spoke of who would die first, yet the question occupied all their thoughts" (6:94). Their unspoken if natural curiosity is satisfied when Yoshiemon dies on the twelfth day of the fourth month. The others seem not far behind. Usaburō can barely stand. (One recalls how robust Manjirō had been; *Castaway Usaburō* is, in this respect as others, a self-consciously postwar work.) Kinroku is the strongest, but he is plagued with problems other than physical. Due to Heishirō's ineptness, the mantle of leadership falls upon Kinroku's shoulders. Consequently he feels responsible for everyone's welfare. His personal guilt over the plight of the *Chōja-maru* finally drives him to commit suicide. The rest of the crew, now abandoned by the only one of their number with any seafaring ability, is too weak even to bail out the hold any longer. They turn to their last hope:

Funadama is the guardian deity of ships. All ships usually install their *funadama* in the hole where the mast stands. The deity's image is fashioned from a paper model, two dice from a board game, and hair taken from the head of the shipowner's wife. It is said that if a ship should be destroyed or its crew killed off, it means that its *funadama* has earlier escaped to someplace else.

Fortunately the *Chōja-maru*'s deity was still safe within its amulet bag. All the men sighed with relief, an expression that their faint hopes were still alive. If the *funadama* had indeed fled, and their divinations had foretold ill fortune, it would have amounted to a promise of a watery death in a hold continuing to fill with brine.

They gathered at the cabin near the ship's bow. Heishirō tore a paper into four pieces, lined them up, and wrote "Thou wilt not die" on one.

186
The
Castaways:
Usaburō
and
the
1950s

On each of the others he wrote "I invoke the Name of Lord Amitabha Buddha" and folded them all. Heishirō patted the folded slips with Shinto paper cuttings from the shrine at Mt. Hakusan to purify them. Believing this would decide whether they should live or die, they put their hands together in supplication and prayed out loud.

While Heishirō joined in the prayers he placed the slips and the paper cutting into a small box and turned it upside down. When he lifted the box one of the slips lay on top of the Shinto cutting. All of their fates would be determined by whatever words were written on it. Heishirō reverently raised it to his forehead and, breathing heavily, unfolded it.

"Thou wilt not die," he read in a quivering voice. [6:95–96]

This divination rite was often conducted by sailors whenever they lacked confidence in their decisions. Used to resolve such questions as a vessel's bearing, or how many days remained until land would be reached, this historical ritual was performed much as Ibuse describes.[28] Within the context of Ibuse's other literature, however, the ritual assumes a significance now familiar to Ibuse's readers. The castaway heroes of *Castaway Usaburō* improve with a mixture of Buddhist and Shinto elements of faith to predicate as well as predict what awaits them. Most typical of Ibuse is the sentence: "All of their fates would be determined by whatever words were written on it." In *Castaway Usaburō* as well as in *Waves,* the written word suggests a magic charged with the authority to sustain or to sentence. the diaries kept by Ibuse's characters intersect with their written prayers, both noting the special province of language as existence.

The desperateness of the *Chōja-maru*'s deteriorating situation—a hold filling with water, a starving crew—dramatizes the importance of such ceremonies as the divination. Ibuse does not betray its power: the prediction that all will survive is fulfilled when, on the very next day, the twenty-fourth day of the fourth month, Rokubei spots a large ship in the distance. Usaburō, in a reference indicative of the mythological world he inhabits, exclaims that it looks like "the ship that the Seven Gods of Good Fortune ride!"

This rescuing ship is an American whaler, the *James Roper.* As were the castaways of *John Manjirō,* those of *Castaway Usaburō* are initially frightened by the presence of non-Japanese. (A heated cauldron on the whaler's deck suggests they might be dinner!) But they are soon calmed by a cordial welcome. (It is, in fact, a bath.) Usaburō has not forgotten, however, in the excitement of his salvation, to bring aboard his two seeds. Even the miracle of a rescue does not daunt his plans to render one day both his rice kernels and his own life fruitful.

Since the castaways number more than the *James Roper* can easily accommodate, they are divided and distributed among other whaling ships nearby. Usaburō finds himself aboard a ship headed directly for Honolulu where he, again like Manjirō, is faced with an important decision. Manjirō, on the one hand, desirous of seeing the world, had argued with reason for the consent of his comrades to leave Hawaii for America. Usaburō, on the other hand, resolves a similar dilemma in his own mind by relying upon pure chance:

> Confused whether to stay on the boat or get off, Usaburō conducted a private divination. He tore a piece of paper into four, wrote "land" on one, "sea" on another, and left the remaining two blank. He folded them, put them in a box atop a table, and prayed for salvation to the Lord Amitabha Buddha. When done, he closed his eyes and selected one of the folded slips. He opened it and read "land." [6:118–19]

His decision thus made for him, Usaburō lets the Honolulu authorities lodge him in the household of a local Chinese, Yoon Jow, originally from Canton. This Cantonese, once married to a native Kanaka woman, is now a widower living with his beautiful daughter "Oiren" (in Usaburō's corruption of her proper Chinese name). The two of them run a clock-repair shop, and Usaburō is to apprentice himself to their trade. But Usaburō speaks very little English (again in marked contrast to Manjirō's precocity), and Yoon Jow cannot read the Chinese characters through which Usaburō then attempts to communicate: little understanding, and even less learning, takes place. With the help of Oiren, Usaburō finally conveys to Yoon Jow that he wishes to build a rice paddy on his property. Yoon Jow not only grants permission but is himself excited by the project, for rice has never before been cultivated in the Sandwich Islands:

> Usaburō did not know how many seeds should be planted in the usual four-square-yard paddy for rice the optimum size. He finally planted his two kernels in a raised wet paddy measuring four square feet. In order that all go well, Usaburō did like the farmers of Echigo. He made a Shinto paper offering, stood it in one ridge of the paddy, and placed the branches of a green-leafed sapanwood tree in its four corners, instead of the customary sacred *sakaki* twigs of his native land. [6:126]

188
The
Castaways:
Usaburō
and
the
1950s

That night Usaburō, Yoon Jow, and Oiren celebrate with a feast of rum and turtle meat. In just a few days' time they have even more cause for rejoicing:

> It surely has something to do with the ocean currents. The good weather on this island varies little throughout the four seasons. January is as warm as June or July would be in Japan. It is a perfect climate for growing rice.
>
> The American word for a rice seed that has begun to grow is "sprout." Yoon Jow, with a look of joy on his face, took Usaburō out to the yard in back.
>
> "Sprout," he said, pointing to the paddy, "All sprout.... "
>
> The kernels planted in this small paddy had both luckily sprouted buds. Their faintly whitish-yellow buds looked so fragile that someone's breath might make them disappear. In Japan, Usaburō would hardly have given such a thing a second look, but the sprouts he was seeing now were a source of strength that made his heart sing. [6:128–29]

The common is suddenly the exceptional; the usual, the unusual. Ibuse is once more inverting hierarchies. Between Lieutenant Okazaki, who saw war in peace, and Shigematsu, who will see regeneration in destruction, stands Usaburō, who perceives "a source of strength" in two tiny rice sprouts. In one sense, Usaburō, the castaway, has made himself less an exile by recreating the scenery of Japan in his new home; in another sense, Usaburō, the lazy brother of Kinroku, enjoys a revitalizing pride in the results of his industry. Usaburō conforms to Ibuse's concept of the historical common man: self-reliant, productive, rewarded by the fruits of his labor. Recalling Yasuoka Shōtarō's characterization of Ibuse's early interest in painting as a projection of the folk impulse to fashion tangible objects, one understands why Ibuse has Usaburō respond to the challenge of a physical dislocation with a physical project, the construction and care of a rice paddy. Its creation leads to a creative definition of self—as Usaburō the farmer, midwife of life, and a necessary accessory to the natural cycle. This is how Usaburō clears a place for himself in far Oahu where, before, there was none. He boasts to Oiren through an interpreter, "I plan to make this island of Oahu into the Land of Abundant Reed Plains and Rice Fields" (*Kono Uwahe no shima o, Toyoashihara no Mizuho no kuni ni suru tsumori ja* [6:135]), a reference both to the mythic past of his old country and to his newfound sense of worthwhile purpose in his new country.

In the seventh chapter of *Castaway Usaburō*, the reader learns that
Usaburō's sprouts thrive; in the eighth, that "the rice plants showed
wonderful progress. . . . [The rice paddy] was the very model of the
Land of Abundant Reed Plains and Rice Fields" (6:151). In the
meantime, however, Usaburō has heard that his fellow castaways
from the *Chōja-maru* have finally also arrived in Hawaii, and that
plans are underway to repatriate them all. Oiren, who has fallen in
love with Usaburō, is understandably dismayed. She weeps over the
prospect of their separation, but for Usaburō, "compared to leaving
Oiren, leaving the rice paddy would be the more difficult" (6:151).
Usaburō's ties to his new home are ties only to the land.

Usaburō and his reunited comrades learn they are to be put aboard
a ship, but they are not apprised of its destination. When Ibuse himself was ordered aboard the *Afurika-maru* in the winter of 1941, his
own terminus was undisclosed; such ignorance is a defining characteristic of the castaway experience. Heinrich Böll once wrote to the
effect that modern man is one who is put on a train in the middle of
the night and sent to some unknown place; similarly, Ibuse remarks
in *Castaway Usaburō* that "being a castaway means that the winds
of fate decide whether one goes or stays" (6:171). Both writers take
the history of the Second World War as proof of their descriptions.
Böll recalls Europe under the Reich; Ibuse, his own journey to Singapore and his later evacuation to remote villages, where his movements, too, were dictated by "the winds of fate."

Usaburō and his shipmates are nonetheless eager to commence
their voyage. Unfortunately they meet with bureaucratic and logistic
delays at every turn. For a while they are disturbed by rumors that
they are to be part of an army sent by the United States to conquer
Japan, but one of Heishirō's divinations reassures them that this will
not come to pass. But Heishirō's oracular talents do not foresee his
own death, which occurs while they await passage. The other castaways mourn and commemorate him:

> They finished making his tomb from wooden boards. They were told,
> because gravestones are shipped from the American mainland, that it
> would take one or two years for a marker to be carved and delivered.
>
> The tomb, four feet high and a foot and a half wide, was made of a
> platform of thick planks with a roof-shaped top. Jirokichi borrowed a
> writing brush from the Cantonese and wrote the epitaph. On the right
> side of the boards he wrote "Heishirō of Japan". . . . [6:181]

190
The
Castaways:
Usaburō
and
the
1950s

The procession of funerals and similar commemorative rites in Ibuse's castaway literature, begun in the Chōhei stories, reaches its destination in this, the most purposefully plotted of his works. The scene of Heishirō's entombment is accordingly rich with an accumulated significance. There is an act of "construction," not only of a wooden coffin and later a fence to surround it, but of a text, the inscription that Jirokichi writes with brush and ink to encode as well as entomb. Both the physical and literary labors of Heishirō's survivors suggest a positive and perhaps seminal response to his death, an attempt to build a symbolic structure that supersedes and salvages their loss. The lives that Ibuse makes most real in this novel, and others, are those of common men isolated on a distant island, tenuously perched on the edge of extinction and forced to face all threats creatively, ritually, faithfully.

In the summer of 1840 the remaining castaways finally board an English merchant vessel on the first leg of their long journey home. They are delivered to a port town (possibly Ust-Kamchatsk) on the Kamchatka peninsula of eastern Siberia. Although they have forsaken far Hawaii for a land much nearer their own, old problems continue to dog them. Shichizaemon falls ill with a debility revealed to be the consequence of his frequent liaisons with women. His fellow castaways reassure him that he will soon recover, but the patient himself knows better:

> "No, Jirokichi, don't tell me not to worry. If foreign doctors could cure this sickness, then it wouldn't be so rampant in their own countries. No, there are neither gods nor Buddhas in foreign lands...." [6:191]

Shichizaemon's lament lies at the heart of *Castaway Usaburō* and is instrumental in understanding Ibuse's purposes in writing such a work. In *John Manjirō,* Ibuse's hero easily abandoned his identity as a Japanese and embraced that of an American, only to revert later with still no evident inner struggle. Ibuse's first castaway novel expresses personal definition as portable; his second, as immobile. The characters of *Castaway Usaburō* are rendered rootless by their separation from Japan. They no longer enjoy the protection of the "gods and Buddhas." They are plagued by a problematic relationship with the foreign nations they visit and their citizens, problematic because they are simultaneously succored and threatened in their bewildering encounters. Partially because of their numbers (as opposed to the solitary Manjirō), Usaburō and his fellow countrymen constitute a community capable of preserving some features of their cultural continuity intact, yet, at the same time, their "Japaneseness" is kept at bay by the new cultures surrounding them. One important tension in their characterizations results, then, from being Japanese where being Japanese is impossible. Ibuse appropriately exploits the potential of this contradiction for a most ambitious purpose, namely, his evolving quest for the definable perimeters of modern humanity itself. Ibuse's view of the human condition is peculiarly contemporary in this historical work, for here, as well as in his wartime memoirs, his heroes are men forced to rationalize the why and how of their survival in an era when others, whether on ships adrift or in cities aflame, die without the solace of any vindicating cultural sanctions.

Due to Shichizaemon's affliction, all the castaways are quarantined and are not permitted to proceed with their voyage on schedule. Suddenly they find themselves residents of, not guests in, remote Czarist Russia. Each is lodged separately in a local home as a servant. Kinzō fares the worst, being placed in a Cossack household. Usaburō is the luckiest, landing in the comparatively genteel home of the representative of a Moscow trading firm.

While in Kamchatka, Usaburō meets a Russian named Rostov who speaks Japanese. He is a graduate of the Japanese language school in Irkutsk. There have been such schools in Russia, Rostov tells Usaburō, for over a century, ever since Peter the Great directed an earlier castaway, Gabriel, *né* Dembei, to organize one in St. Petersburg. Since that time, however, the state of Japanese studies in Russia has declined somewhat, and Rostov wishes to begin to remedy that situation by having the castaways perform a play for the edification of the local populace. Agreeing, the Japanese select the classic story of samurai loyalty, *Chūshingura*, "The Treasury of the Loyal Retainers." They rehearse it and stage their production in front of a packed, enthusiastic house of the town's gentlemen and ladies.

Rostov also slyly suggests that he would welcome a native speaker of Japanese to stay on in Russia as his assistant. To this end, he involves Usaburō in a plot to have Jirokichi (whose stage performance had impressed not only Rostov, but a serving girl named Sonya) marry a Russian. Usaburō is talked into conveying the proposal to Jirokichi, who, angered, resents Usaburō's part in the subterfuge. He tells Usaburō that Rostov intends nothing but to make a "work horse" out of him.

192

The
Castaways:
Usaburō
and
the
1950s

News of Usaburō's implication in Rostov's scheme spreads to the other castaways. In a letter, Kinzō accuses Usaburō not only of abetting a dastardly plot to divide them, but of having been concerned only with his own selfish pursuits ever since the *Chōja-maru* was blown off course. He cruelly reminds Usaburō that his older brother Kinroku had, after all, gotten them into their present predicament. These charges have a deep and unsettling effect on Usaburō. "It was a long letter that said these things. As Usaburō read it to himself over and over again, he began to feel that perhaps it would be better if he did not return to Japan" (6:227).

Usaburō's decision to remain a castaway might spring from a desire to spite Kinzō, or it might reflect a suspicion that Kinzō's accusations are, in fact, true. The growing hostility he encounters from the other Japanese merely adds to Usaburō's doubts about the advisability of repatriating. After deciding that he has no other choice, Usaburō goes to Rostov and tells him that he does not wish to return to Japan. This predictably pleases the Russian, until he learns that Usaburō does not care for Siberia either. Instead, his wish is to return to Oahu, where he can resume work on his rice paddy. Although Rostov scornfully reminds Usaburō that his rice plants have surely matured and withered by now, Usaburō stubbornly believes that Yoon Jow has saved seeds for the next year's paddy, "in that land of constant summer." Rostov relents and agrees that Usaburō may board the next available ship. "As always, the life of a castaway is a matter of fate, much as the leaves are scattered by the wind. That is how Usaburō was forced to accept his lot" (6:229).

In this exchange between Usaburō and Rostov, Ibuse completes his transformation of the castaway (*hyōryūmin*) into the exile (*runin*). Ibuse parenthetically interjects into his description of Usaburō's decision to return to Hawaii the comment: "But [Usaburō] did not particularly wish to return to Oahu" (6:229). The reader is left to assume that Usaburō's true motive is more a desire to depart the company of his fellow castaways, and less, as told Rostov, an enthusiasm for agriculture. Once Ibuse exposes Usaburō's keenness for Oahu as largely feigned, he denies his hero any real place in the world. Afraid to return to Japan for what his comrades might say, and saddened by the prospect of life in a land not wholly his own, Usaburō becomes a reluctant expatriate. One might see in Usaburō's weary resignation the response of an author similarly "scattered by the wind" during the Second World War when he, too, was a castaway abroad and an exile at home. Creative work, both for Ibuse and his hero, can offer only meager consolation.

Kinzō and Tasaburō attempt to reason with Usaburō, but they are acrimoniously dismissed. "Leave me alone. I am destined to rot away in a foreign land.... Leave me alone. I am an alien in an alien land [*tengai no kokaku*]" (6:230). Usaburō's decision to become an exile is irreversible. Yet the others are just as firm in their resolve to return to Japan. In the sixth month of 1841, all save Usaburō and the still incapacitated Shichizaemon board yet another ship, this one taking them to Okhotsk, a major port farther west on the Siberian coast.

Fate, however, soon conspires to reunite Usaburō with his countrymen. One year later, in 1842, Usaburō finds himself aboard a ship headed for Sitka which the other Japanese have also boarded and which will, on its return to Siberia, drop them off near Iturup, one of the Kuril Islands. In Sitka, Usaburō and the others are again forced to wait indefinitely, for the departure dates of their respective vessels are unknown. Idleness leads to boredom and further arguments between Usaburō and his former friends. In a move calculated both to annoy the others and to reject the culture they represent, Usaburō announces that he is converting to Christianity. He angrily explains to Kinzō:

> "It's all your doing that I've been driven to this and now must convert. Once I've switched I won't ever be able to return to Japan, but that's your fault, too. It will be quite a sight when you get back to Japan and have to vindicate yourself before the officials. I may not particularly care for the Russian religion, but I've no choice but to join it." [6:262]

Late in the second month of 1843, Usaburō is baptized in the Russian Orthodox Church as Nikolai. Out of spite and vindictiveness, he purposely becomes less a Japanese if not more a Russian; but abandoning one set of social conventions for another, he finds himself, in a sense, permanently imprisoned. The dilemma is a familiar one for Ibuse's characters. Like the salamander stuck in an underwater cave, Usaburō resigns himself to a lonely exile.

The remaining chapters of *Castaway Usaburō* tell of the castaways' final voyages home. The novel's last two chapters detail the stories of those who repatriate, for Usaburō's refusal to do so reduces him to a "nonperson" in the official records upon which Ibuse's work is based. To the reader of *John Manjirō*, the treatment of Kinzō and his comrades once back in Japan seems cruel indeed.

194
The
Castaways:
Usaburō
and
the
1950s

Although only a few years earlier than Manjirō's return, that of the sailors of the *Chōja-maru* is not welcomed as an opportunity but condemned as a crime. An axiom of government policy holds that castaways are not victims of capricious weather but are willful subversives of authority. Just as Usaburō had predicted, they are regarded as traitors. The Russian ship that had risked much to return them is declared an "enemy intrusion." In the hands of the authorities, the castaways are imprisoned "like birds kept in a cage." They are forbidden the simplest pleasures and are even denied the freedom to speak to others. Unlike Manjirō, but like another of Ibuse's postwar characters, Wabisuke, the returnees are the victims of a law absurdly interpreted. Their confinement and interrogation, detailed in *The Tale of the Clock* and amply quoted by Ibuse in his novel, was to continue for years. The attention paid their troubles at the hands of military and civil authorities suggests a modern parallel perhaps all too clear to Ibuse's postwar, post-Occupation readership.

Meanwhile Usaburō has returned to Oahu. Ibuse is spare with his description of Usaburō once apart from his countrymen:

> Those fortunate enough to return to Japan are expediently documented in the records, but Usaburō, excluded from their number, was utterly obliterated in them. Yet the fact that he does not appear in the records does not mean he was unfortunate. Rather, it was his unhappy life afterwards that was so sad. [6:303]

Ibuse's only clue to Usaburō's later misery, and his final comment on one of his most original fictional characters, comes in the final paragraphs of the novel:

> The first seeds used in the rice paddy were one of the two types discovered aboard the *Chōja-maru*. In time, however, the use of Japanese rice was halted and Cantonese strains were substituted. When Usaburō and Oiren had a child, he thought of attempting to crossbreed Cantonese rice with Japanese, but he was unsuccessful. Rice, unlike human beings, is so diverse in its species that hybridization is impossible. It appears that Japanese and foreign rice split apart so far in the distant past as to seem wholly distinct flora. [6:303–04]

Neither Usaburō nor rice is transplanted easily: as Usaburō had once predicted in a moment of anger, he was indeed destined to "rot away in a foreign land." The parable of the rice reflects Usaburō's predicament: one must be Japanese or not Japanese at all, and he cannot be either. Perhaps Ibuse's most complete tragic character, Usaburō, at the end of *Castaway Usaburō*, must live out the rest of his life on a *zekkai no kotō*, that locale in Ibuse's literature that forms the vital link between his castaways (Chōhei, Usaburō) and his exiles (Wabisuke, Usaburō). Theme echoes theme; work rewrites work. From one salamander and a melancholy youth to the war in Singapore and Edo period castaways, Ibuse's stories align physical separations with psychological alienation, unbridgeable distances with radical displacement. The frequency of this thematic confluence suggests a personal concern early and profound in Ibuse's career: as Yasuoka has recognized, Ibuse was a castaway while still a student in Tokyo.[29] If we include all works that follow men on their confused, directionless journeys through both the geography and history of the world, then many modern writers have written hyōryūmono.[30] Perhaps none but Ibuse, however—as a lonely student in the capital, as a frightened draftee in Southeast Asia, and as the mourner of dead friends and countrymen—has written an entire castaway literature. Chōhei, Manjirō, and Usaburō are figures adrift among nations; watakushi, Tomoakira, and Okazaki, among their fellow men. In fact, the farthest limits of Ibuse's castaway experience stop at neither the geographical nor social. With imaginative insight he has extended the fundamental problem of man's loss of place into his continuing exploration of the authority, and responsibility, of words. A brief look at one more Ibuse story will establish the primacy of the castaway and his condition within his varied literature.

"The Toramatsu Journal"

"The Toramatsu Journal" (*Toramatsu nisshi*, 1949), was written in the early postwar period when Ibuse was much aware that he and his nation had lost certain continuity with their past. It is not a well-known short story, yet it must be considered among the most intriguing of his works classified under a broad definition of castaway literature. As was his castaway novel about Usaburō, "The Toramatsu Journal" purports to be a work of historical fiction based on extant documentation. In the first month of 1796, a peasant by the name of Toramatsu left his village of Ōta in the domain of Aki for a pilgrimage on the island of Shikoku. From various reports authored by contemporary authorities, Ibuse reconstructs as much of Tora-

196
The
Castaways:
Usaburō
and
the
1950s

matsu's story as possible. Prior to his departure, Ōta had suffered a terrible famine, but its lord, who had incurred heavy expenses while in obligatory residence in the shogun's capital, was forced to raise taxes rather than lower them. The peasants suffered greatly. Many fled nocturnally, committing a serious offense against Tokugawa law. Even those who were able to borrow from the landlords and pay their taxes were driven to subterfuge. Left with insufficient means to survive the winter, they would apply for permission to depart Ōta on "religious pilgrimages." These were in fact licenses to roam other areas of the country and beg for food. Toramatsu and his traveling companion, another impoverished peasant named Wakaroku, were two such reluctant itinerants (in Ibuse's terminology, *rurōnin,* a word sharing a common root with his *hyōryūmin* and *runin*). Like Manjirō and Usaburō, they were men forced by circumstance out of their homes to roam from one place to another.

Toramatsu, although a peasant, was literate and kept a journal for part of their journey. This document, the principal among several in the work, provides Ibuse with most of his information. "A copy presently remains among the discarded records of the former Kobatake magistrate's office" (4:237). Toramatsu wrote in *sōrōbun,* the epistolary style, because, Ibuse speculates, "perhaps peasants in remote rural areas those days had no need for any other kind of writing" (4:237). Though authorized only until the following spring, when they had to return to Ōta and resume farming, their pilgrimage was prolonged considerably, first by a peasant uprising in Matsukawa, and then by a serious illness that immobilized Wakaroku. One of the official records Ibuse quotes states that, in their extended absence from their village, the names of the two pilgrims were struck from the local census; thus they became men "outside the register" (*chōgai*). Obliterated from the records no less than was Usaburō, Toramatsu and Wakaroku in effect ceased to exist. Suddenly they, too, were castaways without homes, livelihood, or even legal status. Loss of place, which was geographical for other Ibuse characters is, for those of "The Toramatsu Journal," also textual. The loss becomes doubly profound in its implications.

Approximately two months after crossing over to Shikoku, after spending the night in a pilgrims' shelter in Uwajima, Toramatsu awoke to discover Wakaroku gone. Though he was already seriously overdue, Toramatsu postponed his return to search for his missing friend. Showing passersby a likeness of Wakaroku drawn in his journal, he retraced their route. Meanwhile, as with so many of Ibuse's characters, both had become criminals in the eyes of the law. Delayed pilgrims had once been permitted to return home after an inquiry, but the law had been changed. Such violators were now treated no differently than those who had left their homes without authorization, no small crime. Ibuse's use of the term "pilgrim" now approximates that of "vagrant," "castaway," "exile," and "criminal"; throughout his work, a long line of innocent men are rendered guilty by historical changes they neither know nor understand.

The last *sōrōbun* entry in Toramatsu's journal is dated from the middle of the third month, 1796. Mysteriously, it resumes for two short entries, written in "a corrupted vernacular style laden with regionalisms," over two years later. These final entries describe Toramatsu's discovery of Wakaroku, working as a fish-cake maker in Kōchi, and their painfully inconclusive reunion. All that remains of our knowledge of Toramatsu afterwards, writes Ibuse, is the official record of his 1799 death from natural causes in a Bingo village. Perhaps, like Usaburō, Toramatsu could never return to the place of his birth for reasons known only to him and his one-time friend.

The protagonists in a diverse range of Ibuse's works, particularly those of the postwar period, appear to gravitate towards a common end, a disconnected state of existence in which alienation manifests itself in equally dismal ways. Toramatsu died a lonely vagrant, his very name erased from the records of his village. When officials of the village in which he died sent his few personal effects back to Ōta, Ōta wrote back that no one of that name was listed among them. The final line of "The Toramatsu Journal" reads: "Toramatsu had become a man outside the register" (*Toramatsu wa chōgai no ningen ni natte ita no de aru*) (4:249). It is left to Ibuse, taking note of the journal, sundry papers, and even an unused ferry ticket found on his body, to reassemble Toramatsu's past and to memorialize him in a short story.

The power of "The Toramatsu Journal" comes from its opposing tensions—the denial of a man's existence in a register obliterating his name, against the reaffirmation of that same existence through the official and unofficial texts that supposedly inform the story. The tension between those words that eliminate men and those words that save them reveals "The Toramatsu Journal" to be, in fact, a sophisticated if elliptical restatement of Ibuse's personal poetics.

198
The
Castaways:
Usaburō
and
the
1950s

Much of his earlier work has attempted to save acquaintances of childhood or wartime (Aoki Nampachi, Dazai Osamu, Yanagi Shigenori) from being "outside the register" themselves, which is to say absent from stories, from memories, from significance. If one were to compare the many ways his characters find themselves "shipwrecked," perhaps this sort of textual omission strikes Ibuse as the most terrifying. The fear that what has passed may be separated from what remains—the dead from the words that recall them—may explain in part why Ibuse has written again and again of so many victims.

As one reads repeatedly of men in these and earlier times who were challenged to survive misfortune, a strategy seems to emerge: Ibuse or his heroes apply a variety of remedies—ranging from religious rituals, to rice paddies, to textual reconstructions—all intended to return the literal or figurative castaway to a sense of place. When the critic Yoshida Seiichi claims that Ibuse's hyōryūmono, together with his historical fiction, demonstrate where "his creative method, even his theory of creativity, may lie,"[31] he is saying that the castaway experience and the responses it generates in Ibuse's work are the most original elements of his literary achievement. Yet it is also possible to view Ibuse's hyōryūmono, from the Chōhei stories to such works as "The Toramatsu Journal," as links in a long chain of catastrophe fiction, culminating not in themselves, but in a single masterpiece that encompasses and supersedes them all. Behind Shizuma Shigematsu will stand Chōhei, Usaburō, and Toramatsu; in front of him will loom the same obstacles to physical and psychic survival that they had faced. Ibuse's castaway literature, like his early short stories, his historical fiction, and his wartime memoirs, flows into a broad river of people and themes that will surge with an aggregate force to create one work that completes their common configuration, the novel that in our post-Hiroshima world renders everyone castaways—*Black Rain.*

Ibuse,
Black
Rain,
and the
Present
Day

The black smoke
obscured the sun in the heavens,
and although it was day
it seemed like night.
—*Waves*

The 1960s could have marked Ibuse's first decade of that pleasant, respected retirement Japan reserves for its senior authors. Shortly after he celebrated his sixty-second birthday in 1960, he was made a member of the Japan Art Academy (Nihon Geijutsuin), an honor usually bestowed on artists thought to have reached the pinnacle of their careers. Ibuse could have slipped into a relatively mute and genteel seclusion with no harm to his reputation. At one time, in fact, such a withdrawal from the hectic literary life of Tokyo seemed likely. In his essay "The Banquet Last Night" (*Kinō no kai*, 1959), Ibuse laments that the years now race by, that he wishes he could "apply the brakes... or put up a stop light" to slow down the onslaught of senility, an affliction he fears is approaching because his memory, never good, is rapidly worsening. Moreover he complains of a writer's block in "A Story in Pieces"; unable to write, "no matter what the theme," Ibuse resolves to dedicate his remaining energies to projects begun in the past but not completed. Ibuse numbers these unfinished works as three, the last being the story of a friend named Shigematsu, who was "exposed to the Hiroshima atomic bomb. . . . "

One wonders whether Ibuse had any idea how successful this "final" undertaking would be. *Black Rain,* the tale of that friend, today not only stands as the major achievement of a career with many accomplishments, but looms over the earlier books, not so much illuminating their significance as overshadowing their particular merits. According to 1981 figures announced by the original publisher of the novel, Shinchōsha, the Japanese edition alone has sold over 263,000 hardcover copies and 1,160,000 paperbacks. In addition, a recent poll of leading Japanese intellectuals revealed *Black*

200

Ibuse,

Black

Rain,

and the

Present

Day

Rain as the majority choice for the most significant book published in Japan since 1945.[1]

The reception that greeted *Black Rain* suddenly made the aging Ibuse the focus of renewed attention. In 1966, the year in which the novel appeared as a complete volume, Ibuse won the Noma Prize and was awarded the Order of Cultural Merit, both most prestigious honors. Finally, enthusiastic critics exclaimed, a successful work of art dealing with the atomic bombing has been written. At last, Ibuse's friends rejoiced, he has given the world his masterpiece.

Such praise might make one think that suddenly there had emerged a new Ibuse Masuji, a writer who had worked at less than his whole potential until this new novel had sprung fully grown, as if from the head of Zeus, into his readers' hands to take all by surprise. The Ibuse who wrote *Black Rain*, unlike the one who had written other critically acclaimed works such as *Waves* or *Castaway Usaburō*, became something of a media figure, the unwitting champion of political causes, the eloquent voice of anonymous victims. The glory heaped upon Ibuse may have been deserved, but it was often misleading, since it froze Ibuse and his reputation in a state not wholly literary but political—something of a final irony for a man who had carefully avoided doctrinal and sectarian disputes since his student days. *Black Rain* plunged its author into controversy. Nowadays when Ibuse is interviewed by the press, it is invariably during the first week of August, or on such subjects as the danger of atomic power plants.

But the press and the public it serves cannot be dismissed as insensitive. The theme of *Black Rain* necessarily raises issues beyond those of literary aesthetics; and the partisan attentions paid its author are unavoidable and perhaps justified. Nonetheless, Ibuse's more perceptive critics, and no doubt many of his long-standing readers, realize that this novel is no aberration. Ibuse's work has always been more than the sum of its humorous or quaintly nostalgic stories. Viewed whole, the logical synthesis of his diverse literature, its emphasis on violence and its culture, has consistently pointed the way to the basic theme of *Black Rain*; namely, the social and ethical repercussions of atrocity.

Looking back, it all may have begun with a salamander trapped in a cave. Yet what makes *Black Rain* the paramount achievement of Ibuse's literature of catastrophe is the unprecedented nature of the specific disaster its author seeks to weave into his broad historical fabric. Hiroshima (like Auschwitz, the very name evokes a violence both singular and unprecedented) is the first and only of Ibuse's fiery upheavals to figure as an act of deliberate atrocity as well as of terrific force. Its victims were killed anonymously, indiscriminately, and without the sanction of ceremony. Most important for Ibuse, they died without understanding.

The novelist who would write of Hiroshima is burdened with the special task of explanation as well as communication. Ibuse may have developed effective techniques for integrating floods, earthquakes, and volcanic eruptions into his historical and literary vision, but the advent of Hiroshima presented unique problems of sheer scale—difficulties sometimes linguistic, sometimes formal, often ethical, and always personal. While his stance as a writer, that of a perennial survivor compelled to remember, inevitably led him to the literature of atrocity (one might here recall the characterization of "Wabisuke" as the world's first work of concentration-camp literature), that is not to imply it was a genre easily conceived or executed. Ibuse hesitated twenty years before he made the attempt in earnest, and he has since been most uneasy with his status as Japan's "official" Hiroshima writer. When recently asked to speak about *Black Rain*, he abruptly responded that he had nothing to say on the subject (*"hanasu koto wa nani mo nai desu yo"*).[2]

Ibuse's reaction is one widely shared among A-bomb authors. Hiroshima rightly inspires timidity on the part of writers and critics alike. Ibuse's particular strategy was to write *about* Hiroshima without writing *of* Hiroshima. In other words, he required a formal device that would mediate the experience without distorting it, much as one can view a solar eclipse by its projection through a pin hole onto a blank sheet of paper. Ibuse had envisioned how he might accomplish this long before *Black Rain*, and indeed he had experimented with his methods in a short story about Hiroshima written more than ten years before his celebrated novel. In this early work the reader can discern how Ibuse might one day skirt the pitfalls that had trapped other atomic-bomb writers.[3]

"The Iris"

"The Iris" was published in June 1951 in a special issue of *Chūō kōron*. Like so many of Ibuse's works, it mixes fact and fiction,

202

Ibuse,

Black

Rain,

and the

Present

Day

memoir and invention. Ibuse, characteristically narrating the story's events in the first person as watakushi, begins with the foreshadowing recollection that not long after Hiroshima was bombed, he had spotted in the garden of a friend living in Fukuyama the unusual sight of a single iris "blooming out of season," literally "blooming crazily" (*kuruizaki*). Fukuyama, the city on whose outskirts Ibuse grew up, is the principal setting of "The Iris." It was here that Ibuse, in fact, spent the day of August 6, 1945. Earlier that year he and his family had been reevacuated to the old family estate in nearby Kamo, but on that particular hot summer day, Ibuse felt the urge to go into town:

> On the day of the atomic bombing I rode my bicycle to Fukuyama early in the morning. I thought I would like to see the city one last time before the air raids, which we had heard were coming, destroyed it. I rode over the mountain pass. Once in town I saw that everyone had boarded up their homes in preparation for evacuation. Everything was being offered at very cheap prices, but no one was buying. There was a hemp palm in a very nice pot. There was even a piano for sale. Tea ceremony utensils, too.[4]

This description closely parallels that in "The Iris." Pamphlets dropped from American planes have warned the people below that the Allies have not forgotten Fukuyama. The city, naturally, has panicked. In the midst of the commotion, Ibuse visits three acquaintances busily preparing to flee the targeted town: a druggist, an innkeeper, and a dentist who has recently lost his only son in the fighting. Ibuse well remembers these three social calls, for while he is chatting in Fukuyama, nearby Hiroshima experiences the world's first atomic attack. Ibuse writes in "The Iris":

> I learned of the air raid over Hiroshima some thirty or forty hours after the fact. One injured victim fled from his city home to a village near mine. He reported that Hiroshima had disappeared in a single instant, destroyed by a strange bomb. That rumor spread to my own village. [5:7–8]

News of the Hiroshima devastation slowly reaches Kamo, terrifying in its gradually understood import, and is deftly indexed into the story with Ibuse's own experiences in Fukuyama. On August 7 Fukuyama is bombed and the Allies' promise is kept. Ibuse, safe in his Kamo home that day, recalls in "The Iris" that he goes outdoors to watch: "I saw the glow of Fukuyama burning. The city was hidden behind the hills, blocking my view of the flames, but the edges of the hills were all illuminated, and in one place I could see a pillar of fire soaring into the sky" (5:9).

Perhaps Ibuse has invented this particular scene, but it is consistent with many such descriptions in his literature. Such visions of destruction are no longer merely familiar but nearly rote: that ambiguously powerful image of the beautiful end has accompanied Ibuse back to the garden of his ancestral home. The glow of a burning city and the pillar of fire in the sky above, things seen previously in Tokyo and Singapore, echo like the refrain of a dirge sung by mourners on proximate, but protected, high ground. Any notion of "point of view" in either "The Iris" or *Black Rain* necessarily entails physical as well as literary distance: beneath the narrative constructs of Ibuse's work lie real memories. The destruction of Hiroshima—the actual city burning on the far side of the hills—is both remote and intimate, imagined and real. Ibuse notes in "The Iris" that when cities along the Inland Sea were bombarded, he could feel the earth tremble beneath his home in Kamo. Throughout his entire life, even across the distances that have saved him, Ibuse has felt the repercussions of other people's catastrophes.

"The Iris" explains that refugees from Hiroshima have begun returning to their home villages only to die of a strange illness, dubbed "the volunteer soldier's disease" (*giyūhei no byōki*, literally "the brave soldier's disease"), since the first to manifest its symptoms was in fact such a person. Ibuse, upon hearing details of the bomb from these refugees, realizes with horror that while he was idly engaging the Fukuyama druggist in small talk, this man's son, some miles to the west in Hiroshima, was incinerated. This object of Ibuse's survival guilt is another example of mediation between directly experiencing the event (the dead son) and experiencing knowledge of the event (Ibuse), a process similar to learning that Fukuyama is burning through the observation of far hills silhouetted by its fires.

By this point in "The Iris," the reader understands that Ibuse intends to write about Hiroshima by studying its displaced effects. He places a middle ground simultaneously real and figurative between himself and his theme, permitting the reader a knowledge of what, had Ibuse been in Hiroshima on August 6, would be unknowable—because his narrator would be dead. Although this is not a wholly new technique in Ibuse's works, this does mark the first time it

204

Ibuse,

Black

Rain,

and the

Present

Day

enables a story otherwise technically unfeasible. "The Iris" pioneers the way to *Black Rain*, for both works, albeit in different ways, avoid direct description of the bomb and thus avoid circumscribing or diminishing it. Rather, Ibuse lets the story be told secondhand after it has been carefully articulated and negotiated in the minds of the bomb's victims—first by the refugees of "The Iris" and then by the diarists of *Black Rain*. The choice of Fukuyama in the former and diaries in the latter as the devices of mediation is an important one. Fukuyama is a city with special significance for Ibuse; it belonged to his childhood, and, like Hiroshima, it was targeted to be destroyed. Much like a diary, the setting of Fukuyama makes Ibuse's work easy because of its ties to history, another of the middle grounds that arbitrates for him. He writes in "The Iris":

> Two days later I went into Fukuyama to view the burned remains of the castle tower. Old romances and historical accounts are full of tales of great fires destroying castle towers, but since I had never seen one for myself I decided to go and look at the actual site. What I saw, however, was only scorched earth, with broken roof tiles piled high. People who appeared to be victims of the disaster were sifting through the ruins with shovels and pieces of wood to collect charred spikes. These spikes, which had held end tiles in place, were as big as fire tongs. Indeed, with two you might very well use them as such. [5:11–12]

Fukuyama Castle, one will recall, became Ibuse's childhood introduction to the presence of history when his grandfather took him there sightseeing. Now, forty years later, Ibuse comes sightseeing again, when the course of recent events has leveled the castle, repeating what "old romances and historical accounts" have preserved in their records of medieval times. Ibuse is reconciling catastrophe with the frequent ravages of a cyclical history. One might also recall how, in "Tajinko Village," the village constable Kōda also visited castle ruins, and there learned of the dead voices that once cried out in the night. Fukuyama Castle figures predictably in *Black Rain*, too, when Shigematsu is told by his brother-in-law of the same events described in "The Iris": "An incendiary bomb flew into the third-floor window of the castle's five-story tower and exploded. Great pillars of fire shot up and the structure collapsed" (13:182).

In castles Ibuse seeks those same voices in the past which his fictional constable had inadvertently discovered. In "The Iris" the victims of an air attack comb through rubble for something out of the past that might, even as fire tongs, serve the present; Ibuse's mission seems not so different, for throughout his work the past is "sifted" through the present to link both in a tragic pattern.

After Japan's surrender one week after the raid on Fukuyama, Ibuse begins to think he should return to Tokyo as soon as possible. He visits a friend in Fukuyama to discuss the feasibility of such a move. Ibuse is spending the night at this friend's home when the final, climatic scene of "The Iris" unfolds:

> When I awoke at dawn I opened the window and saw something strange in the pond directly below me. I switched on a lamp, stretched the cord, and directed the light towards the surface of the water. Suddenly I averted my eyes and extinguished the light. I shut the window. Floating on the surface of the water was a human body. A patch of iris was growing near one corner of the pond, and not far away was floating something purple, like a slip of paper. The corpse, face-up, had its cheek nearly touching the purple thing. [5:18]

Added to the castles and pillars of fire is yet another of Ibuse's most familiar images, a corpse floating in a pond. Bodies revolving in water represent another textual invocation of Ibuse's many childhood dreads. The facts surrounding this particular death, however, are of recent and unprecedented origin. Ibuse's host, notified of the grisly discovery, summons the police. An inquiry reveals that the victim, a young girl, had been a factory worker in Hiroshima. She had been driven nearly insane, first by events there and later in Fukuyama. Once that city, too, was bombed, she had lost all her senses and had thrown herself, terror-stricken, into the pond some days before. "They say," the master of the house remarks cavalierly, "that it takes one, maybe two, weeks for a corpse to rise to the surface" (5:20).

Once the body is removed, Ibuse again gazes at the iris patch and notices one suddenly in bloom. "I wonder if that iris has bloomed out of shock from something" (5:21). Ibuse recalls a story about a maid who had drowned herself in a pond out of shame from an unwanted pregnancy. That pond, too had been surrounded by iris. "The Iris" concludes when Ibuse's friend comments, "My iris here have nothing in common with those in your story. Why, the times are completely different. It's crazy for this flower to be blooming!" (5:22).

"The Iris," like the later *Black Rain,* is built with the metaphors of

206

Ibuse,
*Black
Rain*,
and the
Present
Day

a natural world "blooming crazily" upon the transcendent ideal of a recurring history. To this extent neither work appears much different from, for example, *Waves,* a prewar novel nonetheless predicated and executed in a similar fashion (the tree in Rokuhara suddenly blooming; Kakutan's understanding of the inevitable decline of the Taira). But Ibuse has something more, something special, to say about Hiroshima. For that reason he finds it necessary to return to this theme in *Black Rain.*

By the 1960s the meaning of Hiroshima was apparently changing for some Japanese. The sincere mourning of the bomb's victims was increasingly being supplanted by stylized ceremonies staged for the media and even for tourists each August. In an interview with the newspaper *Asahi Shimbun,* Ibuse claimed his inspiration for writing *Black Rain* to be the lament of the bomb's survivors that their memory of Hiroshima was being demeaned in the frenzied "celebrations" that greeted each anniversary of August 6.[5] One slogan of these uneasy survivors—"No more festivals!" (*Omatsuri-sawagi wa mō takusan*)—suggested to Ibuse that the process of neutralizing the significance of atrocity by frivolously ritualizing its remembrance might one day empty the Hiroshima observances of their sincerity and power. Ibuse came to believe he had to preserve—restore—the fact of suffering with a novel that would tell of it from the victims' own perspective, a book that would remain a record of the dead and their survivors, even after they might be forgotten by a public too frightened to remember.

Black Rain

Consequently *Black Rain,* unlike "The Iris," would be a work centrally concerned with the world of the *hibakusha,* or "victims of the bomb." Indeed, as "A Story in Pieces" relates, the impetus for such a novel came from Ibuse's actual acquaintance with a hibakusha. Shigematsu Shizuma (whose family and given names were reversed when he became Ibuse's protagonist) first came to Ibuse's attention just after the war, while he was still in Kamo. Shigematsu offered to show Ibuse the contents of a warehouse of Edo period historical records located in the nearby village of Kobatake, a warehouse suggestive of the repository cited in "The Toramatsu Journal." Later, after Ibuse had moved back to Tokyo and was visiting Hiroshima prefecture on one of his frequent trips, he encountered Shigematsu at an inn often used by fishermen. There Ibuse heard from Shigematsu the story of his stricken niece Yasuko, who, after marrying and bearing two sons, had evidenced symptoms of radiation sickness and died. Shigematsu offered to send Ibuse her two-volume diary, kept while she was infirm. But later, when Ibuse did in fact request the diary, Shigematsu replied that her relatives, tormented by the diary as a reminder of her suffering, had burned both volumes. Ibuse subsequently asked for the woman's hospital charts in lieu of the destroyed journal; these too, Shigematsu regretted, were gone.

Ibuse was forced to broaden his search for sources. In the days following August 6, villages throughout the prefecture had dispatched relief teams into the city to assist the authorities. As Ibuse notes, however, of each village's team, "only one survived."[6] Ibuse assembled five or six of these informants, intending to transcribe their accounts for use in his project, but he had trouble with his tape recorder and had to abandon the idea.

At this point Shigematsu again came to Ibuse's aid. Shigematsu himself had gathered much material on Hiroshima, a collection of records that he, like Ibuse's fictional character, planned to bequeath to future generations. His accumulated documents amounted to over three hundred pages. Once lent to Ibuse, these personal accounts of the atrocity constituted the single greatest source of real data for use in *Black Rain*. As its author has stated, the novel "could not have been written from simple speculation."[7] Additionally, Ibuse personally conducted a detailed investigation of the events of August 1945. He has said in an interview with the *Asahi Shimbun*:

> Since I had no firsthand knowledge of what happened, I was left with no choice but to gather as much material as I could. I collected all there was to be collected, as if I were raking it in. Both before and after I began to write, I went to Hiroshima to hear the stories of more than fifty survivors. I listened to people who, as members of the fire brigades, had gone into the hills. When the talk turned to those who had searched through the "ashes of death," everyone turned silent. The ashes were a forbidden subject. I was told that everyone who passed through them had died.[8]

Ibuse thus commenced his work on *Black Rain* as he would with historical fiction, by researching facts before exercising his imagination upon them. Ibuse has repeatedly stressed the documentary character of this novel, and rightly so, for embedded within it are the per-

208
Ibuse,
*Black
Rain,*
and the
Present
Day

sonal stories of many hibakusha. Yet one is tempted to take issue with Ibuse when he claims that *Black Rain* is merely an assemblage of accounts not his own, for somewhere in the process of creating a work of literature he made this testimony very much his own. Suddenly, or perhaps gradually, it was impossible to remain the objective editor, the detached historian. Ibuse confesses in the same interview:

> Once the writing was under way, I grew quite serious. It was a seriousness that came not from the act of writing, but from the transient world itself. I asked myself: Why did this happen? Everything seemed senseless. I kept thinking to myself that I must continue writing. There was no justice, no humanity, no anything in what happened. Everyone died. The more research I did, the more terrible it became. It was too terrible.[9]

Ibuse found himself drawn ever deeper into the abyss of his morbid material. Soon he neared the absolute depths of that dark vision within his fiction which had for so long been moving towards the light. "Everyone died," Ibuse says, and the fact of his own survival seems to him all the more extraordinary. In one sense Ibuse need never have worried about writing a novel of Hiroshima from "simple speculation"; none of his stories of violent catastrophe could ever have been so completely invented. Somewhere in their inspiration inevitably lies Ibuse's private knowledge of death, abandonment and alienation—a spectrum of acute experiences fictionally magnified and elaborated on a grand historical scale. The reader eventually understands that *Black Rain* is as much a personal novel as it is a public revelation of an immense atrocity.

Black Rain was serialized in *Shinchō* magazine from January 1965 through September 1966. Its twenty chapters, any one of which would be a substantial piece for Ibuse, together constitute his longest work of fiction, numbering nearly three hundred pages in his collected works. One suspects that Ibuse was so engaged by his story that he far exceeded his initial plans for a shorter project. Indeed, many things were altered between the novel's first page and its last. Chapters one through seven were originally entitled *The Marriage of a Niece (Mei no kekkon)* and were renamed *Black Rain* in August 1965 upon the advice of an editor.[10] In hindsight, the change makes poetic sense. Black is a color with frequent and special significance in Ibuse's literature, and water is his most common element. In "The River" the beginnings of a mighty river flowed out from under an enormous black boulder; before that, a salamander was trapped forever in a watery darkness. In *Black Rain,* the image itself is a paradoxical trope of death and life, naming a factual occurrence and symbolizing the lives of Ibuse's characters, who are themselves caught between the destruction of the bomb and their struggles to survive its terror.

The story is difficult to summarize succinctly; its setting regularly shifts between past and present times, encompassing over half a dozen points of view. Perhaps the first sentence of the first chapter best expresses the novel's central issue, if not its plot: "For the past few years Shizuma Shigematsu of Kobatake village had come to think of his niece Yasuko as a burden" (13:3). With this simple opening line, Ibuse accomplishes much. This sentence must rank with "The salamander was sad" as one that perfectly conveys the overall emotional tenor of the work to follow. It also introduces the novel's two major characters and the relationship that contains them both, that of uncle and niece. Yasuko, however, is not only Shigematsu's relative but his ward, which renders her that sort of literary figure guaranteed to inspire a degree of pathos in her function as an observer of her adoptive family's daily life. That life revolves about the triangle of Yasuko, Shigematsu, and Shigeko, who is Yasuko's aunt and Shigematsu's wife. The relationship between Shigematsu and Shigeko, though treated with a masterfully understated and poignant delicacy, figures little in the novel. Their conversations are largely limited to discussions of Yasuko's problems, which are first her marital status and then her health. The first sentence of *Black Rain* also places this small family in the equally small village of Kobatake, an actual locale not far from Ibuse's own in Kamo.

Kobatake possesses a considerable lineage in Ibuse's literature. It is mentioned as one of the impoverished settlements visited by the hapless pilgrims of "The Toramatsu Journal," and it is the subject of an essay entitled "The Story of Kobatake Village" (*Kobatake-mura no hanashi,* 1954). The story Ibuse tells in this essay, that of the Edo period storehouse Shigematsu invited him to view, is fascinating in light of the novel Ibuse was to write a decade later. Perhaps it was when Ibuse saw these records of an old, locally important family, the hereditary magistrates (*daikan*) of Kobatake, that he was moved to memorialize the Shigematsu family in a new record of his own creation. In any case, this history plays an important part in the background of *Black Rain.*

The storehouse explored by Ibuse in Kobatake was filled to its

210

Ibuse,

Black

Rain,

and the

Present

Day

rafters with written relics of the past, reaching back to the late six-teenth century. Ibuse states, in "The Story of Kobatake Village," that he suggested these documents be donated to the local school as refer-ence works, just as both the real and fictionalized Shigematsu sug-gested donating his own records of the atomic bombing. As Ibuse looked through this wealth of information from a time before his own, he thought to himself—anticipating again the protagonist of *Black Rain*—that "you can imagine the lives of peasants long ago when you read [the documents] one by one" (11:47). One text in particular, a voluminous compendium of contemporary events writ-ten in 1798 and 1799, told of crimes, fires, suicides, and flights as well as the story of a pilgrim surely the model for "The Toramatsu Journal," a work thus united with *Black Rain* not only by virtue of their themes—both Toramatsu and Shigematsu may be seen as men set adrift in calamitous times—but of their sources. In that Kobatake storehouse Ibuse again realized the connection between history, violence, and writing, the three pillars upon which numerous of his works rest. In many ways this storehouse lurks behind the writing of *Black Rain*, for in this novel Ibuse meant to build his own vault for his own kind of history, a storehouse of words that might preserve the series of disasters that befell the villagers of Kobatake, not in the eighteenth century but the twentieth.

This is evident even in *Black Rain*'s first chapter. It acts as a preface to the whole novel since it traverses a span of history later reviewed in detail. The narrative is initiated in an indeterminate "present," most likely the early 1950s. Within a few paragraphs, however, the reader is led back to that year of Japan's defeat and the events that ended the Second World War. Soon we learn of one fam-ily's history as well as that of an empire. We are told the background of Shigematsu's chronic radiation sickness and of Yasuko's difficulty in finding a husband owing to persistent rumors that she, too, was exposed to the bomb. This first chapter, moreover, contains a refer-ence to Fukuyama Castle, that recurring sign of a recurring history.

At the novel's outset, then, Ibuse has already established three time lines: distant history, the present of the narrative, and the recent past of the war, a chronology that is both ancient and contemporary. Of these, the only time endowed with specificity is that of August 1945, for that is the only date with absolute reality for the survivors of Hiroshima. In one scene Shigematsu recalls an account of a group from the village Young Men's Association. Armed with bamboo

spears, they were headed into radioactive Hiroshima on August 15 to
look for injured when they heard the Emperor's radio declaration that the war was over. Here Ibuse's three time lines converge: the remote past, implicit in the bamboo spears, which suggest Edo period peasant uprisings; the present day, in which Shigematsu recalls the story; and the month of August 1945, the common ground of all action and all people in the novel.

The narrative device allowing Ibuse to move so easily between past and present is borne out of Shigematsu's concern for his niece's marriage prospects. To counter baseless talk that she was close to ground zero the day the bomb was dropped, Shigematsu decides to transcribe (*seishō suru*, literally "make a clean copy") pertinent entries from his niece's diary to prove to the marriage broker that she was, in fact, far from the blast and its damaging effects.

The entries run from August fifth through the ninth. They represent the first of the many diaries, journals, and testaments that will eventually comprise the greater bulk of the novel. Yasuko's diary anticipates Shigematsu's own, the major diary in *Black Rain*. Not only had Yasuko learned from her uncle to keep a diary, but her diary is the first to introduce graphic descriptions of the destruction later retold with irony in Shigematsu's. Yasuko is on the outskirts of the city when the bomb explodes; only when she reenters Hiroshima later on the morning of the sixth does she see what had happened. In a striking reference, she likens the devastated city to the burning oil tanks of Singapore seen in photographs. She labels Hiroshima first a "city of death" and then a "city of ashes." This shocked reaction and its vocabulary come directly from Ibuse's own experiences in Southeast Asia, experiences that he now associates with those of the hibakusha. Throughout *Black Rain*, in the many accounts heard from survivors, Ibuse will add his own images and expressions to supplement and naturalize an event of which he had no "first-hand knowledge."

Yasuko's diary concludes with a description of the black rain, a radioactive fallout that pelted the city in the late morning of the sixth. The indelible stigmata will not be washed away; here Ibuse foreshadows the damage that will lie dormant in Yasuko until she, years later, is claimed as one of the victims. Yet alongside these references to unprecedented calamity are intimations of a mundane order. Yasuko's entry for August 8 begins "Busy cooking breakfast" (13:11). Her diary combines the routine of a wartime existence with

212

Ibuse,

Black

Rain,

and the

Present

Day

the uniqueness of an atomic attack, an uneasy flow of events mandated by the nature of journal writing and useful for Ibuse's purposes in the novel. Ordinary and extraordinary experiences have been counterpointed before in Ibuse's work—in "Lieutenant Lookeast," for instance—with the similar effect of synthesizing both and thus permitting a curious kind of thematic assimilation. In *Black Rain*, because the book is entirely composed of diaries, this process of tempering traumatic events with domestic ones becomes, in fact, a major theme in itself.

The diary has always, of course, provided Ibuse with a powerful narrative form. He lives in a culture where diary writing enjoys an immensely popular tradition,[11] and it is hardly surprising that such a format for fiction should naturally propose itself. From the early 1930s and in *Waves* Ibuse has exploited the potential of the genre, but in *Black Rain* he expands and deepens that potential in ways unique to his own time and purpose. Once asked why he so often told his stories as diaries, Ibuse replied, only half in jest, that books are easier to write that way. But he went on to say that journals are a particularly "powerful" (*tsuyoi*) genre of literature.[12] By "powerful" Ibuse suggests that diaries (and to some extent all the extratextual materials comprising, or quoted in, his works) confer upon his narratives and their themes an authenticity, a specific and personal historicity. This grounding of the text in an anterior, external chain of denoted events results in a calculated effect crucial to *Black Rain*'s success as a novel of atrocity. Its use of diaries allows the everyday details of conventional life to overlap and thus contrast with the trauma of a nuclear explosion. Much as Shigematsu attempts to arrange a match between his niece and her suitor, so do the diaries mediate the prebomb and postbomb realities of their authors. In this regard Yasuko, the first of *Black Rain*'s diarists, is akin to Tomoakira as he wrote in flight through the Inland Sea, and to Ibuse himself as he carefully transcribed what he wished to remember in Southeast Asia. She and the rest share a common mission, namely, the subjectivization and consequent mastery of experience through making it a story.

The use of diarists as protagonists means that Ibuse has created for the reader of *Black Rain* a textual hall of mirrors. Ibuse coyly defers; he writes about people writing. He avoids direct description of the bomb itself and leaves that to the writers he has borrowed or invented, characters who possess that "first-hand knowledge" of

which he pointedly admits a lack. The function of Fukuyama in "The
Iris," as an extended figure for the impact of the war on people and
their ability to make sense of it, becomes the function of the Shizuma
household in *Black Rain*. Through this family, the novel builds a dialectic in itself, a progressive development first, of life acting upon
writing and then, of writing acting upon life. the reader is led from
text to text, each affirming others and demonstrating the central
work of the novel; namely, the articulation of a new vocabulary of
violence through the creative project of writing. Against the destructive power of the bomb stands the constructive power of words, language, writing. The reader notes, for instance, how, on one hand,
some hibakusha struggle to identify and name the bomb, while, on
the other hand, other characters easily compare names for fish in
their various native dialects. The diaries of *Black Rain* cease to be
vessels for stories and become the story itself. Ibuse makes this most
evident when he turns to Shigematsu's diary.

The Diary of the Bomb

Prompted by his wife's fear that the description of the black rain in
their niece's journal may compromise her chances for marriage,
Shigematsu decides to append his own diary to Yasuko's. If he, only
two kilometers from ground zero, has survived, then surely Yasuko,
many times that distance away, has been spared any ill effects. This
diary (*Hibaku nikki*, literally "The Diary of Being Bombed"), soon
becomes the primary text of *Black Rain*; the reader may easily forget
he is reading an extended quotation inserted into the novel, and not
the novel itself. This cannot be unintended. The indeterminate narrative present of the novel is overwhelmed by the past of the diary,
much as the lives of the hibakusha have been overwhelmed by the actual experience of the bomb. Ibuse is careful, however, to interrupt
Shigematsu's account, periodically returning the reader to the novel's
surface and thereby sponsoring considerable movement within the
story. The nature of this movement suggests nearly random shifts,
which resemble the inner vacillations of memory, as Shigematsu
struggles in the present to write of the past.

Unlike Yasuko's diary, which was merely recopied, Shigematsu's
Diary is, by virtue of the work of memory, essentially rewritten.
Shigematsu adds new interpolations and explanations as he seems to

214

Ibuse,
*Black
Rain,*
and the
Present
Day

relive the experience of the bomb even while safe in his study. Yet far from recoiling, he now rejoices. The diary becomes a project of which Shigematsu is genuinely proud:

> "I've got to recopy this diary sometime soon anyway, since I've already decided to present it to the reference room of the elementary school library. But before I do, I'll let the marriage go-between see it."
>
> "Won't it be enough to show her Yasuko's diary?"
>
> "I'll add my *Diary* to Yasuko's diary. If I'm giving it to the reference room at the school, I've got to copy it out anyway."
>
> "That will be more work, won't it?"
>
> "No matter. I was born to be busy with work. *Diary* will be my own 'history' [*hisutorī*] for the library."
>
> Shigeko fell silent, and Shigematsu, quite satisfied with his explanation, took out a new notebook and began the recopying of his diary. [13:30]

This passage, found early in the novel, establishes that Shigematsu values his diary for reasons beyond the use it might serve in Yasuko's marriage negotiations. *Diary* is both a record of his own suffering and a general history of a major atrocity. Like many of Ibuse's characters, Shigematsu is soon absorbed in the details of documentation. Henceforth, the progress of *Black Rain* revolves as much about the historian seeking to recapture the experience of the bomb as it does about the bomb itself.

In 1943 Ibuse wrote a story entitled "The Fire God" (*Gojinka*). It is an account of the actual volcanic eruption that devastated much of Miyakejima Island in July 1940. The principal character Asanuma who, like the character of the same name in "A General Account of Aogoshima," surveys the damage wrought by the volcano—damage strangely similar to that done Hiroshima by an atomic bomb. Typically, Asanuma writes his observations:

> His was not a record of the actions of the Civil Defense or of administrative personnel, but an account of the entire calamity. [His assistant] Taimei thought that it might be termed one part of the island's history. What Asanuma had seen or heard of various incidents was written down, exactly as they had occurred. There was also one chapter entitled "The Stories of the Victims." [3:157]

Shigematsu is another Asanuma, a victim doubling as witness to preserve the truth of a catastrophe. For both of these typical Ibuse heroes, authenticity is paramount. In the third chapter of *Black Rain*

Shigematsu again refers to *Diary* as his own "part of history," echoing not only his earlier remarks but Asanuma's chronicle of Miyakejima on fire. Shigematsu would like to maintain a scientific objectivity in his writing: in the tenth chapter he is careful to note all the effects found on the corpse of one dead victim, and in the fifteenth he writes, "I even recorded statistically the mortality rate of those who had walked through the burning ruins" (13:217). Those statistics, the reader soon realizes, will include Shigematsu's own niece.

Diary begins where real time begins for many hibakusha, on the morning of August 6. At the moment the bomb exploded, Shigematsu was waiting at Yokogawa Station for a train to take him to his office. A blinding flash was followed by total darkness as he lost consciousness. When he came to, he found the station in rubble all about him. Some victims could be heard crying out for help, but Shigematsu, who had sustained direct injuries only to his face, was ambulatory and made his way out to the street.

At this juncture in the recopying of his diary, Shigematsu stops to discuss with Shigeko whether he should switch from a ball-point pen to the more traditional brush and ink. Shigeko is concerned that words written with a modern pen might fade and be lost. She mentions as evidence a letter sent to Shigematsu's great-grandfather in 1873. Shigematsu is surprised, and curious, on learning that such correspondence exists. Husband and wife go together to the family storeroom. There, in a dank and dark vault which once held bales of rice, in a number of old pine chests inscribed with the family crest, are stored the Shizuma's historical memorabilia. The old magistrate's storehouse of Kobatake has been resurrected in *Black Rain* as the repository of the Shizuma's ancestral past. From one of the chests, Shigeko extracts the Meiji period letter mailed to her husband's forebear in the first year of modern postal service in Japan. This letter, like many documents in the writings of Ibuse Masuji, proves to be its own justification, written by a Tokyo official to demonstrate "Western ink." This official thanks Shigematsu's great-grandfather for a previous gift of seeds from the local *kemponashi,* a kind of Japanese raisin tree.

Like the adolescent Ibuse, who was exhilarated to receive a letter not because it came from Mori Ōgai but because it came from Tokyo, Shigematsu experiences some sense of awe at this discovery from his past. There is an appreciation of the sanctity of these written

216

Ibuse,

Black

Rain,

and the

Present

Day

words, faded though they be. In "The Fire God," Asanuma finds himself revived by the scent of fresh ink on newspapers from Tokyo dropped by plane over his island; Shigematsu feels much the same joy after finding some very old ink from Tokyo in his own home. He decides, right then and there, to resume work on his journal with a brush and ink, tools connoting a renewed and deepened respect for the literary work at hand. This return to a historical means of writing also labels *Diary* a historical document, one that might very well be found in one of the chests in a family storeroom. The storeroom episode is crucial to understanding the scheme of *Black Rain*. Ibuse needs to forge a link between the experience of the bomb and his concept of the historical continuity of life. This he begins to do once he places an old letter, and then a rat-tail brush, in the hands of his protagonist.

Back at work in his study, Shigematsu complains to his wife that he is getting down on paper only a fraction of what he remembers. Perhaps, Shigeko wonders, you are too concerned with style—her exact words are "some sort of 'isms'"—but Shigematsu defensively retorts that his method is nothing but "crude realism" (*akushajitsu to iu bunshō*). Ibuse suggests in this brief exchange that, in writing of atrocity, one fundamental problem is that of a limited imagination confronted by violence of seemingly unlimited dimensions. Shigematsu's solution is to remain literal, no matter how "crude" the result may seem. He wishes his *Diary* to remain an uncomplicated reportage of events told in a simple chronological framework, as autonomous and free from distortion as possible.

This is not, however, Ibuse's own solution. Rather, he deliberately tricks his protagonist and makes *Diary* a most subjective enterprise, one that involves both the diarist and his account in a ritual exorcism. Unconsciously, Shigematsu finds in his journal a patterned activity calculated to effect a sympathetic change in himself, namely, the transition from nonunderstanding to understanding. Writing each day according to a rigidly formal plan, Shigematsu benefits from the reflexivity of ritual. His past is given form and, thus, becomes perceivable and comprehensible. Indeed, if any theme unites the diverse narratives of *Black Rain*, it is the consistent impulse of its characters to restore ritual structure to their lives. This imperative manifests itself in many ways, some of which have nothing to do with writing. There is conventional religious ritual—Shigeko is careful to take the Shizuma ancestral tablets when she flees her destroyed home. There are the smaller rites of everyday life—Yasuko devotes attention to family meals. But perhaps the most telling ritual activity in *Black Rain*, besides that of diary keeping, is Shigematsu's part-time occupation of raising baby carp.

At the beginning of the novel's second chapter, Shigematsu surrenders his recopying to Shigeko so that he might join two other of the village's hibakusha, Shōkichi and Asajirō, at the local pond where they rear fish. This joint project is ostensibly a business venture, but in fact it is rather clever therapy. As these three bomb victims lead the carp through their early life cycle, from the youngest stage of *kego*, through that of *aoko* and *shinko*, to the adult stage of *kirigoi*, they simultaneously lead themselves through a sympathetic healing of the psychological damage done them by the bomb. If the diaries of *Black Rain* establish complex bonds between men and their memories, then the carp of the novel establish parallel bonds between men and the natural world. The second chapter states:

> At dinner the previous evening Yasuko had commented sympathetically, "Inspecting the pond seems like your way of paying respect. It's probably not as much fun as it looks from the outside." But in fact it was a joy that no outsider could know. [13:19]

As did Usaburō from his rice seedlings, so does Shigematsu derive satisfaction and (since such satisfaction is consoling) even succor from his supervision of the baby carp. Another carp, the one given Ibuse by Aoki Nampachi, also has served as a symbol of the vital force flowing through Ibuse's works for many years, until finally in *Black Rain* the baby carp and Shigematsu's relationship with them have become figures of life in the post-Hiroshima world. In his essay "Lake Trout" (*Kosui no ayu*, 1975), Ibuse marks with awe how long fish can survive. One person informs him that trout "can live longer than any of us know. They're like the remnants of the Taira clan in their old villages" (14:4). Ibuse desires a similar power of life for his hibakusha, and so he is drawn back to a pond with carp in it.

Shigematsu, Shōkichi, and Asajirō are the only victims of Hiroshima left alive in Kobatake. They have been warned to avoid overexertion. Thus barred from any usual employment, the men have turned to the raising of carp to remain productive. Moreover, like Shigematsu recopying his journal with a brush and ink, the carp nursery has returned its workers to the context and continuity of a social tradition, and thus to history:

218

Ibuse,

Black

Rain,

and the

Present

Day

Just as Shōkichi had long been saying he would, he brought a bamboo pole with an abalone shell dangling from it to ward off weasels. He stood it near the pond.

"Oh, an abalone shell!" exclaimed the young owner of the hatchery as he rested from scooping out the baby carp. "I haven't seen one of those in quite a while. An abalone shell. The old folks around these parts would remember that custom fondly." [13:26]

Along with idle gossip and roadside naps, raising fish "is a custom going back hundreds, even thousands of years." It is thus an activity with the potential of restoring those who practice it to social, and thereby psychic, wholeness. At one point in the novel, Ibuse calls both diary writing and carp raising "affirming" (*kōdōteki*) pastimes, a characteristic pointing to a common regenerative function.

Every chapter of *Black Rain* is similarly enriched by Ibuse's emphasis on ritual, custom, and tradition. This broad motif permeates the lives of his characters at every stage of the story. Even as Shigematsu and his family were fleeing the burning city on August 6, he paused long enough to reflect that the parched rice they were eating was a foodstuff travelers in older times were certainly wise to carry. Returning to events earlier that same day, Shigematsu notes in his diary that when he had stumbled out of Yokogawa Station he had found himself in front of a shrine, or rather what remained of it. Within the shrine grounds lay bleeding, disfigured victims of the explosion. The scene suggests the disintegration of religious structures (in both literal and abstract senses) under the force of the bomb, and their subsequent replacement by images of violence defying faith. Many of the victims, including Shigematsu, soon suffered from a terrible thirst, that unquenchable desire for water characteristic of severe burn victims. Shigematsu wandered about searching for something potable until he came upon a water tank by the Yokogawa Elementary School:

Without using my hands I washed my face by immersing it in a bucket of water and shaking it left and right. I filled the bucket to the brim, took a deep breath, dunked my face again, and exhaled slowly as I shook it. It felt good to have the bubbles brush against my cheeks as they rose to the surface.

My thirst knew no limits. I filled the bucket again and drank from it after gargling three times. Although I was never taught to do so as a child, I
nonetheless gargled three times whenever I drank water from a spring or
a well away from home. My childhood friends had told me to do this not
only to prevent upset stomachs but, they said, to demonstrate respect for
the god of the water. [13:41–42]

This passage defines Shigematsu's postbomb world in several important ways. First, he is suddenly rendered a castaway, a man
"away from home," in a world made unrecognizable by a nuclear
flash. That moment of heat and pressure transfigures a modern urban center into a raw, primitive vastness. Shigematsu is as "lost" in
downtown Hiroshima as Chōhei had been on Torishima. Shigematsu recognizes neither the landscape nor the blackened survivors
who shuffle past him; even their gender is a mystery to him. One
might think that Ibuse has finally written an urban novel, a work
treating modern man in his modern abode. But this is not so. *Black
Rain* transforms city into country—buildings and streets into a
leveled plain. What was once Hiroshima is now another representa-
tion of Ibuse's dark and dangerous natural world—a fiery delta, a
lethal river, all locales his readers have toured before.

This parallel between the worlds of Ibuse's exiles and the hibakusha continues. Shigematsu improvises a figurative "shrine" by gargling three times in deference to the water spirit; the castaways of the
Chōhei stories build an actual shrine on their deserted island. Such
characters, though widely separated in time, space, and the dimensions of their calamities, are consistent in their responses. All invoke
a mythic structure to compensate for the loss of a civil one; all revert
to the ceremonies of Ibuse's *homo ritualis*. Water remains vital
throughout Ibuse's castaway and Hiroshima stories, the crucial sub-
stance of their characters' rites. In *Castaway Usaburō*, the crew of
the *Chōja-maru* pray for water; in *Black Rain*, Shigematsu prays to
it. An ordinary bucket of water suffices to create, in the seared world
of Hiroshima, a ritual context that must replace the loss, only an
hour earlier, of the social context.

After Shigematsu completes his lengthy draught at the water tank,
he moves on aimlessly in the general direction of Mitaki Park. Soon
he leaves the world of Ibuse's castaway imagery and enters that of his
beautiful end. Overhead, Shigematsu sees the pillars of fire, the bil-

220

Ibuse,
*Black
Rain,*
and the
Present
Day

lowing black smoke, the swirling vortexes, and the hypnotizing colors that inevitably accompany Ibuse's vision of terrible destruction. In Hiroshima, as well as in Tokyo or Singapore, there rises an unusual cloud in the sky:

When I arose from the ground, what first caught my eye was a gigantic cumulonimbus cloud. In texture it looked just like the one I had seen in photographs of the Great Kantō Earthquake, except that this had a fat stem and rose much higher in the sky. Flat at the top, it grew bigger and bigger, as if it were a mushroom opening its cap.... Just as one thought that the top was billowing towards the east, the wind would shift and move it towards the west, then back again to the east. Each time different parts of its mushroom body would change colors—red, purple, azure, and green. It emitted an intense light. At the same time it continued to expand in size as its insides constantly billowed to its outsides. Its stem, which resembled bundled veils, kept getting stouter. It seemed ready to attack above the city. My whole body withered from fear. I wondered if I were not about to collapse.... [13:48]

... The cloud, once a mushroom, now resembled more the shape of a jellyfish. Yet even more beastlike than that, it shook its tentacles and changed the color of its head red, purple, lavender, and green. Its direction turned to the southeast and then hung low in the sky. Smoke kept pouring out from within it as bubbles do from boiling water. It appeared crazed, as if it still might attack at any moment. [13:50]

Clouds have long been more than mere meteorological phenomena to Ibuse. Just before *Black Rain* he published an essay, "Umbrella Clouds" (*Kasagumo,* 1964), in which he tells of encountering a fortune-teller who openly wonders what mushroom-shaped clouds, in fact, portend. Ibuse has his own theory, one he has held since he first saw these omens of destructive power looming over a Tokyo rocked by earthquakes and ravaged by fires in 1923. "Beastlike," these clouds signal the release of a malevolent energy bent on sweeping away all that lies beneath. Yet closely allied with their evil is their beauty. In *Black Rain,* the changing colors that fascinate Shigematsu also maximize his terror, for in Ibuse's imagination violence has often taken the form of patterns attractive in their abstraction.

Shigematsu's fear and confusion have the effect of driving him back into the reassuring rites of his prebomb existence. For instance, he is suddenly inspired to do his usual morning calisthenics as if they were a "Shinto purification ceremony" (*misogi-shiki to iu hōshiki de*). Dazed, he continues to wander aimlessly, "entrusting his fate to the heavens."

At the end of the third chapter, the novel returns to the present, yet the emphasis on ritual activity persists. Shigematsu, done with his recopying for the day, is having dinner with his wife when he recalls how poorly they ate during the war. Perhaps, he suggests, Shigeko should write her own account of their deprivations as an appendix to his *Diary*. Shigeko has her own idea: why not commemorate Hiroshima by having every August 6 the same breakfast they had on that day in 1945. This would preserve, and ritualize, their suffering in a kind of reverse feast of thanksgiving. Shigeko remembers exactly what she prepared that day, and indeed, she remembers much else. She does decide to record her own journal.

Soon the entire Shizuma household is busy writing. Shigeko's contribution to the family project, though brief, is rather resplendently entitled "Dietary Life in Wartime Hiroshima" (*Hiroshima nite senjika ni okeru shokuseikatsu*). It is a fascinating summary of the largely nutritional hardships endured by the civilian population in the last years of the war. This journal, like all others in *Black Rain*, provides interesting details on how cleverly people respond when faced with serious shortages. By obtaining foodstuffs in the country or on the black market, or by substituting homemade concoctions for hard-to-get necessities, the women of Shigeko's neighborhood exhibit the resourcefulness that has interested Ibuse since his first castaway stories, and which he has made a hallmark of his folk characters. Shigeko includes lists of foods in her account, as did Shigematsu of disfigured hibakusha in his, and, moreover, as eighteenth-century officials did of a dead pilgrim's personal effects in "The Toramatsu Journal." Through the accumulation of such impoverished or even grotesque details there emerges dark realism, different in both technique and significance from that of other writers. Shigeko's little memoir, though easy to overlook in the immense scope of *Black Rain,* is as valuable a lesson as any in the novel in how survivors do, indeed, survive.

Shigematsu approves of his wife's literary labors. After reading her account, which notes how hungry children were given insects to eat, it is with no little irony that he leaves to attend a ritual dedicated to the souls of vermin:

> The insect rites [*mushi kuyō*] are a ceremony always held two days after the traditional observance of *bōshū* [June 5]. This day was set aside to

222

Ibuse,

*Black
Rain,*
and the
Present
Day

make fancy rice dumplings to honor insects inadvertently killed by farmers working in the fields. [13:67]

Such historical agrarian customs are some of the traditions of the prebomb world which Shigematsu brings with him into the postbomb world. They are modes of symbolic behavior, validated by centuries of common observances intimately connected with a social sense of full integration. They ensure, to whatever extent, the continuity of cultural structures. Shigematsu, stripped of those structures by the Hiroshima bomb, now realizes what subtle purposes such old folklore can serve. The belief is one in the sanctity of life, the most important of all faiths for Ibuse's hibakusha. Throughout *Black Rain*, the hero will find himself recalling a host of obscure rites from the past, all serving as powerful talismans against further attacks on a social economy already weakened by atrocity. Ibuse writes at the beginning of chapter seven:

> Shigematsu continued to make a clean copy of his *Diary*.
> This month there were a number of festivals. The rice-seedling celebration and the memorial service for dead insects had already passed. On the eleventh would be the planting festival, on the fourteenth, the old iris festival, and on the twentieth, the bamboo-cutting festival. Each of these simple ceremonies seemed to symbolize how the peasants of long ago, impoverished as they were, held life in high regard. As Shigematsu continued his copying, and as he continued to recall the holocaust [*abikyōkan*], he realized that the poorer the peasants' festivals were, the more we should treasure them. [13:98]

Shigematsu treasures the "simple ceremonies" of modern life as well—Shigeko's celebration of her August 6 repast; his own attention to raising carp. One of the festivals observed by everyone in Kobatake, however, bodes ill for Yasuko. Just before her prospective fiancé breaks off negotiations because of disturbing talk that will not subside, Ibuse writes:

> June 30 was the Sumiyoshi Festival in Onomichi harbor. It is an observance in which lanterns are set afloat to beseech Sumiyoshi that Kobatake village suffer no floods. Four floats, each of plain wood and named after one of the seasons, carry lit candles and drift in calm pools along the valley stream. It is reportedly best if they slowly drift on the dark water for a long time: should, for instance, the one marked "Autumn" flow too soon from its pool, then floods were to be feared at that time of year. [13:123]

Ritual in *Black Rain* is tied not only to the private regeneration of one hibakusha family, but to the general movement of the human, and natural, world. Indeed, Shigematsu's recopying of the diary is itself an activity that, conspicuously marked with words found like those on the Sumiyoshi Festival floats, functions much as a modern, literary amulet.

The fifth through ninth chapters are largely excerpts from the August 6 entry of *Diary*. Shigematsu is still wandering about the center of the city in a dazed mental state. Fire, more destructive than the original blast, drives him and his fellow refugees first this way and then that. In the melee, Shigematsu encounters an old acquaintance. He often seems to encounter such acquaintances, frequently from his native Kobatake. Even in a novel chronicling a nuclear attack, Ibuse's most frequent setting—the village—somehow remains intact. At one point Shigematsu and his friend, Miyaji, look up into the sky together:

> From the center of the city swirled an incredible whirlpool of flames that pierced the heavens. It was a huge, huge pillar of fire. It sucked up smoke and fire that spewed from all the city streets and made a whirlpool out of them. It changed into a cloud that trailed smoke. Around this whirlwind of fire, soaring through the clouds, were little fiery lumps and other things in flames that rained down upon the ground. It was as in a dream. We realized that these were in fact the supports, beams, and doorsills of houses that had been sucked up into the swirling winds. Ignited by the heat, they were only now plummeting back to earth. [13:78]

Pillars of fire and swirling whirlpools, the two kinetic elements of Ibuse's vision of violence, are joined in *Black Rain* to destroy every corner of Hiroshima. Yet, true to the rules of Ibuse's beautiful end, Shigematsu is able, though not far from the center of the city, to witness the display of abstract force as if distantly removed. In this scene, more than any other, Shigematsu perhaps seems most like his creator Ibuse: the possible vicariousness of the experience is at the core of so much of Ibuse's writing. "It was as in a dream." Others die—Miyaji, for instance, soon disappears in a fire—but never Shigematsu. He is left alive to remember, and to write.

Leaving the fiery vortexes behind, Shigematsu finally makes his way across the city to the sports ground near his home, where Shigeko, following a prearranged plan, has taken refuge. Together they return to their house in the Senda-machi neighborhood to sur-

224

Ibuse,

Black

Rain,

and the

Present

Day

vey the damage. Immediately catching Shigematsu's perceptive eye are the dead fish floating in the small pond in their back yard. Strange, he thinks to himself, that human beings should live while aquatic life dies. Somehow it seems a reversal of the "natural order"; it is certainly a reversal of Ibuse's order, for until now his literature has indeed been filled with living fish ("The Carp") and dead people ("The River") in its many ponds. This scene is also the reverse of the final scene of the novel, when Shigematsu will be busying himself with the baby carp in his pond while Yasuko lies dying in a hospital.

This is foreshadowed when their niece is reunited with them at their Senda-machi home. She bears the mark of the black rain, the consequence of her unwise decision to reenter the city earlier in the day. The Shizuma family, now complete, leaves their neighborhood and first crosses the Kyōbashi River for Ujina, an outlying district initially thought to have been spared destruction but, in fact, as devastated as elsewhere. At this point Shigematsu makes a fateful determination. They will traverse the very center of the city in the hope of reaching his firm—the Japan Textile Company—in the suburb of Furuichi. In this case, the shortest route is also the most dangerous. Their journey through Hiroshima is a revelation of hell. They walk, run, stumble, and crawl past grotesque creatures, both human and not, both dead and dying. "An endlessly varied series of corpses lay scattered about" (13:105). They make their way over the red-hot coals beneath their feet and against the searing winds that blow radioactive ash in their faces. No matter which way they turn, they are met with the same terrible sights.

Hiroshima becomes, like Albert Camus's Oran or Elie Wiesel's Auschwitz, a closed environment of death, an underworld of seemingly infinite damnation. Ibuse's narrative of their passage gives no clue of their presence in what, only a few hours earlier, was a city; rather, the Shizumas seem, as they read the shattered inscription on a stone pillar, to be in a "dream." Everything they experience is unbelievable, fantastic, nightmarish. Remarking upon this stone pillar, which belonged to an important family and once was thought beautiful, Ibuse writes, "Both style and sophistication mean nothing in times such as these" (13:100). The inversion or utter collapse of conventional standards and expectations signaled by this entry into the dream world is further emphasized when Shigematsu notices a pond surrounded with flowers and resting birds, a common sight in earlier Ibuse works that now appears absolutely extraordinary. The reader is reminded of iris about the pond in Fukuyama, or the miraculousness of his Hawaiian rice paddy to the stranded Usaburō.

Black Rain advances a theme germane to Ibuse's postwar work, best known perhaps in "Lieutenant Lookeast," namely, the reversal of terms such as "normal" and "abnormal" in order to effect a transcendental world view. Indeed, in this novel what seems most "normal" in the lives of its characters is the vision of the fiery holocaust that pursues wherever they run. The beautiful end is seen not only in whirlwinds above but in whirlpools below:

> Countless corpses had tumbled down into the grasses that grew below the river bank to our right. In the river itself, body after body came floating by. Some, caught in the willow roots on the river's edge, would be dragged by the current, swung around, and suddenly made to rear their heads out of the water. Some came down the river with either the upper or lower half of their lifeless bodies bobbing. And some, those who revolved in circles below the willow trees, seemed to be alive as they raised their arms almost as if to grasp at the branches above. [13:104]

Like the childhood playmate eulogized in his memoirs, or the tragic suicide told in "The River," the victims of *Black Rain* link in death to form an image of natural mechanics turned grotesque; burnt corpses revolving endlessly in the eddies of a river. The image oddly recalls that of the candle floats launched by Shigematsu's fellow villagers in their Sumiyoshi Festival. What floats here, however, is the consequence of calamity, not a magical injunction against it.

Finally, after crossing Aioi Bridge only meters from ground zero, the Shizumas make their way up along the Ōta River to Yamamoto Station, where they hope to catch a train to Furuichi. They are fortunate enough to find one waiting to depart—but it will be a long wait, indeed, as they soon realize once they have pushed their way aboard an already packed carriage. What follows in the narrow confines of this stalled train is one of the most powerful, and certainly most ghastly, passages of the novel.

Its details come not from any of Ibuse's Hiroshima informants, nor from any of the written testimonies he gathered; rather, it is reconstructed from an incident Ibuse himself had witnessed in Fukuyama after the sixth. Ibuse reveals in the *Asahi Shimbun* interview:

> I first realized that the atomic bomb had been dropped over Hiroshima when I returned to Fukuyama Station in the evening. Hiroshima is ap-

226
Ibuse,
*Black
Rain*,
and the
Present
Day

proximately one hundred miles from Fukuyama, and one can see the city from Mihara, only twenty-five miles from Fukuyama. Train after train came rolling into the station, each packed with grisly victims of the bomb. The trains continued to discharge their passengers even though all the inns near the station were filled to capacity. The riders were furious at the National Railways, but of course neither the train nor the station personnel had the least idea of what was going on. One of the passengers began to parody the railways by announcing, "For the present we are sorry to inconvenience our passengers with this deterioration in National Railways' service." He was a very good mimic.[13]

The sight of injured and humiliated victim-passengers pouring out of trains in Fukuyama Station—Ibuse's first introduction to what had happened in Hiroshima—is incorporated with few changes into "The Iris." In the later *Black Rain*, Ibuse extends the train journey back to its point of departure in the bombed city, dramatizing it as one of the most unforgettable moments of the novel.

While his family waits for the hot, overcrowded train to pull out of the station, Shigematsu begins to take horrified stock of the degraded humanity huddled nearby. A mother embraces her lifeless baby, refusing to believe it dead; others vomit and defecate where they stand; many are simply stunned and silent. The train lurches forward, but it is only a false start. One of the passengers parodies the ridiculously polite apologies of the conductor. The tensions thus lessened, some of the waiting strangers strike up conversations among themselves. This train, like many trains in modern fiction, becomes a place where people of different backgrounds can meet and mingle for the author's expository purposes. Ibuse makes the scene aboard the train a microcosm of his entire novel: Shigematsu listens attentively to the various accounts traded among his fellow riders:

> Everyone spoke of today's bombing attack. Yet, since each told only what he himself had seen or heard, with no connection to anyone else's story, I found it impossible to get a clear picture of the entire disaster. I record here their stories just as I recall them. [13:113]

The first story is told by a man from the Fukushima-chō district of the city, which in turn leads to the story of an acquaintance of his. Next speaks a boy whose father had abandoned him in order to save himself, then a man who blames the arrogance of the army for all that has happened, and finally a woman who numbly explains how her only child had died the instant the bomb exploded. Ibuse has previously used this technique of assembling strangers together in one place and making them talk; in fact, some works seem hardly more than such extended montages. In "No Consultations Today" the common ground is a doctor's office; in *The Station Hotel,* a hotel. In *Black Rain,* however, Ibuse's method engenders a distinctly morbid mood, a mood ensured by the use of a train as the meeting place of Hiroshima hibakusha. Trains, so often important venues for nineteenth-century literature both east and west, could no longer suggest only vehicles in which genteel people traveled in comfort; war had changed that. After German cattle cars, and then a Hiroshima commuter train, had been used to transport dehumanized people "jammed like sardines," the romance of such travel was gone forever.

Eventually the train starts sluggishly rolling and arrives in Furuichi. With the Shizuma family's safe arrival at his company's facilities there, Shigematsu's entry for August 6 comes to its long-delayed conclusion. The August 7 entry of *Diary* begins almost immediately with the ninth chapter of *Black Rain*. Shigematsu wakes in great pain in the company dormitory, but still he endeavors to make himself useful. There is much to do. The refugees, most of whom have no association with the firm, crowd the facilities, dying at an alarming rate. Soon, disposal of the bodies becomes an indelicate problem. Shigematsu's superior debates whether they ought to be burned or buried, eventually opting for the former out of, one suspects, practicality. Still, he cannot bring himself to let these victims pass from this world without the benefit of a funeral. Shigematsu, close by at the moment of his boss's decision, is ordered to take the place of a priest and read memorial prayers over the dead. A rather irreligious layman lacking any clerical qualifications, Shigematsu at first demurs. His superior admonishes:

> "Well then, who would you say has the power to lead the dead into salvation? There's no difference between amateurs and professionals in this matter. Reading the sutras for the deceased is in a different class from administering the sick medicine. And it certainly isn't illegal. If you don't care for the Shinshū sect, then Zen or Nichiren rites will do just as well." [13:129]

Shigematsu dutifully acquiesces. Other Ibuse characters have done so before. In the bomb shelters of Singapore, Mr. Burrough per-

228

Ibuse,
*Black
Rain*,
and the
Present
Day

formed marriage ceremonies; in "Voyage South," and again in "Yanagi Shigenori and the Three-Forked Road at Bukit Timah," Ibuse pointed to a precedent drawn directly from his own experience:

> The sound of gunfire all day. With [Nakamura] Chihei and others, bathed in the pure, lush waters of a hillside spring.... The farewell ceremony for the late Yanagi Shigenori. The deceased died a hero's death on a battlefield near the Bukit Timah Road on February 12, and his remains have come back to us. A lieutenant read the sutras while we military journalists placed offerings of fruit and flowers before his ashes and a photograph. Later we all spoke of the deceased's fine character. [10:49]

This lieutenant of the Second World War described in "Voyage South" becomes Shigematsu in *Black Rain*. Both don the mantle of a priest, and both respond intuitively to the needs of the survivors, offering ceremonies for the dead. In the broadest sense this is the mission of all Ibuse's survivors, a large cast of fictional and real characters united by the simple circumstance of their staying alive. In *Black Rain*, no one survivor is any better qualified than another to memorialize the dead. Just remaining among the living is talent enough.

Shigematsu prepares himself for the task ahead by visiting an old priest in a nearby Shinshū temple for some condensed instruction in the funeral liturgy. He learns of several lengthy sutras often read for the dead, but, realizing no doubt how often he would have to recite them, he decides instead that the "Sermon on Mortality" (*Hakkotsu no gobunshō*, literally "A Treatise on Skeletons") will suffice.[14] Shigematsu constructs his makeshift rites about its words:

> I lacked the power to guide the dead to salvation, but I did resolve at least to conduct the memorial services. I do believe that some repose must be offered them. I realized that I would have to read the prayer with all my heart and soul. [13:131]

In a fashion typical of Ibuse and his heroes, Shigematsu takes careful notes on the old priest's reading of the prayers. Notebook in hand, he returns to the factory and immediately puts his lesson to work, reading over one corpse, then another and another, the words he has just heard recited. His services, though those of a neophyte, are required near and far. The dead now seem numberless. Some bereaved survivors even offer Shigematsu remuneration for his chari-

table work, so deep is their need to believe that he is a real priest
reading real prayers and delivering their dead relatives or friends to a real paradise. Form, even an improvised one, is paramount. After the violence of Hiroshima, such rituals are all that seem to retain any importance, perhaps even any reality. The last line in Shigematsu's diary entry for August 7 reads, "It was a day that dawned and darkened with funerals" (13:133).

The journal for August 8 makes a similar point. By the end of this third day of his postbomb world, Shigematsu has discarded his notes. He recites his prayer for the dead by heart. His services are, however, no longer conducted for the benefit of a single deceased and his mourners. They are now direct pleas to God: the number of dead is so great that their bodies are disposed of in anonymous mass pyres. "The sight of tongues of fire at work on the bodies of men," writes Shigematsu of this day, "flickered before my eyes like a waking dream" (13:136).

Shigematsu's duties as resident priest include maintaining records, an activity that often figures importantly in Ibuse's stories but doubly so here, for Shigematsu's records are records of the dead. As one preliminary for the funerals, Shigematsu enters into his notebook whatever salient details are known of the deceased. In a narrative method much resembling that found in "The Toramatsu Journal," bits and pieces of a human existence are strung together to form a pathetically moving and powerful text within a text. Why Shigematsu should do this is part of his nature as an Ibuse hero: Ibuse makes his writer-protagonists attempt to impose structure—literary "logic"—upon a body of fragmentary and unordered data. It is one hallmark of such characters that Shigematsu is scrupulously objective, at times nearly scientific, in his observations and inferred explanations of atomic Hiroshima. Earlier in the novel he had written of a cucumber, half burned by the bomb's flash, in such terms as "physical process' (*butsuriteki sáyō*), "metachromatism" (*henshoku*), and "chemical mutation" (*kagakuteki henka*). His is the same rationally descriptive approach to catastrophe exploited in "The River." In *Black Rain*, more refined and deftly combined in the figure of a priest with a kind of intuitive spirituality, this objectivity seems at some times absurd and at other times comforting. The imposition of a pseudoscientific language upon the events and aftermath of Hiroshima, by a man who recites ancient prayers even while his life is destroyed by the ad-

230

Ibuse,

Black

Rain,

and the

Present

Day

vance of modern physics, is paralleled by the similar imposition of Ibuse's familiar historical principles. Shigematsu writes in the August 9 entry of his *Diary:*

> Hadn't the whole world seemingly fallen into disarray since the bomb was dropped on Hiroshima? Someone once told me an old saying— regions where wars have been especially terrible need one hundred years for their people to recover from the damage done their characters. That is probably true. [13:146–47]

Shigematsu's speculative remarks on the ethical as well as physical harm done in Hiroshima are prompted by theft. Some company supplies are stolen by soldiers purporting to be acting under orders. By discovering precedents in "an old saying," Shigematsu helps to reconcile the Hiroshima disaster to a general pattern of historical experience. In this particular instance, Ibuse appears on the verge of concluding, as have other writers describing other atrocities, that the victim is in ever-present danger of degenerating morally as much as the victimizer. Although in Hiroshima there can be no complicity (the "victimizer" is, at first anyway, an ungraspable inhuman energy, seemingly without willful direction), there is still betrayal when one victim ensures his survival at the cost of another's. This is symptomatic of the general collapse of the social economy, which, in more ordered times, holds the baser human impulses in check.

Elaborating on this idea that once the bomb fell, all normal rules of the natural world were suspended, Shigematsu notes that "war paralyzes men's power of judgment" (13:140). "Since the *pikadon* [atomic bomb; literally "flash-boom"] of August 6, the soldiers . . . no longer know how to act" (13:286). Moreover, he quotes his niece to the effect that "after the bomb fell, the military chain of command quickly disintegrated. Law was thrown aside. There were reputedly officers who trembled before their men" (13:155).

Shigematsu's response to the breakdown of order is to emphasize proportionately his social and professional identities. He reminds himself that he is a husband, an uncle, a company official. On August 10 he begins a quixotic errand for his firm, one which will keep him fruitlessly busy for days as he tries to secure a supply of coal. This development in the story serves two purposes, one that allows Shigematsu a dignity in being considered useful, and one that allows the reader to reenter Hiroshima with him and see it once more through his eyes.

Returning to what he had fled only days before, Shigematsu sees much the same destruction, but he realizes much more of its vast reality—no longer "dreamlike." "Hiroshima has disappeared. I never dreamed that the city, with this tragedy, could have come to this" (13:160). The sight of countless corpses still left exactly where they have died makes Shigematsu recite "involuntarily" to himself the Sermon on Mortality. He sits stunned among the smoldering ruins and idly sketches in the ashes as had Kakutan in *Waves* when he, too, realized what history had wrought. As he etches both words and swirls (*uzu*, a frequent term in Ibuse's vocabulary, suggesting the historical vortex that controls the motion of human and natural events), he recalls his school days in Kobatake as Kakutan the monk-warrior had recalled his own at the academy. Shigematsu's memory in this passage combines with Ibuse's own. He rises and continues on his way through the city to seek out the authorities. He writes in *Diary:*

> Fate had not been kind to the city of Hiroshima. Corpses floated in a pond filled with lotus flowers. In the grasses that grew alongside the pond cowered a single white pigeon. When I quietly approached it and picked it up in my hands, I discovered that it had lost its right eye and had scorched the feathers on its right shoulder. I felt the urge to eat it broiled with soy sauce, but instead I let it escape by tossing it into the air. The bird flapped its wings vigorously and flew over the leaves of the lotus plants, making a parabola from left to right.
>
> Then suddenly it dove into the water. [13:169]

Ibuse's literary imagination again leads his readers to a pond of death. This passage suggests much already encountered in his literature: over a pond surrounded by flowers ("The Iris") flies an injured bird ("Sawan on the Roof") in an irregular pattern ("Wabisuke") until it plunges into the water and dies ("The River").

The irony of the pigeon's death prefigures another irony. When Shigematsu returns from Hiroshima to Furuichi, he learns that he has been supposed dead. This he hears from two of his wife's brothers, who rushed to the city from Kobatake when they learned of its destruction. The night is late, however, and it is not until the next day, after an exhausting schedule of more funerals and more inquiries into the coal supplies, that Shigematsu is apprised of all the details.

The villagers of Kobatake first heard of the raid on Hiroshima

232
Ibuse,
*Black
Rain*,
and the
Present
Day

early on the evening of the sixth, and soon afterwards injured refugees began arriving. Thoroughly alarmed, Shigeko's brothers decided that, even if only to confirm their deaths, they must go into the city to look for the remains of the Shizumas. Laden with offerings for the Shizumas' souls, the brothers began their trek:

> On their way out of the village they stopped off at my mother's to say good-bye. There they found my younger sister and her two children who had returned to the village from Fukuyama. Mother thought that we had surely been blown to pieces or killed under the weight of our own house. She had placed our three photographs on the Buddhist altar alongside three cups of water and a vase of dahlias.
>
> "If you are going to Hiroshima, then at the very least take some incense sticks with you. And some of the village's water or green leaves. Place the incense among the ruins of the house. Scatter the water and the leaves. And since Shigematsu liked *kemponashi* nuts so much, take some of those along, too."
>
> As she spoke she poured some well water into an empty vinegar bottle. Then she wrapped the incense and leaves from a *fukurashi* tree in paper. She entrusted all this to [Shigeko's older brother] Masao. He told me that my mother also picked up two or three green *kemponashi* nuts that had fallen to the ground and put them in a little pocket of his backpack. [13:181]

When the brothers arrived at the Shizumas' former home in Sendamachi, they lit the incense and scattered the other offerings before a neighbor told them that those they honored were, in fact, still alive and in Furuichi. Shigematsu, like the hero of "Chōhei's Grave" before him, was consecrated in ceremonies by relatives who thought themselves his dutiful survivors.

There is irony here, but there is also a sincere comment on the powers of commemorative rituals in the lives of *Black Rain*'s characters. Most intriguing in this particular funeral rite is the *kemponashi*, a tree established earlier in the book as a symbol of history when its seeds were mentioned in a nineteenth-century letter. When the tree recurs later in the narrative, it suggests a suprahistorical tie cutting across all three tenses of the novel to connect disparate experiences in a common theme, namely, the vigor of regenerative responses to destruction. "Seeds" and "green nuts" suggest rebirth: the transcendental symbol is simultaneously the resurgence of nature. The symbolism and power of the organic world, evident early in Ibuse's work, begins in *Black Rain* with the pond of baby carp but develops fully only in the latter part of the novel. When Shigematsu reenters Hiroshima on the eleventh, he makes a startling discovery in the still smoldering city:

> The bomb had spurred the growth of such things as plants and flies even while it checked human powers of life. Plants and flies, in fact, were rampant. Yesterday behind the charred ruins of the noodle shop on this street, a *bashō* tree grew new shoots a foot and a half in length. The original stems had been cleanly ripped off by the explosive force of the bomb, leaving no traces behind. Yet now something new, growing as fast as bamboo shoots, had taken their place. By today they were over two feet long. The fact that this tree was growing by more than fives each day surprised even me, a man born on a farm and familiar with trees. [13:188–89]

The invigorated *bashō* tree that Tomoakira mentions in his *Waves* diary foreshadows disaster for the *Heike*. But that described in Shigematsu's *Diary* seems somehow encouraging, perhaps a symbol of a rebirth. Indeed, much of the Hiroshima landscape increasingly appears as a metaphoric range of the power of Ibuse's natural world. Shigematsu takes careful note of the postbomb flora, a descriptive emphasis that renders the city noticeably less a metropolis and more, again, a village. Much like villages elsewhere in Ibuse's literature, Hiroshima is then the site of those traditions and values largely identified with rural folk.

Chapter fourteen, a chapter in which such traditions and values figure prominently, includes an encounter between Shigematsu and friends from Kobatake who have come to aid in the relief work. Shigematsu joins them and looks for fellow Kobatake villagers among the hospitalized. From these villagers Shigematsu learns news not only of home, but of the entire world. Nagasaki has also been destroyed by a bomb. The Soviet Union has entered the war. Moreover, the dreadful news that Shigematsu relives as he recopies his diary seems to lead to further dreadful news in the present. As if writing of Hiroshima has somehow precipitated a recurrence of its horrors, Yasuko, years after the actual explosion, has begun to exhibit the symptoms of the radiation disease from which her uncle had sought to convince himself she was safe.

With this crucial development in the novel, the reader's attentions are shifted from the events of 1945 to those of the narrative present.

234

Ibuse,

Black

Rain,

and the

Present

Day

Excerpts from Shigematsu's diary now alternate with details of a calamity related to, but delayed after, that of the original bomb. Two stories now parallel each other, deepening the tragedy of both. Shigematsu is fully aware of the pathos of the coincidence:

> Yasuko's vision gradually deteriorated, and she said there was a constant ringing in her ears. I was first told of these symptoms while in the parlor. For a second the room disappeared and was replaced by a big jellyfish cloud in the clear sky above me. I saw it very clearly. [13:217]

Yasuko

For some time Shigematsu is far too upset to go on recopying his *Diary*. Writing about the bomb when he feels responsible for his niece's exposure to it could only aggravate his guilt. As Yasuko's condition worsens, so do Shigematsu's personal recriminations. This theme—Shigematsu's responsibility for Yasuko—has lurked in the background throughout *Black Rain*. But it is now given full play, encouraged perhaps by Ibuse's own guilt over the loss of those for whom he, too, has felt responsible. Shigeko takes Shigematsu outdoors to sit beneath a *kemponashi* tree while she tells him the details. Yasuko had been experiencing the dread symptoms for a while, but at first she had ignored them. Later, admitting the truth to herself, she had tried treating the disease on her own with the help of folklore and some medical texts. "By the time Shigeko took Yasuko to the general clinic in Kobatake for her first examination, her condition had become quite serious" (13:218). The clinic's Dr. Kajita then arranged for Yasuko to be cared for at home by the Shizumas.

Shigematsu leaves the nursing of his sick niece to his wife. He is embarrassed by Yasuko's illness, for he, once the only victim in the family, now appears nearly robust by comparison. Ibuse's hero (much as Ibuse himself has done in the very writing of this novel) turns his attention to a text of the A-bomb casualty rather than to the casualty herself:

> Shigeko told him in detail about the sick girl's condition. She also showed him the diary of their niece's illness that she kept every night before retiring. It was not like the charts maintained by hospital staffs, but more like an ordinary diary with descriptions and personal impressions penned in here and there. Yet this diary was nothing to be read lightly.

Shigematsu fell into deep thought over Yasuko's illness. He decided to go ask the head of the Hosokawa Clinic in Yūda, where he himself had had hemorrhoid surgery, what might be done. He took the diary along as a record of her case.

Dr. Hosokawa read a few pages and then spoke.

"How about sending this to the Atomic Bomb Casualty Commission in Hiroshima? This diary tells of a hospital doctor, a patient suffering sickness, and a nurse. A typical trio. Three people, the one in the middle a victim, all exhausted from their confusion over what to do. In fact, they are a trio of victims; that much is clear. The Hiroshima ABCC maintains records on bomb victims and occasionally publishes reports on the subject." [13:222–23]

Dr. Hosokawa's advice might seem insensitive. Perhaps he sees in Yasuko merely an interesting case, one that should be referred to the ABCC, an American facility that at one time only examined hibakusha and never treated them. Yet Shigematsu accepts Dr. Hosokawa's suggestion with enthusiasm. What the doctor proposes, after all, is much what Shigematsu has already done. His own *Diary*, too, was an "ordinary diary" written only to be sent to the local school where it would be kept among other records. Shigematsu sees another opportunity to augment his documentation in this new diary. He starts to work at once.

"Shigematsu copied onto lined paper what Shigeko had written in her scrawl. He changed the words and sentences to suit his own taste" (13:224). In one sense this new diary is a reverse image of *Diary*. It hopes to detail the course of regeneration, not destruction; it may be meant both as medicine and memoir. Yet over the six days it documents, Yasuko's condition worsens continually, interrupted only by momentary rallies that offer a false, and cruel, hope. "The Diary of the Illness of Takamaru Yasuko" begins on July 25, the day of the Tenjin Festival. A fever leaves her listless and bedridden, but two days later she feels better, so much so that the whole family decides to enjoy the evening air in the garden under the *kemponashi* tree. A neighbor comes by with a gift of eels (thought to be a restorative food) for Yasuko and stays to entertain the Shizumas with his stories. "Old man Takizō took the feelings of the sick girl into account and did not touch upon illness in his legends and fantastic tales handed down from long ago" (13:227). Within a story within a story, there are now more stories—tales of old Kobatake intended to

236
Ibuse,
*Black
Rain*,
and the
Present
Day

lighten the low spirits of the Shizuma family. The old tales transport everyone into the nostalgic past of the village, a time before the atomic bomb when all one had to worry about were clever badgers, snakes, and wolves.

On July 28 Yasuko goes out of the house to find a new doctor, since Dr. Kajita has been called away indefinitely. She decides to admit herself to the Kuishiki Hospital located in a neighboring village, no doubt because she feels she has become too much a burden to her aunt and uncle. Within days everything seems to go wrong with the girl. She is now severely stricken with acute radiation sickness, an affliction once termed by Dr. Kajita as "the monster of illnesses."

By chapter seventeen, when it is the middle of an August as hot as that of 1945, Yasuko's condition seems beyond hope. She is still hospitalized and is in terrible pain. Shigematsu's feelings of guilt are now almost unbearable:

> Yasuko's radiation sickness was due not only to the black rain but also to her having wandered through the ashes of the burning ruins. She had scraped her left elbow while crawling on the ground from Aioi Bridge to Sakan-chō. It did not seem impossible that this wound had allowed the deadly ashes to do their work. Now of course nothing could be done, but he felt it had been wrong to drag her from the Ujina branch of the Japan Transport Company to the Furuichi factory. If only he had begged Sugimura, head of the Ujina office, he would have let Yasuko stay with him for two or three days. Shigematsu felt the responsibility for this. Moreover, it was Shigematsu who had brought Yasuko to Hiroshima in the first place. [13:234]

This latent guilt, exacerbated by Yasuko's illness, makes Shigematsu desperate to help her. He cannot stand to see her die, for her death would be a replay of the death of Hiroshima, one calamity he had already barely survived. To survive another would make living seem dishonest, a lie. Shigematsu again turns to the only means of help he seems to know: words, language, writing. He finds both consolation and direction in the diary of another hibakusha, Iwatake Hiroshi, sent him by Dr. Hosokawa. Iwatake, also a doctor, was drafted at the age of forty-five only a little over a month before the war ended. Unfortunately he was in Hiroshima on August 6 and was very seriously injured by the bomb. At first he was taken to a school converted to a reception center in the suburb of Hesaka, then later to his native village of Shōbara. His wife eventually found him there,

though his face was so disfigured that she could recognize him only
by his name. Once reunited with his wife, however, Iwatake began a miraculous recovery. Ibuse writes:

> With [Dr. Iwatake's] account was included Mrs. Iwatake's recollection of those same days. It appeared to be a transcription of an interview conducted into her husband's amazing recovery. Perhaps it might serve as a reference for Yasuko's own treatment. [13:252]

First Mrs. Iwatake begged to have her husband moved to a more private room. Then she obtained medical supplies to treat the burns covering his body. Yet even with such preferential treatment, his condition began to deteriorate. Maggots infested his right ear, and on August 15, the day the war ended, he nearly expired from a high fever. At this point Mrs. Iwatake decided to take her husband away to Yūda village where, aided by the local peaches that he ate to the near exclusion of all else, he began to improve. Eventually he was completely restored to health. Shigematsu learns that he practices medicine this very day in Tokyo.

This story—a true one quoted nearly verbatim by Ibuse from the Iwatakes' actual journal—inspires Shigematsu and his wife to keep their niece's spirits high. The sheer will to live, it seems, might effect a cure. Perhaps that power of human will, Shigematsu wonders, can be inspired empathically. With that in mind, he redoubles his efforts at the carp pond where the fish are now, like Yasuko, at a crucial stage. Many have died, but that was expected: those will live that most want to live. The survivors concern Shigematsu, for they are the carp that have beaten the odds. Perhaps Yasuko, too, will be among the fortunate ones. Somehow his labors at the pond with Shōkichi and Asajirō will make that all the more possible.

Chapters nineteen and twenty comprise the climax of *Black Rain;* as Ibuse writes—"Now is the critical moment" (13:264). The reader is in suspense over Yasuko's fate; Shigematsu, over that of his carp. Worried that he and his partners have erred fatally in their timing, he turns to a traditional source of wisdom for advice and reassurance:

> When Shigematsu returned home he consulted the *Treasure Almanac* compiled by Katō Daigaku. According to the old lunar calendar, today would be the seventeenth day of the sixth month, or the traditional day of the Seventeen-Day-Old Moon, when it was customary to plant such things as radishes, kidney beans, and round Chinese cabbages in ground

238

Ibuse,

Black

Rain,

and the

Present

Day

where earlier there had been ginseng and melons. This was a valuable bit of knowledge, learned from the peasants' experience of the warm weeks in early autumn. Yes, of course the baby carp would be all right. Three days from now would be August sixth on the new calendar, Hiroshima Memorial Day, and then, on the ninth, Nagasaki Memorial Day.

"Yes, only three days left. I've got to hurry with my writing." [13:269]

In this brief passage, the cosmological world of calendrical observances, the inherited lessons of human history, the animal life cycle of carp, and Shigematsu's dairy with its need to memorialize Japan's incinerated cities are all juxtaposed to combine in a complex wheel of ritual dynamism. The two atomic bomb anniversaries become dates on the new calendar, to be honored like the traditional days of old, taking their cue from the "valuable bit of knowledge, learned from the peasants' experience." Shigematsu's *Diary,* the liturgy of these new rites, must be completed before these new festivals arrive. Throughout *Black Rain* Ibuse's hero has restored—and created anew—ceremonies in the impaired lives of the Hiroshima hibakusha. With this in mind, particularly as it might benefit Yasuko, Shigematsu resumes the copying of his diary.

It is now the entry for August thirteenth. For the fifth day in a row, Shigematsu leaves for Hiroshima in search of coal for the Furuichi factory. He passes by more smoke and fire, more people on the road silently dying. He fords a river full of corpses—another of Ibuse's deadly streams—while reciting to himself the Sermon on Mortality. When he returns to his temporary home in Furuichi empty-handed, his boss comes not to reprimand him but to give Yasuko and Shigeko a farewell banquet, for both of them are leaving for Kobatake in the morning. While feasting on home-brewed liquor and fried mulberry leaves, the Shizumas learn from their benefactor that what destroyed their city is called an "atomic bomb." Shigematsu observes:

> I know that the names for the *pikadon* had progressed from the initial "new weapon," to "new-type bomb," to "secret weapon," to "new-type special bomb," to "extra-powerful special bomb," and now today to "atomic bomb." But it could not be true that nothing would grow in Hiroshima for seventy-five years. I had seen grasses growing everywhere in the burned ruins. [13:279]

Earlier in the novel Shigematsu had traded different names for fish with a man who had grown up outside of Kobatake. Now he again ponders names, this time for the very device that has devastated his life and, until now, has remained unidentified. Language works constructively, even when its theme is destruction, naming things that can destroy names. The dinner party concludes with everyone singing ridiculous childhood songs. Of his favorite, Shigematsu writes, "I still have no idea what it means." Perhaps he is summing up the predicament of all words, not only the newly coined "atomic bomb," in his post-Hiroshima world.

The twentieth and final chapter of *Black Rain* begins with the August 14 entry of the *Diary*. Now alone in Furuichi, Shigematsu again sets off for Hiroshima. More than a week has passed since the sixth, but smoke still rises, not from the direct effects of the bomb itself but from the many crematoria. Suddenly Shigematsu spots something else:

> When I happened to look back over my shoulder I saw a single-band white rainbow that pierced the morning sun, shining hot in the overcast sky. It was a very unusual rainbow. I remember as a child I once saw a silver rainbow appear between me and the mountains late one night. I thought it strange. But this was the first time I had seen a white rainbow in the daytime. [13:285]

The white smoke of the crematoria is followed by the white rainbow of the daytime sky: both are images beautiful in themselves but signifying a nefarious past and future. Another incarnation of Ibuse's beautiful end—white like the waterspout that consumed Wabisuke's Hadakajima and as tall as the pillars of fire that also pierce the sky—the white rainbow of *Black Rain* is a sign of calamity still to come. Rainbows may be a new feature of Ibuse's cataclysmic vision, but they are known elsewhere in his literature. In a story entitled "Stray Dogs" (*Yaken,* 1961), Ibuse writes of a friend who strives to catch a glimpse of the legendary silver rainbow reputed to appear over a mountain near Ibuse's hometown of Kamo, possibly the rainbow that *Black Rain*'s Shigematsu "remember[s] as a child." Ibuse further explains in "Stray Dogs," however, that the villagers consider such silver rainbows evil omens. "The dark shadows of men's hearts, the disasters of the planet, all are reflected in the heavens as rainbows" (13:377). So it certainly seems in Ibuse's novel. When Shigematsu mentions to his boss what he has seen, the latter recalls his own experience of several years earlier:

> "Yes, it is a sign that something bad will happen," said the factory manager in all seriousness.

240
Ibuse,
Black
Rain,
and the
Present
Day

"The next day [after I saw one] was the day of the February 26 Incident [of 1936, when young Army officers attempted a coup]. That's why there had been a silver rainbow in the sky earlier. When I told my boss that I had seen one, he was taken quite aback. He told me there's a saying 'The white rainbow pierces the sun.' It's a sign from nature that foretells an armed uprising. That's what it says in the Chinese *Records of the Historian.* As for me, well, I thought that was rather unlikely. But at dawn the following day the February 26 Incident began."

"The one I saw was a rather thin rainbow that seemed to go right through the sun."

"Right, not too wide, but white and streamlined. I'm not superstitious, but a white rainbow is a sign. It sure seems that way." [13:290]

Ibuse, for one, is convinced. In another essay, "All About Rainbows" (*Niji no iroiro,* 1974), he writes that the book of Genesis holds rainbows to be the sign of the promises God makes to men, but that the Early Han *Shih Chi*—the *Records of the Historian* referred to by Shigematsu's manager—conversely argues that rainbows portend military insurrections. Ibuse himself admits in "All About Rainbows" that he saw a white rainbow over Miyakejima just before the February 26 Incident, and he further claims that citizens of Hiroshima reportedly spotted some soon after their city was bombed. Perhaps, Ibuse speculates, the spottings occurred on the day before Japan surrendered to the Allies.

In his novel, where he is free to arrange events as he pleases, Ibuse does place the surrender on the day after Shigematsu sees the rainbow. August 15 marks the last of the *Diary* entries—and it is the most dramatic. Shigematsu rises early in his Furuichi quarters, but he does not make the trip into Hiroshima. Instead, he and others spend a very long morning simply waiting for the news everyone both anticipates and dreads. They have been told to stand by for an important broadcast. When the hour finally comes to gather in the company cafeteria before the radio set, Shigematsu hesitates. "I shrank from the important events that the words coming out of the radio would signal. My feelings were just the reverse of the common compulsion to look straight into something one fears" (13:293).

Intimidated by the gravity of the moment, Shigematsu leaves the company building for the world outside, an outdoors of cool breezes and lush vegetation, a land naturally blessed with a river of clear, refreshing waters. Shigematsu is fleeing into Ibuse's natural world, a place where "baby eels swim blithely upstream against the current."

There he remains, among the positive and beautiful forces of nature, while the others huddle about a crackling radio and listen to an unfamiliar voice whose words they hardly comprehend. Shigematsu does not rejoin his coworkers until he is sure the broadcast is over. When he does, he is incapable of sharing their excited consternation. Their puzzled debate over the meaning of the Emperor's *mikotoba*, or "august words," recalls earlier debates in the novel over the appropriate words for certain species of fish and bombs: even the proclamation to end the war is devoid of clear meaning. Indeed, for Shigematsu as for so many survivors, nothing can ever again attain the reality of that one day—August 6—the day that not only defeated Japan but also, in some sense, defeated the full potential of language to signify.

Black Rain comes to a hurried conclusion once the Emperor has broadcast the surrender. When Shigematsu's diary for the fifteenth ends, so does the novel. Finished with all his recopying—completed for reasons now distinctly different from those with which he began —he leaves his study to make a quick check on his baby carp. On the way to the pond he prays to himself that a colorful rainbow, and not a white one, may arch across the skies, foretelling a recovery for his dying niece. "Although he knew it could never be, Shigematsu gazed at the far mountains and prayed it might come true" (13:298). Out of the pond where his carp now vigorously swim rises a single purple flower: the image is not of a world gone insane, as in "The Iris." Rather, like the black rain itself, the image combines regenerative strength with the hue of death.

This ending has left some people dissatisfied. Dissatisfaction, however, might very well have been what Ibuse intended for his readers— an emotion not uncommon or always accidental in the literature of atrocity; it would be hard to imagine what "satisfaction" in such a context would mean. Yet what troubles most is not the disarray in which Ibuse has left his characters per se, but the disarray of his narrative, the absence of a distinct "sense of an ending." The same seems true of *Waves*, another novel in which the story ends simultaneously with the main character's literary labors. Yet even if one grants to the abrupt conclusion of *Black Rain* consistency by reason of Ibuse's own precedent, or by reason of a thematic logic that ends the world of the novel when it ends the novelistic activities of its inhabitants, disgruntled readers might still object to the shifts in (even disintegration of) what begins as a unified point of view.

In the first chapters of *Black Rain,* Shigematsu, a character distinct

242

Ibuse,

Black

Rain,

and the

Present

Day

from Ibuse, is in firm control of the story. He is obviously the central figure. Before long, however, he abandons any active role and assumes a passive one. As the writer of diaries, an amateur historian, a record keeper, Shigematsu increasingly resembles his maker. Rather predictably, it is precisely when the novel enters the world of diaries, of extratextual texts, that the roles of Ibuse and his hero are confused. When the action of the story shifts from Shigematsu's present to the journals' collective past, the documentation assumes a privileged authority over the direction of the novel.

At times the reader cannot be absolutely certain whether first-person pronouns refer to a particular diarist, the recopier Shigematsu, or Ibuse himself. Perhaps Ibuse found the return to his typical narrative stance irresistible and surrendered to the urge to replace Shigematsu's omniscience with his own. Especially from the seventeenth chapter onwards, when Dr. Iwatake's account begins, Shigematsu ceases to serve as a narrator at all and is reduced to being one important character among several. Finally it is Ibuse who, though never named, seems to emerge most forcefully from the page. In hindsight, the reader must realize that it would have been impossible for Ibuse to remain outside his story, for once he had made Shigematsu pick up his pen, he had created in his novel a world of writers that demanded his own participation. *Black Rain*, Ibuse's greatest work, is thus a work about the work of literature.

That in itself is not unusual, either for Ibuse or for other modern writers. In *Black Rain,* as elsewhere, the characters are diarists, note takers, and list makers. All are searching in various, but always literary, ways to describe a grammar and a rhetoric of cataclysm. For Ibuse, such work began long before 1945 and achieved success long before *Black Rain*. The striking parallels of people and places found in other works are not hard to discern. Yet even while Ibuse was gathering material for *Black Rain,* he was writing another novel. Not only is it structurally and thematically similar to this most famous one, but it intersects with Ibuse's study of Hiroshima in ways indicative of his larger mission as a writer.

The Hachigata Castle of Musashi

The Hachigata Castle of Musashi (Bushū Hachigata-jō, 1961– 1962) is a historical novel that, like *Black Rain,* studies the past from

the point of view of the present. Serialized in *Shinchō* magazine in the
1960s—also like *Black Rain*—it appeared during the same period that Ibuse wrote and published his essay "Death in the Field, Death in the Field Hospital," his seminal short piece on the state of being a survivor. This theme seems to have especially preoccupied him at that time, for *Hachigata Castle* is a fascinating journey back in time to meet earlier veterans of earlier wars, and to understand in history what Ibuse had come to understand in his own life.

Whether it be Kuchisuke in his valley, Tomoakira on the Inland Sea, or Ibuse himself in Singapore, many of his characters have been men placed under a sometimes absurd, but always omnipotent, fate. Ironically, most of these same characters have never understood just how absurd and how omnipotent their fate is: in *Hachigata Castle* Ibuse sets his story in just such an unaware time. Referring to himself as watakushi, in the manner of an essayist, Ibuse begins his novel with the story of an acquaintance, the head priest of a Buddhist temple in Saitama Prefecture. The temple, Kōkōji, is located not far from the ruins of Hachigata Castle, the site of a famous siege during the civil wars of the late sixteenth century. The year before, this priest had sent Ibuse a gift of some red pine. Red pine is the wood of which the Shizuma family chests were made, chests that had contained historical records. This red pine, too, will be found to yield a kind of historical evidence of its own. The note accompanying the priest's gift explains that the temple is being rebuilt. The present structure, dating from the Edo period, admits too little light and leaks when it rains. Remembering that on one of his visits Ibuse had said he would like to have a desk made from the old wood, he has sent some along for just that purpose.

The temple records note that Kōkōji was first built in the eighth century and survived "many years of vicissitude" (*uitempen no iku-seisō*) until a fire destroyed it in the early nineteenth century. The buildings now being replaced were put up in the decades shortly thereafter; their wood, which Ibuse receives as a gift, is then well over one hundred years old. The priest says near the end of his letter that, although the wood looks worn, "I believe that once it is planed the surface will be quite lustrous" (8:408). The same may be said of *Hachigata Castle*. Ibuse will "plane" layer after layer of recorded history to expose whatever might shine below; here, as in Ibuse's other historical fiction, ugly times may harbor hidden lessons.

Ibuse takes the wood to a lumber yard to be sawed into planks.

244

Ibuse,
Black
Rain,
and the
Present
Day

Within the wood, however, the yardman finds embedded bits of metal and arrow barbs. Ibuse supposes that this wood must have grown on a battlefield to yield such souvenirs. His curiosity predictably excited, he dashes off a letter to the Kōkōji priest asking for any information he might have about this. The priest will reply, Ibuse will write again, and other correspondents will make their contributions. *Hachigata Castle* develops as a compendium of letters, as *Black Rain* was a summation of diaries. No other Ibuse work, however, including *Black Rain,* so conspicuously emphasizes its sources or so skillfully exploits their special status within the narrative.

When the priest's reply to Ibuse's first letter arrives, it speculates that the lumber was originally gathered from the old Hōjō castle at Hachigata in the former region of Musashi. If any battle took place there that might have left bullets and arrows embedded in the trees, it must have been during Hideyoshi's allies' successful siege of the castle in the summer of 1590. The castle's lord was Hōjō Ujikuni. The siege was part of Hideyoshi's campaign against the main forces of the Hōjō led by Ujinao in Odawara. For his correspondent's perusal, the priest sends four dense and voluminous histories of this campaign. They are *A Brief Genealogy* (*Kanki bukan,* literally *A Short-Sighted Book of Heraldry*), described by the priest as "a record of the battles in Toyotomi Hideyoshi's conquest of Odawara"; *The Hachigata Castle of Musashi* (*Musashi Hachigata-jō*), and *The Tragic History of the Fall of Hachigata* (*Hachigata rakujō aishi*), both "documents that research and record the actions of the castle troops during its siege"; and *The Life of Inomata Noto* (*Inomata denki*), a biography of the general who led the defense of Hachigata Castle, a handwritten account borrowed from one of Kōkōji's old patron families. This last document, perhaps because its story is the most personal, most interests Ibuse.

Its author appears to have been an obscure samurai, Heihachi, who simply recorded what he had heard from others of the castle events. In this respect, Heihachi resembles none more than Ibuse himself and his many other fictive heroes, culminating in Shizuma Shigematsu, who also have served as the witness-scribes of troubled times. Moreover, the facts he preserves in his record seem vaguely familiar: as in the Second World War, this fighting in the late sixteenth century was a man-made calamity, putting five thousand men within the castle walls against almost sixty thousand on the outside. As in all of Ibuse's catastrophes, the world is turned topsy-turvy at the moment of historical change:

Those soldiers within the castle under General Inomata Noto acted in an unusual way. They split into two types—those who became heroes and those who went to the opposite extreme. *The Life of Inomata* tells us this in true accounts. Officers normally of lofty character weakened as they turned day by day to lazy pleasures. Although street vendors regularly came to the castle gates, on rainy days those officers would go into town and steal eggs from homes, or would even force their way in to do worse. It was unspeakable. Yet, other soldiers, ordinarily cowards, struck at Maeda Toshiie's camp and brought back the heads of enemy soldiers so highly placed that their teeth were blackened [in the manner of aristocrats]. [8:416]

Ibuse's gaze is drawn to these men within the walls rather than those without, especially when he comes to the appendixes of this history. "I was more interested in the social standings [*bungenroku*] of Inomata's men than I was in the military history of *The Life of Inomata* itself" (8:416). These records, which included each samurai's status, income, and origin, revealed that nearly all the warriors came from regions other than Musashi. "One can only imagine that in coming here they sought a place to live and work after their own defeats elsewhere" (8:416). Hachigata Castle was thus defended by drifters—castaways—who, like the father of the narrator in "An Old Man Speaks of the Mountain," had joined the battle for lack of any other employment.

With great excitement, Ibuse discovers two of the Hachigata defenders to be from his own Bingo village of Kamo. Kitayama Mimbu and Momotani Kindayū were both middle-aged soldiers who, like Toramatsu and Wakaroku, had been drawn into the events of history far from their native land. When Mōri Motonari attacked in the vicinity of Kamo in the middle of the sixteenth century, all the villagers had fled, in what Ibuse terms an "emergency evacuation," to the head of the Ashidagawa River. There most of the town had remained even after the fighting had subsided. Ibuse speculates that eventually no more than two or three families had returned to Kamo. He writes:

Aside from what is written in the official histories, this is all I know of my village before the Sengoku period. It is far too little. This is why I wish more than anything else to acquire a knowledge of my village in olden times. When, who, where, what—I want to know first of all the names of the people who actually existed and what remains of their lives. I do not care how trivial the facts might be. Tragic tales are fine; anything that is

246
Ibuse,
Black
Rain,
and the
Present
Day

not myth. I am a man born into a village where history has vanished. [8:417–18]

Ibuse's intense confession establishes *Hachigata Castle* as an important personal work in his career. Perhaps all of his historical literature has been a private search for a lost past. At the very least, it is a literature now starkly illuminated by this admission of ignorance, this mighty complaint that Ibuse has harbored against events that long ago severed the continuity of his village and its people. *Hachigata Castle* is arguably Ibuse's strongest work of historical fiction for its cogency in joining the distant past with the immediate present. The reader can now surmise Ibuse's thoughts when he, too, had participated in an "emergency evacuation" in the 1940s. This novel provides a key to Ibuse's most profound and obsessive motives as a writer in a time as historically dislocated as those his old documents recall.

Impatient to learn more, Ibuse pores through the many historical records the priest continues to acquire and send him. He hopes that each successive one might reveal further details of his fellow villagers Kitayama and Momotani. He struggles to match the names, dates, and places that he encounters in his reading with those he recalls hearing in his childhood. There is a sense of urgency in Ibuse's labors, as if this will be his only chance to rescue a world long lost, much as he has salvaged the lives of other men in other stories. This retrieval of the past is Shigematsu's mission, too, but he is Ibuse's creation and not Ibuse himself. Here in *Hachigata Castle*, the castaway, the exile, is Ibuse; and the deserted island, the refuge, is his own personal past. He makes several telling connections between his search in history with his search for an understanding of his own uncanny survival, as when he sympathetically remarks how lucky Kitayama and Momotani are to have escaped from Mōri's attack. "I bless the fact that Mimbu got away safely" (8:419).

Ibuse becomes curious as to what sort of life two masterless samurai such as these might have led in Hideyoshi's day. Consequently, he writes to another friend—an ex-army officer, amateur historian, and expert on weapons who lives in a town not far from Kamo. This older man joins the exchange of letters and texts between Ibuse and the priest, expanding the basis of the novel into a triangular flow of theory and fact. He first replies to Ibuse not so much with learning but with a lament: probably, he writes, noting the irony, the lives of sixteenth-century samurai without commission were little different from his own after the postwar purges of former military personnel. Castaways, exiles, masterless samurai, hibakusha, and now purged officials all retrace a common pattern of defeat, loss, and alienation—a pattern Ibuse almost appears eager to confirm as he combs through the information that continues to come from Kōkōji.

He asks the priest to check whether any of Kitayama's or Momotani's descendants might be among his temple's congregation. Unfortunately not, answers the priest, but—"miraculously"—records do remain of many Hachigata Castle defenders originally from Bingo. He writes to Ibuse:

> These men [from Bingo] unaccounted for after the battle were likely among the numberless dead, or else they went off in search of another commission. Even for an age known as the "Warring States" period, it does seem that they were treated far too badly after coming all the way from Bingo. It was in vain. All that remains now are their names on just so many scraps of paper. I shall copy down the names I have written for you on a separate piece of paper so that tonight, when I recite the sutras, I may read their names and mourn for their souls. I will read them in a loud voice. Sometimes I do this just for myself. It has nothing to do with anyone else. I beg your indulgence. [8:424]

With the assistance of this priest—who increasingly sounds like Ibuse himself—he is gradually able to map out the probable histories of Kitayama and Momotani. More of his information comes from a history that reads much like a sequel to *The Life of Inomata*, entitled *More Military Chronicles* (*Zoku gunki*). According to the priest, Momotani, who was used by Inomata as a messenger, is described not as an accomplished warrior but rather as a "clever talker with a fondness for women." Ibuse insists upon more details, but when he learns that the priest suspects that *More Military Chronicles* may, in fact, have been Momotani's own diarylike account, he decides at once to travel to Kōkōji to study the document himself.

After stopping to tour the ruins of Hachigata Castle, Ibuse arrives at Kōkōji. He and the priest take out *More Military Chronicles* and start to go through it together. It is another handwritten document lent by the owner of *The Life of Inomata*, and it details not only Hideyoshi's intrigues perpetrated against the Sanada, but many of the military campaigns and private deceits of that time. It also details

248

Ibuse,
Black
Rain,
and the
Present
Day

the lives of ordinary men like Kitayama and Momotani, who, Ibuse learns, came from questionable backgrounds. *More Military Chronicles* appears to be a history written by Momotani as a diary and left with a woman, presumably his lover. Since she knew she would have to return it one day, she copied it for herself as a memento. Like *Black Rain, Hachigata Castle* features diaries and copied diaries, texts meant to substitute for their authors. Yet Ibuse's painstaking reading of this history/diary/memorial, nearly illegible in its scrawled hand, uncovers little of import. The chronicle scarcely touches upon Momotani's, and his own, native country of Bingo, which is the knowledge Ibuse most desires:

> I want to know what his impressions were of my village centuries ago—the landscape, people, customs, language, religion, legends, anything. Does he not mention such things even in one or two places? . . . As I have said before, the history of my village was utterly destroyed. [8:441]

Unfortunately, Ibuse is to be disappointed. His trip to Kōkōji and the examination there of *More Military Chronicles* reveals nothing of Bingo other than that many of its men drifted east to fight in the battles of the late sixteenth century. *More Military Chronicles* states, "It is unknown what happened to Momotani Kindayū after the fall of Hachigata Castle, or to Kitayama Mimbu after the surrender to Fujita Nobuyoshi" (8:474). Ibuse ends his novel with the line, "I would like to think that Kindayū, of whom so little is noted, was one of the men missing in action and not accounted for in these documents" (8:474). Momotani Kindayū is another in history's long line of victims relegated to eternal obscurity.

The ending of this novel resembles that of many other Ibuse works, but perhaps none more than *Black Rain*. In both, the conventional concept of a "story" is spurned for a story about stories. In both, the failure of the tale to conclude happily (Yasuko will die; Momotani is lost to history) is seized upon to reaffirm a central principle of Ibuse's world. Both novels begin with an objective historical fact (the bombing of Hiroshima; the destruction of Hachigata Castle) which they exploit imaginatively with highly subjective, very interpretive, first-person accounts, some real and some invented. In *Black Rain*, Ibuse's hand is heavy, and it is fairly easy to discern which passages are his and which are borrowed, but *Hachigata Castle* requires some research in order to separate the truth from the fiction.

Indeed, none of the important documents mentioned in *Hachigata Castle* actually exists. *The Life of Inomata*, the record of samurai origins, and *More Military Chronicles* are entirely products of Ibuse's need to pretend such men as Momotani and Kitayama once lived: their names, in fact, are taken from actual places found near his childhood home of Kamo, almost as if he means to emphasize the ties between his literature and his own history—or the lack thereof. The impetus for the novel—a gift of red pine embedded with bullets and arrows—is also a fabrication, but one inspired from a story Ibuse once heard. Lumber imported to Japan from Southeast Asia often does have bullets buried within, the legacy of a war Ibuse recalls often, even in works set centuries earlier.[15] Ibuse has never met the priest of Kōkōji, although he has visited the temple. It does indeed exist, and it figures as the subject of an Ibuse essay.

In "The Cedar Doors of Kōkōji Temple" (*Kōkōji no sugido*, 1965), Ibuse describes the beautiful and finely crafted doors of the temple, and he speculates about the carpenter who hewed them and the painter who painted them. What had they intended by their labors? Through these doors, Ibuse travels back into the world of their makers, just as he visits the sixteenth century through some bits of iron and arrow barbs, and just as he vicariously experiences Hiroshima through the diaries of its victims. A souvenir arrow from Fukuyama Castle long ago launched Ibuse on his historical sojourns: now he returns to arrows and castles with lessons learned in the meantime. From such works as *Black Rain* and *Hachigata Castle* comes the most complete expression of Ibuse's vision of the world, its past and its future, as he creatively rediscovers its wandering souls, be they soldiers in the sixteenth century or an unmarried niece in the twentieth.

Two compelling qualities in *Black Rain*—the mediation of the past and the present through found or invented texts, and the dynamic tension between historical fact and imaginative truth—are equally salient in *Hachigata Castle*. Shigematsu's *Diary* finds its equivalent in *More Military Chronicles;* the reality of Hiroshima confronts the reader's natural hesitancy to accept it, and the fall of Hachigata Castle contrasts with the historical obscurity of its Bingo defenders. This coincidence of method and meaning makes *Black Rain* seem less a statement about the singular or "new" reality of the atomic age and more an argument that even the atrocities of the Second World War are historically consistent with past tragedies. Perhaps *Black Rain* is

250

Ibuse,

Black

Rain,

and the

Present

Day

better praised as the greatest of its author's catastrophe literature rather than as the greatest of his country's atomic-bomb literature.

Continuing in a parallel vein, Ibuse's plea for details of his own history in *Hachigata Castle* allows a deeper understanding of Shigematsu's work in *Black Rain*—each is the work of the survivor. The experience of disaster is often like the experience of personal loss or abandonment;[16] in this one sense, it makes little difference that Shigematsu survives an atomic holocaust and Ibuse survives Aoki Nampachi, the war, Dazai Osamu, and, as he continues to age, most of his peers. Personal tragedy and modern history have conspired to place Ibuse in a position to write *Black Rain,* an intensely personal novel that nonetheless has attracted readers throughout the world.

For Ibuse, the work of writing has often been the work of mourning. *Black Rain* disguises within itself the sad themes of his entire oeuvre. This panoramic novel encompasses the alienation and ambivalence first articulated in his early short stories, the dark natural and historical worlds of "The River" and *Waves,* the pain of a war that has decimated his generation, the strengths of men set adrift on alien seas, and the beautiful end that both beckons and repels. In addition, there is the theme of which Ibuse has written best and most profoundly in *Black Rain,* namely, the legacy of the dead and the memorialization of their souls. The horrors of the atomic holocaust have struck his imagination as another ghastly event in a life spent on the edge of history, watching those he has known and even loved fall into its deep abyss. Unlike other writers, Ibuse has found Hiroshima to be not an incomprehensible aberration, but part of a paradigm, one that assumes the world is capable of great and cruel crimes that will occur again and again. Usaburō drifts away from his home; Shigematsu's is literally burned out from under him. Yasuko is the tragic victim of circumstances she has neither caused nor understood; and the salamander is not so very different. The author of "The Salamander," *Castaway Usaburō* and *Black Rain,* however, lives on to survive the sufferings of all his characters. The burden left him is the pacification of their spirits.

Like Shigematsu reciting his prayer over the dead of the city or the Kōkōji priest reciting his over the lost soldiers of long ago, Ibuse has performed with his writing a subtle and artful litany for the consecration both of those he has outlived and those he lives to remember. The logic behind his writings is bared in a short essay entitled "Early

March" (*Sangatsu jōjun,* 1954). At age fifty-six Ibuse sadly notes
that all his friends have left him behind. "Makino, Yokomitsu,
Hayashi, Dazai... all of them are dead" (11:22). In his loneliness
Ibuse treasures his little gifts and knickknacks that once belonged to
his departed friends.

Upon cataloguing them, however, he discovers that many of his
letters from these dead writers are missing. An investigation reveals
that they somehow fell into the hands of a stranger during the
turmoil of his extended evacuation in the last year of the war. Meanwhile, Ibuse hears almost daily of more deaths and more funerals to
be attended. He dreads the obituaries. Suddenly he is seized by a need
to have those letters back in his possession. The imperative to
preserve even an epistolary vestige of his friends' existences becomes
an obsession that will not lessen. These letters, constituting a "literature," represent for Ibuse more the men themselves than simply the
correspondence they left behind. He would collect the letters as he
did the testimonies of the hibakusha; both become precious *katami,*
or mementos of the dead, that are central to Ibuse's textual ritual of
chinkon, the pacification of the dead and the consecration of their
souls.

Ibuse, apparently a man of no particular institutional religion, has
authored a religious literature. A spiritual transcendence implicit in
his work saves it from total gloom, for in that transcendence lies the
possibility of reconciliation. This possibility is suggested in *Black
Rain,* but it is beautifully realized a decade later in yet another work
about war and its ravages. With this work, Ibuse succeeds in bringing
to a thematic close the lengthy rites of a mournful literature begun
well over half a century before.

"The Pond at Kenkōji Temple"

"The Pond at Kenkōji Temple" (*Kenkōji no ike,* 1978) is, like
most of Ibuse's work after *Black Rain,* a piece which is part essay,
part story, but largely memoir. It is a memoir of a journey, both actual and figurative, through the themes, settings, and images of much
of his writing. "The Pond at Kenkōji Temple" opens with a typical
recollection of a trip. Ibuse writes that he has recently visited a remote mountain village called Kanae in northern Japan, his interest

252
Ibuse,
Black
Rain,
and the
Present
Day

having been sparked by a report that the priest of its temple, Kenkōji, raises wild ducks in the pond behind the main hall. Fascinated, Ibuse decides to see these ducks for himself.

Upon his arrival, he finds Kanae a cold and snowbound hamlet, a place he describes as a "ruined village." Over half its families have moved to more prosperous areas, and those who have remained are, like the temple they support, quite poor. Other such villages come to mind: Toramatsu's famine-stricken Ōta in the eighteenth century, or Ibuse's evacuated village of Kamo in the sixteenth. Kanae is another of Ibuse's archetypal landscapes, barren and deserted, a place history has forgotten ever since a war—in this instance the Second World War—has murdered its young, leaving it a village of old and bereaved survivors.

The priest renowned for his ducks is not on hand to greet his visitor; he is busy conducting Buddhist memorial services throughout the village. This year marks the thirty-third annual observances of the war dead, and Kanae, which sacrificed many of its men, is, for the time being, a village of smoldering incense and intoned prayers. "When the young men left for the front, their families decorated their homes with signs proclaiming the human contribution they were making. By the end of the war the young men had almost all come home, in telegrams from the government, as dead spirits."[17] Kanae is typical of Ibuse in its tragic history. In a few pages the reader is plunged into the midst of his ceremonial worlds, a fiction full of "dead spirits" and the rites with which they are surrounded. The village priest, even with only half the congregation he once had, is kept hurrying about in his robes. He never does, in fact, have the time to show Ibuse his ducks.

Ibuse checks into his inn and, after a nap, rises to view the preparations for a memorial service to be held soon at the inn itself, whose proprietress had lost her first husband in the war. Ibuse is told that since this is such a special observance, services will be lengthy. Indeed, a look at the schedule for another such service shows that it will begin at nine in the morning and continue into the evening. Resigned to never being able to see the priest, Ibuse decides to go alone to see the ducks in the temple pond.

An old women in the employ of the temple takes Ibuse out back to see the fowl. She explains that although the pond may now be muddy and ill tended, before the war it had been surrounded with beautiful flowers: the reader feels in a very familiar place. In these waters the temple's ducks swim, oblivious to the human history implicit in the wild growth around them.

Somewhat tired by his sightseeing, Ibuse returns to the inn and retires for the night. When he arises the next morning, the memorial service is about to begin in the downstairs rooms. Ibuse writes, "In these parts they call memorial services 'invocations.' One gets the feeling that centuries of understanding have gone into that word."[18] Here is more of the "valuable knowledge" that Shigematsu has recognized in farmers' old festivals.

Ibuse decides to watch the ceremony unobserved, through a slit in the sliding door separating the main room from one on the side. Thus, he places himself physically in the narrative of "The Pond at Kenkōji Temple" precisely where he so often places the point of view in his mature fiction: off to one side, away from the action, but where all is visible. Moreover, he does as his heroes do; he takes notes of what he sees. Ibuse again assumes the role of historian:

> The priest said that guests attending services for his Kanae parishioners almost all come in suits and carry small flasks. The women wear black mourning clothes. In this respect things are not much different from Tokyo. The priest himself will bring some expensive saké, and while the guests are settling down in the room he will approach the statue of Buddha, bow reverently, and place the saké to one side of the altar. Then, suddenly spinning around, he will face the chief mourner and greet him. At precisely the instant he swings around from the statue, that chief mourner will never fail to be waiting for him—ready.
>
> "It is at just such moments," the priest once said, "that I feel especially good. It is hundreds of years of tradition which achieves such perfect timing. I am never nervous."
>
> I decided to write down in my notes that very scene.[19]

Ibuse serves as the recording witness to "hundreds of years" of "perfect" ceremonies. From his hidden position, Ibuse documents the dead and their survivors joined in one moment of practiced communion. He describes it in more detail than perhaps any other actual ritual found in his work. First, photographs of the dead are put on display. Some are in uniform; others, not. Then the priest appears in his purple robes and begins the liturgy by reciting an unintelligible, yet somehow meaningful, sutra. Ibuse notes:

254

Ibuse,

Black

Rain,

and the

Present

Day

I listen to sutras, but I have no idea what they mean. I am especially dumbfounded by those of the Shingon sect. Yet there is a dignity in the fact that the sutras are not translated. Perhaps we should be grateful for parts we do not understand. Sutras perform the function of distancing the profane from the sacred.[20]

After more than an hour of steady recitation, the priest turns to the assembled mourners and begins his sermon. Just as Ibuse would, the priest combines references to the past with those of the present, intertwining his homily with significant allusions to history both ancient and recent:

> *Namu daishi henjō kongō, namu daishi henjō kongō.* . . . Ladies and gentlemen, during the war the *Asahi Shimbun* published poems from their readers. I wrote them down in my notes at the time, and now, when I give a sermon in a memorial service for the war dead, I use some of them in my prefatory remarks:
>
>> I ask for my dear child
>> I ask only for my dear child
>> A letter from the army
>> I show to no one
>> Tears
>> How many years.
>
> And another one;
>
>> "I want to drink
>> All the water from our well"
>> A scrawled note is delivered
>> Older brother is dead in battle.
>
> These two poems are like something in the ancient *Manyōshū* anthology that might have been sung by the mother of a distant soldier. They are, I think, the work of amateur poets.[21]

The priest continues his unusually personal and thoughtful sermon as Ibuse remains in the adjoining room, watching silently. The priest comments, "War is like a terrible whirlpool. Once you are caught in it, there is no escape."[22] A few minutes later he is finished. The chief mourner expresses his thanks movingly and at length. Bottles of saké are opened. Toasts, at first ceremonial but soon libatory, follow in quick succession. The mood of the mourners relaxes. Jackets are shed, and the conversation is enlivened by the alcohol. Eventually the room is alive with singing meant not to celebrate so much as commemorate. The bereaved recall with songs and stories—in this informal ritual following the more sober one—those whom they have, through fate, survived to honor this day. One man thinks back to the send-off they gave his brother in this very same room; another remembers the day that the war ended. A Chinese poem about battle is recited. A veteran recites a Mongolian horse-driving song that he learned in Manchuria. A woman sings a Niigata children's song. Everyone in the room has the opportunity to recall, share, and memorialize. In this small room in an inn in a remote "ruined village," Ibuse has created another sort of *Black Rain*—a collection of memories rather than diaries, but nonetheless a compilation of the stories of survivors.

Sensing that the day's activities are nearly over, Ibuse decides to slip away quietly and return to Tokyo. Just as he leaves the inn and gets into a cab, however, he impulsively adds to his itinerary one more look at the Kenkōji ducks. His cab driver offers to act as guide:

> The driver got out of the car and led me to the front of the temple's main hall. Then he directed me to the cemetery in back and to the right. Just as I had seen yesterday, a mother pheasant was leading her young this way and that among the gravestones. They appeared to be walking idly but were, in fact, quite alert. The chicks were about the size of turtle doves, though two or three were even larger than that. . . . They say that anyone who sees such a procession will have a lucky day. I learned that as a child from my neighbors.[23]

Ibuse's readers are again among the dead, but this time, unlike all times before, the omens bode well. Ibuse and his guide continue around to the pond, where they find the old woman picking weeds. They talk and watch the wild ducks in the water, but eventually their voices send the ducks flying from the pond to a nearby hill. Ibuse signals his driver and they depart for the train station. Here the story ends.

"The Pond at Kenkōji Temple" cannot help but remind its readers of earlier Ibuse works. Instead of Shigematsu and the carp empathically reinforcing the regenerative potential in each other, there is the priest and his domesticated wild ducks; instead of a wish for a rainbow that would augur healing, there is a parade of pheasants through a graveyard; instead of hibakusha, there are mourners, the

256

Ibuse,
Black
Rain,
and the
Present
Day

conventional victims of war. "The Pond at Kenkōji Temple" and *Black Rain* are both works of faith and ceremony. They are religious in nature, but not in any sectarian way, for Ibuse's heroes are invariably men with the resources to create their own individual relationships with the dead. Where Ibuse's style achieves its greatest success is not in its humor or irony—these are, in fact, the easiest of his accomplishments—but in its imparting of harmony, warm and appropriate, human and spiritual, to his readers. This harmony intensifies over the decades of his career, and by the time of "The Pond at Kenkōji Temple," one might suggest that his work as a writer is done: the literature of Ibuse Masuji, no matter what further stories may follow, has attained its thematic apotheosis.

Finally, the dark energy driving his pen seems spent. The painful wisdom of the solitary survivor has become the confirmed wisdom of the universal survivor. The world of catastrophic violence is now provisionally inoculated with Ibuse's seamless historical vision. His work can return full circle to this desolate pond from where it began, to other bodies of water which once trapped salamanders and held beloved white carp. What has transpired in the decades distancing the beginnings from the end of Ibuse's journey through his watery world has been, most simply put, the evolution of its fire. In "The Pond at Kenkōji Temple," no fiery pillars soar through the heavens. There is no beautiful end to enthrall the viewer. There is, to be sure, still light in his words, but there is no longer the blaze of destruction. Instead, one finds the brilliance of a small reflection—mentioned long ago in the first few lines of his poem "Fish Prints" (*Gyotaku*, 1947):

> Memorial services tomorrow at Gorosaku's house
> His oldest son died in the war
> His second son died in the war
> His third son died in the war
> He will pray for them together
>
> Adorning the altar
> Is a bowl filled with offerings of devil's-tongue
> Each piece of root shining in the light [10:119]

This light also illuminates "The Pond at Kenkōji Temple," a work whose pond harbors no corpses, only serene fowl. Finally, after the tragedies of his youth, after the years of war when so many were killed, after the loss of a friend and writer who killed himself, Ibuse has entered a tranquil world of satisfied ghosts where no man need feel remorse for having lived.

Conclusion

I am a man born into a village
where history has vanished.
—*The Hachigata Castle of Musashi*

"The Pond at Kenkōji Temple" in 1978, as a statement of how culture can creatively preserve the rituals, and thus the moral structure,
of human society, may have lyrically brought Ibuse's writing to its
principal thematic conclusion. But it is a conclusion that Ibuse has
reiterated *sotto voce* throughout the 1980s. As he nears ninety—
older than any of his fictional old men—his particular insistence, always important in his widely diverse stories and novels, has come
forward to stand alone and make itself starkly plain; longevity has
awarded Ibuse a clarity of vision graced with the sagacity of experience. Unlike many writers of fiction, but very much like the best historians, Ibuse's last work might well be judged his most gifted.

Since the 1981 collection of stories and essays *Up from the Sea*,
Ibuse has, despite illness, steadily published a variety of brief works
in such journals as *Shinchō, Bungakukai* and *Kaien* (*The Storm
Petrel*). Additionally, he has edited a collection of essays by his early
admirer Kobayashi Hideo and has issued the definitive editions of a
number of his own best-known first works. In March 1985, Waseda
University, where sixty-five years earlier he had been something less
than a good student, awarded Ibuse a prize and put some of his memorabilia on public display. Recent years have, in fact, seen something
of an Ibuse revival, a "boom" as the Japanese would say. Not only
have several of his novels, both in the original and in English translation, been reissued, but in 1985 and 1986 a major publisher brought
out a new thirteen-volume collection of his works.[1] This series,
which has sold spectacularly, created a stir. Ibuse, typically, used the
opportunity to rewrite a number of his most familiar and canonized
pieces, including "The Salamander." This latest version of Ibuse's

most famous story now reads more like its 1923 prototype,
"Confinement," with the role of the frog reduced. While his critics
may find his penchant for tinkering with his prose exasperating,
Ibuse insists upon reviewing what he has written in the past as
thoughtfully now as then. Ibuse remains a writer unusually anxious
over his words, even when those words are universally acclaimed.

This acclaim has resulted in a cottage industry of Ibuse studies.
The number of book-length critical works in Japanese on Ibuse has
at least quadrupled in the 1980s. Academia, perhaps in light of his
undiminished production, has had to update and reevaluate Ibuse's
place in the fluid scholarly consensus on the history of modern, especially postwar, Japanese literature. At the same time, the Ibuse
revival has taken on some of the characteristics of pop culture; one
can go into a bookstore today and buy cassette tapes of Ibuse works
read aloud by famous actors, or even video tapes of a television documentary on him. But if Ibuse has been made into a commodity, he is
a controversial one. He has publicly supported opposition to the
building of atomic power plants, and he is perhaps the most distinguished signatory to the 1982 call by over three hundred writers
for the abolition of nuclear weapons—a call harshly criticized by
many highly placed people in Japan.[2] All in all, one hears more
from—and about—Ibuse Masuji today than at any time since the
publication of *Black Rain*.

It would be wrong to suspect, however, that Ibuse has been
reduced to the signing of petitions or the raking over of old textual
ground in lieu of any genuine literary creativity. First, it is in perfect
keeping with the thrust of his writing that Ibuse should participate in
a movement of public figures committed to disarmament. Surely no
other Japanese writer of his stature has been so concerned with the
issue of survival as he. Small creatures trapped in caves, young aristo-
crats fleeing for their lives, a generation decimated in an impossible
war, whole cities leveled—the writings of Ibuse Masuji cite this
theme almost redundantly. What continually excites his reader's imagination is his method, his way of approaching an otherwise rote
history through its human marginalia. Ibuse examines the tragedies
of those who have suffered more obscurely from the violent turns of
events, not those who have profited. He does so by distinguishing between what the victors may say their skill and bravery have wrought,
and what their victims, now gone, cannot say.

This particular insistence has, indeed, come forward to stand alone, and it is articulated succinctly in Ibuse's most recent novel. Although it makes subtle and wide reference to many of his prior themes, Ibuse's personal reading of history is restated in an especially original and fascinating way. In the early 1980s Ibuse had come across a rare work entitled *A Record of Tea Parties* (*Chakaiki*) by the late sixteenth- and early seventeenth-century tea connoisseur Kamiya Sōtan. Sōtan, in addition to his famous interest in the rapidly aestheticizing art of tea, played a small but significant role in the political and military upheavals of his time. Acquainted with the colorful unifier of Japan, Toyotomi Hideyoshi, through their mutual appreciation of tea, Sōtan—by profession a wealthy merchant in Hakata—served as a supplier of matériel to Hideyoshi's armies during their invasions of the nearby Korean peninsula in the last decade of the sixteenth century. As both an important businessman and devotee of tea, Sōtan hosted, and was hosted at, a number of elaborate tea parties—elegant dinners, really—whose broad range of courses, and conversations, he noted in *A Record of Tea Parties*.

Ibuse was quite taken with this unusual resource for historical detail of the latter and most violent part of what the Japanese refer to, after the Chinese fashion, as their own Warring States period—a time of extended bloody civil war and overseas adventures. In 1982 Ibuse published in *Kaien* his notes on *A Record of Tea Parties*, in an essay entitled "The Diary Left by Kamiya Sōtan" (*Kamiya Sōtan no nokoshita nikki*). By July of the following year, he had begun serializing in the same journal what, when published as a separate volume in 1986, would be his own imaginative tea diary of the same period of history, *The Record of Tea Parties at Tomonotsu* (*Tomonotsu chakaiki*).

Tomonotsu is mentioned in Ibuse's memoirs—the small seaside town in extreme eastern Hiroshima Prefecture where his grandfather Tamizaemon would take him as a child for a summer holiday. In his brief preface to *Tomonotsu*, Ibuse notes that even back then Ankokuji, the town's famous temple, lay in ruins before the ruins of its once equally renowned castle, Tomonotsu-jō. By Ibuse's day the grand buildings had largely been subdivided into private homes. The proud days of the past were gone, days when the well known Ashikaga Yoshiaki, last of the Ashikaga shoguns and a player in the intrigues surrounding his patron Hideyoshi in the last years of his life, has resided within. Ibuse notes in *Tomonotsu* that only broken tiles remain; Tomonotsu, like Kanae of "The Pond at Kenkōji Temple," is a forgotten place that wars, be they recent or long ago, have slighted.

It is here, in this port significant both to history and to himself, that Ibuse has situated this fanciful novel, or perhaps better put, this diary-novel—as with so many Ibuse works, the brief preface gives way to a succession of chronologically arranged entries. In *Tomonotsu*, half a dozen invented authors trace fifteen dinner parties hosted in and around the closed setting of Tomonotsu from 1588 to 1599. During these years Hideyoshi ruthlessly consolidated his power throughout Japan. He sought to rid himself of all opposition—whether that meant crucifying Christians or driving such longtime friends as Sen no Rikyū, Japan's greatest tea master, to suicide—and to expand his empire by inconclusively invading Korea (allied with Ming China) not once, but twice. The guests (i.e., the diarists) are predominantly local gentry and priests. Many, by dint of their samurai class, had once been required to take up arms in the service of their lords, who are, in turn, in service of the great Lord Hideyoshi. Their tea parties, given both their positions and the turmoil throughout the country, never lack for topics of conversation.

The account commences in 1588, six years after the assassination of Oda Nobunaga and the sudden rise of Hideyoshi to the position of leading contender for control. It concludes in 1599, one year after his equally sudden death and one year before the decisive battle at Sekigahara, when Tokugawa Ieyasu, once Hideyoshi's rival, would emerge as his heir. *Tomonotsu*, then, much like Toromatsu's, is a journal that reads as a shadow account of small events mirroring greater ones. The choreographed play of a tea party ironically plots the dramatically unpredictable course of armies. The samurai discuss what they have seen, or heard of: the siege of castles, the machinations of Japanese and Jesuit missionaries alike at the centers of power, the eccentricities of Hideyoshi; but most of all they speak of the Korean campaigns. The vicissitudes of Japan's military fortunes on the continent seem to typify their era, a time when, as one of them notes, "the entire world is changing rapidly."

As the novel progresses, its mood, much like that of *Waves*, darkens. Anecdotes about Hideyoshi become pointed criticisms. His ambition is seen as megalomania. Once he is dead, he is scorned as well as eulogized at the tea parties. The scorn comes not from lesser men who have resented his success; it comes from tired soldiers who have suffered his defeat. Samurai declaim him as one who "seemed to enjoy the frenzy of war." Ankokuji Ekei, once a representative of the Mōri clan in its negotiations with Hideyoshi when the Mōri opposed him, and later one of Hideyoshi's advisers (and one of the few historical figures in Ibuse's otherwise fanciful novel), surveys the sweep of history, as did his fellow priest-warrior Kakutan in *Waves*. Ekei remarks at a tea party held the fourth month of 1599: "The war that has gone on for seven years has ended. Whatever one thinks, it was an empty and vain battle. Everyone who fought in it was exhausted by it."[3] Ekei's candor allows others present to wonder aloud why Hideyoshi had bled the nation dry to finance his schemes; still others reflect on how vicious a war it was, one in which ally was hardly distinguishable from foe.

The late sixteenth century and its disillusionments are described in numbed and demoralized terms, much as postwar Japanese have spoken of their own imperial folly, or as Americans have until recently spoken of Vietnam. In writing of an era of epic violence heretofore neglected in his works, Ibuse has drawn, in this cleverly executed novel, much the same conclusion as found elsewhere: as Lance-Corporal Tomomura remarks in "Lieutenant Lookeast," war "is a waste. An absolute waste." Hideyoshi's ill-advised expeditions abroad are viewed as belonging to that depressingly regular pattern of history, the recurring spiral of human institutions to willful self-destruction. They are viewed thus, as always, by men and women who barely survive at the edges of the vortex.

Black Rain, as noted earlier, contains a moving scene told in the August thirteenth entry of Shigematsu's journal. His company boss, Mr. Fujita, is dressed in a formal kimono and brings to Shigematsu and his family a carefully packed box of meager but much appreciated foods from the factory canteen. Fujita wishes them to enjoy one pleasant meal before Yasuko and Shigeko return to the country the following day. Treats as scarce as canned meat and improvised saké are unwrapped and divided with a care and ceremony suggestive of the tea ceremony; Fujita and the Shizumas mean to imbue their rare feast with a dignity heretofore impossible in the aftermath of Hiroshima. The samurai of *Tomonotsu*, while enjoying far better fare, nonetheless are seated at a ceremony equally indicative of an enforced calm protected from a violence without. As Ibuse has aged, he has increasingly emphasized the quiet rites of our lives, treasuring them ever more highly; perhaps it is only in such artificial moments

that the absolute scale of either natural or human violence can, as if
in silhouette, be intimated; perhaps it is only in such moments that
the dignity of an individual life retains any significance.

I hope that each of this study's five chapters has contributed to an
understanding of Ibuse's career as thematically cumulative, of his
achievement as one composed of complementary pieces. In the late
1920s, the loneliness and insecurities of Ibuse's youth led to his
cathartic use of the third-person narrator to observe, at second hand,
the world and its terrors; the dispassionate tone of *Black Rain* might
be traced back to how skillfully Ibuse described the predicament of a
hapless salamander. In the 1930s, Ibuse imagined the topography of
his imminently catastrophic natural and historical worlds, and he
forged their rhetorical lexicon in "The River" and *Waves;* in the
1940s, real catastrophes, told in such works as "A Young Girl's
Wartime Diary" and "Lieutenant Lookeast," forced Ibuse to draw
upon that lexicon in often ironic ways.

His castaway works (to which *Tomonotsu* nods with its anecdote
about Tokugorō, a Japanese castaway found in Korea by Hideyoshi's soldiers) explore a particular kind of historical disaster, which
nonetheless illuminates the portability, the resilience, and the adapt-
ability of culture—a requisite step before Ibuse's A-bomb victims
would be able to reconstruct a post-Hiroshima culture distinctly
their own. In later works, such as "The Pond at Kenkōji Temple,"
this human capacity for manipulating the literal and metaphoric systems that surround us provides the basis for hope, which is spared
the sentimentality that would otherwise compromise it; Ibuse's
portrait of the mourners in Kanae inspires not so much our indulgent
sympathy as our respect for the completeness of their secluded rites,
the wholeness of their survival.

The question remains, however: Why should the world construed
by Ibuse Masuji after nearly seventy years of writing be considered
by readers as anything but eccentric? After all, few of us have been
through an atomic attack; even fewer, surely, aboard a shipwrecked
boat. How does he speak to us? Ibuse's projection of philosophically
simple formulas for living onto the complexity of modern society
can, admittedly, seem uselessly reductive, or worse, naïve. While
conceding that some degree of faith is required to read Ibuse with
enthusiasm—his work is characterized more by the presence of faith
than by anything else—I would maintain that the diverse survivals of
which he writes comprise a flexibly true trope of history as well as

history itself. Survival, I would argue, is the paramount issue of our century—and that is why we read Ibuse best when we read him perhaps a little frightened for our own lives.

The majority of Ibuse's audience today has come of age always aware that life on this planet hinges on the mutual and constant restraint of a few powerful men; that same audience is more recently threatened by uncontrollable ecological change and the spread of unfathomable viruses. Perhaps every age thinks itself the least likely to survive; then again, perhaps not. The writings of Ibuse Masuji intercede with blind assurances that someone will always be on hand to restore, rebuild, and remember; I find myself, in spite of what I know, eager to believe that he is right and not I. I am prepared to accept that the world is probably not what Ibuse believes it to be. But belief, and the irrepressible human thirst for it, is exactly what Ibuse's work is all about.

Notes

Preface

1. Anonymously quoted in Robert Jay Lifton, *Death in Life: Survivors of Hiroshima* (New York: Simon and Schuster, 1967), p. 369.

Introduction

1. Makino Shin'ichi, "Shin-sakka no purōfīru I: Ibuse Masuji o kataru—kare ni tsuite no sōwa," *Shinchō* (January 1931), p. 79.

2. Numbers in parentheses refer to volume and page in Ibuse's standard collected works, *Ibuse Masuji zenshū*, 14 vols. (Tokyo: Chikuma Shobō, 1964–1975).

Quote is from Ibuse memoir "The Pipe" (*Paipu ni tsuite*, 1951), from the first line of a poem Ibuse attributes to "someone." The style and sentiment strongly suggest it is his own: "In each and every leaf, there is history/Each has its own story/I want to make each and every leaf tell it to me/I want to make at least one leaf tell it to me/I want to cock my ear to hear its whisper now/For tomorrow, I may not want to listen anymore. . . . "

3. Kaikō Takeshi, *Hito to kono sekai* (Tokyo: Kawade Shobō, 1970), p. 260.

4. Author's interview with Ibuse, November 15, 1980.

The First Three Decades: 1898–1929

1. From an essay entitled "Soil" (*Tsuchi*, 1934): "I am still un-accustomed to the soil of the Tokyo area. First of all, when I look at my garden it is hard to believe that such black grit could really be solid earth. If I plant pine saplings in it, they grow straight without the least elegant

deviation. The ground of my hometown was generally pale in color. After a rain the darker sand in the roads would form knotlike spots similar to those on dyed *Iyo* textiles. It made me want to walk barefoot" (9:133).

2. Itō Sei, *Sakka ron* (Tokyo: Chikuma Shobō, 1961), p. 243.

3. In fact they seem hardly faded. Even an incomplete list of the childhood memoirs would include several dozen works, principally "Miscellany" (1936), *The First Half of My Life* (1970), and *An Ogikubo Almanac* (1981–1982). Much of my information about Ibuse's early years, however, was gathered from two interviews, one conducted by Onuma Tan (see note 7, this chapter), and the other by Kawamori Yoshizō (see note 5, this chapter).

4. *Keiroku,* literally "chicken rib," is found in early Chinese literature as a metaphor for things—like the scant meat found on a rib—that one finds trifling yet difficult to discard.

5. See Kawamori Yoshizō, "'Sanshōuo' made," in Ibuse, *Hito to hitokage* (Tokyo: Chikuma Shobō, 1972), pp. 313–32.

6. Ibid., p. 315.

7. Known as "Nakandē" in the local Kamo dialect. See Onuma Tan, "Ibuse Masuji (sakka to sakuhin)," in *Ibuse Masuji Fukazawa Shichirō,* ed. Nihon bungaku kenkyū shiryō kankōkai (Tokyo: Yūseidō, 1977), p. 7.

8. "Miscellany" (9:244).

9. "Memories of an Injury" (*Kega o shita kioku,* 1946) (10:275–76).

10. Quoted in Ban Toshihiko, "Ibuse-san kara kiita koto, sono san," in *Ibuse Masuji zenshū daigokan geppō* 5 (June 1967), p. 3.

11. Onuma, "Ibuse Masuji (sakka to sakuhin)," pp. 9–10.

12. Ibid., p. 10.

13. Ibid., p. 21.

14. Ibid., p. 9.

15. Ibuse Masuji, "A Carp for My Sixtieth Birthday" (*Kanreki no koi,* 1959), quoted in Kawakami Tetsutarō, "Ibuse Masuji no shi to shijitsu," *Gunzō* (March 1961), p. 169.

16. Onuma, "Ibuse Masuji (sakka to sakuhin)," p. 8.

17. Yanagawa Shun'yō (1877–1918), originally one of Ozaki Kōyō's most promising disciples, became well-known for ornately sentimental works, such as *Yume no yume, Nishikigi,* and *Nasanu naka* (about which Fumio teased Masuji). Shun'yō's reputation suffered later as his name was increasingly associated with cheap popular fiction, thus prompting Fumio's acid—and mistaken—comment on his younger brother's taste in authors.

18. Mori Ōgai, *Mori Ōgai zenshū* (Tokyo: Iwanami Shoten, 1979), 3:199.

19. Kawamori, "'Sanshōuo' made," p. 322.

20. Yasuoka Shōtarō, *Shōsetsuka no shōsetsuron* (Tokyo: Kawade Shobō, 1970), p. 100–01. By "mimetic realism" perhaps Yasuoka means Ibuse's impulse to exist completely in the world by "mirroring" it in his literature.

21. Author's interview with Ibuse, November 15, 1980.

22. Henry Dewitt Smith II, *Japan's First Student Radicals* (Cambridge: Harvard University Press, 1972), p. 25.

23. Ibuse writes, for example, in "Arriving in the Capital": "I entered Waseda in early September, but a great struggle had arisen on campus between the Takada and Amano factions [of the student movement]. They broke windows in the school's offices and forced the employees out. Professors were standing outside the main gate in a drizzling rain making fiery speeches. A protest meeting was held in the Waseda Theater. I had just enrolled and could not distinguish on sight the Amano and Takada factions. One day, as I was on my way to school, a husky student stationed by the main gate grabbed me by the collar and barked, 'Hey! You can't attend classes!' Perhaps he was a member of the judo team. He did not let go of my collar. However, another husky student looked at my clothing and said, 'You're not a Waseda student, are you? You're here to take the entrance exam. Well, good. If you had been a Waseda student, we'd have half killed you.' I was permitted to pass. I was wearing a felt hat and formal kimono that day: my Waseda student hat had not yet arrived. If it had, I would have been in for some trouble" (9:242–43).

24. Kawamori, "'Sanshōuo' made," p. 330.

25. Ibid., p. 325.

26. Ibid., p. 326.

27. See Wakuda Yū's discussion of this episode in Ibuse's life, in his *Shichū Ibuse Masuji* (Toyko: Meiji Shoin, 1981), pp. 1–3.

28. "Miscellany" (9: 236).

29. Ibuse, quoted to this effect in Nakano Yoshio, *Gendai sakka* (Tokyo: Iwanami Shoten, 1964), p. 132.

30. Shiga especially influenced Ibuse. See, for example, "Events Surrounding the Story 'Tale of a Kidnapping'" (14:96–101).

31. Ibuse, *An Ogikubo Almanac* (*Ogikubo fudoki* [Tokyo: Shinchōsha, 1982]), p. 99.

32. Terada Tōru, "Ibuse Masuji ron," in *Ibuse Masuji Fukazawa Shichirō*, p. 29.

33. Yasuoka, quoted in Ishizaki Hitoshi, "Ibuse Masuji no buntai," in *Ibuse Masuji*, ed. Gendai kokugo henshū iinkai (Tokyo: Tōkyō Shoseki, 1980), p. 24.

34. Ibuse, quoted in Nakamura Akira, *Sakka no buntai* (Tokyo: Chikuma Shobō, 1977), p. 24.

35. Isogai Hideo, "Ibuse Masuji—kindai bungaku ni okeru warai no teichaku," in *Ibuse Masuji Fukazawa Shichirō*, p. 101.

36. Ibuse, *An Ogikubo Almanac*, pp. 28–29.

37. Throughout this study, I use the Japanese first-person singular pronoun *watakushi* as a proper name to identify the narrative voice adopted by Ibuse in his early works. I would justify this "coinage" not only because of the continuity of this narrative voice from story to story in the 1920s and 1930s, but because such usage follows Japanese practice and spares the reader from my constantly devising such English equivalents as "I," or "the narrator," or "Ibuse's voice."

38. Onuma, p. 25.

39. Ibuse, quoted by Ban, "Ibuse-san kara kiita koto, sono jūni," in *Ibuse*

Masuji zenshū daijūyonkan geppō 14 (March 1975), p. 1.

40. *Hanseiki* (13:434).

41. Ibuse, quoted in Ōkoshi Kishichi, *Ibuse Masuji no bungaku* (Tokyo: Hōsei Daigaku Shuppankyoku, 1980), p. 54.

42. Kobayashi Hideo, "Ibuse Masuji no sakuhin ni tsuite," anthologized in Kobayashi, *Bungei hyōron (jōkan)* (Tokyo: Chikuma Shobō, 1974), pp. 117–20.

43. Ibuse, *Tanaka Kōtarō-sensei no koto,* in *Hito to hitokage,* p. 80.

44. See Ibuse's description of Satō in "Faces and Features, Part Three" (*Fūbō —shisei, sono san,* 1969) (13:353–84).

45. Tanizaki Seiji, "Ibuse Masuji ron," in *Ibuse Masuji Fukazawa Shichirō,* p. 4.

46. "Miscellany" (9:292).

47. "Lingering Flavors" (14:25).

48. Hasegawa Izumi, "'Yane no ue no Sawan,'" in *Kindai meisaku kanshō* (Tokyo: Shibundō, 1968), p. 282.

49. Ibid.

50. Ibid., p. 272.

51. Kamei Katsuichirō, "Suiko no majutsu," *Bungakukai* (August 1956), p. 37.

52. See, for example, Ibuse's memoir "The Bird's Nest" (*Tori no su,* 1950) (10:285–99).

53. "The Salamander" (1:3).

54. Kawakami, quoted in Onuma, p. 26.

55. Ibuse, quoted in Ban, "Ibuse-san kara kiita koto, sono ichi," in *Ibuse Masuji zenshū daisankan geppō* 3 (April 1967), p. 2.

56. "Recess" (1:88).

57. Tōgō Katsumi, "Ibuse Masuji no seishun," *Kokubungaku kenkyū* (October 1965), p. 88.

Rivers, the Sea, an Island: The 1930s

1. Two of the contributors to *Sakuhin* in particular, Nakajima Kenzō and Kawakami Tetsutarō, were to become two of Ibuse's closest friends.

2. Ibuse, "Rivers and Ravines" (*Kawa to tanima,* 1939), quoted in Hasegawa Kōhei, "Ibuse Masuji," *Kindai Nihon bungaku kenkyū—Shōwa sakka ron* (Tokyo: Shōgakukan, 1944), 1:232.

3. Ibuse, *Waves* (*Sazanami gunki* [Tokyo: Kawade Shobō, 1938]), quoted in Tōgō, "*Sazanami gunki* ron," in *Ibuse Masuji Fukazawa Shichirō,* p. 187.

4. Matsumoto Tsuruo, *Ibuse Masuji ron* (Tokyo: Tojūsha, 1978), pp. 93–188.

5. Ibid., pp. 98–99.

6. Ibuse, quoted in Onuma, p. 22.

7. Ibuse claims to know a Kyūshū family who possesses the diary upon which he based *Waves,* but he also says that they wish to remain anonymous

to avoid the attention that the discovery of such a historical resource would bring them. I suggest this is another of Ibuse's fanciful stories meant to persuade the reader of his writing's pretended relationship with fact, and thus manipulate that reader's ironic response to the text.

8. Taira no Tomoakira (1169–1184) was the son of the historically important Taira no Tomomori (1152–1185). Given the title of Lord of Musashi, he fought courageously in the battle of Ichinotani (1184) and was killed after enabling his father to flee. Although he was only sixteen at the time, he was immortalized in chapter 17 of the Ninth Book of the *Heike monogatari*, where it is written: "Tomomori was in command of the Heike force at the woods of Ikuta. After all his men had fled, he made his way to the beach to retreat by boat. He was escorted by only two men, his son Tomoakira and one of his retainers, Yorikata. Catching sight of the three, about ten horsemen of the Kodama clan came galloping up with a shout. Yorikata, a strong bowman, let fly an arrow at the standard-bearer riding at the head of the band. The shaft pierced the standard-bearer's neck and toppled him from his horse. The leader of the band, urging his horse, started to gain on Tomomori. But Tomoakira, spurring his charger, thrust himself between them, grappled with his foe, fell with him to the ground, pressed him down, and cut off his head. While Tomoakira was getting to his feet, his opponent's retainer fell upon him and struck off his head" (*The Tale of the Heike*, 2 vols., trans. Hiroshi Kitagawa and Bruce T. Tsuchida [Tokyo: University of Tokyo Press, 1977], 2:564). In Ibuse's novel, Tomoakira is not killed, but only thought to be so; he lives on to continue his witness of history, if not his actual participation within it.

9. The reader is referred to the translation by Kitagawa and Tsuchida, cited in note above, for the complete text of this classic.

10. Although that particular claim might be hard to believe, it does seem true that the *Heike* is the most important work in the classical canon for Ibuse: not only did he subtitle the 1939 edition of *Waves* "Shin-Heike monogatari" (*The New Tale of the Heike*), but he published in 1959, through Kawade Shobō, his own modern Japanese translation of the classical *Heike monogatari*.

11. Ibuse, quoted in Matsumoto, p. 95.

12. Ōoka Shōhei, quoted in Ōkoshi, "Ibuse Masuji *Sazanami gunki*—Ibuse Masuji no ninshiki kōzō," in *Ibuse Masuji Fukazawa Shichirō*, p. 154.

13. Here Ibuse radically departs from the traditional story told of Tomoakira. See note 8, this chapter.

14. Ibuse, quoted in Matsumoto, p. 113.

15. Ōoka, quoted in Takada Kin'ichi, "*Sanshōuo* no henshin—Ibuse Masuji ron," *Mita bungaku* (August 1973), p. 77.

16. Nakamura Mitsuo, "Ibuse Masuji ron," in *Ibuse Masuji Fukazawa Shichirō*, p. 53.

17. Ibuse, quoted in Ban, "Ibuse-san kara kiita koto, sono ni," in *Ibuse Masuji zenshū daiyonkan geppō* 4 (May 1967), p. 2.

18. Ibuse, quoted in Ōkoshi, *Ibuse Masuji no bungaku*, p. 66.

19. Yasuoka, "Ibuse Masuji no bunshō to rekishi," in Ibuse, *Sazanami gunki* (Tokyo: Sakuhinsha, 1980), pp. 179–80.

20. See Ishimoda Shō, *Heike monogatari* (Tokyo: Iwanami Shoten, 1980), pp. 10–11.

21. Ōoka, *Rekishi shōsetsu no mondai* (Tokyo: Bungei Shunjū Shuppansha, 1974), p. 196.

22. Tōgō, "Ibuse Masuji no sengo," *Nihon bungaku* (January 1978), p. 33.

Beautiful Endings: The Second World War

1. Yasuoka, quoted in Kaikō, p. 263.

2. Author's interview with Ibuse, June 8, 1981.

3. See, for example, Tōgō, "Sensōka no Ibuse Masuji—ryūri to teikō," in *Ibuse Masuji Fukazawa Shichirō*, p. 196.

4. Ibid., p. 196.

5. Asami Fukashi, quoted in Tanabe Kenji, "*Tajinko-mura ron*," *Kindai bungaku shiron* (September 1954), p. 29.

6. Ibid.

7. Author's interview with Ibuse, November 15, 1980.

8. Ibuse, quoted in Ban, p. 4.

9. *An Ogikubo Almanac*, p. 152.

10. Ibuse, *Under Arms, Umi* (September 1978), p. 136.

11. Ibuse, *Up From the Sea (Umi-agari* [Tokyo: Shinchōsha, 1981]), p. 8.

12. Tōgō, p. 197.

13. *Under Arms, Umi* (March 1978), p. 116.

14. Tōgō, p. 200.

15. Ibuse humorously confesses his fright in "Ashihei's Water-Imp Drawings" (*Ashihei-san no kappa-zu*, 1960) (12:40–44).

16. In private conversation, Ibuse has expressed remorse over his employment by a newspaper that cooperated with, and even aided in, Japanese atrocities against Singapore's civilians.

17. *Under Arms, Umi* (December 1978), p. 171.

18. Terada, quoted in Tōgō, p. 202.

19. *Up From the Sea*, p. 95.

20. See Ibuse, "The Day of a Memorial Service for a Bell," in *Nihon teikō bungaku sen* (Tokyo: San'ichi Shobō, 1955), pp. 215–20. The fact that the same work could be published in a wartime military organ and a postwar anthology of protest literature further demonstrates the subtlety of Japanese ideological distinctions.

21. Ibuse, quoted in Ōkoshi, pp. 87–88.

22. Nakamura Mitsuo, p. 59.

23. Saeki Shōichi, *Nihon o kangaeru* (Tokyo: Shinchōsha, 1966), p. 164.

24. See "Ten Years Ago" (10:233–49).

25. Tōgō, "Ibuse Masuji to Dazai Osamu," in *Ibuse Masuji*, p. 44.

26. Dazai Osamu, "Kōki," in Ibuse, *Ibuse Masuji senshū* (Tokyo: Chikuma Shobō, 1948), 2:324.

27. See Sōma Shōichi, *Dazai Osamu to Ibuse Masuji* (Tsugaru: Tsugaru Shobō, 1972), pp. 131–34.

28. See "The Ways of Women" (10:306–23).

29. Sōma, pp. 128–30.

30. See "Ten Years Ago" (10:233) for Ibuse's reference to his first mention of Dazai.

31. Makino Shin'ichi (1896–1936) holds a distant, but related, second place. In his early years as a writer, Ibuse was a friend of Makino. He broke with him one night after a humiliating argument in a restaurant. After Makino's suicide, Ibuse characteristically felt guilty about their soured relationship. See Ibuse, "Makino Shin'ichi" (*Makino Shin'ichi*, 1955); "About Makino Shin'ichi" (*Makino Shin'ichi no koto*, 1950); and "A Trip in Late Spring" (*Banshun no tabi*, 1952).

32. *An Ogikubo Almanac* p. 178.

33. *Up From the Sea*, pp. 8–9.

34. Ibid., p. 90.

35. Usui Yoshimi, *Sakka ron hikaechō* (Tokyo: Chikuma Shobō, 1977), p. 488.

36. Ibuse, quoted in Ban, "Ibuse-san kara kiita koto, sono go," in *Ibuse Masuji zenshū daishichikan geppō 7* (August 1967), pp. 3–4.

37. See "Death in the Field, Death in the Field Hospital" (8:270–87).

The Castaways: Usaburō and the 1950s

1. Ibuse began publishing his translations of Hugh Lofting's children's stories in 1941 with *Doritoru-sensei Afurika-yuki* [Doctor Dolittle Goes to Africa, the Japanese title of *The Story of Doctor Dolittle*] (Tokyo: Hakurin Shōnenkan, 1941). This was followed by *Doritoru-sensei no sākasu* [Doctor Dolittle's Circus] (Tokyo: Iwanami Shoten, 1952), *Doritoru-sensei kōkai ki* [The Voyages of Doctor Dolittle] (Tokyo: Kōdansha, 1952), *Doritoru-sensei no yūbinkyoku* [Doctor Dolittle's Post Office] (Tokyo: Iwanami Shoten, 1952), *Doritoru-sensei no kyaraban* [Doctor Dolittle's Caravan] (Tokyo: Iwanami Shoten, 1953), *Doritoru-sensei tsuki e yuku* [Doctor Dolittle in the Moon] (Tokyo: Iwanami Shoten, 1955), and finally the twelve-volume *Doritoru-sensei monogatari zenshū* [The Complete Stories of Doctor Dolittle] (Tokyo: Iwanami Shoten, 1961–62).

2. Daniel Defoe, *Robinson hyōryūki*, trans. Ibuse Masuji (Tokyo: Tsuru Shobō, 1961).

3. Yasuoka, *Shōsetsuka no shōsetsuron*, p. 106.

4. Kamei, *Bungaku to shinkō* (Tokyo: Buntaisha, 1949), p. 160.

5. Katsuragawa Hoshū (1751–1809), a scholar of the West, was ordered by the central government in Edo in 1794 to draft an account of the *Kambō-maru*, a ship out of Ise that had drifted to Asiatic Russia in the late eigh-

teenth century. The result was *A Report of Siberia*, a twelve-volume work with an additional two volumes consisting solely of charts. In 1937 the Sanshūsha publishing house issued an abridged version.

6. Like *A Report of Siberia*, *Strange Tales of the Seas* was written by a scholar of "Dutch Learning," but under orders of the *bakufu* rather than of the local Sendai *han*. An account of the Mutsu vessel *Wakamiya-maru* marooned in Russia, it was even longer than *A Report of Siberia*. It comprised sixteen volumes of text and one of charts upon its completion in 1806 by Ōtsuki Gentaku (1757–1827).

7. Arakawa Hidetoshi, *Nihonjin hyōryūki* (Toky   Jimbutsu Ōraisha, 1964), p. 1.

8. Ibid., p. 22.

9. Ibuse's essay entitled "The Russian Ship" (*Oros. sen*, 1935) tells the story of a vessel that drifted to Miyakejima in the E   period. Because it concerns Russian, not Japanese, sailors, I do not inclu e it for the purposes of this study, among Ibuse's castaway stories, which otherwise explore a particularly Japanese response to the experience of cul ural separation. See Ibuse, "The Russian Ship," *Shinchō* (December 1935), p. 183–95.

10. Anthologized in *Ikoku hyōryūki shū*, ed. Arakawa (Tokyo: Yoshizawa Hiroshi Bunkan, 1972), pp. 239–58.

11. Ibid., pp. 259–75.

12. Arakawa, *Nihonjin hyōryūki*, p. 22.

13. Ibuse, quoted in Shōno Junzō, "Jishin, kaminari, kaze," in *Ibuse Masuji zenshū daisankan geppō 3* (April 1967), pp. 7–8.

14. One such biography—so similar to Ibuse's that both seem drawn from the same sources—is Emily V. Warinner's *Voyage to Destiny* (New York: Bobbs-Merrill, 1956).

15. *Ikoku hyōryūki shū*, pp. 131–58.

16. Anthologized in *Ikoku hyōryū kidan shū*, ed. Ishii Kendō (Tokyo: Fukuei Shoten, 1927), pp. 420–50.

17. Published privately in 1936.

18. *Kiroku bungaku sōsho* (Tokyo: Kawade Shobō, 1937).

19. Ibuse, quoted in Ban, "Ibuse-san kara kiita koto, sono ni," p. 3.

20. Ibuse, "'But,' 'Then,' 'However,'" *Bungakukai* (August 1956), p. 30.

21. Ibid., p. 32.

22. Wakuda, p. 183.

23. *Tales of the Barbarians* was written in 1849 by the scholar of Western studies Koga Kin'ichirō (1816–1884). The tale of the *Chōja-maru* and its crew, *Barbarians* is one of the most renowned of all Japanese castaway accounts and was edited and re-issued most recently by Heibonsha in 1965.

24. Maeda Nariyasu (1811–1884), the *daimyō* of Kanazawa, ordered the mathematician Endō Takanori (1784–1864) to compile an account of the *Chōja-maru* because Toyama, where the castaways had returned, was a branch domain. The result, *The Tale of the Clock*, was a ten-volume work completed in 1850.

25. Author unknown. Wakuda Yū, the critic who has done the most re-

search into Ibuse's *hyōryūmono*, has convincingly argued that it is, in fact, the clever product of his own imagination. See Wakuda, pp. 195–97.

26. Although Ibuse credits this to a scholar posthumously known as Sorō Sei [?], who traveled to Hawaii to interview Usaburō in his later years, it, too, seems an invented work. Ibid.

27. In fact, Usaburō himself is an imaginary character: like the works that supposedly detail his life, Ibuse created him to tell a story historically truthful—in the sense of its consistency with lives actually led—if not historically accurate. Ibid., pp. 183–213.

28. See Kawai Hikomitsu's description of this rite in his *Nihonjin hyōryūki* (Tokyo: Shakai Shisōsha, 1967), pp. 101–03.

29. Yasuoka, ibid., pp. 107–08.

30. Perhaps one example of a modern "castaway account" would be Ōoka Shōhei's *Furyoki* (*Journal of a P.O.W.*, 1948), in which a Japanese soldier taken prisoner by the Americans in the Second World War considers his own fate, and self-identity, much as Ibuse's sailors did.

31. Yoshida Seiichi, "Ibuse Masuji to hyōryūki mono," in *Ibuse Masuji Fukazawa Shichirō*, p. 141.

Ibuse, *Black Rain,* and the Present Day

1. "*Kuroi ame* no Ibuse Masuji-shi ni kiku," *Asahi Shimbun*, Evening Edition, August 3, 1981, p. 4; *Bungei shunjū* (January 1987), pp. 101–32.

2. *Asahi Shimbun*.

3. Fur further information concerning these A-bomb writers and others, see Nagaoka Hiroyoshi, *Gembaku bungaku shi* (Nagoya: Fūbaisha, 1973).

4. *Asahi Shimbun*.

5. Ibid.

6. Ibid.

7. Ibid. Ibuse's words are, "I cannot write of this from the imagination."

8. Ibid.

9. Ibid.

10. Ibuse, quoted in Ban, "Ibuse-san kara kiita koto, sono jūichi," in *Ibuse Masuji zenshū daijūsankan geppō* 13 (March 1975), p. 3.

11. One impressive example of the ubiquity of diaries among Japanese is told in an Ibuse essay entitled "Older Friends" (*Sempai,* 1964). Ibuse writes that once his own diary and that of a friend disagreed over some detail of a dinner party they both had attended. Ibuse resolves the discrepancy by asking the waitress who had served them at the party to consult *her* diary; the point being that Ibuse could have assumed with little worry that she would have one.

12. Nakamura Akira, p. 23.

13. *Asahi Shimbun*.

14. A prayer written by the Shinshū priest Rennyo in the Muromachi period. In chapter 19 Shigematsu recites its first line to himself: "Whether it is

I or whether it is someone else, whether it is today or whether it is tomorrow, those of us who die and those who survive shall all pass from this life, a life more fragile than the dew. And so, we who are in the prime of life this morning shall be dry bones by night. As soon as the winds of this transient world blow, our eyes shall close forever" (13:274).

15. See Matsumoto, p. 168.

16. Martha Wolfenstein has written on this connection in her work *Disaster: A Psychological Essay* (Glencoe, Ill.: The Free Press, 1957). Lifton, who is indebted to Wolfenstein, observes in *Death in Life:* "Psychologically speaking, the survivor's actual death immersion is itself a symbolic reactivation of earlier 'survivals'. . . . [I]n adult life images of death, loss and separation remain, to a considerable extent, psychologically interchangeable. A survivor's death encounter, therefore, may be symbolically reactivated by exposure to any of the three, as well as by experiences specifically reminiscent of that encounter" (p. 485).

17. *Up From the Sea,* p. 159.

18. Ibid., p. 166.

19. Ibid., p. 176.

20. Ibid., p. 178.

21. Ibid., p. 180.

22. Ibid., p. 181.

23. Ibid., p. 205.

Conclusion

1. Ibuse, *Ibuse Masuji jisen zenshū,* 13 vols. (Tokyo: Shinchōsha, 1985–86).

2. This controversy over the "Writers' Declaration on the Danger of Nuclear War" has been discussed many places, but the principal arguments against participation have been summed up by Yoshimoto Takaaki in his *"Han-kaku" iron* (Tokyo: Shin'ya Sōshosha, 1982).

3. Ibuse, *The Record of Tea Parties at Tomonotsu,* in *Ibuse Masuji jisen zenshū,* 13:107.

Chronology

For the most complete chronology of the principal events and publications in Ibuse's life and career, see Matsumoto Takeo, "Nempu," in Ibuse, *Ibuse Masuji jisen zenshū* (Tokyo: Shinchōsha, 1986), 13:349–74. For the most complete chronology of all of Ibuse's publications, including his translations, see Maeda Sadaaki et al., "Ibuse Masuji chosaku nempyō," in Isogai Hideo, ed., *Ibuse Masuji kenkyū* (Tokyo: Keisuisha, 1984), pp. 525–50.

The chronology included here lists those original works mentioned in this study. They are organized alphabetically within each year of initial publication (or first year of serialization for serialized works), and are followed with location references. Unless otherwise noted, volume and page numbers refer to the *Ibuse Masuji zenshū*, 14 vols. (Tokyo: Chikuma Shobō, 1964–1975).

1923   "Confinement" (*Yūhei; Seiki* [July 1923])

1925   "Plum Blossom by Night" (*Yofuke to ume no hana;* 1:18–33)

1926   "The Carp" (*Koi;* 1:12–17)

1927   "An Elliptical Design" (*Ibitsu na zuan; Fudōchō* [February 1927])

1929   "Kuchisuke's Valley" (*Kuchisuke no iru tanima;* 1:34–60)
        "Mining-Town Clinic" (*Tankōjitai byōin;* 1:61–71)
        "The Salamander" (*Sanshōuo;* 1:3–11)
        "Sawan on the Roof" (*Yane no ue no Sawan;* 1:72–79)

1930   "A Delicate Canary" (*Hoso-kanariya;* 9:8–9)
        "Recess' (*Kyūkei jikan;* 1:80–88)
        Waves (*Sazanami gunki;* 1:370–480)

1931   "A Practical Joke" (*Itazura* 9:19–22)
        "The River" (*Kawa;* 1:181–226)

1932   "The Chinese Ink Stick" (*Seimakkan;* 9:27–32)

"Takachiho in Hyūga" (*Hyūga Takachiho;* 9:461–67)
"Turtles" (*Kame;* 9:442–49)

1940　"Enshin's Conduct" (*Enshin no gyōjō;* 2:451–58)
　　　"Tajinko Village Continued" (*Tajinko-mura hoi;* 2:344–88)

1941　"Morikichi from Beppu Village on Oki Island" (*Oki Beppu-mura no Morikichi;* 3:22–30).
　　　"The Notions Shop" (*Komamonoya;* 3:10–21)

1942　*City of Flowers (Hana no machi;* 3:31–118)
　　　"Singapore Diary" (*Shōnan nikki;* 10:57–73)
　　　"A Talk with Abu Bakr" (*Abubaka to no hanashi;* 10:3–9)

1943　"An Account of My Voyage South" (*Nankō taigaiki;* 10:10–56)
　　　"The Day of a Memorial Service for a Bell" (*Kane kuyō no hi;* 3:186–95)
　　　"The Fire God" (*Gojinka;* 3:119–65)
　　　"From Gemas to Keluang" (*Gemasu kara Kurūan e;* 10:77–86)
　　　"Inns and Barracks" (*Ryokan—heisha;* 10:95–97)
　　　"Late July of 1942" (*Jūshichinen shichigatsu gejungoro;* 10:74–76)
　　　"When We Published the *Shōnan Times*" (Shōnan taimuzu *hakkan no koro;* 10:87–94)
　　　"A Young Girl's Wartime Diary" (*Aru shōjo no senji nikki;* 10:98–116)

1946　"The Hashimoto Inn" (*Hashimotoya;* 3:348–63)
　　　"Memories of an Injury" (*Kega o shita kioku;* 10:275–76)
　　　"The Sutra Case" (*Kyōzutsu;* 3:251–68)
　　　"Tales of Thieves" (*Oihagi no hanashi;* 3:310–27)
　　　"Wabisuke" (*Wabisuke;* 3:269–309)

1947　*Always Moving (Hikkoshi-yatsure;* 3:364–450)
　　　"Fish Prints" (*Gyotaku;* 10:117–20)
　　　"Letters" (*Tegami no koto;* 10:150–60)

1948　"Dazai" (*Dazai-kun no koto;* 10:192–94)
　　　"A Guide to the Ravine" (*Sankyō fūbutsu shi;* 4:3–30)
　　　"My Birdcage" (*Watakushi no torikago;* 10:223–26)
　　　"My Fountain Pen" (*Watakushi no mannenhitsu;* 10:255–61)
　　　"One Cold Night I Remember Mother" (*Kan'ya haha o omou;* 9:334–36)
　　　"Parting Regrets" (*Sekibetsu;* 10:366–68)
　　　Room for Rent (Kashima ari; 4:47–217)
　　　"Talk of the Returnees" (*Fukuinsha no uwasa;* 4:31–46)
　　　"Ten Years Ago" (*Jūnenmae goro;* 10:233–49)

1949　"Evacuation Diary" (*Sokai nikki;* 10:277–80)
　　　"The Flashlight" (*Kaichū dentō;* 10:262–66)
　　　"No Consultations Today" (*Honjitsu kyūshin;* 4:335–413)

"Mother" (*Ofukuro*; 12:56–63)
"The Tale of the Koto" (*Koto no ki*; 12:45–53)

1961 *The Hachigata Castle of Musashi* (*Bushū Hachigata-jō*; 8:407–74)
"On the Road Relocating Again" (*Saisokai tojō*; 11:156–58)
"Scents" (*Nioi*; 12:115–18)
"Stray Dogs" (*Yaken*; 8:372–78)

1963 "Birthdays" (*Tanjōbi*; 13:299–314)
"Death in the Field, Death in the Field Hospital" (*Senshi—
sembyōshi*; 8:270–87)
"A Story in Pieces" (*Kataware sōshi*; 8:301–12)
"A Watch and the Naoki Prize" (*Tokei to Naoki-shō*; 14:460–63)

1964 "About Abe Shinnosuke" (*Abe Shinnosuke no koto*; 14:449–51)
"Older Friends" (*Sempai*; 7:10–32)
"Umbrella Clouds" (*Kasagumo*; 8:393–406)

1965 *Black Rain* (*Kuroi ame*; 13:3–298)
"The Cedar Doors of Kōkōji Temple" (*Kōkōji no sugido*;
12:436–37)

1969 "Faces and Features, Part Three" (*Fūbō—shisei, sono san*;
13:353–84)

1970 *The First Half of My Life* (*Hanseiki*; 13:374–454)
"Fishermen" (*Tsuriudo*; 14:294–324)
"Hirano Naomi, A Wartime Draftee" (*Sensōchū no chōin—Hirano
Naomi*; 14:285–89)
"A Town Under the River" (*Kawazoko no machi*; 14:280–84)

1971 "The Waseda Woods" (*Waseda no mori*; 14:200–07)

1972 "Practice Period" (*Shūsaku jidai*; in *Ibuse Masuji Kambayashi Aka-
tsuki—Gendai Nihon bungaku taikei 65* [Tokyo: Chikuma Shobō,
1970; pp. 369–73])
"Tanaka Kōtarō, My Teacher" (*Tanaka Kōtarō-sensei no koto*;
14:223–42)

1973 "Events Surrounding the Story 'Tale of a Kidnapping'" ("*Ko o
nusumu hanashi*" *no shūhenji*; 14:96–101)

1974 "All About Rainbows" (*Niji no iroiro*; 14:45–47)
"Lingering Flavors" (*Atoaji no yosa*; 14:24–25)
"Someone I Miss" (*Oshii hito*; 14:11–14)

1975 "Lake Trout" (*Kosui no ayu*; 14:3–7)

1977 *Under Arms* (*Chōyōchū no koto*; Umi [September 1977–January
1980])

1978 "The Pond at Kenkōji Temple" (*Kenkōji no ike*; in Ibuse, *Umi-agari*

[Tokyo: Shinchōsha, 1981; pp. 149–213])

"Yanagi Shigenori and the Three-Forked Road at Bukit Timah" (*Bukitema sansaro to Yanagi Shigenori no koto; Umi-agari*, pp. 87–108)

1979   "Up from the Sea" (*Umiagari; Shinchō* [December 1979])

1981   *An Ogikubo Almanac (Ogikubo fudoki; Shinchō* [February 1981–June 1982])

1982   "The Diary Left by Kamiya Sōtan" (*Kamiya Sōtan no nokoshita nikki; Kaien* [January 1982–September 1982])

1983   *The Record of Tea Parties at Tomonotsu (Tomonotsu chakaiki; Kaien* [July 1983–April 1985])

Bibliography

Critical Materials in Japanese

For complete bibliographies of the secondary materials on Ibuse available in Japanese, see Ōkoshi Kishichi, "Ibuse Masuji sankō bunken mokuroku," *Kokubungaku kaishaku to kanshō* (March 1985), pp. 136–44; and Terayoko Takeo, "Ibuse Masuji sankō bunken nempyō," in Isogai Hideo, ed., *Ibuse Masuji kenkyū* (Tokyo: Keisuisha, 1984), pp. 465–524. Below are listed only the book-length studies and anthologies of Ibuse criticism:

Bungaku kyōiku kenkyūsha shūdan cho. Kumagai Takashi, ed. *Ibuse bungaku techō*. Tokyo: Mizura Shobō, 1984.

Bungaku kyōikusha kenkyū shūdan. *Bungakushi no naka no Ibuse Masuji to Dazai Osamu*. Tokyo: Bungaku kyōikusha kenkyū shūdan, 1977.

Isogai Hideo, ed. *Ibuse Masuji kenkyū*. Tokyo: Keisuisha, 1984.

Isogai Hideo et al. *Ibuse Masuji—sakka sakuhin shirizu 7*. Tokyo: Tōkyō Shoseki, 1980.

Kasei Tadao. *Ibuse Masuji shiron*. Tokyo: Rindōsha, 1985.

Kumagai Takashi. *Ibuse Masuji—kōen to taidan*. Tokyo: Hato No Mori Shobō, 1978.

Matsumoto Takeo. *Ibuse Masuji hito to sakuhin*. Tokyo: Shimizu Shoin, 1981.

Matsumoto Tsuruo. *Ibuse Masuji ron*. Tokyo: Tōjusha, 1978.

Nagata Ryūtarō. *Ibuse Masuji bungaku shoshi*. Tokyo: Nagata Shobō, 1972.

Nihon bungaku kenkyū shiryō kankōkai. *Ibuse Masuji Fukazawa Shichirō—Nihon bungaku kenkyū shiryō sōsho*. Tokyo: Yūseidō, 1977.

Ōkoshi Kishichi. *Ibuse Masuji no bungaku*. Tokyo: Hōsei Daigaku Shuppankyoku, 1980.

Ōkubo Tsuneo et al. *Ibuse Masuji gendai kokugo kenkyū shirizu 11*. Tokyo: Shōgaku Tosho, 1981.

Shimizu Shōzō. *Ibuse Masuji sono bungaku to sekai.* Tokyo: Sōjusha, 1984.
Sōma Seiichi. *Dazai Osamu to Ibuse Masuji.* Tsugaru: Tsugaru Shobō, 1972.
Wakuda Yū. *Ibuse Masuji no sekai.* Tokyo: Shūeisha, 1983.
———. *Shichū Ibuse Masuji.* Tokyo: Meiji Shoin, 1981.

Critical Materials in English

Kimball, Arthur G. "After the Bomb." In *Crisis in Identity and Contemporary Japanese Novels.* Rutland and Tokyo: Charles E. Tuttle Company, 1973. Pp. 43–59.
Lifton, Robert J. "Black Rain." In *Death in Life: Survivors of Hiroshima.* New York: Simon and Schuster, 1967. Pp. 543–55.
Liman, Anthony V. "Ibuse's Black Rain." In *Approaches to the Modern Japanese Novel,* edited by K. Tsuruta and T. Swann. Tokyo: Waseda University Press, 1976. Pp. 45–72.
———. "Carp." "Pilgrims' Inn." In *Approaches to the Modern Japanese Short Story,* edited by T. Swann and K. Tsuruta. Tokyo: Waseda University Press, 1982. Pp. 83–101.
———. "*The River:* Ibuse's Poetic Cosmology." In *Essays on Japanese Literature,* edited by Takeda Katsuhiko. Tokyo: Waseda University Press, 1977. Pp. 129–45.
Rimer, J. Thomas. "Tradition and Contemporary Consciousness: Ibuse, Endō, Kaikō, Abe." In *Modern Japanese Fiction and Its Traditions.* Princeton: Princeton University Press, 1978. Pp. 245–70.

Ibuse Works in English Translation

"Hakuchō no uta." "Swan Song." Translated by G. W. Sargent. *Eigo seinen.* 102. nos. 9–12 (1956).
"Henrō yado." "Pilgrims' Inn." Translated by John Bester. In *Lieutenant Lookeast and Other Stories.* Tokyo: Kodansha International, 1971; London: Secker and Warburg, 1971. Pp. 53–58.
"Honjitsu kyūshin." "No Consultation Today." Translated by Edward Seidensticker. *Japan Quarterly.* 8, no. 1 (1961): 50–79. Reprinted in *No Consultation Today.* Tokyo: Hara Shobō, 1964. Pp. 8–128.
"Iwata-kun no kuro." "Kuro, the Fighting-cock." Translated by Yokichi Miyamoto with Frederick Will. *Chicago Review.* 19, no. 1 (1966): 83–89.
Jon Manjirō hyōryūki. John Manjiro, the Castaway: His Life and Adventure. Translated by Hisakazu Kaneko. Tokyo: Hokuseido, 1940.
"John Manjirō: A Castaway's Chronicle." Translated by David Aylward and Anthony Liman. In *Castaways: Two Short Novels.* Tokyo, New York, and San Francisco: Kodansha International, 1987. Pp. 68–138.

"Kaikon mura no Yosaku." "Yosaku, the Settler." Translated by John Bester. In *Lieutenant Lookeast and Other Stories*. Tokyo: Kodansha International, 1971; London: Secker and Warburg, 1971. Pp. 113–29.

"Kakitsubata." "The Crazy Iris." Translated by Ivan Morris. *Encounter*. 6, no. 5 (1956): 92–93. Reprinted in *The Crazy Iris and Other Stories of the Atomic Aftermath*, edited by Ōe Kenzaburō. New York: Grove Press, 1985. Pp. 17–35.

"Kan'ya." "A Cold Night." Translated by George Saito. *Japan P.E.N. News*. 18 (March 1966): 1–6.

"Kappa sōdō." "Catching a Kappa or Water Imp." Translated by Kiyoaki Nakao. *Two Stories by Masuji Ibuse*. Tokyo: Hokuseido, 1970. Pp. 4–28.

"Koi." "Carp." Translated by John Bester. In *Lieutenant Lookeast and Other Stories*. Tokyo: Kodansha International, 1971; London: Secker and Warburg, 1971.

"Kuchisuke no iru tanima." "Kuchisuke's Valley." Translated by John Whittier Treat. In *The Shōwa Anthology, 1929–1961*, edited by Van C. Gessel and Tomone Matsumoto. Tokyo, New York and San Francisco: Kodansha International, 1985. 1:1–20.

Kuroi ame. Black Rain. Translated by John Bester. *Japan Quarterly*. 14, nos. 2–4 (1967); 15, nos. 1–3 (1968). Tokyo: Kodansha International, 1969; London: Secker and Warburg, 1971.

"Noheiji no Mutsugorō ryakuden." "The Life of Mutsugoro of Noheiji." Translated by Kiyoaki Nakao. In *Two Stories by Masuji Ibuse*. Tokyo: Hokuseido, 1970. Pp. 32–72.

"Noriai jidōsha." "The Charcoal Bus." Translated by Ivan Morris. In *Modern Japanese Short Stories*, edited by I. Morris. London: Spottiswoode, 1961; Tokyo: Tuttle, 1962. Pp. 212–22.

"Oshima no zonnengaki." "A Geisha Remembers." Translated by David Aylward and Anthony Liman. In *Castaways: Two Short Novels*. Tokyo, New York, and San Francisco: Kodansha International, 1987. Pp. 17–58.

"Sanshōuo." "The Salamander." Translated by Tadao Katayama. *The Reeds*. 2 (1956): 51–64.

"The Salamander." Translated by Leon Zolbrod. *The East*. 1, no. 2 (1964): 21–23.

"Salamander." Translated by Sadamichi Yokoo and Sanford Goldstein. *Japan Quarterly*. 13, no. 1 (1966): 71–75.

"Salamander." Translated by John Bester. In *Lieutenant Lookeast and Other Stories*. Tokyo: Kodansha International, 1971; London: Secker and Warburg, 1971. Pp. 59–65.

Sazanami gunki. Waves: A War Diary. Translated by David Aylward and Anthony Liman. In *Waves: Two Short Novels*. Tokyo, New York, and San Francisco: Kodansha International, 1986. Pp. 26–103.

"Tajinko mura." "Tajinko Village." Translated by John Bester. In *Lieutenant Lookeast and Other Stories*. Tokyo: Kodansha International, 1971; London: Secker and Warburg, 1971. Pp. 135–247.

"Tange-shi tei." "At Mr. Tange's." Translated by Sadamichi Yokoo and Sanford Goldstein. *Literature East and West.* 13, nos. 1–2 (1969): 167–81.

"Life at Mr. Tange's." Translated by John Bester. In *Lieutenant Lookeast and Other Stories.* Tokyo: Kodansha International, 1971; London: Secker and Warburg, 1971. Pp. 97–111.

"Ushitora jiisan." "Old Ushitora." Translated by John Bester. In *Lieutenant Lookeast and Other Stories.* Tokyo: Kodansha International, 1971; London: Secker and Warburg, 1971. Pp. 67–89.

"Wabisuke." *Isle-on-the-Billows.* Translated by David Aylward and Anthony Liman. In *Waves: Two Short Novels.* Tokyo, New York, and San Francisco: Kodansha International, 1986. Pp. 115–42.

"Yane no ue no Sawan." "Sawan on the Roof." Translated by Yokichi Miyamoto with Frederick Will. *Chicago Review.* 19, no. 1 (1966): 51–54.

"Sawan on the Rooftop." Translated by Tadao Katayama. *The Reeds.* 11 (1967): 127–34.

"Sawan on the Roof." Translated by John Bester. *Lieutenant Lookeast and Other Stories.* Tokyo: Kodansha International, 1971; London: Secker and Warburg, 1971. Pp. 129–34.

"Yofuke to ume no hana." "Plum Blossom by Night." Translated by John Bester. In *Lieutenant Lookeast and Other Stories.* Tokyo: Kodansha International, 1971; London: Secker and Warburg, 1971. Pp. 11–22.

"Yōhai taichō." "A Far-worshipping Commander." Translated by Glenn Shaw. *Japan Quarterly.* 1, no. 1 (1954): 53–73. Reprinted in *No Consultation Today.* Tokyo: Hara Shobō, 1964. Pp. 126–213.

"The Far-worshipping Commander." Translated by Glenn Shaw. In *The Shadow of Sunrise,* edited by Shoichi Saeki. Tokyo: Kodansha International, 1966; London: Ward Lock, 1966. Pp. 157–86.

"Lieutenant Lookeast." Translated by John Bester. In *Lieutenant Lookeast and Other Stories.* Tokyo: Kodansha International, 1971; London: Secker and Warburg, 1971. Pp. 23–51.

Index